The Habermas Reader

The Habermas Reader

EDITED BY WILLIAM OUTHWAITE

Polity Press

First published in 1996 by Polity Press
in association with Blackwell Publishers Ltd

Editorial office:
Polity Press
65 Bridge Street
Cambridge CB2 1UR, UK

Marketing and production:
Blackwell Publishers Ltd
108 Cowley Road
Oxford OX4 1JF, UK

ISBN 0–7456–13934
ISBN 0–7456–13942 (pbk)

A CIP catalogue record for this book is available from the British Library.

Typeset in Times 10/11 pt
by CentraCet Limited, Cambridge
Printed in Great Britain by Hartnolls Ltd, Bodmin, Cornwall

This book is printed on acid-free paper.

Contents

Contents

Acknowledgements

I am extremely grateful to Jürgen Habermas for his support for this project and his comments on various drafts, and to Anthony Giddens and John Thompson for their guidance and encouragement.

The author and publishers wish to thank Beacon Press and MIT Press for their cooperation and kind permission to reproduce material previously co-published with them.

Beacon Press for material from *Toward a Rational Society* in chapters 3, 4 and 5; *Theory and Practice* in chapters 6 and 7; *Knowledge and Human Interests* in chapter 8; *Communication and the Evolution of Society* in chapters 10, 21 and 23; *The Theory of Communicative Action*, Volumes I and II, in chapters 11, 12, 13, 14, 24, 25, 26, and 27; *Legitimation Crisis* in chapter 22.

MIT Press for material from *The Structural Transformation of the Public Sphere* in chapters 1 and 2; *On the Logic of the Social Sciences* in chapter 9; *Moral Consciousness and Communicative Action* in chapters 15 and 17; *Justification and Application* in chapter 16; *Between Facts and Norms* in chapters 18, 19 and 20; *The Philosophical Discourse of Modernity* in chapters 28 and 29.

PART I

General Introduction

General Introduction

The work of Jürgen Habermas is central to many of the most pressing intellectual and practical concerns of the contemporary world. There is a widely perceived crisis both of philosophy and sociology, the two academic specialisms with which Habermas is most closely identified, and of historical materialism, of which he has also attempted a "reconstruction." The boundaries between normative political theory and analytical social theory have become increasingly indistinct, for good reasons. More broadly, "modernity" itself has been revived as a theoretical category at the same time as its status as a project has been radically questioned by "postmodernists" and others.

Habermas's thought ranges from linguistics to moral, political, and social theory, via political economy, philosophy, and the history of ideas. Modernity, however, seen as offering a highly conditional promise of autonomy, justice, democracy, and solidarity, now seems increasingly the organizing category with which to understand his thought. As early as the late 1950s, he has claimed in an interview, "My problem was a theory of modernity, a theory of the pathology of modernity, from the viewpoint of the realization – the deformed realization – of reason in history." Poised, as he once described Marxism, between philosophy and social science, Habermas is also himself poised between Marxism and non-Marxist thought, between the critical theory of the earlier Frankfurt School (discussed below) and modern social and political theory, between the critique of modernity and its affirmation as a still valid, indeed inescapable project. This tension, which he has most recently thematized as one between "facticity and validity" in legal and democratic theory, runs through all his work, from his early studies of the public sphere* and of technocratic positivism in theory and practice

---

*In order to avoid repetition I have chosen to provide a general glossary of problematic terms, and brief biographical details of some of the less well-known thinkers referred to by Habermas. Terms included in the glossary are indicated by an asterisk when they first appear, as are names included in the biographical notes. A useful source for further information on concepts and thinkers is *The Blackwell Dictionary of Twentieth-Century Social Thought* (1993), edited by the late Tom Bottomore and myself.

down to his later development of a theory of discourse* which underpins his challenging reformulation of the foundations of ethics.

Habermas has always affirmed the need for serious intellectual engagement, not only with the philosophical tradition of Kant, Hegel, and Marx, and its development into later social and political theory, but also with the principal theoretical movements in the human and social sciences. At the center of these intersections, Habermas has pursued, over the past 35 years, a coherent intellectual and political project: to reanimate in new and expanded forms the critical thrust and the practical impulse of Marxist philosophy and social theory, recombining theory and practice in a manner which can be defended in the modern world.

Born in 1929, Jürgen Habermas studied philosophy, history, psychology, and German literature at the University of Göttingen, and then in Zürich and Bonn, where he obtained his doctorate in 1954. After working as a journalist, he became, in 1956, Adorno's assistant in the reconstituted Institute for Social Research, where he participated in an empirical study on the political awareness of students, *Student und Politik*, published in 1961. From 1959 to 1961 he worked on his *The Structural Transformation of the Public Sphere* (1962).

After a period as Professor of Philosophy at Heidelberg, Habermas returned to Frankfurt in 1964 as Professor of Philosophy and Sociology, where he delivered the inaugural lecture on "Knowledge and Interest" which prefigures the book with the same title, published in 1968. His other works of this period are the essays entitled *Theory and Practice* (1963), a survey work *On the Logic of the Social Sciences* (1967), and some further essays grouped under the title *Technology and Science as Ideology* (1968).

The year 1968 was also, of course, the time of major student-led protest, in West Germany as elsewhere. Habermas participated very fully in the movement, welcoming its intellectual and political challenge to the complacency of German democracy (and incidentally its supersession of the gloomy diagnosis, in *Student und Politik*, of the unpolitical orientation of West German students). Although he came to criticize its extremism, he has continued to take a very positive view of the long-term effect of the movement on values in the Federal Republic, while deploring the short-term legacy of its failure: a decline into apathy or desperate terrorism.

In 1971 Habermas left Frankfurt for Starnberg, Bavaria, to take up, along with the natural scientist C. F. von Weizsäcker, the directorship of the newly created Max Planck Institute for the Study of the Conditions of Life in the Scientific-Technical World. Surrounded by some of the most brilliant younger sociologists in the country, he published an enormous amount of material, including the well-known *Legitimation Crisis* (1973) and the essays published in English as *Communication and the Evolution of Society* (1979), and culminating in

The Theory of Communicative Action (1981). In 1982 he returned to Frankfurt, to the chair in Sociology and Philosophy which he occupied until his retirement in 1994.

In the 1980s and early 1990s, Habermas continued to develop the implications of his theory of communicative action in three main areas. The first was that of moral philosophy, with *Moral Consciousness and Communicative Action* (1983) and *Justification and Application* (1991). The second was that of the critical history of philosophy, with *The Philosophical Discourse of Modernity* (1985) and *Postmetaphysical Thinking* (1988). Finally, in "Law and Morality" (lectures delivered 1986) and *Between Facts and Norms* (1992), he extended his discourse ethics to the theory of law and the democratic state. His occasional writings include numerous essays, newspaper articles, and interviews, some of which have appeared in English in *The New Conservatism* (1989), *The Past as Future* (1991), and a volume of interviews edited by Peter Dews, *Habermas: Autonomy and Solidarity* (London: Verso, 1986, 1992).

If Max Weber has been described as a bourgeois Marx, Habermas might be summarily characterized as a Marxist Max Weber. Like Weber, he is basically a thinker rather than a man of action, but one who intervenes in political issues when something, as he often puts it, "irritates" him. His collected "political writings" – a broad category which includes occasional lectures and interviews – run to several volumes. Although he rejects Weber's doctrine of the value-freedom* of science, he insists, like Weber, on the distinction between scholarly and political discourse. Like Weber, and the existentialist philosopher and psychologist Karl Jaspers* in the postwar period, he has operated in some way as the intellectual conscience of the country, with a public profile higher than one would expect of someone who has not sought out a political role.

Habermas combines a deep grounding in the philosophical tradition with a remarkable openness to a wide variety of contemporary philosophical and social theories. Entire books could be written about the respective influences on his thought of Kant and Hegel, Marx and Weber, Parsons* and Piaget,* and so on. The most important source is, however, without question the broad Marxist tradition which also inspired the original Frankfurt Institute for Social Research.

The history of Marxist thought in the twentieth century is in large part a process for which the pejorative term is "revisionism," involving the abandonment or relegation of certain Marxist principles, the incorporation of, or at least engagement with, non-Marxist theories such as those of Kant, Nietzsche, and Freud, and a tendency to pay more attention to "superstructural" processes, whether political, ideological, or more particularly artistic, than to those in the so-called "base."

The Hungarian Marxist Georgy Lukács was a crucial figure in this development, offering one channel at least through which German idealism, with important modifications by the sociologist Georg Simmel, was transmuted into "critical theory." Although Lukács considered himself to be an "orthodox" Marxist, his enormously creative elaboration of some of the more Hegelian themes in Marx, subsequently discovered in Marx's own early writings, was the decisive influence on what has come to be known as "Western Marxism." The two intellectual linchpins of this movment are Lukács's concept of reification, which generalized Marx's analysis of commodity fetishism, and his emphasis on the idea of totality. The term "critical theory" is used in this context (as opposed to a broader usage in literary theory) in two main ways: first, to refer to the tradition which began with Simmel and Lukács; and second, more narrowly, to refer to the work of some of the writers associated with the Frankfurt Institute for Social Research. (The term "Frankfurt School," which tends to be used interchangeably with "critical theory" in the English-speaking world, was used in West Germany to refer to the Institute after its re-establishment there in 1950.)

The Institut für Sozialforschung was established as a private foundation in 1923 to develop interdisciplinary Marxist research, and when the philosopher Max Horkheimer succeeded the historian Carl Grünberg as Director in 1930 he inaugurated the conception of a distinctive "critical theory." The Institute provided a base or looser forms of support for many of the most brilliant neo-Marxist thinkers of the twentieth century, spanning and linking philosophy and the social sciences. As well as Max Horkheimer, Theodor Adorno, and Herbert Marcuse,* those associated with the Institute included Walter Benjamin, Horkheimer's close associate the economist Friedrich Pollock, and two other economists, Henryk Grossman and Arkady Gurland, the psychologists Bruno Bettelheim and Erich Fromm, and the literary theorist Leo Lowenthal. Although the rise of Nazism meant that the Institute had to move, first to Geneva and Paris, and then, in 1934, to New York, its work survived all these vicissitudes. Its journal, the *Zeitschrift für Sozialforschung*, published from 1932 to 1941 (the last three parts in English), remains one of the richest intellectual documents of the period. In the 1950s Horkheimer and Adorno returned to Germany and re-established the Institute, though with a rather more traditional emphasis on work in philosophy and social theory.

The distinctive Frankfurt School perspective is essentially that of Adorno, Horkheimer, and Marcuse. Their flexible neo-Marxism developed in response to three major challenges: those of fascism, Stalinism, and managerial capitalism, whose perceived similarities and apparent invincibility pushed the Frankfurt thinkers into a position of permanent and increasingly desperate opposition. Their ever more negative philosophy of history is epitomized by Adorno and Horkheimer's *Dialectic of Enlightenment*, written at the height of World War II, in which they argued that the Enlightenment critique of myth and domination,* and the pursuit of rational mastery over nature, themselves contribute to new forms of domination.

Habermas's relationship to Frankfurt critical theory was rather less immediate than is often assumed. In intellectual terms, he is closer to the Institute's earlier program, grounding his critique in an interdisciplinary synthesis drawn from various social sciences and avoiding the temptations of the negative philosophy of history. But if Habermas was dissatisfied with the form of Adorno and Horkheimer's thought from *Dialectic of Enlightenment* onward, he shared their substantive preoccupation with the way in which enlightenment, in the form of instrumental or means–end rationality, turns from a means of liberation into a new source of enslavement.

In Habermas's early work, this preoccupation took three forms. First, there was a working-through of the classical philosophical texts: Marx and Weber, but also Kant, Fichte, and Hegel – not to mention the Greeks. Second, there was a preoccupation with technology and the attempt to construct a "left" alternative to the technological determinism arising in part from Heidegger and, in postwar Germany, from the philosopher Arnold Gehlen* and the sociologist Helmut Schelsky.* Third, and relatedly, there was a concern with rational political discussion or practical reason in modern technocratic democracy. The first of these themes predominates in *Theory and Practice*; the second can be found in Habermas's early journalism and in *Technology and Science as Ideology*; the third theme occurs in both these works, but is first addressed in *Student und Politik* and *The Structural Transformation of the Public Sphere*. They are in any case interrelated, since the transformation of public opinion from a critical perspective on state policy into an object of technical manipulation is intimately linked to the tendency to treat political decisions as a whole as a technical matter to be decided on expert advice. And this in turn raises issues about the theoretical and practical relations between theory and practice in the modern world.

In his first major book, *The Structural Transformation of the Public Sphere*, Habermas relates the concept of public opinion back to its historical roots in the idea of the public sphere or public domain. The literate bourgeois public of the eighteenth century took on a political role in the evaluation of contemporary affairs and, in particular, state policy. With the growth of trade and industry, state policy came to have an importance for the growing bourgeoisie which it had not had in a society of small-scale household production and retailing; hence the enormous growth in the newspaper market. In addition to any independent desire for greater democratic influence, people needed to know what the state was doing or failing to do and to influence it as far as they could. What Habermas calls the transformation of the public sphere involves a shift from publicity in the sense of openness to the modern sense of the term in journalism, advertising, and politics

(p. 140). The reading public, which had prefigured the political public, also prefigures its decline into "minorities of specialists who put their reason to use publicly and the great mass of consumers whose receptiveness is public but uncritical" (p. 175). The same is true of the political process, split between a small number of party activists and a basically inactive mass electorate; public opinion ceases to be a source of critical judgment and checks, and becomes a social psychological variable to be manipulated. The result is a "gap between the constitutional fiction of public opinion and the social-psychological dissolution of its concept" (p. 244).

Just as, in Horkheimer and Adorno's *Dialectic of Englightenment*, the Enlightenment critique of myth turned into another myth, so here the principle of the bourgeois public sphere, the critical assessment of public policy in rational discussion, oriented to a concept of the public interest, turns into what Habermas calls a manipulated public sphere in which states and corporations use "publicity" in the modern sense of the word to secure for themselves a kind of plebiscitary acclamation. Habermas's analysis, however, is both more carefully grounded in the results of historical, sociological, and political scientific research, and also somewhat less pessimistic in its conclusions. Although the bureaucratization of administration seems, as Max Weber had noted in relation to parliamentary politics, to remove the activity of specialists from rational control, it might yet be possible to create, by means of public communication within these organizations, "an appropriate relation between bureaucratic decision and quasi-parliamentary deliberation" (p. 234). This cautious conclusion seems to point in two main directions: (1) the critique of technocratic ideology and (2) the attempt to work out an intellectual and practical basis for public discussion and effective control of public policy. The first theme points toward Habermas's essays in *Theory and Practice* and *Technology and Science as Ideology* and toward the philosophical critique of positivism which dominated his work in the 1960s; the second theme finds its full development in the *Theory of Communicative Action* and in *Between Facts and Norms*.

Taken as a whole, *Theory and Practice* has three main themes which recur in Habermas's later work: (1) a critical evaluation of the Marxist tradition, (2) some reflections on the possibility of what he later called the "reconstruction" of historical materialism, and (3) a methodological comparison between the unity of empirical and normative, or technical and "practical"* issues to be found in Aristotle, in natural law* theory, and in Marxism, and the scientistic, ostensibly value-free approach of the modern social sciences. Habermas has recalled reading Lukács's *History and Class Consciousness* in the 1950s with a mixture of admiration and a sense that this sort of orthodox Marxism, however creative, belonged to a different world. In *Theory and Practice* he notes some familiar facts which count "against Marx" in the modern world. The interpenetration of state and society in organized capitalism has made the base/superstructure distinction inapplicable; the exploitation of labor has taken on subtler forms in affluent welfare capitalism, and therefore the proletariat no longer exists in its traditional form.

For these and other reasons we can no longer accept Marxism wholesale as a valid scientific theory. Equally unsatisfactory, however, is the response by some social scientists, such as the economist Joseph Schumpeter* or the sociologist Ralf Dahrendorf, to filter out the useful bits of economics or sociology from the overall model. Marxism has been denatured by this kind of asset stripping, as much as by official Soviet dogmatism. To do this is to lose sight of Marxism's powerful vision of a social totality and also its peculiar methodological status. Marxism is suspended "between philosophy and science," taking up and concretizing the philosophical concept of critique in the service of a program of social and political emancipation, yet also scientifically falsifiable. Marxists have themselves often misunderstood the status of Marx's critique, construing it on the model of the other sciences. The dependence of ideas on interests arising from a system of production is originally a dialectical notion, linking ideas and material interests in a model of the process of social reproduction. But Engels, and Marx from 1850 onward, turn this into a naturalistic theory; thus "the correct ideology was distinguished from the false solely according to the criteria of a realist theory of knowledge" (p. 238). Marxism, in other words, failed to uphold its "philosophical" content in setting itself up as one positive science among others. "Marx never explicitly asked himself the epistemological question concerning the conditions of the possibility of a philosophy of history with a political intent" (p. 242).

It was another ten years before Habermas offered a systematic "reconstruction" of historical materialism, but the methodological model which he attributed to Marx is also the one which governs his early conception of his own work. Treating the positivist separation of facts and values as "less a result than a problem" (*Theory and Practice*, p. 31; cf. part III, sections 6 and 7, below), he attempts to carve out a role for critical social science between a modern but simplistic positivism and superseded traditions of orthodox idealist and Marxist philosophy and political theory.

Habermas pursued these issues more systematically in two other major books published in the late 1960s. The first, *On the Logic of the Social Sciences*, is a detailed working through of the antipositivist and antifunctionalist implications of the three variants of an interpretive methodology which had recently come to prominence. The first of these was the "phenomenological" sociology developed by Alfred Schutz out of Edmund Husserl's phenomenological philosophy, in a book originally published in 1932 and reissued in 1960, and in his collected essays, also published in the early 1960s. Second was Peter Winch's sociological reworking of Ludwig Wittgenstein's later philosophy, in an influential book of 1958, based on the idea that to understand a culture is to understand the conceptual framework shared by members of that culture. Third was Hans-Georg Gadamer's* reformulation in 1960 of the hermeneutic tradition. Gadamer drew on Martin Heidegger's philosophy and stressed that our understanding of texts (and for Gadamer all humanly experienced reality is mediated through language) involves a crucial element of existential encounter which leaves both us and the text changed.

These three traditions, as Habermas showed, raised once again the issue of the dualism traditionally argued to exist between the natural sciences and the sciences of mind or spirit (*Geisteswissenschaften*): "there would be no reason to touch on the well-buried complex of the dualism of science if it did not in one area continually produce symptoms that demand analytic resolution: in the social sciences, heterogeneous aims and approaches conflict and intermingle with one another" (*On the Logic of the Social Sciences*, p. 2). The positivist thesis of unified science fails, in Habermas's view, because of the intimate relationship between the social sciences and history, and the fact that they are based on "a situation-specific understanding of meaning that can be explicated only 'hermeneutically'" (*On the Logic of the Social Sciences*, p. 43). As he put it some ten years later: "the problem of 'understanding' [*Verstehen*] in the human and social sciences only achieved its great methodological importance because access to a symbolically prestructured reality cannot be gained by observation alone, and because the understanding [*Verständnis*] of a participant cannot be so easily subjected to methodological control as the perception of an observer" ("Objektivismus in den Sozialwissenschaften," p. 549).

Having modestly presented this work as a "literature survey," Habermas published in the following year what is widely considered to be still his best work, *Knowledge and Human Interests*, an enormously ambitious critical history of the philosophical origins of modern positivism in the natural and human sciences. In a brilliant argument which ranged over Kant and Fichte, Hegel and Marx, Comte and Mach, Peirce* and Dilthey, and finally Freud, Habermas moved toward a conception of a critical or emancipatory social science, exemplified by Freudian and Marxian theory and distinguished both from the empirical methods of the natural sciences, oriented to the prediction and control of objectified processes, and from the hermeneutic methods of the humanities, which are unable on their own to uncover causal obstacles to understanding and the effects of systematically distorted communication. This is the task of critical social sciences, effecting what in the philosophical tradition had been conceived as the union of reason and universalizable human interests.

Habermas had by now abandoned his earlier description of critical theory as a practically oriented and falsifiable philosophy of history, and replaced it by this more substantial model of the methodology of critical science. Soon, however, he began to feel that the path he had traced through epistemology and methodology in order to establish a foundation for critical social theory had been something of a detour, and retained too much of the traditional notion of the primacy of philosophy. More concretely, the way in which he had specified the status of the interests governing the various sciences was unstable. They were supposed to be factually present, empirically given interests of the human species as a whole, but they also performed a transcendental role in setting the conditions of the possibility of meaningful statements in these sciences. This "quasi-transcendental" status led to paradoxes in, for example, the analysis of nature, which both was constituted as an object of inquiry and was itself the grounds of constituting activity and the interests which animated it. Habermas felt also that in stressing the theoretical constitution of the object-domains of the social sciences he had not adequately distinguished between the origins and the validity of statements, between the context of discovery and the context of justification. Nor, he conceded, did the neat division between three types of science do justice to a large body of interesting and important work in history, linguistics, and the other social sciences, which could not be assigned to one of these categories.

Having decided against the illusory attractions of the philosophy of history, and failed to get what he wanted out of the philosophy of science, Habermas turned more substantially to the philosophy of language. Of the two directions of research which interested him, one turned out to be a false trail. The other, however, formed the basis for all his subsequent work from the mid-1970s to the present. It is therefore important to examine this "linguistic turn" in some detail.

Habermas had been attracted for some time by the idea of grounding the social sciences in a theory of language, and devoted the Gauss lectures which he delivered at Princeton in 1971–2 to this program. Noam Chomsky's* theory of linguistic competence could, he believed, be generalized into a broader notion of communicative competence, a "universal pragmatics" which would "allow one to find and reconstruct the systems of rules according to which we produce complexes of interaction, i.e. the symbolic reality of society itself." He soon abandoned this project as originally conceived, concluding that social theory must stand on its own and give up the search for foundations of knowledge in either a direct or an indirect, linguistic form, but he retained the idea of a theory of communicative action, now grounded in an analysis of the presuppositions of meaningful speech.

Habermas's central idea is remarkably simple. It is that every standard use of language to make statements involves certain presuppositions: that what the speaker says is true, that it is sincerely meant, and that it is normatively appropriate. Joking apart, talking about things, including ourselves, only has a point if we are serious about it and can at least envisage the possibility of reaching agreement, as autonomous and equal partners in discussion. I can make you believe what I want by hypnosis, or by deception, or perhaps by appealing to authority, but this isn't playing the game: our discussion in this case is merely a simulated one.

Thus the analysis of communication gives us a concept of which Habermas calls action oriented to reaching mutual understanding or agreement, and also of action guided by that understanding. What distinguishes a suggestion or request formulated in a communicative orientation from a simple command is that the former's presuppositions are in practice open to challenge. Habermas gives the example of a professor asking a seminar participant to fetch a glass of water. The participant may question the factual presupposition that there is water available, the professor's sincerity in asking for it, or the normative appropriateness of such a request.

Agreements reached in advance, in discourse, are one way of coordinating action; another is via the consequences of action. Markets and legal systems characteristically operate in this second way, penalizing those who step out of line by producing more goods than are needed or by violating a duly enacted law; only in exceptional circumstances are you expected to give an undertaking in advance to obey the law. But democracy means, among other things, that all should have the opportunity to participate at some level in decisions which concern them.

Habermas has worked out the implications of this "formal" or "universal" pragmatics in a number of different areas. First, at the level of language use itself, it may be possible to examine the systematic distortion of communication. Such distortions characteristically result from unresolved external conflicts which impinge on the communicative encounter. In discussions between slaves and masters, for example, systematic distortion is likely to be the rule rather than the exception. Habermas has not so far written much about these issues, though there are some suggestive papers, notably one from a manuscript written in 1974.

Second, and controversially, Habermas has developed, along with his associate Karl-Otto Apel,* a discourse-based or communicative ethical theory. The agreements aimed at in speech concern not only matters of fact but also, Habermas believes, moral questions. *Contra* a tradition of thought which is still influential, especially in the English-speaking countries, moral judgments are not just expressions of preference, or prescriptions based on an ultimately arbitrary choice between alternative values (see part V, section 15). We can distinguish, he suggests, between ethical dilemmas related to concrete ways of life and core moral questions about which our reasoning must take a universalistic form. A discourse ethics steers a path between the formal and communitarian traditions of ethical thought: moral judgments are neither just expressions of social conventions, nor reached deductively by individuals who are in principle isolated from one another and alone with their consciences. The agreement must be one which is or could have been reached *in discussion.*

Habermas has recently argued that the same principles can be extended to the fields of law and the state. Law and morality are distinct, but both moral and legal norms depend implicitly on what Habermas calls the discourse principle, that those affected by them could agree to them as participants in a rational discourse (*Between Facts and Norms*, p. 138). Modified to fit the three contexts of morality, law, and political democracy, the intuition embodied in the discourse principle underpins the structural relations between them. Although they developed independently, the rule of law in the constitutional state (*Rechtsstaat* in German) and political democracy now presuppose each other. Legal forms are not self-legitimating;* they presuppose, while also reinforcing, the support afforded by the public sphere of a legal and political community. "The rational quality of political legislation does not only depend on how elected majorities and protected minorities work within parliaments. It also depends on the level of participation and school education, the degree of information and the precision with which controversial issues are articulated – in short, on the discursive character of non-institutionalized opinion formation in the political public sphere" (*Faktizität und Geltung*, p. 570).

It may be helpful here to outline the basic conceptual choices underlying Habermas's arguments. Take two extreme opposing principles:

A Everyone affected by legal and political decisions should discuss them until there is complete agreement about them.
B Legal and political decisions are complicated matters which should be left to experts.

The first might be called radical anarchism; the second is a very compressed version of one of the conclusions of Niklas Luhmann's* politically conservative system theory. Habermas has sometimes been misunderstood as advocating (A), but in fact, as his recent work makes clear beyond any doubt, his position is a much more nuanced one. It is true, however, that, while he rejects (A) on grounds of practicality, his objection to (B) is one of principle. Habermas has argued against technocracy from the beginning of his career; he now makes it clear that he accepts something like the existing institutional framework of law and representative democracy in a society such as his own, while insisting that the appropriateness of such arrangements, the fairness of conventions, and so forth should be open to, and determined by, the widest possible public discussion. And to outline the formal model of law and democracy, and the interrelations between them, is also to show how lamentably modern societies have failed to live up to these principles.

As the above discussion indicates, Habermas sees his analysis of communicative action in part as a normative theory, yielding moral and political prescriptions, but also as a social theory expressing or, in his terms, reconstructing certain features of modernity. As he put it in an interview, he is not:

> saying that people ought to act communicatively, but that they *must* . . . When parents educate their children, when living generations appropriate the knowledge handed down by their predecessors, when individuals cooperate, i.e. get on with one another without a costly use of force, they must act communicatively. There are elementary social functions which can only be satisfied by means of communicative action. (*The Past as Future*, p. 11)

In his most substantial work to date, *The Theory of Communicative Action*, Habermas uses this basic model to reconstruct Western Marxism's critique of bureaucracy and capitalist reification. In shorter works in the 1970s he had outlined what he called a "reconstruction" of historical materialism as a two-stage evolutionary theory of history based not just on the advance of the productive forces, the aspect stressed in most Marxist thought, but on a complementary learning process in morality and forms of social integration. As human beings learn to control natural processes, and to develop new forms of material production, they also learn new ways of conceptualizing and ordering their social relations.

Habermas develops this theme via a detailed analysis of Max Weber. He suggests that what Weber analyzed as the rationalization of action in fact has two aspects. The first is the replacement of traditional world-views and forms of social action by new forms which are more reflexive, explicit, ordered, and calculable: the specification of life-projects, whether religious or economic, and the extension of the areas of social life which are seen as open to agreement rather than having been laid down as part of a religiously legitimated order. Social contract theory can be viewed as a paradoxical, because mythical, expression of this rationalizing tendency, and the codification of law is one of its principal aspects. The individual becomes a kind of proprietor or manager of himself or herself.

But the rationalization of world-views is increasingly overshadowed by a second form of rationalization, involving the growing independence of market and administrative structures which are again removed from the domain of discussion and possible agreement. The growth of these self-sufficient structures and the reduction of individuals to impotent cogs in these machines is captured in Weber's metaphor of the "iron cage." Georg Lukács, fusing Marx's concept of commodity fetishism, which involves the transformation of social relations (in particular, those between "capital" and "labor") into relations between things, and Weber's analysis of rationalization, used the term "reification," taken up by Habermas himself.

Both Weber and the Marxist tradition, however, have conceptualized this situation with reference to the individual subject* and its rationality. In so doing, they have weakened the explanatory power of their theories, the force of their critiques, and the plausibility of possible alternatives. For Weber, the rationalization process is inevitable, and is in part the expression of an individualism which we cannot fail to value; yet it also undermines individuality and risks reducing human beings to a condition of servitude comparable with that in ancient Egypt. Similarly, in what Max Horkheimer and Theodor Adorno called the dialectic of enlightenment, the very process by which human societies emerge from slavery to natural forces and mythical beliefs turns back on itself and creates a new realm of universal domination. If rationalization is seen in this way, as the performance of an individual or collective *subject*, mastering itself as part of the extension of its power, there is no obvious way out of such traps. Only a fuller understanding of the way in which objectified market and administrative structures come to dominate the lifeworld* of human beings allows for the possibility of re-establishing democratic control over these processes.

This replacement of a subject-centered conception of rationality by a communicative one grounded in interactions *between* human subjects also has crucial implications for philosophy, which Habermas has brought out in a series of lectures published in 1985 as *The Philosophical Discourse of Modernity*, and a volume of essays, *Postmetaphysical Thinking*, published three years later. As we saw in relation to *Knowledge and Human Interests*, Habermas has ceased to see philosophy as having any special privilege in relation to the sciences; and in an essay of 1971, "Does Philosophy Still Have a Purpose?," he had sketched out a model of cooperation between philosophy and the individual sciences. Attempts to rehabilitate metaphysics, whether in the traditional mode of transcendental philosophy, as in the work of Dieter Henrich, or in more innovative and fashionable variants building on Heidegger's later philosophy, attribute to philosophy a privileged method and domain which it can no longer aspire to without anachronism.

This does not mean, however, that we should, like the American pragmatist philosopher Richard Rorty, cease to take seriously the concept of truth and the idea of possible agreement as the goal of rational discourse. When Rorty claims that we cannot mean by truth anything more than truth "for us," though we can aim to extend the scope of "us" by pursuing intersubjective agreement, Habermas argues that we could not understand the way we criticize and modify our established standards of rationality and justification if we did not take seriously the idea of a possible consensus which would transcend the opposition of "us" and "them." In other words, although our validity*-claims are always made in specific contexts, the validity which they claim transcends time and space.

It is this model which Habermas used in *The Philosophical Discourse of Modernity* as the basis of an ambitious critique of the Western philosophical tradition since Hegel. This, too, is marked by the sense that philosophy is at an end, whether in Hegelian absolute knowledge, Marxian communism, Nietzsche's will to power, Wittgenstein's fly in the fly-bottle, Heidegger's "turn" to poetry in his later philosophy, or Derrida's "deconstruction." Despite the diversity of these thinkers, in what is a relatively unprofessionalized field, there is a common feature: a (partially justified) suspicion of the narrowness of the original Enlightenment conception of rationality. Western philosophy, says Habermas, takes basically three directions from Hegel. The left Hegelians and Marxists aimed to generalize and realize the rationality of the Enlightenment in a new society of freedom; the right Hegelians aimed to tame and incorporate it in secure institutional forms; Nietzsche, by contrast, turned reason against itself, unmasking it as an expression of the will to power and mocking the rationalistic and moralistic illusions of modernity.

Habermas's response is that thinkers such as Heidegger, Derrida, and Foucault are right to reject the philosophy of consciousness centered on the subject, but wrong to draw on conclusions they do. There is "another way out of the philosophy of the subject," via a reflection on human *inter*subjectivity and communication. In other words, rather than oscillating between the inflation of the human knowing subject and a radical skepticism about its reality, we should hold on to a model in which "participants in interaction ... coordinate their plans for action by coming to an understanding about something in the world" (p. 296). "Communicative reason finds its criteria in the argumentative procedures for ... redeeming claims to propositional truth, normative rightness, subjective truthfulness, and aesthetic harmony" (p. 314). It thus "recalls older ideas of logos" in its orientation to consensus and "a decentered understanding of the world" (p. 315). This also yields a more balanced view of the ambiguous achievements of modernity than that offered by Horkheimer and Adorno and later by Michel Foucault – suggesting that we should see it as an incomplete project rather than a misguided and discredited one.

It will be clear from this discussion of Habermas's work that he has always situated himself in relation to one or more traditions of thinking, often working out and presenting his own theoretical innovations via detailed critical expositions of other writers. This means that an assessment of the significance of his work also turns in part on whether one shares his judgments about the insufficiencies of earlier and competing traditions. Someone who believes, for instance, in the continued viability of an orthodox Kantian, Hegelian, or Marxist position, or that the important issues in contemporary philosophy are located somewhere on the axis from Nietzsche to Heidegger and Derrida or Lyotard, or that there is nothing much wrong with Gadamer's hermeneutics or Luhmann's system theory – or, for that matter, with neo-positivism or rational action theory – will not see the point of the theoretical questions to which Habermas has attempted to provide answers. Similarly, someone who takes a more optimistic view than he does of the current state of liberal democracy, or a more pessimistic view of its prospects, or who considers that in any case the "life and times of liberal democracy" are an irrelevant preoccupation compared to more serious global crises, both natural and social, will fail to see the point of his practical-political concerns. I shall concentrate here on neo-Marxism and system theory as the most plausible competing theories of similar scope to Habermas's own, while also paying some attention to the work of Michel Foucault, the other social thinker of perhaps comparable importance in the late twentieth century.

As we have seen, Habermas has a number of principled objections to standard versions of Marxism. First, he shared with earlier critical theorists, and a number of other postwar socialist thinkers, a sense that capitalism had changed so as to render inapplicable the traditional accounts of the relation between base and superstructure, and also the basic crisis theorems of Marxism, in which the economic contradictions of capitalism, together with the immiseration and estrangement of the proletariat, made the system both economically and politically unstable. Second, Marxism was in any case flawed as a theory of society, in that it paid too much attention to productive resources and not enough to the development of normative structures. Third, Marxism misunderstood itself as empirical science, rather than as a theory of a more complex methodological character.

Habermas worked in the 1970s on all three dimensions. On the first point, he developed, and published as *Legitimation Crisis* (1973), an outline model in which economic crisis tendencies in late capitalism were displaced onto other parts of society, giving rise to more diffuse crises of legitimation and motivation. Habermas came to reject this model in its details, but he restates many of the same themes in *Between Facts and Norms*. "The independent establishment of illegitimate power and the weakness of civil society and the political public sphere can come to a head in a 'legitimatory dilemma' . . . Then the political system is sucked into mutually reinforcing legitimacy and steering deficits" (*Faktizität und Geltung*, p. 466).

In relation to the second theme, the excessive materialism or "productionism" of Marxist theory, Habermas developed an ambitious model of evolutionary learning which mapped the stages of cognitive development identified by developmental psychology onto stages of social development. Here he spells out in more detail the notion that Marxism should pay as much attention to learning processes in the domain of norms, ethics, and social regulation in general as to the mastery of natural processes and the development of the forces of production. He had always accepted Karl Kautsky's* suggestion that the base–superstructure model applied mainly to the analysis of social change; he now argued that changes in normative structures are often the stimulus to major social changes. The emergence of family structures, for example, may have been more important than labor or the use of tools in what Engels called the "transition from ape to man."

This model inspired some important work in historical sociology, which, however, left it looking less rather than more plausible. At the same time, more orthodox Marxists were themselves paying more and more attention to the "relative autonomy" of political processes, and thus converging to some extent with earlier Frankfurt School models of culture (which Habermas has himself criticized for being too orthodox) and his own more flexible system model.

Habermas's view of the methodological status of Marxism has also changed as his thought developed, while retaining the basic theme that it was something more than an ordinary science. The aspect of Marxism which had always played the largest part in his thinking was the critique of ideology, especially when, in his "middle period," he moved from characterizing it as a practically oriented philosophy of history to seeing it as an exemplar of an emancipatory social science. As he subsequently developed the model of reconstructive sciences, like Noam Chomsky's linguistics, which uncover the structures which make possible capacities (such as language use) that we already know we have, he presented his version of historical materialism as a reconstructive science of human social evolution.

Finally, we should look at Habermas's attitude to Marxism as a guide to political projects. His politics were always reformist rather than revolutionary, social democratic rather than communist. He had no illusions about the state socialist dictatorships in the East, and his response to their sudden collapse focussed more on the future consequences for the West than on the past and current state of the ex-communist societies themselves. (In Germany, of course, the two issues largely coincided.) He has, however, spelled out, more explicitly than in the past, his view that modern societies cannot realistically hope to replace market structures as a whole without risking worse problems than those of capitalism itself. He now defines what he means by socialism as radical democracy, with at best the hope that this will be able to keep in check some of the worst excesses of capitalism. To some this will seem a realistic accommodation to the fact that capitalism is "the only game in town"; others will see it as opportunism or surrender. But in the current state of fundamental rethinking of Marxism and socialism as a whole – so far as this has taken place at all – Habermas's revisions no longer seem particularly extreme.

The system theorist Niklas Luhmann is not just Habermas's contemporary, and a competitor for the attention of the sociological public in Germany and elsewhere; he has also been a more or less constant reference point for Habermas's own thinking. Habermas displayed a rather nuanced attitude to functionalist theory in *Logic of the Social Sciences*, suggesting that functionalists were at least confronting the issues of societies as a whole. Shortly afterwards, he embarked on a lengthy exchange with Luhmann which led to several further volumes of papers by their respective supporters. At the same time, he was making substantial use of the terminology of system theory in *Legitimation Crisis* and other works. He returned more substantially to the theme of system theory in *The Theory of Communicative Action* and again at the end of *The Philosophical Discourse of Modernity*.

In brief, Habermas largely accepts Luhmann's diagnosis of the growth of relatively autonomous subsystems in modern societies, but whereas Luhmann sees this as a beneficial advance in differentiation and in the reduction of complexity, Habermas sees it as pathological in its consequences for the lifeworld and for democratic self-rule. He has, however, taken over from system theory the idea that societies cannot be understood as subjects (*Theory and Practice*, pp. 303ff, n. 67), and that, more particularly, the public sphere in modern societies must necessarily be conceived in a fairly abstract manner, as a structure of mediated communication rather than as a group of individuals who in principle could meet and discuss in a single space. One can ask, however, as Thomas McCarthy and Hans Joas have done, if Habermas has not taken too seriously the pretensions of system theory and whether one really needs, as he believes, to move from theories of human action to theories of social systems in order to address the processes which he identifies in modernity. And it is clear that Luhmann's system theory does not offer a political or normative alternative to Habermas's.

The direct relationship between Foucault and Habermas was marred by mutual misunderstanding. Foucault seems to have had for a long time a very basic and undifferentiated understanding of critical theory, and Habermas tended to pay more attention in his own writings to Foucault's provocative metatheoretical reflections than to the tremendous power of his critical thinking. Both Foucault and Habermas were of course committed to what Axel Honneth has called the "critique of power" and, more specifically, to examining certain pathological consequences of the operation of state welfare bureaucracies. Of course Foucault's thought is full of inconsistencies and contradictions, and there is a tension between his evident partisanship in favour of the oppressed and his antinormative stance, as there is in his critique of knowledge systems in the name of just another knowledge system. Foucault needs a model to oppose to that of the undifferentiated universality of power relations, and this might well be found in the concept of communicative power which Habermas derives from the political philosopher Hannah Arendt,* in which power results from the self-empowerment of a political collectivity. But Foucault has also identified, as Harry Kunneman has shown, a crucially important area of pseudo-communication between social-scientifically trained members of the welfare state "therapeutocracy" and their clients. Habermas is too quick to label as a deviant and pathological case the "latently strategic action" of those who enter a discourse with an ulterior purpose; but this is the norm when the discourse is rigged in advance by inequalities of power and knowledge which are constitutive of the therapeutic role as conventionally institutionalized.

These considerations suggest that Habermas's thought is not so radically divergent in many areas from that of thinkers with whom he is often sharply contrasted. Often, as for example with Lyotard, what seems at first sight a serious disagreement may be largely a matter of differences in emphasis and intellectual style. As the initial controversies, direct and indirect, between critical theory and "postmodernism" fade into the past, some of these underlying commonalities are becoming clearer.

Habermas has developed a theory of action which will take its place alongside those of Max Weber and Talcott Parsons as one of the central elements of social theory, and he has used this to construct a critical theory of modernity, and of the philosophical discourse of modernity, of enormous scope and power. His discourse ethics has put his work at the center of contemporary discussions in moral philosophy, and his emergent theory of law and the democratic state seems to be having a similar impact. There can be little doubt that Habermas's thinking will be as influential in the twenty-first century as it has been in the second half of the twentieth.

My aim in this *Reader* has been to bring out the diversity of Habermas's work, the moments at which he has taken new directions as well as the very substantial elements of continuity. The selection follows a roughly chronological order of presentation. Habermas now considers his work up to about 1976, represented here by the extracts in parts II and III, to have been superseded in its basic orientation by his subsequent model of communicative action (see part IV), and it is important to bear this in mind when reading these works. On the other hand, his abiding concern with the quality of public debate in modern democracies, illustrated in part II by an extract from *The Structural Transformation of the Public Sphere* and some essays published a few years later, returns as a major theme in his most recent work on law and the state. The short extracts in part V and much of the analysis in parts VII and VIII reformulate some aspects of his earlier analysis in *Legitimation Crisis*. Finally, the epistemological and methodological issues which loomed large in his work of the late 1960s have returned in a different form, both in *The Theory of Communicative Action* and, more broadly, in his conception of reconstructive sciences and his assertion of a complementary relation between critical social theory and "postmetaphysical" philosophy. A striking feature of Habermas's intellectual production is his readiness to engage with criticisms of his work, and his responses to critics, in the volumes listed under "Further Reading" below, are important both for an understanding of his underlying orientations and as a way into his work.

Notes

I have reduced the volume of notes in the extracts which make up this *Reader*, especially where they refer to relatively inaccessible untranslated sources. I have also occasionally added notes, or added to existing ones.

Further Reading

The most recent introductory book which covers the whole of Habermas's theoretical work to date is my *Habermas: A Critical Introduction* (1994), whose structure corresponds roughly to that of this *Reader*. Of the large number of earlier texts, I particularly recommend Thomas McCarthy's superb *The Critical Theory of Jürgen Habermas* (1978). Stephen White's *The Recent Work of Jürgen Habermas: Reason, Justice and Morality* (1988) and Kenneth Baynes's *The Normative Grounds of Social Criticism: Kant, Rawls, Habermas* (1991) are outstanding critical discussions of Habermas's work on these issues. There are several recent books focussing on *The Theory of Communicative Action*, notably those by David Ingram and Arie Brand. Robert Holub's *Jürgen Habermas: Critic in the Public Sphere* (1991) provides a good introduction to Habermas's thought by way of his many critical exchanges with other thinkers.

A second route into Habermas is via the many volumes of essays devoted to his work. The first of these to appear in English, and still well worth reading, is John Thompson and David Held's *Habermas: Critical Debates* (1982). This was followed in 1985 by R. J. Bernstein's *Habermas and Modernity* and in 1991 by the English version of Axel Honneth and Hans Joas's 1986 volume on *Communicative Action*. In each of these books, Habermas replies to the other contributors. Finally, the Festschrift published by Honneth, McCarthy, Claus Offe, and Albrecht Wellmer to mark Habermas's 60th birthday is now available in English in two volumes, *Philosophical Interventions in the Unfinished Project of the Enlightenment* and *Cultural-Political Interventions in the Unfinished Project of the Enlightenment* (1992). An excellent volume of a similar kind focussing on Habermas's ethical theory is Seyla Benhabib and Fred Dallmayr's *The Communicative Ethics Controversy* (1990).

Perhaps the best way into Habermas's thought is through the interviews which he has given over the past ten or twenty years. Many of these are available in English, with an extremely useful introduction, in Peter Dews's volume, *Habermas: Autonomy and Solidarity* (1986, 2nd edn 1992), and in *The Past as the Future* (1994). Dews's book *Logics of Disintegration* (1987) is an excellent critique of post-structuralism from a Habermasian point of view.

Three recent books which engage substantially with Habermas and are themselves major contributions to the continuing tradition of critical theory are Honneth's *Critique of Power*, Benhabib's *Critique, Norm and Utopia*, and Jay Bernstein's *The Politics of Transfiguration*. Also highly relevant, of course, are the works of Karl-Otto Apel and Albrecht Wellmer,* developed in close association with Habermas. Readers interested in the historical background to critical theory as a whole are well served with a number of excellent books, ranging from Tom Bottomore's brief introduction (1984) to Rolf Wiggershaus's massive history (1986, tr. 1993). Of intermediate dimensions, and still extremely useful, are Martin Jay's *The Dialectical Imagination* (1973) and David Held's *An Introduction to Critical Theory* (1980).

PART II

Rationality and the Public Sphere

Introduction

One of Habermas's first academic projects was his "Habilitation" thesis on the origins of the public sphere in eighteenth-century Europe and its transformation in the twentieth century. Habermas outlines the transformation of the eighteenth-century bourgeois public sphere which had operated as a site for the critical discussion of state policy by informed outsiders. This critical concept of public opinion is replaced, he argues, in the twentieth century by something more like publicity in the modern sense of the term, in which a mass public is manipulated by commercial and party political interest groups. The academic counterpart to this process is the abandonment by positivistic social science of the original critical concept of public opinion in favor of an empirically measurable and value-free "social-psychological" concept.

In readings 1–2, taken from the final chapters of The Structural Transformation of the Public Sphere, Habermas draws some conclusions from his analysis. The interpenetration of state and society changes both. The simple contrast between a private domain (which includes what Habermas calls the public sphere of critically reasoning citizens) and the closed domain of the state gives way to a multiplicity of intermediate, semi-private, and semi-public organizations. The state is opened up to influence by political parties and other organized groups. At the same time it extends its influence into the private sphere; it has to do so precisely in order to formally guarantee the independence of non-state institutions, where earlier states had simply exercized benign neglect or respected traditional privileges. The state rewrites and extends private law as well as public law.

Habermas describes all this as a process of "refeudalization." The public sphere becomes dominated by a smaller number of large and powerful organizations, and only organized publics can have any influence. The tension between genuine "publicness" and manipulative "publicity" runs through these organizations; it is mirrored in the concept of public opinion itself, in the tension between an empirical or "social-psychological" concept and one where public opinion is transfigured as a normative concept in constitutional law. The same public servants, in *other words, who speak reverently about the public, the public interest, and public opinion will spend a good deal of time manipulating public opinion through public relations work.*

Structural Transformation *inspired a great deal of political as well as academic discussion in Germany when it was published in 1962, and the English translation in 1989 sparked off a number of very active debates among historians and other social scientists. The book also points forward to several issues which run through the rest of Habermas's work; these include not only the concept of critical rationality and the conditions for its exercise, the critique of ideology and the politics of the modern state, but also some more institutional themes which recur in his later work. The "hollowing out" of the intimate sphere of the family, for example, as outside influences on family members become stronger with the growth of labor markets and social insurance, and developments in suburban architecture tend to open up the family house to public gaze, is discussed in language which anticipates the later theme, in* Theory of Communicative Action, *of the "colonization" of the lifeworld by the market economy and legal-bureaucratic regulation.*

The critique of technocratic social science which animates Habermas's account of the social-scientific "dissolution" of the concept of public opinion is developed more fully in several essays published in Theory and Practice *(1963) and* Technology and Science as Ideology *(1968). An early influence on his thinking had been Heidegger's critique of technology, taken up by Arnold Gehlen, Helmut Schelsky, and others. In the three essays from which excerpts are reproduced in this part, Habermas explores the dangers of "technocracy" (the term popularized in Jacques Ellul's book of 1954). At the same time, however, he attacks the notion, found both among the conservative thinkers named above and in the work of critical theorists such as Herbert Marcuse, whose* One Dimensional Man *appeared in 1964, that the rule of technology and the "scientization" of politics were an unavoidable fate for mid-twentieth-century advanced capitalist societies.*

In the first of the essays excerpted here as readings 3–5, "Technical Progress and the Social Lifeworld," Habermas begins from the "two cultures" debate initiated by the scientist and novelist C.P. Snow about the gulf between science and the humanities and the general ignorance of natural science. For Habermas, this points to an even more pressing problem for modern societies: the integration of technical progress into other areas of human life. In the second essay, "The Scientization of Politics and Public Opinion," he attacks the reduction of practical-political issues to technical problems, and in the third he asks how far technology and science have themselves become the dominant ideology of the times. The last paragraph of the extract from "Technology and Science as 'Ideology'" relates directly to Knowledge and Human Interests *but also points forward to the model Habermas presented over ten years later in* The Theory of Communicative Action.

Further Reading

Craig Calhoun has edited an exceptionally useful collection of essays under the title *Habermas and the Public Sphere* (Cambridge, Mass.: MIT Press, 1992). This includes Habermas's preface to the new German edition of *The Structural Transformation of the Public Sphere* and his response to the other essays in the book. Note also the excellent earlier discussions by Peter Hohendahl in "Habermas' Critique of the Frankfurt School," *New German Critique*, 35, 1985: 3–26 and in *The Institution of Criticism* (Ithaca, N. Y.: Cornell University Press, 1982), and the recently translated book by Oskar Negt and Alexander Kluge, *The Public Sphere and Experience* (Minneapolis: Minnesota University Press, 1993), first published in 1972.

1

The Transformation of the Public Sphere's Political Function

To the extent that state and society penetrate each other and bring forth a middle sphere of semi-public, semi-private relationships ordered by social legislation still emerging, the constitutional tenets of a private sphere that precedes the state and of a public sphere that connects society with the state and thus has a function in the political realm are changed in their significance (as regards their sociological import and actual constitutional function) by virtue of a concurrent set of constitutional norms. For what can no longer be vouchsafed indirectly by means of exemption is now in need of being positively granted: a share in social benefits and participation in the institutions of the political realm's public sphere. The legitimate scope of this participation has to be expanded simultaneously to the degree to which this participation is to become effective. Hence societal organizations are active in a state-related fashion in the public sphere of the political realm, be it indirectly through parties or directly in interplay with public administration. In part these are economic associations in the narrower sense that now collectively organize those formerly individual interests of owners operating out of their original private autonomy; in part they are mass organizations that by means of the collective representation of their interests in the public sphere have to obtain and defend a private status granted to them by social legislation. In other words, they have to obtain and defend private autonomy by means of political autonomy. Together with the politically influential representatives of cultural and religious forces this competition of organized private interests in the face of the "neomercantilism" of an interventionist administration leads to a "refeudalization" of society insofar as, with the linking of public and private realms, not only certain functions in the sphere of commerce and social labor are taken over by political authorities but conversely political functions are taken over by societal powers.

Consequently, this refeudalization also reaches into the political public sphere itself. Here organizations strive for political compromises with the state and with one another, as much as possible to the exclusion of the public; in this process, however, they have to procure plebiscitary agreement from a mediatized* public by means of a display of staged or manipulated publicity. In opposition to this factual trend toward the weakening of the public sphere as a principle stands the redefinition of the functions of constitutional rights by a state committed to social rights and, in general, the transformation of the liberal constitutional state into a social-welfare state. The mandate of publicity is extended from the organs of the state to all organizations acting in state-related fashion. In the measure that this is realized, a no longer intact public of private people dealing with each other individually would be replaced by a public of organized private people. *Only such a public could, under today's conditions, participate effectively in a process of public communication via the channels of the public spheres internal to parties and special-interest associations and on the basis of an affirmation of publicity as regards the negotiations of organizations with the state and with one another.* The formation of political compromises would have to be legitimated by reference to this process.

The political public sphere of the social-welfare state is marked by two competing tendencies. Insofar as it represents the collapse of the public sphere of civil society, it makes room for a *staged and manipulative* publicity displayed by organizations over the heads of a mediatized public. On the other hand, to the degree to which it preserves the continuity with the liberal constitutional state, the social-welfare state clings to the mandate of a political public sphere according to which the public is to set in motion a *critical* process of public communication through the very organizations that mediatize it. In the constitutional reality of the social-welfare state this form of critical publicity is in conflict with publicity merely staged for manipulative ends. The extent to which the former type prevails gauges the degree of democratization of an industrial society constituted as a social-welfare state – namely, *the rationalization of the exercise of social and political authority.* The state committed to social rights has abandoned the fiction of the liberal constitutional state that with its establishment as an organ of state the public sphere had actually become a reality in the realm of politics. From the very start, indeed, the parliament was rent by the contradiction of being an institution opposing all political authority and yet established as an "authority" itself. In contrast, publicity operating under the conditions of a social-welfare state must conceive of itself as a self-generating process. Gradually it has to establish itself in competition with that other tendency which, within an immensely expanded public sphere, turns the principle of publicity against itself and thereby reduces its critical efficacy.

Naturally, the question of the degree to which the forces active in the political public sphere can effectively be subjugated to the democratic mandate of publicity – and to what extent it is thus possible to achieve the rationalization of political domination and social authority to which the social-welfare state lays claim – ultimately leads back to the problem which from the very beginning was implicit in the idea of the bourgeois public sphere. The notion of society as liberalism's ambivalent conception made evident had supposed the objective possibility of reducing structural conflicts of interest and bureaucratic decisions to a minimum. One aspect of the problem is technical, the other can be reduced to an economic one. Today more than ever the extent to which a public sphere effective in the political realm can be realized in accord with its critical intentions depends on the possibility of resolving these problems. Here I would like to confine myself to two provisional remarks.

With the mounting bureaucratization of the administration in state and society it seems to be inherent in the nature of the case that the expertise of highly specialized experts would necessarily be removed from supervision by rationally debating bodies. Max Weber analyzed this tendency with respect to the inevitably precarious relationship between the parliament and the executive.[1] Against this, however, it must be taken into account that in the meantime a partner equal to the administration has grown within the administration itself: "The control of the state's political bureaucracy today is possible only by means of society's political bureaucracy, in the parties and pressure groups [*Interessenverbände*]".[2] Of course, the latter themselves would have to be subject to a control within the framework of their intraorganizational spheres. Inasmuch as this is a matter of the technical aspect within one and the same organization, it should not be impossible on structural grounds to arrive at an appropriate relationship between bureaucratic decisions and a quasi-parliamentary deliberation by means of a process of public communication.

To be sure, this problem does not present itself today as primarily technical. The disappearance of publicity inside large organizations, both in state and in society, and even more their flight from publicity in their dealings with one another result from the unresolved plurality of competing interests; this plurality in any event makes it doubtful whether there can ever emerge a general interest of the kind to which a public opinion could refer as a criterion. A structurally ineradicable antagonism of interests would set narrow boundaries for a public sphere reorganized by the social-welfare state to fulfill its critical function. Neutralization of social power and rationalization of political domination in the medium of public discussion indeed presuppose now as they did in the past a possible consensus, that is, the possibility of an objective agreement among competing interests in accord with universal and binding criteria. Otherwise the power relation between pressure and counterpressure, however publicly exercised, creates at best an unstable equilibrium of interests supported by temporary power constellations that in principle is devoid of rationality according to the standard of a universal interest.

In our day, nevertheless, two tendencies are clearly visible which could add a new twist to the problem. On the basis of the high (and ever higher) level of forces of production, industrially advanced societies have attained an expansion of social wealth in the face of which it is not unrealistic to assume that the continuing and increasing plurality of interests may lose the antagonistic edge of competing needs to the extent that the possibility of mutual satisfaction comes within reach. Accordingly, the general interest consists in quickly bringing about the conditions of an "affluent society" which renders moot an equilibrium of interests dictated by the scarcity of means. On the other hand, the technical means of destruction increase along with the technical means of satisfying needs. Harnessed by the military, a potential for self-annihilation on a global scale has called forth risks so total that in relation to them divergent interests can be relativized without difficulty. The as yet unconquered state of nature in international relations has become so threatening for everybody that its specific negation articulates the universal interest with great precision. Kant argued that "perpetual peace" had to be established in a "cosmopolitan order."

Be that as it may, the two conditions for a public sphere to be effective in the political realm – the objectively possible minimizing of bureaucratic decisions and a relativizing of structural conflicts of interest according to the standard of a universal interest everyone can acknowledge – can today no longer be disqualified as simply utopian. The dimension of the democratization of industrial societies constituted as social-welfare states is not limited from the outset by an impenetrability and indissolubility (whether theoretically demonstrable or empirically verifiable) of irrational relations of social power and political domination. The outcome of the struggle between a critical publicity and one that is merely staged for manipulative purposes remains open; the ascendancy of publicity regarding the exercise and balance of political power mandated by the social-welfare state over publicity merely staged for the purpose of acclamation is by no means certain. But unlike the idea of the bourgeois public sphere during the period of its liberal development, it cannot be denounced as an ideology. If anything, it brings the dialectic of that idea, which had been degraded into an ideology, to its conclusion.

The Structural Transformation of the Public Sphere, ch. VI, pp. 231–5.

Notes

1 See especially Max Weber, "Parliament and Government in a Reconstructed Germany," *Economy and Society* (New York: Bedminster Press, 1968), vol. III, Appendix II.

2 H. Sultan, *Burokratische Verwaltungsstaat und soziale Demokratie* (Hannover and Frankfurt, 1955), p. 32.

2

On the Concept of Public Opinion

"Public opinion" takes on a different meaning depending on whether it is brought into play as a critical authority in connection with the normative mandate that the exercise of political and social power be subject to publicity or as the object to be molded in connection with a staged display of, and manipulative propagation of, publicity in the service of persons and institutions, consumer goods, and programs. Both forms of publicity compete in the public sphere, but "the" public opinion is their common addressee. What is the nature of this entity?

The two aspects of publicity and public opinion do not stand in a relationship of norm and fact – as if it were a matter of the same principle whose actual effects simply lagged behind the mandated ones (and correspondingly, the actual behavior of the public lagged behind what was expected of it). In this fashion there would be a link between public opinion as an ideal entity and its actual manifestation; but this is clearly not the case. Instead, the critical and the manipulative functions of publicity are clearly of different orders. They have their places within social configurations whose functional consequences run at cross-purposes to one another. Also, in each version the public is expected to behave in a different fashion. Taking up a distinction introduced earlier it might be said that one version is premised on public opinion, the other on non-public opinion. And critical publicity along with its addressee is more than merely a norm. As a constitutionally institutionalized norm, no matter what structural transformation its social basis has undergone since its original matrix in the bourgeois constitutional state, it nevertheless determines an important portion of the procedures to which the political exercise and balance of power are factually bound. This publicity, together with an addressee that fulfills the behavioral expectations set by it, "exists" – not the public as a whole, certainly, but surely a workable substitute. Further questions, to be decided empirically, concern the areas in which these functions of publicity are in force and to what extent and under which conditions its corresponding public exists today. On the other hand, the competing form of publicity along with its addressee is more than a mere fact. It is accompanied by a specific self-understanding whose normative obligatoriness may to a certain extent also be in opposition to immediate interests of "publicity work." Significantly, this self-understanding borrows essential elements precisely from its publicist antagonist.

Within the framework of constitutional law and political science, the analysis of constitutional norms in relation to the constitutional reality of large democratic states committed to social rights has to maintain the institutionalized fiction of a public opinion without being able to identify it directly as a real entity in the behavior of the public citizens. [. . .] If, without a naïve faith in the idea of a rationalization of domination, the mandate implicit in the constitutional norms of a public sphere as an element in the political realm cannot be simply abandoned to the facticity of a public sphere in a state of collapse, two paths toward defining the concept of public opinion become evident.

One of these leads back to the position of liberalism, which in the midst of a disintegrating public sphere wanted to salvage the communication of an inner circle of representatives capable of constituting a public and of forming an opinion, that is, a critically debating public in the midst of one that merely supplies acclamation. [. . .] The element of publicity that guarantees rationality is to be salvaged at the expense of its other element, that is, the universality guaranteeing general accessibility. In this process, the qualifications that private people once could attain within the sphere of commerce and social labor as social criteria of membership in the public become autonomous hierarchical qualities of representation, for the old basis can no longer be counted on. Sociologically, a representativeness of this kind can no longer be determined in a satisfactory fashion under the existing conditions.

The other path leads to a concept of public opinion that leaves material criteria such as rationality and representativeness entirely out of consideration and confines itself to institutional criteria. [. . .] By replacing the public as the subject of public opinion with agencies in virtue of which alone it is still viewed as capable of political activity, this concept of public opinion becomes peculiarly nondescript. It is impossible to discern whether this "public opinion" has come about by way of public communication or through opinion management, whereby it must remain undecided again whether the latter refers merely to the enunciation of a mass preference incapable of articulating itself or to the reduction to the status of a plebiscitary echo of an opinion that, although quite capable of attaining enlightenment, has been forcibly integrated. As a fiction of constitutional law, public opinion is no longer identifiable in the actual behavior of the public itself; but even its attribution to certain political institutions (as long as this attribution abstracts from the level of the public's behavior altogether) does not remove its fictive character. Empirical social research therefore returns with positivist pathos to this level, in order to establish "public opinion" directly. Of course, it in turn abstracts from the institutional aspects and quickly accomplishes the social-psychological liquidation of the concept of public opinion as such.

Already a problem for liberalism by the middle of the century, "public opinion" came fully into view as a problematic entity in the final quarter of the nineteenth century. [...] The normative spell cast by constitutional theory over the concept was [...] broken – public opinion became an object of social-psychological research. Tarde* was the first to analyze it in depth as "mass opinion;"[1] separated from the functional complex of political institutions, it is immediately stripped of its character as "public" opinion. It is considered a product of a communication process among masses that is neither bound by the principles of public discussion nor concerned with political domination.

When, under the impression of an actually functioning popular government, political theoreticians like Dicey in England and Bryce in the United States[2] nevertheless retained this functional context in their concepts of public opinion (which, to be sure, already show the traces of social-psychological reflection), they exposed themselves to the accusation of empirical unreliability. The prototype of this kind of objection is A.C. Bentley's early critique. He misses "a quantitative analysis of public opinion in terms of the different elements of the population," which is to say, "an investigation of the exact things really wanted under the cover of the opinion of each group of the people, with time and place and circumstances all taken up into the center of the statement." Hence Bentley's thesis: "There is no public opinion ... nor activity reflecting or representing the activity of a group or set of groups."[3]

Public opinion became the label of a social-psychological analysis of group processes, defining its object as follows: "Public opinion refers to people's attitude on an issue when they are members of the same social group."[4] This definition betrays in all clarity what aspects had to be positivistically excluded from the historic concept of public opinion by decades of theoretical development and, above all, of empirical methodological progress. To begin with, "public," as the subject of public opinion, was equated with "mass," then with "group," as the social-psychological substratum of a process of communication and interaction among two or more individuals. "Group" abstracts from the multitude of social and historical conditions, as well as from the institutional means, and certainly from the web of social functions that at one time determined the specific joining of ranks on the part of private people to form a critical debating public in the political realm. "Opinion" itself is conceived no less abstractly. At first it is still identified with "expression on a controversial topic,"[5] later with "expression of an attitude,"[6] then with "attitude" itself.[7] In the end an opinion no longer even needs to be capable of verbalization; it embraces not only any habit that finds expression in some kind of notion – the kind of opinion shaped by religion, custom, mores, and simple "prejudice" against which public opinion was called in as a critical standard in the eighteenth century – but simply all modes of behavior. The only thing that makes such opinion a public one is its connection with group processes. The attempt to define public opinion as a "collection of individual opinions"[8] is soon corrected by the analysis of group relations: "We need concepts of what is both fundamental or deep and also common to a group."[9] A group opinion is considered "public" when subjectively it has come to prevail as the dominant one. The individual group member has a (possibly erroneous) notion concerning the importance of his opinion and conduct, that is to say, concerning how many and which ones of the other members share or reject the custom or view he embraces.[10] [. . .]

Yet just as the concept of public opinion oriented to the institutions of the exercise of political power does not reach into the dimension of informal communication processes, a concept of public opinion social-psychologically reduced to group relations does not link up again with that very dimension in which the category once developed its strategic function and in which it survives today, leading the life of a recluse not quite taken seriously by sociologists: precisely as a fiction of constitutional law. Once the subject of public opinion is reduced to an entity neutral to the difference between public and private spheres, namely, the group – thus documenting a structural transformation, albeit not providing its concept – and once public opinion itself is dissolved into a group relationship neutral to the difference between reasonable communication and irrational conformity, the articulation of the relationship between group opinions and public authority is left to be accomplished within the framework of an auxiliary science of public administration. [. . .]

The material for opinion research – all sorts of opinion held by all sorts of population group – is not already constituted as public opinion simply by becoming the object of politically relevant considerations, decisions, and measures. The feedback of group opinions, defined in terms of the categories employed in research on governmental and administrative processes or on political consensus formation (influenced by the display of staged or manipulative publicity), cannot close the gap between public opinion as a fiction of constitutional law and the social-psychological decomposition of its concept. A concept of public opinion that is historically meaningful, that normatively meets the requirements of the constitution of a social-welfare state, and that is theoretically clear and empirically identifiable can be grounded only in the structural transformation of the public sphere itself and in the dimension of its development. The conflict between the two forms of publicity which today characterizes the political sphere has to be taken seriously as the gauge of a process of democratization within an industrial society constituted as a social-welfare state. Non-public opinions are at work in great numbers, and "the" public opinion is indeed a fiction. Nevertheless, in a comparative sense the concept of public opinion is to be retained because the constitutional reality of the social-welfare state must be conceived as a process in the course of which a public sphere that functions effectively in the political realm is realized, that is to say, as a process in which the exercise of social power and political domination is effectively subjected to the mandate of democratic publicity. The criteria by which opinions may be empirically gauged as to their degree of publicness are therefore to be developed in reference to this dimension of the evolution of state and society; indeed, such an empirical specification of public opinion in a comparative sense is today the most reliable means for attaining valid and comparable statements about the extent of democratic integration characterizing a specific constitutional reality.

Within this model, two politically relevant areas of communication can be constrasted with each other: the system of informal, personal, non-public opinions on the one hand, and on the other that of formal, institutionally authorized opinions. Informal opinions differ in the degree of their obligatoriness. The lowest level of this area of communication is represented by the verbalization of things culturally taken for granted and not discussed, the highly resistant results of that process of acculturation that is normally not controlled by one's own reflection – for example, attitudes toward the death penalty or sexual morality. On the second level the rarely discussed basic experiences of one's own biography are verbalized, those refractory results of socialization shocks that have again become subreflective – for example, attitudes toward war and peace or certain desires for security. On the third level one finds the often discussed things generated as self-evident by the culture industry, the ephemeral results of the relentless publicist barrage and propagandist manipulation by the media to which consumers are exposed, especially during their leisure time.

In relation to those matters taken for granted in a culture (which as a kind of historical sediment can be considered a type of primordial "opinion" or "prejudice" that probably has scarcely undergone any change in its social-psychological structure), the matters whose taken-for-granted status is generated by the culture industry have both a more evanescent and more artificial character. These opinions are shaped within the medium of a group-specific "exchange of tastes and preferences." Generally, the focus for this stratum of other-directed opinions is the family, the peer group, and acquaintances at work and in the neighborhood – each with its specific structures of information channeling and opinion leadership ensuring the binding nature of group opinions. To be sure, matters that are taken for granted in a culture also become topical in the exchanges of opinion of such groups, but they are of a different sort from the ideas sustained by conviction, which in anticipation of their inconsequentiality circulate, so to speak, until recalled. Like those "opinions," they too constitute systems of norms demanding adaptation, but they do so more in the manner of a social control through "fashions" whose shifting rules require only a temporary loyalty. Just as those things that are taken for granted in a culture because of deep-seated traditions may be called subliterary, so those generated by the culture industry have reached a post-literary stage, as it were. The contents of opinion managed by the culture industry thematize the wide field of intrapsychic and interpersonal relationships first opened up psychologically by the subjectivity which during the eighteenth century, within the framework of an intact bourgeois domain of interiority, required a public and could express itself through literature. At that time the private spheres of life were still protected in their explicit orientation to a public sphere, since the public use of reason remained tied to literature as its medium. In contrast, the integration culture delivers the canned goods of degenerate, psychologically oriented literature as a public service for private consumption – and something to be commented on within the group's exchange of opinions. Such a group is as little a "public" as were those formations of pre-bourgeois society in which the ancient opinions were formed, secure in their tradition, and circulated unpolemically with the effect of "laws of opinion." It is no accident that group research and opinion research have developed simultaneously. The type of opinion that emerges from such intragroup relations – picked up ready-made, flexibly reproduced, barely internalized, and not evoking much commitment – this "mere" opinion, a component of what is only "small talk" anyway, is per se ripe for research. The group's communication processes are under the influence of the mass media either directly or, more frequently, mediated through opinion leaders. Among the latter are often to be found those persons who have reflected opinions formed through literary and rational controversy. However, as long as such opinions remain outside the communication network of an intact public, they too are part of the non-public opinions, although they clearly differ from the three other categories.

Over and against the communicative domain of non-public opinion stands the sphere of circulation of quasi-public opinion. These formal opinions can be traced back to specific institutions; they are officially or semi-officially authorized as announcements, proclamations, declarations, and speeches. Here we are primarily dealing with opinions that circulate in a relatively narrow circle – skipping the mass of the population – between the large political press and, generally, those publicist organs that cultivate rational debate and the advising, influencing, and deciding bodies with political or politically relevant jurisdictions (cabinet, government commissions, administrative bodies, parliamentary committees, party leadership, interest-group committees, corporate bureaucracies, and union secretariats). Although these quasi-official opinions can be addressed to a wide public, they do not fulfill the requirements of a public process of rational-critical debate according to the liberal model. As institutionally authorized opinions, they are always privileged and achieve no mutual correspondence with the non-organized mass of the "public."

Between the two spheres, naturally, exists a linkage, always through the channels of the mass media; it is established through that publicity, displayed for show or manipulation, with the help of which the groups participating in the exercise and balancing of power strive to create a plebiscitary follower-mentality on the part of a mediated public. We also count this vehicle of managed publicist influence among the formal opinions; but as "publicly manifested" they have to be distinguished from "quasi-public" opinions.

In addition to this massive contact between the formal and informal communicative domains, there also exists the rare relationship between publicist organs devoted to rational-critical debate and those few individuals who will seek to form their opinions through literature – a kind of opinion capable of becoming public, but actually non-public. The communicative network of a public made up of rationally debating private citizens has collapsed; the public opinion once emergent from it has partly decomposed into the informal opinions of private citizens without a public and partly become concentrated into formal opinions of publicistically effective institutions. Caught in the vortex of *publicity that is staged for show or manipulation*, the public of non-organized private people is laid claim to not by public communication but by the communication of publicly manifested opinions.

An opinion that is public in the strict sense, however, can only be generated in the degree that the two domains of communication are mediated by a third, that of *critical publicity*. Today, of course, such a mediation is possible on a sociologically relevant scale only through the participation of private people in a process of formal communication conducted through intraorganizational public spheres. Indeed, a minority of private people already are members of the parties and special-interest associations under public law. To the extent that these organizations permit an internal public sphere not merely at the level of functionaries and managers but at all levels, there exists the possibility of a mutual correspondence between the political opinions of the private people and that kind of quasi-public opinion. This state of affairs may stand for a tendency that for the time being is on the whole insignificant; the extent and actual impact of this tendency need to be established empirically – that is, whether we are dealing in general with a growing or declining tendency. For a sociological theory of public opinion this tendency is nevertheless of decisive importance, for it provides the criteria for a dimension in which alone public opinion can be constituted under the conditions of a large democratic state committed to social rights.

In the same proportion as informal opinions are channeled into the circuit of quasi-public opinions, seized by it, and transformed, this circuit itself, in being expanded by the public of citizens, also gains in publicity. Since, of course, public opinion is by no means simply "there" as such, and since it is at best possible to isolate tendencies that under the given conditions work in the direction of generating a public opinion, it can be defined only comparatively. The degree to which an opinion is a public opinion is measured by the following standard: the degree to which it emerges from the intraorganizational public sphere constituted by the public of the organizations' members and how much the intraorganizational public sphere communicates with an external one formed in the publicist interchange, via the mass media, between societal organizations and state institutions.

C.W. Mills,* by contrasting "public" and "mass," obtained empirically usable criteria for a definition of public opinion:

> In a *public*, as we may understand the term, (1) virtually as many people express opinions as receive them. (2) Public communications are so organized that there is a chance immediately and effectively to answer back any opinion expressed in public. Opinion formed by such discussion (3) readily finds an outlet in effective action, even against – if necessary – the prevailing system of authority. And (4) authoritative institutions do not penetrate the public, which is thus more or less autonomous in its operation.[11]

Conversely, opinions cease to be public opinions in the proportion to which they are enmeshed in the communicative interchanges that characterize a "mass:"[12]

> In a *mass*, (1) far fewer people express opinions than receive them; for the community of publics becomes an abstract collection of individuals who receive impressions from the mass media. (2) The communications that prevail are so organized that it is difficult or impossible for the individual to answer back immediately or with any effect. (3) The realization of opinion in action is controlled by authorities who organize and control the channels of such action. (4) The mass has no autonomy from institutions; on the contrary, agents of authorized institutions penetrate this mass, reducing any autonomy it may have in the formation of opinion by discussion.[13]

These abstract determinations of an opinion process that takes place under the conditions of a collapse of the public sphere can be easily fitted into the framework of our historical and developmental model.[14] The four criteria of *mass* communication are fulfilled to the extent that the informal domain of communication is linked to the formal merely through the channels of a publicity staged for the purpose of manipulation or show; via the "culture industry's unquestioning promulgations," the non-public opinions are then integrated through the "publicly manifested" ones into an existing system; in relation to this system the non-public opinions are without any autonomy. In contrast to this, under conditions of the large democratic social-welfare state the communicative interconnectedness of a *public* can be brought about only in this way: through a critical publicity brought to life within intraorganizational public spheres, the completely short-circuited circulation of quasi-public opinion must be linked to the informal domain of the hitherto non-public opinions.

In like measure the forms of consensus and conflict that today determine the exercise and equilibration of power would also be altered. A method of public controversy which came to prevail in that manner could both ease the forcible forms of a consensus generated through pressure and temper the forcible forms of conflicts hitherto kept from the public sphere. Conflict and consensus (like domination itself and like the coercive power whose degree of stability they indicate analytically) are not categories that remain untouched by the historical development of society. In the case of the structural transformation of the bourgeois public sphere, we can study the extent to which, and manner in which, the latter's ability to assume *its* proper function determines whether the exercise of domination and power persists as a negative constant, as it were, of history – or whether as a historical category itself, it is open to substantive change.

The Structural Transformation of the Public Sphere, ch. VII, pp. 236–50.

Notes

1 G. Tarde, *L'Opinion et la Foule* (Paris, 1901).
2 A.V. Dicey, *Law and Public Opinion in England* (London, 1905); J. Bryce, *The American Commonwealth*, 2 vols (1889); A. L. Lowell's famous study *Public Opinion and Popular Government* (New York, 1913) stands in Bryce's tradition; he also emphasized: "Public opinion to be worthy of the name, to be the proper motive in a democracy, must be really public; and popular government is based upon the assumption of a public opinion of that kind" (p. 5).
3 Cited after P.A. Palmer, "The Concept of Public Opinion in Political Theory," in B.R. Berelson and M. Janowitz (eds), *Reader in Public Opinion and Communication* (New York: Free Press, 2nd edn 1966), p. 11.
4 L.W. Doob, *Public Opinion and Propaganda* (New York, 1948), p. 35; similarly, N.J. Powell, *Anatomy of Public Opinion* (New York, 1951), pp. 1ff.
5 W. Albig, *Public Opinion* (New York, 1938), p. 3.
6 M.B. Ogle, *Public Opinion and Political Dynamics* (Boston, 1950), p. 48.
7 Doob, *Public Opinion and Propaganda*, p. 35: "In this sense it might appear as though public opinion exists whenever people have attitudes."
8 H.L. Child, cited after Powell, *Anatomy of Public Opinion*, p. 4.
9 H. Hyman, "Towards a Theory of Public Opinion," *Public Opinion Quarterly*. 21, 1, 1957: 58.

10 P.R. Hofstatter, *Psychologie der öffentlichen Meinung* (Vienna, 1949), pp. 53ff.

11 C.W. Mills, *The Power Elite* (New York, 1956), pp. 303–4.

12 On the political sociology of the "mass" see the study of W. Kornhauser, *The Politics of Mass Society* (Glencoe, Ill., 1959).

13 Mills, *The Power Elite*, p. 304; and *The Sociological Imagination* (New York, 1959), pp. 81ff.

14 H. Blumer, "The Mass, the Public, and Public Opinion," in Berelson and Janowitz, *Public Opinion and Propaganda*, pp. 34ff.

3

Technical Progress and the Social Lifeworld

How can the relation between technical progress and the social life-world, which today is still clothed in a primitive, traditional, and unchosen form, be reflected upon and brought under the control of rational discussion?

To a certain extent practical questions of government, strategy, and administration had to be dealt with through the application of technical knowledge even at an earlier period. Yet today's problem of transposing technical knowledge into practical consciousness has changed not merely its order of magnitude. The mass of technical knowledge is no longer restricted to pragmatically acquired techniques of the classical crafts. It has taken the form of scientific information that can be exploited for technology. On the other hand, behavior-controlling traditions no longer naïvely define the self-understanding of modern societies. Historicism* has broken the natural-traditional validity of action-orienting value systems. Today, the self-understanding of social groups and their world-view as articulated in ordinary language is mediated by the hermeneutic appropriation of traditions as traditions. In this situation questions of life conduct demand a rational discussion that is not focussed exclusively either on technical means or on the application of traditional behavioral norms. The reflection that is required extends beyond the production of technical knowledge and the hermeneutical clarification of traditions to the employment of technical means in historical situations whose objective conditions (potentials, institutions, interests) have to be interpreted anew each time in the framework of a self-understanding determined by tradition. [. . .]

Culture and education can then no longer indeed be restricted to the ethical dimension of personal attitude. Instead, in the political dimension at issue, the theoretical guidance of action must proceed from a scientifically explicated understanding of the world.

The relation of technical progress and social lifeworld and the translation of scientific information into practical consciousness is not an affair of private cultivation. [. . .]

Today, in the industrially most advanced systems, an energetic attempt must be made consciously to take in hand the mediation between technical progress and the conduct of life in the major industrial societies, a mediation that has previously taken place without direction, as a mere continuation of natural history. This is not the place to discuss the social, economic, and political conditions on which a long-term central research policy would have to depend. It is not enough for a social system to fulfill the conditions of technical rationality. Even if the cybernetic dream of a virtually instinctive self-stabilization could be realized, the value system would have contracted in the meantime to a set of rules for the maximization of power and comfort; it would be equivalent to the biological base value of survival at any cost, that is, ultra-stability. Through the unplanned sociocultural consequences of technological progress, the human species has challenged itself to learn not merely to affect its social destiny, but to control it. This challenge of technology cannot be met with technology alone. It is rather a question of setting into motion a politically effective discussion that rationally brings the social potential constituted by technical knowledge and ability into a defined and controlled relation to our practical knowledge and will. On the one hand, such discussion could enlighten those who act politically about the tradition-bound self-understanding of their interests in relation to what is technically possible and feasible. On the other hand, they would be able to judge practically, in the light of their now articulated and newly interpreted needs, the direction and the extent to which they want to develop technical knowledge for the future.

This *dialectic of potential and will* takes place today without reflection in accordance with interests for which public justification is neither demanded nor permitted. Only if we could elaborate this dialectic with political consciousness could we succeed in directing the mediation of technical progress and the conduct of social life, which until now has occurred as an extension of natural history; its conditions being left outside the framework of discussion and planning. The fact that this is a matter for reflection means that it does not belong to the professional competence of specialists. The substance of domination is not dissolved by the power of technical control. To the contrary, the former can simply hide behind the latter. The irrationality of domination, which today has become a collective peril to life, could be mastered only by the development of a political decision-making process tied to the principle of general discussion free from domination. Our only hope for the rationalization of the power structure lies in conditions that favor political power for thought developing through dialogue. The redeeming power of reflection cannot be supplanted by the extension of technically exploitable knowledge.

Toward a Rational Society, pp. 53–61.

4

The Scientization of Politics and Public Opinion

The scientization of politics is not yet a reality, but it is a real tendency for which there is evidence: the scope of research under government contract and the extent of scientific consultation to public services are primary examples. From the beginning the modern state, which arose from the need for central financial administration in connection with the market patterns of an emerging national and territorial economy, was dependent on the expertise of officials trained in the law. However, their technical knowledge did not differ fundamentally in form from professional knowledge of the sort possessed by the military. Just as the latter had to organize standing armies, so the officials had to organize a permanent administration. Both were practicing an art more than applying a science. It is only recently that bureaucrats, the military, and politicians have been orienting themselves to strictly scientific recommendations in the exercise of their public functions – indeed, this practice has only existed on a large scale since World War II. This marks a new or second stage of that "rationalization" which Max Weber had already comprehended as the basis for the development of bureaucratic domination. It is not as though scientists had seized state power; but the exercise of power domestically and its assertion against external enemies are no longer rationalized only through the mediation of administrative activity organized through the division of labor, regulated according to differentiated responsibilities, and linked to instituted norms. Instead they have been structurally transformed by the objective exigencies of new technologies and strategies.

Following a tradition that goes back to Hobbes, Weber found clear definitions for the relation of expertise and political practice. His famous confrontation of administration by officials versus political leadership served to separate strictly the functions of the expert from those of the politician.[1] The latter makes use of technical knowledge, but the practice of self-assertion and domination requires in addition that a person or group with specific interests make decisions and carry them out. In the last analysis political action cannot rationally justify its own premises. Instead a decision is made between competing value orders and convictions, which escape compelling arguments and remain inaccessible to cogent discussion. As much as the objective knowledge of the expert may determine the techniques of rational administration and military security and thereby subject the means of political practice to scientific rules, practical decision in concrete situations cannot be *sufficiently* legitimated through reason. Rationality in the choice of means accompanies avowed irrationality in orientation to values, goals, and needs. According to Weber only complete division of labor between the objectively informed and technically schooled general staffs of the bureaucracy and the military on the one hand and leaders with a power instinct and intense will on the other will make possible the scientization of politics.

Today we are confronted with the question whether this *decisionistic* model* is valid for the second stage of the rationalization of domination. Systems analysis and especially decision theory do not merely make new technologies available, thus improving traditional instruments; they also rationalize choice as such by means of calculated strategies and automatic decision procedures. To this extent the objective necessity disclosed by the specialists seems to assert itself over the leaders' decisions.

Following a tradition that extends back through Saint-Simon to Bacon, the decisionistic definition of the relation of expertise to political practice is being abandoned by many in favor of a *technocratic model*.[2] The dependence of the professional on the politician appears to have reversed itself. The latter becomes the mere agent of a scientific intelligentsia, which, in concrete circumstances, elaborates the objective implications and requirements of available techniques and resources as well as of optimal strategies and rules of control. If it is possible to rationalize decisions about practical questions, as a choice in situations of uncertainty, to the point where the "symmetry of uncertainty" (Rittel) and thus the problems of decision in general are reduced step by step, then the politician in the technical state is left with nothing but a fictitious decision-making power. The politician would then be at best something like a stopgap in a still imperfect rationalization of power, in which the initiative has in any case passed to scientific analysis and technical planning. The state seems forced to abandon the substance of power in favor of an efficient way of applying available techniques in the framework of strategies that are objectively called for. It appears to be no longer an apparatus for the forcible realization of interests that have no foundation in principle and can only be answered for decisionistically. It becomes instead the organ of thoroughly rational administration.

But the weaknesses of this technocratic model are evident. On the one hand, it assumes an immanent necessity of technical progress, which owes its appearance of being an independent, self-regulating process only to the way in which social interests operate in it – namely through continuity with unreflected, unplanned, passively adaptive natural history. On the other hand, this model presupposes a continuum of rationality in the treatment of technical and practical problems, which cannot in fact exist. For the new methods that characterize the rationalization of power in its second stage do not bring about the disappearance of the problem-complex connected with the decision of practical issues. Within the framework of research operations that expand our power of technical control we can make no cogent statements about "value systems," that is, about social needs and objective states of consciousness, about the directions of emancipation and regression. Either there are still other forms of decision than the theoretical-technical for the rational clarification of practical issues that cannot be completely answered by technologies and strategies, or no reasons can be given for decisions in such issues. In that case we would have to return to the decisionistic model. [. . .]

In the *pragmatistic model* the strict separation between the function of the expert and the politician is replaced by a critical interaction. This interaction not only strips the ideologically supported exercise of power of an unreliable basis of legitimation but makes it accessible *as a whole* to scientifically informed discussion, thereby substantially changing it. Despite the technocratic view, experts have not become sovereign over politicians subjected to the demands of the facts and left with a purely fictitious power of decision. Nor, despite the implications of the decisionistic model, does the politician retain a preserve outside of the necessarily rationalized areas of practice in which practical problems are decided upon as ever by acts of the will. Rather, reciprocal communication seems possible and necessary, through which scientific experts advise the decision-makers and politicians consult scientists in accordance with practical needs. Thus, on the one hand the development of new techniques is governed by a horizon of needs and historically determined interpretations of these needs, in other words, of value systems. This horizon has to be made explicit. On the other hand, these social interests, as reflected in the value systems, are regulated by being tested with regard to the technical possibilities and strategic means for their gratification. In this manner they are partly confirmed, partly rejected, articulated, and reformulated, or denuded of their ideologically transfigured and compelling character.

So far we have considered the three models of the relation of expertise and politics without reference to the structure of modern mass democracy. Only one of them, the pragmatistic, is necessarily related to democracy. If the division of power and responsibility between experts and leaders is carried out according to the decisionistic pattern, then the politically functioning public realm of the citizenry can serve only to legitimate the ruling group. The election and confirmation of governing individuals, or those capable of governing, are as a rule plebiscitary acts. The reason that democratic choice take the form of acclamation rather than public discussion is that choice applies only to those who occupy positions with decision-making power and not to the guidelines of future decisions themselves. At best these decision-makers legitimate themselves before the public. Decisions themselves, according to the decisionistic view, must remain basically beyond public discussion. The scientization of politics then automatically accords with the theory developed by Weber, extended by Schumpeter, and now unquestioned by modern political sociology, a theory that in the last analysis reduces the process of democratic decision-making to a regulated acclamation procedure for elites alternately appointed to exercise power. In this way power, untouched in its irrational substance, can be legitimated but not rationalized.

The claim to rationalization, in contrast, is upheld by the technocratic model of scientized politics. Of course, the reduction of political power to rational administration can be conceived here only at the expense of democracy itself. If politicians were strictly subjected to objective necessity, a politically functioning public could at best legitimate the administrative personnel and judge the professional qualifications of salaried officials. But if the latter were of comparable qualifications it would in principle be a matter of indifference which competing elite group obtained power. A technocratic administration of industrial society would deprive any democratic decision-making process of its object. This conclusion has been drawn by Helmut Schelsky: "the people's political will is supplanted by the objective exigencies that man produces as science and labor."[3]

In contrast, the successful transposition of technical and strategic recommendations into practice is, according to the pragmatistic model, increasingly dependent on mediation by the public as a political institution. Communication between experts and the agencies of political decision determines the direction of technical progress on the basis of the tradition-bound self-understanding of practical needs. Inversely it measures and criticizes this self-understanding in the light of the possibilities for gratification created by technology. Such communication must therefore necessarily be rooted in social interests and in the value-orientations of a given social lifeworld. In both directions the feedback-monitored communication process is grounded in what Dewey* called "value beliefs." That is, it is based on a historically determined pre-understanding, governed by social norms, of what is practically necessary in a concrete situation. This pre-understanding is a consciousness that can only be enlightened hermeneutically, through articulation in the discourse of citizens in a community. Therefore the communication provided for in the pragmatistic model, which is supposed to render political practice scientific, cannot occur independently of the communication that is always already in process on the pre-scientific level. The latter type of communication, however, can be institutionalized in the democratic form of public discussions among the citizen body. The relation of the *sciences* to *public opinion* is constitutive for the scientization of politics.

It is true that this relation has never been made explicit in the tradition of pragmatistic thought. For Dewey it seemed self-evident that the relation of reciprocal guidance and enlightenment between the production of techniques and strategies on the one hand and the value-orientations of interested groups on the other could be realized within the unquestionable horizon of common sense and an uncomplicated public realm. But the *structural change in the bourgeois public realm* would have demonstrated the naïveté of this view even if it were not already invalidated by the internal development of the sciences. For the latter have made a basically unsolved problem out of the appropriate translation of technical information even between individual disciplines, let alone between the sciences and the public at large. Anyone who adheres to the notion of permanent communication between the sciences, considered in terms of their political relevance, and informed public opinion becomes suspect of wanting to put scientific discussion on a mass basis and thus to misuse it ideologically. This position in turn provokes a critique of ideology that opposes the simplified and over-extended interpretation of scientific results in accordance with a *Weltanschauung*, and instead firmly insists upon the positivistic separation of theory and practice. Weber's thesis of the neutrality of the sciences with regard to pre-existing practical valuations can be convincingly employed against illusionary rationalizations of political problems, against *short-circuiting* the connection between technical expertise and a public that can be influenced by manipulation, and against the distorted response which scientific information meets with in a deformed public realm.

Nevertheless, as soon as this critique calls into question a more extensive rationalization of the power structure as such, it succumbs to the limitations of positivism and to an ideology that makes science impervious to self-reflection. For then it confuses the actual difficulty of effecting permanent communication between science and public opinion with the violation of logical and methodological rules. True, as it stands the pragmatistic model cannot be applied to political decision-making in modern mass democracies. However, this is not because discussing practical questions both with reference to available techniques and strategies and within the horizon of the explicated self-understanding of a social lifeworld would require the illusory rationalization of unfounded acts of will. The reason is rather that this model neglects the specific logical characteristics and the social preconditions for the reliable translation of scientific information into the ordinary language of practice and inversely for a translation from the context of practical questions back into the specialized language of technical and strategic recommendations. [. . .]

The direction of technical progress today is still largely determined by social interests that arise spontaneously from the compulsion to reproduce social life; they are not reflected as such and confronted with the declared political self-understanding of social groups. Consequently new technical potentials intrude unprepared into existing forms of life conduct. They only make more evident the disproportion between the results of the most intensive rationality and unreflected goals, petrified value systems, and obsolete ideologies. The advisory bodies concerned with research policy give rise to a new type of interdisciplinary, future-oriented research, which ought to clarify the immanent developmental state and social preconditions of technical progress in connection with the cultural and educational level of society as a whole. They would thus offer a viewpoint different from that bounded by pre-existing, unreflected social interests. These investigations, too, obey a hermeneutic interest in knowledge. For they make it possible to confront given social institutions and their self-understanding with the technology that is actually used and potentially available. Inversely, as part of this projected clarification by means of the critique of ideology, they make it possible to reorient social needs and declared goals. The formulation of a long-term research policy, the preparation of new industries that utilize future scientific information, and the planning of an educational system for a qualified younger generation whose jobs are yet to be created are part of an endeavor to direct consciously what has previously taken place spontaneously and without planning: the mediation of technological progress with the conduct of life in large industrial societies. This endeavor embodies the dialectic of enlightened will and self-conscious potential.

The communication between experts at major research and consulting organizations and political authorities about individual projects take place within an objectively delimited problem area, and discussion between consulting scientists and the government remains bound to the constellation of given situations and available potentials. But for this third task of programming social development as a whole, the dialogue between scientists and politicians is freed from the influence of *specific* problems. It must of course link up to a concrete situation, namely to a historical phase of tradition and to concrete social interests on the one hand, and to a given level of technical knowledge and industrial utilization on the other. Beyond this, however, the attempt at a long-term research and education policy oriented to immanent possibilities and objective consequences must be left up to the dialectic which we have become acquainted with in its earlier phases. It must enlighten those who take political action about their tradition-bound self-understanding of their interests and goals in relation to socially potential technical knowledge and capacity. At the same time it must put them in a position to judge practically, in the light of these articulated and newly interpreted needs, in what direction they want to develop their technical knowledge and capacity in the future. This discussion necessarily moves within a circle. For only to the extent that, knowing the technical potential of our historically determined will, we orient ourselves to the given situation can we know in turn what specifically oriented expansion of our technical potential we want for the future.

In the last analysis the process of translation between science and politics is related to public opinion. This relation is not external to it, as though it were a question of taking prevailing constitutional norms into account. Rather it follows immanently and necessarily from the requirements of the confrontation of *technical knowledge and capacity* with *tradition-bound self-understanding*. The latter forms the horizon within which needs are interpreted as goals and goals are hypostatized as values. An element of anticipation is always contained in the integration of technical knowledge and the hermeneutical process of arriving at self-understanding. For it is set in motion by discussion among scientists isolated from the citizenry. The enlightenment of a scientifically instrumented political will according to standards of rationally binding discussion can proceed only from the horizon of communicating citizens themselves and must lead back to it. The consultants who would like to find out what will is expressed by political organizations are equally subject to the hermeneutic constraint of participating in the historical self-understanding of a social group – in the last analysis, in the conversations of citizens. Such an explication is, of course, bound to the methods of the hermeneutic sciences. But the latter do not destroy the dogmatic core of traditional, historically generated interpretations, they only clarify them. The two additional steps of employing the social sciences to analyze this self-understanding in connection with social interests on the one hand, and of ascertaining available techniques and strategies on the other, lead beyond this area of public discourse. But the result of these steps, as the enlightenment of political will, can become effective only within the communication of citizens. For the articulation of needs in accordance with technical knowledge can be ratified exclusively *in the consciousness of the political actors themselves*. Experts cannot delegate to themselves this act of confirmation from those who have to account with their life histories for new interpretations of social needs and for accepted means of mastering problematic situations. With this reservation, however, the experts must anticipate the act of confirmation. Insofar as they assume this representative role, the experts necessarily think within the context of the philosophy of history, but in an experimental way and without being able to share the teleology and dogma of the tradition.

   While integrating technology into the hermeneutically explicated self-understanding of a given situation, the process of the scientization of politics could be realized only if we had the guarantee that political will had obtained the enlightenment it wanted and simultaneously that enlightenment had permeated existing political will as much as it could under given, desired, and controllable circumstances. This could be guaranteed only by the ideal conditions of general communication extending to the entire public and free from domination. These considerations of principle must now, however, disguise the fact that the empirical conditions for the application of the pragmatistic model are lacking. The depoliticization of the mass of the population and the decline of the public realm as a political institution are components of a system of domination that tends to exclude practical questions from public discussion. The bureaucratized exercise of power has its counterpart in a public realm confined to spectacles and acclamation. This takes care of the approval of a mediatized population. But even if we disregard the limits established by the existing system and assume that a social basis could be found today for public discussion among a broad public, the provision of relevant scientific information would still not be simple. [. . .]

However, neither the inner scientific requirement of translation nor the external requirement of free exchange of research information would actually suffice to set in motion a discussion of the practical consequences of scientific results among a responsive public, if the responsible scientists themselves did not ultimately take the initiative. The third tendency that we should like to adduce in favor of such discussion arises from the role conflict in which representative scientists become involved as scientists on the one hand and citizens on the other. To the extent that the sciences are really taken into the service of political practice, scientists are objectively compelled to go beyond the technical recommendations that they produce and reflect upon their practical consequences. This was especially and dramatically true for the atomic physicists involved in the production of the atomic and hydrogen bombs.

Since then there have been discussions in which leading scientists have argued about the political ramifications of their research practice, such as the damage that radioactive fallout has caused to the present health of the population and to the genetic substance of the human species. But the examples are few and far between. They show at least that responsible scientists, disregarding their professional or official roles, cross the boundaries of their inner scientific world and address themselves directly to public opinion when they want either to avert practical consequences connected with the choice of specific technologies or to criticize specific research investments in terms of their social effects.

Nevertheless, one would scarcely know from these small beginnings that the discussion that has begun in the offices of scientific consultants to government agencies basically has to be transferred to the broader political forum of the general public. The same holds for the dialogue now going on between scientists and politicians about the formulation of a long-term research policy.

As we have seen, the preconditions are unfavorable on both sides. On the one hand we can no longer reckon with functioning institutions for public discussion among the general public. On the other, the specialization of a large-scale research and a bureaucratized apparatus of power reinforce each other only too well while the public is excluded as a political force. The choice that interests us is not between one elite that effectively exploits vital resources of knowledge over the heads of a mediatized population and another that is isolated from inputs of scientific information, so that technical knowledge flows inadequately into the process of political decision-making. The question is rather whether a productive body of knowledge is merely transmitted to men engaged in technical manipulation for purposes of control or is simultaneously appropriated as the linguistic possession of communicating individuals. A scientized society could constitute itself as a rational one only to the extent that science and technology are mediated with the conduct of life through the minds of its citizens.

There is a special dimension in which the controlled translation of technical into practical knowledge and thus the scientifically guided rationalization of political power is possible. Political rationalization occurs through the enlightenment of political will, correlated with instruction about its technical potential. This dimension is evaded when such enlightenment is considered either impossible because of the need for authoritative decisions or superfluous because of technocracy. In both cases, the objective consequences would be the same: a premature halt to possible rationalization. And the illusory attempts of the technocrats to have political decisions be directed only by the logic of objective exigency would justify the decisionists by leaving sheerly arbitrary what remains an irreducible remnant of practice on the periphery of technological rationality.

Toward a Rational Society, pp. 62–86.

Notes

1 Max Weber, "Bureaucratic nomination and Political Leadership," *Economy and Society*, III.
2 Jacques Ellul, *The Technological Society* (New York, 1967).
3 Helmut Schelsky, *Der Mensch in der wissenschaftlichen Zivilisation* (Cologne–Opladen, 1961), p. 22.

5

Technology and Science as "Ideology"

In order to reformulate what Weber called "rationalization," I should like to go beyond the subjective approach that Parsons shares with Weber and propose another categorial framework. I shall take as my starting point the fundamental distinction between *work* and *interaction*.[1]

By "work" or *purposive-rational action* I understand either instrumental action or rational choice or their conjunction. Instrumental action is governed by *technical rules* based on empirical knowledge. In every case they imply conditional predictions about observable events, physical or social. These predictions can prove correct or incorrect. The conduct of rational choice is governed by *strategies* based on analytic knowledge. They imply deductions from preference rules (value-systems) and decision procedures; these propositions are either correctly or incorrectly deduced. Purposive-rational action realizes defined goals under given conditions. But while instrumental action organizes means that are appropriate or inappropriate according to criteria of an effective control of reality, strategic action depends only on the correct evaluation of possible alternative choices, which results from calculation supplemented by values and maxims.

By "interaction," on the other hand, I understand *communicative action*, symbolic interaction. It is governed by binding *consensual norms*, which define reciprocal expectations about behavior and which must be understood and recognized by at least two acting subjects. Social norms are enforced through sanctions. Their meaning is objectified in ordinary language communication. While the validity of technical rules and strategies depends on that of empirically true or analytically correct propositions, the validity of social norms is grounded only in the intersubjectivity of the mutual understanding of intentions and secured by the general recognition of obligations. Violation of a rule has a different consequence according to type. *Incompetent* behavior, which violates valid technical rules or strategies, is condemned per se to failure through lack of success; the "punishment" is built, so to speak, into its rebuff by reality. *Deviant* behavior, which violates consensual norms, provokes sanctions that are connected with the rules only externally,

Table 5.1

	Institutional framework: symbolic interaction	*Systems of purposive-rational (instrumental and strategic) action*
Action-orienting rules	Social norms	Technical rules
Level of definition	Intersubjectively shared ordinary language	Context-free language
Type of definition	Reciprocal expectations about behavior	Conditional predictions conditional imperatives
Mechanisms of acquisition	Role internalization	Learning of skills and qualifications
Function of action type	Maintenance of institutions (conformity to norms on the basis of reciprocal enforcement)	Problem-solving (goal attainment, defined in means-ends relations)
Sanctions against violation of rules	Punishment on the basis of conventional sanctions: failure against authority	Inefficacy: failure in reality
"Rationalization"	Emancipation, individuation; extension of communication free of domination	Growth of productive forces; extension of power of technical control

that is, by convention. Learned rules of purposive-rational action supply us with *skills*, internalized norms with *personality structures*. Skills put us in a position to solve problems; motivations allow us to follow norms. Table 5.1 summarizes these definitions. They demand a more precise explanation, which I cannot give here. It is above all the bottom row which I am neglecting here, and it refers to the very problem for whose solution I am introducing the distinction between work and interaction.

In terms of the two types of action we can distinguish between social systems according to whether purposive-rational action or interaction predominates. The institutional framework of a society consists of norms that guide symbolic interaction. But there are subsystems such as (to keep to Weber's examples) the economic system or the state apparatus, in which primarily sets of purposive-rational action are institutionalized. These contrast with subsystems such as family and kinship structures, which, although linked to a number of tasks and skills, are primarily based on moral rules of interaction. So I shall distinguish generally at the analytic level between (1) the *institutional framework* of a society or the sociocultural lifeworld and (2) the *subsystems of purposive-rational action* that are "embedded" in it. Insofar as actions are determined by the institutional framework they are both guided and enforced by norms. Insofar as they are determined by subsystems of purposive-rational action, they conform to patterns of instrumental or strategic action. Of course, only institutionalization can guarantee that such action will in fact follow definite technical rules and expected strategies with adequate probability.

With the help of these distinctions we can reformulate Weber's concept of "rationalization."

The term "traditional society" has come to denote all social systems that generally meet the criteria of civilizations. The latter represent a specific stage in the evolution of the human species. They differ in several traits from more primitive social forms: (1) a centralized ruling power (state organization of political power in contrast to tribal organization); (2) the division of society into socioeconomic classes (distribution to individuals of social obligations and rewards according to class membership and not according to kinship status); (3) the prevalence of a central world-view (myth, complex religion) to the end of legitimating political power (thus converting power into authority). Civilizations are established on the basis of a relatively developed technology and of division of labor in the social process of production, which make possible a surplus product, i.e. a quantity of goods exceeding that needed for the satisfaction of immediate and elementary needs. They owe their existence to the solution of the problem that first arises with the production of a surplus product, namely, how to distribute wealth and labor both unequally and yet legitimately according to criteria other than those generated by a kinship system.[2]

In our context it is relevant that despite considerable differences in their level of development, civilizations, based on an economy dependent on agriculture and craft production, have tolerated technical innovation and organizational improvement only within definite limits. One indicator of the traditional limits to the development of the forces of production is that until about 300 years ago no major social system had produced more than the equivalent of a maximum of $200 per capita per annum. The stable pattern of a pre-capitalist mode of production, pre-industrial technology, and pre-modern science makes possible a typical relation of the institutional framework of subsystems of purposive-rational action. For despite considerable progress, these subsystems, developing out of the system of social labor and its stock of accumulated technically exploitable knowledge, never reached that measure of extension after which their "rationality" would have become an open threat to the authority of the cultural traditions that legitimate political power. The expression "traditional society" refers to the circumstance that the institutional framework is grounded in the unquestionable underpinning of legitimation constituted by mythical, religious, or metaphysical interpretations of reality – cosmic as well as social – as a whole. "Traditional" societies exist as long as the development of subsystems of purposive-rational action keeps within the limits of the legitimating efficacy of cultural traditions.[3] This is the basis for the "superiority" of the institutional framework, which does not preclude structural changes adapted to a potential surplus generated in the economic system but does preclude critically challenging the traditional form of legitimation. This immunity is a meaningful criterion for the delimitation of traditional societies from those which have crossed the threshold to modernization.

The "superiority criterion," consequently, is applicable to all forms of class society organized as a state in which principles of universally valid rationality (whether of technical or strategic means–ends relations) have not explicitly and successfully called into question the cultural validity of intersubjectively shared traditions, which function as legitimations of the political system. It is only since the capitalist mode of production has equipped the economic system with a self-propelling mechanism that ensures long-term continuous growth (despite crises) in the productivity of labor that the introduction of new technologies and strategies, i.e. innovation as such, has been institutionalized. As Marx and Schumpeter have proposed in their respective theories, the capitalist mode of production can be comprehended as a mechanism that guarantees the *permanent* expansion of subsystems of purposive-rational action and thereby overturns the traditionalist "superiority" of the institutional framework to the forces of production. Capitalism is the first mode of production in world history to institutionalize self-sustaining economic growth. It has generated an industrial system that could be freed from the institutional framework of capitalism and connected to mechanisms other than that of the utilization of capital in private form.

What characterizes the passage from traditional society to society commencing the process of modernization is *not* that structural modification of the institutional framework is necessitated under the pressure of relatively developed productive forces, for that is the mechanism of the evolution of the species from the very beginning. What is new is a level of development of the productive forces that makes permanent the extension of subsystems of purposive-rational action and thereby calls into question the traditional form of the legitimation of power. The older mythic, religious, and metaphysical world-views obey the logic of interaction contexts. They answer the central questions of men's collective existence and of individual life history. Their themes are justice and freedom, violence and oppression, happiness and gratification, poverty, illness and death. Their categories are victory and defeat, love and hate, salvation and damnation. Their logic accords with the grammar of systematically distorted communication and with the fateful causality of dissociated symbols and suppressed motives.[4] The rationality of language games, associated with communicative action, is confronted at the threshold of the modern period with the rationality of means-ends relations, associated with instrumental and strategic action. As soon as this confrontation can arise, the end of traditional society is in sight: the traditional form of legitimation breaks down.

Capitalism is defined by a mode of production that not only poses this problem but also solves it. It provides a legitimation of domination which is no longer called down from the lofty heights of cultural tradition but instead summoned up from the base of social labor. The institution of the market, in which private property owners exchange commodities – including the market on which propertyless private individuals exchange their labor power as their only commodity – promises that exchange relations will be and are just owing to equivalence. Even this bourgeois ideology of justice, by adopting the category of reciprocity, still employs a relation of communicative action as the basis of legitimation. But the principle of reciprocity is now the organizing principle of the sphere of production and reproduction itself. Thus on the base of a market economy, political domination can be legitimated henceforth "from below" rather than "from above" (through invocation of cultural tradition).

If we suppose that the division of society into socioeconomic classes derives from the differential distribution among social groups of the relevant means of production, and that this distribution itself is based on the institutionalization of relations of social force, then we may assume that in all civilizations this institutional framework has been identical with the system of political domination: traditional authority was political authority. Only with the emergence of the capitalist mode of production can the legitimation of the institutional framework be linked immediately with the system of social labor. Only then can the property order change from a *political relation* to a *production relation*, because it legitimates itself through the rationality of the market, the ideology of exchange society, and no longer through a legitimate power structure. It is now the political system which is justified in terms of the legitimate relations of production: this is the real meaning and function of rationalist natural law from Locke to Kant.[5] The institutional framework of society is only mediately political and immediately economic (the bourgeois constitutional state as "superstructure").

The superiority of the capitalist mode of production to its predecessors has these two roots: the establishment of an economic mechanism that renders permanent the expansion of subsystems of purposive-rational action, and the creation of an economic legitimation by means of which the political system can be adapted to the new requisites of rationality brought about by these developing subsystems. It is this process of adaptation that Weber comprehends as "rationalization."

Within it we can distinguish between two tendencies: rationalization "from below" and rationalization "from above."

A permanent pressure for adaptation arises from below as soon as the new mode of production becomes fully operative through the institutionalization of a domestic market for goods and labor power and of the capitalist enterprise. In the system of social labor this institutionalization ensures cumulative progress in the forces of production and an ensuing horizontal extension of subsystems of purposive-rational action – at the cost of economic crises, to be sure. In this way traditional structures are increasingly subordinated to conditions of instrumental or strategic rationality: the organization of labor and of trade, the network of transportation, information, and communication, the institutions of private law, and, starting with financial administration, the state bureaucracy. Thus arises the substructure of a society under the compulsion of modernization. The latter eventually widens to take in all areas of life: the army, the school system, health services, and even the family. Whether in city or country, it induces an urbanization of the *form* of life. That is, it generates subcultures that train the individual to be able to "switch over" at any moment from an interaction context to purposive-rational action.

This pressure for rationalization coming from below is met by a compulsion to rationalize coming from above. For, measured against the new standards of purposive rationality, the power-legitimating and action-orienting traditions – especially mythological interpretations and religious world-views – lose their cogency. On this level of generalization, what Weber terms "secularization" has two aspects. First, traditional world-views and objectivations lose their power and validity *as* myth, *as* public religion, *as* customary ritual, *as* justifying metaphysics, *as* unquestionable tradition. Instead, they are reshaped into subjective belief systems and ethics which ensure the private cogency of modern value-orientations (the "Protestant ethic"). Second, they are transformed into constructions that do both at once: criticize tradition and reorganize the released material of tradition according to the principles of formal law and the exchange of equivalents (rationalist natural law). Having become fragile, existing legitimations are replaced by new ones. The latter emerge from the critique of the dogmatism of traditional interpretations of the world and claim a scientific character. Yet they retain legitimating functions, thereby keeping actual power relations inaccessible to analysis and to public consciousness. It is in this way that ideologies in the restricted sense first came into being. They replace traditional legitimations of power by appearing in the mantle of modern science and by deriving their justification from the critique of ideology. Ideologies are coeval with the critique of ideology. In this sense there can be no pre-bourgeois "ideologies."

In this connection modern science assumes a singular function. In distinction from the philosophical sciences of the older sort, the

empirical sciences have developed since Galileo's time within a methodological frame of reference that reflects the transcendental viewpoint
of possible technical control. Hence the modern sciences produce
knowledge which through its *form* (and not through the subjective
intention of scientists) is technically exploitable knowledge, although
the possible applications generally are realized afterwards. Science and
technology were not interdependent until late into the nineteenth
century. Until then modern science did not contribute to the acceleration of technical development or, consequently, to the pressure toward
rationalization from below. Rather, its contribution to the modernization process was indirect. Modern physics gave rise to a philosophical
approach that interpreted nature and society according to a model
borrowed from the natural sciences and induced, so to speak, the
mechanistic world-view of the seventeenth century. The reconstruction
of classical natural law was carried out in this framework. This modern
natural law was the basis of the bourgeois revolutions of the seventeenth, eighteenth, and nineteenth centuries, through which the old
legitimations of the power structure were finally destroyed.[6]

[. . .] Since the last quarter of the nineteenth century two developmental
tendencies have become noticeable in the most advanced capitalist
countries: an increase in state intervention in order to secure the
system's stability, and a growing interdependence of research and
technology, which has turned the sciences into the leading productive
force. Both tendencies have destroyed the particular constellation of
institutional framework and subsystems of purposive-rational action
which characterized liberal capitalism, thereby eliminating the conditions relevant for the application of political economy in the version
correctly formulated by Marx for liberal capitalism. I believe that
Marcuse's basic thesis, according to which technology and science today
also take on the function of legitimating political power, is the key to
analyzing the changed constellation.
   The permanent regulation of the economic process by means of state
intervention arose as a defense mechanism against the dysfunctional
tendencies, which threaten the system, that capitalism generates when
left to itself. Capitalism's actual development manifestly contradicted
the capitalist idea of a bourgeois society, emancipated from domination,
in which power is neutralized. The root ideology of just exchange, which
Marx unmasked in theory, collapsed in practice. The form of capital
utilization through private ownership could only be maintained by the
government corrective of a social and economic policy that stabilized
the business cycle. The institutional framework of society was repoliti-
cized. It no longer coincides immediately with the relations of production, i.e. with an order of private law that secures capitalist economic
activity and the corresponding general guarantees of order provided by
the bourgeois state. But this means a change in the relation of the

economy to the political system: politics is no longer *only* a phenom-
enon* of the superstructure. If society no longer "autonomously"
perpetuates itself through self-regulation as a sphere preceding and
lying at the basis of the state – and its ability to do so was the really
novel feature of the capitalist mode of production – then society and
the state are no longer in the relationship that Marxian theory had
defined as that of base and superstructure. Then, however, a critical
theory of society can no longer be constructed in the exclusive form of
a critique of political economy. A point of view that methodically
isolates the economic laws of motion of society can claim to grasp the
overall structure of social life in its essential categories only as long as
politics depends on the economic base. It becomes inapplicable when
the "base" has to be comprehended as in itself a function of governmental activity and political conflicts. According to Marx, the critique
of political economy was the theory of bourgeois society only as *critique
of ideology*. If, however, the ideology of just exchange disintegrates,
then the power structure can no longer be criticized *immediately* at the
level of the relations of production. [. . .]

Old-style politics was forced, merely through its traditional form of
legitimation, to define itself in relation to practical goals: the "good life"
was interpreted in a context defined by interaction relations. The same
still held for the ideology of bourgeois society. The substitute program
prevailing today, in contrast, is aimed exclusively at the functioning of a
manipulated system. It eliminates practical questions and therewith
precludes discussion about the adoption of standards; the latter could
emerge only from a democratic decision-making process. The solution
of technical problems is not dependent on public discussion. Rather,
public discussions could render problematic the framework within which
the tasks of government action present themselves as technical ones.
Therefore the new politics of state interventionism require a depoliticization of the mass of the population. To the extent that practical
questions are eliminated, the public realm also loses its political
function. At the same time, the institutional framework of society is still
distinct from the systems of purposive-rational action themselves. Its
organization continues to be a problem of *practice* linked to communication, not one of *technology*, no matter how scientifically guided.
Hence, the bracketing out of practice associated with the new kind of
politics is not automatic. The substitute program, which legitimates
power today, leaves unfilled a vital need for legitimation: how will the
depoliticization of the masses be made plausible to them? Marcuse
would be able to answer: by having technology and science *also* take on
the role of an ideology.

Since the end of the nineteenth century the other developmental
tendency characteristic of advanced capitalism has become increasingly
momentous: the scientization of technology. The institutional pressure

to augment the productivity of labor through the introduction of new technology has always existed under capitalism. But innovations depended on sporadic inventions, which, while economically motivated, were still fortuitous in character. This changed as technical development entered into a feedback relation with the progress of the modern sciences. With the advent of large-scale industrial research, science, technology, and industrial utilization were fused into a system. Since then, industrial research has been linked up with research under government contract, which primarily promotes scientific and technical progress in the military sector. From there information flows back into the sectors of civilian production. Thus technology and science become a leading productive force, rendering inoperative the conditions for Marx's labor theory of value. It is no longer meaningful to calculate the amount of capital investment in research and development on the basis of the value of unskilled (simple) labor power, when scientific-technical progress has become an independent source of surplus value, in relation to which the only source of surplus value considered by Marx, namely the labor power of the immediate producers, plays an ever smaller role.

As long as the productive forces were visibly linked to the rational decisions and instrumental action of men engaged in social production, they could be understood as the potential for growing power of technical control and not be confused with the institutional framework in which they are embedded. However, with the institutionalization of scientific-technical progress, the potential of the productive forces has assumed a form owing to which men lose consciousness of the dualism of work and interaction.

It is true that social interests still determine the direction, functions, and pace of technical progress. But these interests define the social system so much as a whole that they coincide with the interest in maintaining the system. *As such* the private form of capital utilization and a distribution mechanism for social rewards that guarantees the loyalty of the masses are removed from discussion. The quasi-autonomous progress of science and technology then appears as an independent variable on which the most important single system variable, namely economic growth, depends. Thus arises a perspective in which the development of the social system *seems* to be determined by the logic of scientific-technical progress. The immanent law of this progress seems to produce objective exigencies, which must be obeyed by any politics oriented toward functional needs. But when this semblance has taken root effectively, then propaganda can refer to the role of technology and science in order to explain and legitimate why in modern societies the process of democratic decision-making about practical problems loses its function and "must" be replaced by plebiscitary decisions about alternative sets of leaders of administrative personnel. This technocracy thesis has been worked out in several versions on the intellectual level. What seems to me more important is that it can also become a background ideology that penetrates into the consciousness of the depoliticized mass of the population, where it can take on legitimating power. It is a singular achievement of this ideology to detach society's self-understanding from the frame of reference of communicative action and from the concepts of symbolic interaction and replace it with a scientific model. Accordingly the culturally defined self-understanding of a social lifeworld is replaced by the self-reification of men under categories of purposive-rational action and adaptive behavior.

The model according to which the planned reconstruction of society is to proceed is taken from systems analysis. It is possible in principle to comprehend and analyze individual enterprises and organizations, even political or economic subsystems and social systems as a whole, according to the pattern of self-regulated systems. It makes a difference, of course, whether we use a cybernetic frame of reference for analytic purposes or *organize* a given social system in accordance with this pattern as a man–machine system. But the transferral of the analytic model to the level of social organization is implied by the very approach taken by systems analysis. Carrying out this intention of an instinct-like self-stabilization of social systems yields the peculiar perspective that the structure of one of the two types of action, namely the behavioral system of purposive-rational action, not only predominates over the institutional framework but gradually absorbs communicative action as such. If, with Arnold Gehlen, one were to see the inner logic of technical development as the step-by-step disconnection of the behavioral system of purposive-rational action from the human organism and its transferral to machines, then the technocratic intention could be understood as the last stage of this development. For the first time man can not only, as *Homo faber*, completely objectify himself and confront the achievements that have taken on independent life in his products; he can in addition, as *Homo fabricatus*, be integrated into his technical apparatus if the structure of purposive-rational action can be successfully reproduced on the level of social systems. According to this idea the institutional framework of society – which previously was rooted in a different type of action – would now, in a fundamental reversal, be *absorbed* by the subsystems of purposive-rational action, which were embedded in it.

Of course this technocratic intention has not been realized anywhere even in its beginnings. But it serves as an ideology for the new politics, which is adapted to technical problems and brackets our practical questions. Furthermore it does correspond to certain developmental tendencies that could lead to a creeping erosion of what we have called the institutional framework. The manifest domination of the authoritarian state gives way to the manipulative compulsions of technical-operational administration. The moral realization of a normative order is a function of communicative action oriented to shared cultural meaning and presupposing the internalization of values. It is increasingly supplanted by conditioned behavior, while large organizations as such are increasingly patterned after the structure of purposive-rational action. The industrially most advanced societies seem to approximate the model of behavioral control steered by external stimuli rather than guided by norms. Indirect control through fabricated stimuli has increased, especially in areas of putative subjective freedom (such as electoral, consumer, and leisure behavior). Sociopsychologically, the era is typified less by the authoritarian personality than by the destructuring of the superego. The increase in *adaptive behavior* is, however, only the obverse of the dissolution of the sphere of linguistically mediated interaction by the structure of purposive-rational action. This is paralleled subjectively by the disappearance of the difference between purposive-rational action and interaction from the consciousness not only of the sciences of man, but of men themselves. The concealment of this difference proves the ideological power of the technocratic consciousness.

[. . .] Technocratic consciousness is, on the one hand, "less ideological" than all previous ideologies. For it does not have the opaque force of a delusion that only transfigures the implementation of interests. On the other hand today's dominant, rather glassy background ideology, which makes a fetish of science, is more irresistible and farther-reaching than ideologies of the old type. For with the veiling of practical problems it not only justifies a *particular class's* interest in domination and represses *another class's* partial need for emancipation, but affects the human race's emancipatory interest as such.

Technocratic consciousness is not a rationalized, wish-fulfilling fantasy, not an "illusion" in Freud's sense, in which a system of interaction is either represented or interpreted and grounded. Even bourgeois ideologies could be traced back to a basic pattern of just interactions, free of domination and mutually satisfactory. It was these ideologies which met the criteria of wish-fulfillment and substitute gratification; the communication on which they were based was so limited by repressions that the relation of force once institutionalized as the capital–labor relation could not even be called by name. But the technocratic consciousness is not based in the same way on the causality of dissociated symbols and unconscious motives, which generates both false consciousness and the power of reflection to which the critique of ideology is indebted. It is less vulnerable to reflection, because it is no longer *only* ideology. For it does not, in the manner of ideology, express a projection of the "good life" (which, even if not identifiable with a bad reality, can at least be brought into virtually satisfactory accord with it). Of course the new ideology, like the old, serves to impede making the foundations of society the object of thought and reflection. Previously, social force lay at the basis of the relation between capitalist and wage-laborers. Today the basis is provided by structural conditions which predefine the tasks of system maintenance: the private form of capital utilization and a political form of distributing social rewards that guarantees mass loyalty. However, the old and new ideology differ in two ways.

First, the capital–labor relation today, because of its linkage to a loyalty-ensuring political distribution mechanism, no longer engenders uncorrected exploitation and oppression. The process through which the persisting class antagonism has been made virtual presupposes that the repression on which the latter is based first came to consciousness in history and *only then* was stabilized in a modified form as a property of the system. Technocratic consciousness, therefore, cannot rest in the same way on collective repression as did earlier ideologies. Second, mass loyalty today is created only with the aid of rewards for *privatized needs*. The achievements in virtue of which the system justifies itself may not in principle be interpreted politically. The acceptable interpretation is immediately in terms of allocations of money and leisure time (neutral with regard to their use), and mediately in terms of the technocratic justification of the occlusion of practical questions. Hence the new ideology is distinguished from its predecessor in that it severs the criteria for justifying the organization of social life from any normative regulation of interaction, thus depoliticizing them. It anchors them instead in functions of a putative system of purposive-rational action.

Technocratic consciousness reflects not the sundering of an ethical situation but the repression of "ethics" as such as a category of life. The common, positivist way of thinking renders inert the frame of reference of interaction in ordinary language, in which domination and ideology both arise under conditions of distorted communication and can be reflectively detected and broken down. The depoliticization of the mass of the population, which is legitimated through technocratic consciousness, is at the same time men's self-objectification in categories equally of both purposive-rational action and adaptive behavior. The reified models of the sciences migrate into the sociocultural lifeworld and gain objective power over the latter's self-understanding. The ideological nucleus of this consciousness is *the elimination of the distinction between the practical and the technical*. It reflects, but does not objectively account for, the new constellation of a disempowered institutional framework and systems of purposive-rational action that have taken on a life of their own.

The new ideology consequently violates an interest grounded in one of the two fundamental conditions of our cultural existence: in language, or more precisely, in the form of socialization and individuation determined by communication in ordinary language. This interest extends to the maintenance of intersubjectivity of mutual understanding as well as to the creation of communication without domination.

Technocratic consciousness makes this practical interest disappear behind the interest in the expansion of our power of technical control. Thus the reflection that the new ideology calls for must penetrate beyond the level of particular historical class interests to disclose the fundamental interests of mankind as such, engaged in the process of self-constitution.

Toward a Rational Society, pp. 91–113.

Notes

1 On the context of these concepts in the history of philosophy, see "Work and Interaction," in *Theory and Practice*.
2 Gerhard E. Lenski, *Power and Privilege: A Theory of Social Stratification* (New York: McGraw-Hill, 1966).
3 See Peter L. Berger, *The Sacred Canopy* (New York: Doubleday, 1967).
4 See *Knowledge and Human Interests*.
5 See Leo Strauss, *Natural Right and History* (Chicago: University of Chicago Press, 1963; C.B. McPherson, *The Political Theory of Possessive Individualism* (London: Oxford University Press, 1962); and "The Classical Doctrine of Politics in Relation to Social Philosophy," in *Theory and Practice*.
6 See "Natural Law and Revolution," in *Theory and Practice*.

PART III

Epistemology and Methodology

Introduction

The extracts in this section show how Habermas's critique of positivistic social science developed in the 1960s into an ambitious social theory of knowledge based on the concept of cognitive or knowledge-guiding interests. Reading 6, based on a lecture delivered in 1960, is an early attempt to locate Marxism in terms of the philosophy of science, as well as a critique of positivism. In this extract, Habermas contrasts Marx's program with that of modern sociology, which in the 1950s had focussed to a considerable degree on role theory.[1] As Habermas, shows, in an argument later taken up by, for example, Pierre Bourdieu, sociology as traditionally conceived has often failed to reflect on its own activity.[2]

The critique of positivism is developed further in reading 7, "Dogmatism, Reason, and Decision," written for Theory and Practice in 1963. At about the same time, Habermas was joining in the long-running "positivism dispute" (Positivismusstreit) begun by Theodor Adorno and Karl Popper* at the conference of the German Sociological Association held in 1961.[3] This article also points to some of the themes of Habermas's inaugural lecture at Frankfurt in 1965, "Knowledge and Human Interests: A General Perspective," and his book with the same title published in 1968. (The lecture is reprinted in the English translation as Reading 8.) In Knowledge and Human Interests, Habermas uses his model of knowledge-guiding interests as the basis of a brilliant critical reconstruction of the origins of modern positivism. Habermas aims both to combat the positivistic reduction of epistemology, the philosophical theory of knowledge, to methodology, and to outline a model of critical social science, illustrated by Freudian psychoanalytic theory and the Marxist critique of ideology and explicitly oriented to emancipation. In this model, the conception of critical social science replaces Habermas's earlier account of Marxism and of his own emergent critical theory as a "philosophy of history with a practical purpose." In the 1970s this is in turn replaced by a model of reconstructive science of which Habermas's own theory of communicative action is the paradigmatic example.

Habermas has since come to see Knowledge and Human Interests as something of a detour, and no longer aims to combine epistemology with *social theory in such a direct manner. The book remains, however, one of his most impressive and inspiring, showing how the heritage of German critical philosophy could ground the project of an interdisciplinary critical social science as inaugurated by Horkheimer and Adorno. Habermas was working at the same time on a "literature survey",* On the Logic of the Social Sciences, *published in 1967 with a new edition in 1970. Habermas has always presented this work as merely an exercise in self-clarification, but it provides an excellent guide to the principal methodological dilemmas in the social sciences and to Habermas's development of his own conception via engagement with, in particular, analytic philosophy, phenomenology, hermeneutics, and system theory. (It was around this time that he conducted two important intellectual debates with the hermeneutic philosopher Hans-Georg Gadamer and the system theorist Niklas Luhmann.) The book as a whole, like the opening pages reproduced here as reading 9, is concerned with the perennial questions of naturalism (the methodological unity of the social and natural sciences), and the relation between understanding and explanation.*

Notes

1 See, in particular, Ralf Dahrendorf, "Homo Sociologicus," in Dahrendorf, *Essays in the Theory of Society* (London: Routledge, 1968).
2 See Pierre Bourdieu and Loïc Wacquant, *An Invitation to Reflexive Sociology* (Chicago: University of Chicago Press, 1982).
3 See T.W. Adorno, R. Dahrendorf, H. Pilot, H. Albert, J. Habermas, and K.R. Popper, *The Positivist Dispute in German Sociology* (London: Heinemann, 1976).

Further Reading

On naturalism and interpretive understanding, see Roy Bhaskar, *The Possibility of Naturalism* (Hemel Hempstead: Harvester Wheatsheaf, 1979, 2nd edn 1989) for the most important recent contribution to these issues, based on Bhaskar's critical realist philosophy of science. William Outhwaite, *Understanding Social Life: The Method called Verstehen* (London: Allen & Unwin 1975; 2nd edn Lewes: Jean Stroud 1986), is a more a historical account, strongly influenced by Habermas's *Logic of the Social Sciences*. See also William Outhwaite, *New Philosophies of Social Science: Realism, Hermeneutics and Critical Theory* (London: Macmillan, 1987). F.R. Dallmayr and T. McCarthy (eds), *Understanding and Social Inquiry* (Notre Dame: University of Notre Dame Press, 1977) includes some of the principal contributions to the debate over *Verstehen*.

6

The Positivistic Dissolution of the Claimed Unity of Theory and Praxis

Within the concept of society as a historical totality Marx could still hold together what later fell apart into the specific subjects of the separate social sciences. The consoling promise of a "synthesis" *post festum* cannot restore what must be lost in the gaps between the various sectors of economics, sociology, political science, and jurisprudence: the system of human social life as such. [. . .]

Certainly, on the basis of their division of labor, several of the social sciences have meanwhile made the proud advance in knowledge that enables them to draw abreast of the natural sciences. However, this progress has exacted a price which is imposed on the natural sciences to a lesser degree than on the sciences of society, especially when they themselves are no longer in any way aware of this cost. In terms of one single example we should like to demonstrate how a science, in this case modern sociology, has to constrict the range of its possible insights more severely, the more rigorous the criteria to which it subjects its specific results.

(1) Today sociology views human beings as the bearers of social roles. With the operational introduction of this category it opens up domains of social behavior to exact analysis. Insofar as role, defined as the behavioral expectation of a reference group, represents a historical magnitude, its variations during the course of the historical development of mankind must remain closed to sociological investigation. This imposes a limit even on dynamic theories, which seek to do justice to the process and conflictual character of social events. In this respect the experience which they represent is in no way historical. Only in an advanced stage of industrial society, with what Max Weber called the rationalization of social relations, has the functional interdependence of institutions grown to such an extent that the subjects, claimed for their part by an increasing and varying multiplicity of social functions, can be interpreted as the points of intersection of social obligations. It is only

the multiplication, the growing independence, and the accelerated interchangeability of dissociated behavior patterns that endow the "roles" with a quasi-reified existence with respect to the persons who "externalize" themselves in these roles, and develop the demands for inwardness within this externalization, as it comes to their consciousness – as the history of bourgeois consciousness, especially during the eighteenth century, has shown. Marx was convinced that the reification of modes of conduct could be traced back to the expansion of the relation of exchange and, ultimately, to the capitalistic mode of production. Be that as it may, this much is certain in any case: the analytical fruitfulness of the category "role" is not independent of the stage of development of the society, in terms of the relations of which society must first prove itself. If, however, it is generalized to apply to social relations as such and thus becomes a universal historical category, then role analysis, with its historical dependency, must ignore social evolution as a historical process altogether – as though it were wholly external to the individuals whether they are subsumed under a few natural roles, like the medieval serfs, or whether, like the employees in an industrially advanced civilization, they are subsumed under multiple, rapidly changing, and somewhat dissociated roles. In this dimension of development, there is a growing opportunity to relate to the roles as roles. This brings about increased freedom of scope for mobility in accepting and exchanging roles as well as of a new sort of lack of freedom, insofar as one sees oneself forced to take on externally assigned roles; and perhaps the more external these roles become, the more deeply they have to be internalized.

A sociology committed to role analysis will ignore this dimension, and will therefore be forced to reduce historical development to a social modification of basic relations which remain eternally the same. The roles as such are posited as constant in their relationship to their bearers, as though the complex of social life were as external to the life of the human beings themselves as in Kant's relation of the empirical character to the intelligible character.

(2) But the price which sociology pays for the advancement of knowledge is not only a methodological blindness with respect to the historical character of society. Together with its methodological abstinence with respect to the practical consequences of its own activity, it must also accept a limitation which obstructs its view not only of its object but even of the discipline itself. This can be demonstrated by the same example. To separate rigidly the scientific construction of the role bearer from the dimension of moral decision, when confronting the real human beings (as in Kant's distinction between the phenomenal and the noumenal domains), is intended to help clarify the conflicting positions into which the sociologist gets, as scientist and politician in one person. According to the well-known resolution of the controversy

about value judgment, he must strictly separate the two: on the one side, keep the answers to technical questions which he has discovered by empirical, theoretical means, in pursuing explanatory problems; and on the other side, keep those answers to ethical and political questions which he had attained by traditional or philosophical means in pursuing normative problems. Today, however, sociology, to a growing degree, is becoming an applied science in the service of administration. The technical translation of research results is not applied to analytic schemata, but instead to a social reality which has already been schematized. Therefore the isolation between the two domains remains a fiction. With a view to its sociopolitical consequences, sociology, in spite of its methodical distance from its object, still deals with actual human beings, with the living interrelationships of society.

Only when role theory is referred back to the activity of the sociologists themselves do its fundamental problematics begin to emerge: how can a mediation of the construction of phenomena, on the one hand, and of social existence, on the other, be incorporated in this reflection itself? And how can the relation of theory to praxis be dealt with adequately in theory, and if possible, incorporated into theory itself? Some have sought to do justice to this problem on the basis of value-free method, with the postulate that the sociologist must select his problems from the viewpoint of their relevance to the freedom of the individuals:

> There can be no danger to the purity of scientific activity, if sociology prefers such verifiable theories, which take into account the right and the fullest value [*Fülle*] of the individual. Not to lose sight of the thought about the possible application of the results, for the uses and the well-being of the free individual, when pursuing scientific activity that has society as its subject matter is completely above suspicion.[1]

However, how can these specific goals be rationally applied to concrete situations? And indeed, beyond that, are the interests which guide inquiry determining only for the selection of the problems, or do they also impinge on the selection of the fundamental categories of the system? Does not a prior understanding of intelligible character always necessarily enter into the sociological construction of empirical character, in the sense in which this Kantian distinction has been subjected to Hegel's general critique? For the latter quite correctly points out that Kant cannot wholly eradicate the substantial elements from his functional concept of truth (defined by the transcendental conditions of the possibility of knowledge), that he must also presuppose a prior correspondence of reason and nature, subject and object.[2] Of course, Marx removes the idealistic basis for the dialectical relation between the two. The self-movement of the spirit, in which subject and object are interwoven, he interprets as the self-generation of man by means of social labor. Man does not have in his possession the "unity of subject and object" from the outset [*von Haus aus*], either as spirit or as a being of nature; only in the exchange, by labor, with nature as the reciprocal self-formative process of nature is this unity practically constituted. All possible experience is confined within the horizon of this praxis; at its root it is structured by specific interests.

Though indeed the unity of subject and object, given in interested experience, is formalized by the separation between subject and object which science brings about methodologically, it is never wholly suspended. The kinds of experience and the degree of their scientific character are distinguished only by the degree to which their links to interest can be formalized. Now the interest in acquiring control over real processes is indeed susceptible to a high degree of formalization: it is fundamental and powerfully active in all historical and social situations. And beyond that, the interest is confirmed to the degree to which it actually leads to domination, of nature, to begin with, and is thus confirmed retroactively by its successes; it is stabilized through positive feedback. Therefore this interest can become so self-evident that, once it has been fully invested in the initiative toward knowledge, it "disappears." Still, in the domain of the social sciences it must become problematic. We have no experience of what happens within nature "itself" as it comes under the control of the categorial apparatus of the sciences (physics) and the technical apparatus of the applied sciences (technology), nor do we need to, as we are not "practically" interested in the "fate" of nature as such. But we are practically interested in society. For even if we place ourselves (fictitiously) outside the social interrelationships of life in order to confront them, we still remain part of them, even in the act of insight, as subject and object in one. The interest in attaining control over society initially invested in the cognitive initiative of scientific theories interferes with the simultaneous interest in society "in itself." Therefore a prior understanding originating in interested experience always infiltrates the fundamental concepts of the theoretical system.

But if experiences dependent on the situation must necessarily also enter into the strictly scientific approach, then the interests which direct knowledge must be brought under control, they must be legitimized as objective interests, unless one wants to arbitrarily break off the process of rationalization. Whether the theory of social integration (arising out of the experience of the insecurity produced by social crises) seeks to understand the social system as a structure of a harmoniously equalized and enduring order, or whether the theory of social conflict (arising out of the experience of how deceptive the security of compulsive political integration can be) seeks to understand that same system as an association of domination [*Herrschaftsverband*] kept open and in flux by internal oppositions – no matter which approach is chosen, an anticipatory interpretation of society as a whole always enters into the selection of the fundamental categories. Significantly, this is a prior understanding of how the society is and, at the same time, of how it ought to be – for the interested experience of a situation in which one lives separates the "is" from the "ought" just as little as it dissects what it experiences into facts, on the one hand, and norms, on the other.

The dialectical interpretation comprehends the knowing subject in terms of the relations of social praxis, in terms of its position, within both the process of social labor and the process of enlightening the political forces about their goals. According to Horkheimer, this twofold reflection distinguishes "critical theory" from "traditional theory:"

> The traditional conception of theory is abstracted from the scientific enterprise, and this is carried on within the division of labor at a given level. This conception corresponds to the activity of scholars, as it is carried out side by side with all the other activities in society, without any direct insight into the connections between these separate activities being attained. In this conception, therefore, the real social function of science does not appear, thus, not what the theory means for human existence, but only what it means within the detached sphere in which it is being produced under historical conditions ... The professional scholar, as scientist, views social reality, with all its products, as external to him, and, as citizen, perceives his interest in this society in terms of political articles [he may write], membership in parties or benevolent organizations, and participation in elections, without connecting these two, as well as several other modes of conduct, in any way, except, at most, by psychological interpretations; while critical thinking is motivated by the actual attempt to overcome this tension, to resolve [sublate] the opposition between the consciousness of goal, the spontaneity, the rationality immanent within the individuals, and the relations to the labor process which are fundamental for society.[3]

For Marx the problem of such a "materialistic" self-consciousness on the part of critique arose not out of the immanent difficulties of the positive sciences, but out of the consideration of the political consequences that flowed from the philosophy of his time – or rather, its lack of consequences. At that time the social sciences had by no means achieved a status in which they could have held up before dialectical theory the mirror of the inheritance salvaged from the bankruptcy of philosophy. So much philosophical substance had been incorporated into the approach of economic theory of the eighteenth and the early nineteenth centuries that the critique of political economy met it on its own scientific ground and from there delivered its judgment on the false scientific claims of philosophy. The ideological self-understanding of the phenomenological experience of spirit was to be condemned by means of the critical experience of the social interrelations of life; philosophy was to be superseded *as* philosophy. Today, on the contrary, the positive sciences are at one with the philosophy of that time in the "idealistic" aspect, by which traditional theory in general is distinguished from critical theory. The latter occupies its distinctive position between philosophy and positivism in such a manner that a critical self-enlightenment of positivism leads into the same dimension at which Marx arrived, so to speak, from the opposite direction.

Theory and Practice, pp. 206–12.

Notes

1 R. Dahrendorf, "Homo Sociologicus," in Dahrendorf, *Essays in the Theory of Society* (London: Routledge, 1968).
2 Kant, *Critique of Pure Reason*, tr. N.K. Smith (New York: 1928), A651, pp. 537ff.
3 Max Horkheimer, "Traditional and Critical Theory," in *Critical Theory* (New York: Seabury Press, 1972).

7

Dogmatism, Reason, and Decision: On Theory and Praxis in Our Scientific Civilization

In the major tradition of philosophy, the relation of theory and praxis always referred to the good and the righteous – as well as the "true" – and to the life, both private and collective, of individuals as well as of citizens. In the eighteenth century this dimension of a theoretically guided praxis of life was extended by the philosophy of history. Since then, theory, directed toward praxis and at the same time dependent on it, no longer embraces the natural, authentic, or essential actions and institutions of a human race constant in its essential nature; instead, theory now deals with the objective, overall complex of development of a human species which produces itself, which is as yet only destined to attain its essence: humanity. What has remained is theory's claim of providing orientation in right action, but the realization of the good, happy, and rational life has been stretched out along the vertical axis of world-history; praxis has been extended to cover stages of emancipation. For this rational praxis is now interpreted as liberation from an externally imposed compulsion just as the theory which is guided by this interest of liberation is interpreted as enlightenment. The cognitive interest of this enlightenment theory is declaredly critical; it presupposes a specific experience, which is set down in Hegel's *Phenomenology of Mind*, just as it is in Freud's psychoanalysis – the experience of an emancipation by means of critical insight into relationships of power, the objectivity of which has as its source solely that the relationships have not been seen through. Critical reason gains power analytically over dogmatic inhibition.

Reason takes up a partisan position in the controversy between critique and dogmatism, and with each new stage of emancipation it wins a further victory. In this kind of practical reason, insight and the explicit interest in liberation by means of reflection converge. The higher level of reflection coincides with a step forward in the progress toward the autonomy of the individual, with the elimination of suffering and the furthering of concrete happiness. Reason involved in the argument against dogmatism has definitely taken up this interest as its own – it does not define the moment of decision as external to its sphere. Rather, the decisions of the subjects are measured rationally against that one objective decision, which is required by the interest of reason itself. Reason has not as yet renounced the will to the rational.

Now this constellation of dogmatism, reason, and decision has changed profoundly since the eighteenth century, and exactly to the degree to which the positive sciences have become productive forces in social development. For as our civilization has become increasingly scientific, the dimension within which theory was once directed toward praxis has become correspondingly constructed. The laws of self-reproduction demand of an industrially advanced society that it look after its survival on the escalating scale of a continually expanded technical control over nature and a continually refined administration of human beings and their relations to each other by means of social organization. In this system, science, technology, industry, and administration interlock in a circular process. In this process the relationship of theory to praxis can now only assert itself as the purposive-rational application of techniques assured by empirical science. The social potential of science is reduced to the powers of technical control – its potential for enlightened action is no longer considered. The empirical, analytical sciences produce technical recommendations, but they furnish no answer to practical questions. The claim by which theory was once related to praxis has become dubious. Emancipation by means of enlightenment is replaced by instruction in control over objective or objectified processes. Socially effective theory is no longer directed toward the consciousness of human beings who live together and discuss matters with each other, but to the behavior of human beings who manipulate. As a productive force of industrial development, it changes the basis of human life, but it no longer reaches out critically beyond this basis to raise life itself, for the sake of life, to another level.

But, of course, the real difficulty in the relation of theory to praxis arises not from this new function of science as a technological force, but rather from the fact that we are no longer able to distinguish between practical and technical power. Yet even a civilization that has been rendered scientific is not granted dispensation from practical questions; therefore a peculiar danger arises when the process of scientification transgresses the limit of technical questions, without, however, departing from the level of reflection of a rationality confined to the techno-logical horizon. For then no attempt at all is made to attain a rational consensus on the part of citizens concerning the practical control of their destiny. Its place is taken by the attempt to attain technical control over history by perfecting the administration of society, an attempt that is just as impractical as it is unhistorical. When theory was still related to praxis in a genuine sense, it conceived of society as a system of action by human beings, who communicate through speech and thus must realize social intercourse within the context of conscious communication. Through this communication they must form themselves into a collective subject of the whole that is capable of action – otherwise, the fortunes of a society ever more rigidly rationalized in its particular parts must slip away as a whole from that rational cultivation, which they require all the more urgently. On the other hand, a theory which confuses control with action is no longer capable of such a perspective. It understands society as a nexus of behavioral modes, for which rationality is mediated solely by the understanding of sociotechnical controls, but not by a coherent total consciousness – not by precisely that interested reason which can only attain practical power through the minds of politically enlightened citizens.

In industrially advanced society, research, technology, production, and administration have coalesced into a system which cannot be surveyed as a whole, but in which they are functionally interdependent. This has literally become the basis of our life. We are related to it in a peculiar manner, at the same time intimate and yet estranged. On the one hand, we are bound externally to this basis by a network of organizations and a chain of consumer goods; on the other hand, this basis is shut off from our knowledge, and even more from our reflection. The paradox of this state of affairs will, of course, only be recognized by a theory oriented toward praxis, even though this paradox is so evident: the more the growth and change of society are determined by the most extreme rationality of processes of research, subject to a division of labor, the less rooted is this civilization, now rendered scientific, in the knowledge and conscience of its citizens. In this discrepancy, scientifically guided techniques and those of decision theory – and ultimately even cybernetically controlled techniques – encounter a limitation which they cannot overcome; this can only be altered by a change in the state of consciousness itself, by the practical effect of a theory which does not improve the manipulation of things and of reifications, but which instead advances the interest of reason in human adulthood, in the autonomy of action and in the liberation from dogmatism. This it achieves by means of the penetrating ideas of a persistent critique.

Committed reason and the interest of the Enlightenment: Holbach, Fichte, and Marx

[...] In the concept of reason active as critique of ideology, knowledge and commitment are related dialectically: on the one hand, it is only possible to see through the dogmatism of a congealed society to the degree to which knowledge has committed itself to being guided by the anticipation of an emancipated society and actualized adult autonomy for all human beings; at the same time, on the other hand, this interest demands that insight into the processes of social development be already attained, because only in these processes can such insight be constituted as objective. On the level of the historical self-reflection of a science with critical intent, Marx for the last time identifies reason with a commitment to rationality in its thrust against dogmatism.

In the second half of the nineteenth century, during the course of the reduction of science to a productive force in industrial society, positivism, historicism, and pragmatism, each in turn, isolate one part of this all-encompassing concept of rationality. The hitherto undisputed attempt of the great theories to reflect the complex of life as a whole is henceforth itself discredited as dogmatic. Reason, once it is particularized, is assigned to the level of subjective consciousness, whether as the capacity for the empirical verification of hypotheses, for historical understanding, or for the pragmatic control of behavior. At the same time, interest and inclination are banished from the court of knowledge as subjective factors. The spontaneity of hope, the act of taking a position, the experience of relevance or indifference, and above all, the response to suffering and oppression, the desire for adult autonomy, the will to emancipation, and the happiness of discovering one's identity – all these are dismissed for all time from the obligating interest of reason. A disinfected reason is purged of all moments of enlightened volition; external to itself, it has externalized – alienated – its own life. And life deprived of spirit leads an existence of arbitrariness that is a ghostly spirit indeed – all under the name of "decision."

The positivistic isolation of reason and decision [*Entscheidung*]

Prior to positivism, critical knowledge referred to a scientific orientation in action. Even the knowledge of nature (physics in the classical sense) had its role to play with respect to praxis (to ethics and politics). However, after the empirical sciences of the new type, so successful since the time of Galileo, had attained a consciousness of themselves in positivism, and after analytic philosophy, inspired by the Vienna circle* as well as by Peirce and Dewey, had explicated this self-understanding in terms of the philosophy of science, especially in the work of Carnap,* Popper, and Morris,* the two cognitive functions were distinctly separated – and both deprived of their power of orientation for action.

The *affirmative* achievement of the modern sciences consists in statements about empirical uniformities. The hypothetical laws, gained from a deductive connection among statements and tested by controlled experiments, refer to regular covariances of empirical variables in all the domains accessible intersubjectively to experience. Under given individual initial conditions, universal laws of this kind serve as explanations. The theoretical statements which permit the causal explanation of effects in the same way make possible the prediction of effects, given the causes. This predictive application of the theories of experimental science reveals the interest of knowledge which guides these generalizing sciences. As artisans were formerly guided, in working on their materials, by rules of experience which had been proven in the tradition of their trade, so in the same way engineers in all sectors can rely on such scientifically tested predictions in the choice of the means they employ, of their instruments and operations. To be sure, the reliability of the rules distinguished the exercise of technique [*techne*] in the old sense from what we call technique [technology] today. The function of the knowledge of modern science must therefore be understood in connection with the system of social labor: it extends and rationalizes our power of technical control over the objects or – which comes to the same thing – objectified processes of nature and society.

From this affirmative achievement of knowledge reduced to empirical science derives also its other function, its *critical achievement*. For when this type of science attains a monopoly in the guidance of rational action, then all competing claims to a scientific orientation for action must be rejected. This activity is now reserved for a positivistically circumscribed critique of ideology. It is directed against dogmatism in a new guise. Any theory that relates to praxis in any way other than by strengthening and perfecting the possibilities for purposive-rational action must now appear dogmatic. The methodology of the empirical sciences is tacitly but effectively rooted in a technical cognitive interest that excludes all other interests; consequently all other relations to life-praxis can be blocked out under the slogan of ethical neutrality or value-freedom. The economy in the selection of purposive-rational means which is guaranteed by conditional predictions in the form of technical recommendations is the sole admissible "value,"[1] and it too is not seen explicitly as a value, because it simply seems to coincide with rationality as such. In fact, we have here the formalization of one sole relevance to life, namely, the experience of success as feedback control, built into the systems of social labor and already realized in every successful elementary performance of labor.

According to the principles of an analytic philosophy of science, empirical questions which cannot be posed and solved in the form of technical tasks cannot therefore expect to receive a cogent theoretical answer. From the outset, all practical questions, which cannot be answered adequately by technical prescriptions, but which instead also require a self-understanding within their concrete situation, go beyond the cognitive interest invested in empirical science. The only type of science admitted by the positivistic approach is one that is not capable of investigating such questions rationally. And theories which in spite of that offer such solutions can be convicted of dogmatism by these criteria. The goal of a critique of ideology abbreviated in this manner is to respond to every dogmatic assertion with the decisionistic [*dezision-istisch*] thesis that practical questions (in our sense) cannot be discussed cogently and in the final instance must be simply decided upon, one way or another. The magic word for release from the spell of dogmatism is "decision," decision that has been painfully isolated from reason: practical questions are not "capable of truth" [*wahrheitsfähig*].

At this point in the positivistic confrontation with the new lineaments of dogmatism,[2] the inverse side of such a critique of ideology is revealed. It is correct in removing the veil of a false rationalization of what has been derationalized in value ethics [*Wertethik*] such as Scheler's* and Hartmann's* philosophy and in referring ideal objects back to the subjectivity of needs and inclinations, value judgments and commitments. But the result of its labors is monstrous enough: from the mainstream of rationality the pollutants, the sewage of emotionality, are filtered off and locked away hygienically in a storage basin – an imposing mass of subjective value-qualities. Every single value appears as a meaningless agglomeration of meaning, stamped solely with the stigma of irrationality, so that the priority of one value over the other – thus the persuasiveness which a value claims with respect to action – simply cannot be rationally justified. Thus on this level the critique of ideology involuntarily furnishes the proof that progress of a rationalization limited in terms of empirical science to technical control is paid for with the corresponding growth of a mass of irrationality in the domain of praxis itself. For action still demands an orientation, as it did before. But now it is dissected into a rational implementation of techniques and strategies and an irrational choice of so-called value-systems. The price paid for economy in the selection of means is a decisionism set wholly free in the selection of the highest-level goals.

The positivistically cleansed demarcation set between knowing and evaluating of course represents less a result than a problem. For the detached domain of values, norms, and decisions is now seized upon anew by philosophic interpretations, precisely on the basis of that division of labor shared with a reduced science.

The *subjective philosophy of value* is no longer as assured of the reference to meaning split off from the context of life, and hypostatized, as the objective value ethics was, which had immediately made of this a domain of ideal being, transcending sense experience. It too sought to reclaim the existence of orders of value (Max Weber) and of forces of faith [*Glaubensmächte*] (Jaspers) in a sphere elevated above history. But scientifically-controlled knowledge cannot simply be complemented by intuitive knowledge. The philosophic belief that remains midway between pure commitment and rational comprehension must pledge itself to one of the competing orders, without, however, revoking the pluralism of these orders, and without being able wholly to resolve the dogmatic core which is the source of its own life. Polemic, responsible although in principle indecidable, between philosophers, as the intellectually honest and existentially committed representatives of spiritual forces, appears as the only permissible form of discussion in this domain of practical questions. *Decisionism* as a world-view today no longer is ashamed to reduce norms to decisions. In non-cognitive ethics, in the form of linguistic analysis, the decisionistic complement to a positivistically limited science is itself still conceived positivistically (R.M. Hare).* As soon as certain fundamental value-judgments are posited as axioms, a deductive chain of statements can be analyzed cogently for each; at the same time, such principles themselves are not accessible to rational comprehension: their acceptance is based solely on a decision, a commitment. Such decisions can then be interpreted either in an existential-personal sense (Sartre) or in a public, political sense (Carl Schmitt)* or institutionally from anthropological presuppositions (Gehlen), but the thesis remains the same: that decisions relevant to the praxis of life, whether they consist in the acceptance of values, in the selection of biographical [*lebensgeschichtlich*] design, or in the choice of an enemy, are not accessible to rational consideration and cannot form a rationally substantiated consensus. But if practical questions, eliminated from knowledge that has been reduced to empirical science, are dismissed in this way entirely from the controlling powers of rational investigation, if decisions on questions touching on the praxis of life must be pronounced as beyond any and every authority committed to rationality, then we cannot be astonished by the ultimate desperate attempt to secure socially binding precommitments on practical questions institutionally by a return to the closed world of mythical images and powers (Walter Bröcker).* As Adorno and Horkheimer have shown, this complementing of positivism by *mythology* is not devoid of its logically compelling character, whose abysmal irony can be turned to laughter only by dialectics.

Sincere positivists, in whom such perspectives choke off laughter – thus, positivists who recoil before the half-concealed metaphysics of an objective value ethics and a subjective philosophy of value, as they do before the proclaimed irrationality of decisionism and the resurrection of mythology – seek their foothold in a reified critique of ideology with self-understanding, which, however, in the primitive form of nullifying projections, as developed from the time of Feuerbach down to Pareto, has itself congealed into the program of a *Weltanschauung*. For the one thing that remains unclarified in all this radicalism is the root: the motive of the critique of ideology itself. If the goal of the latter consists only in differentiating in principle the scientifically rationalized shaping of reality from the "value-laden forms of a world-view seeking interpretation of the world and self-interpretation of man"[3] – where such attempts at "enlightening consciousness" cannot make a claim to demonstrable rationality – then the critique of ideology closes off for itself the possibility of justifying its own endeavours theoretically. For as critique, it too is making an attempt to enlighten consciousness, and certainly not to shape reality; it does not produce new techniques; at best it could prevent given techniques from being misapplied in the name of a merely alleged theory. But from what source does this critique draw its power, if reason divorced from commitment must be wholly devoid of any interest in an emancipation of consciousness from dogmatic constraint?

Certainly science must be allowed to exercise its affirmative function as knowledge – it is, so to speak, itself recognized as a value. This is served by the separation, performed by the critique of ideology, of knowing from commitment, and such a separation, once carried out, would have abolished dogmatism. But even so, science in its critical function of knowledge, the combating of dogmatism on a positivistic level, is possible only in the form of a science which reflects on itself and wills itself as an end – thus again a kind of committed reason, the *justified* possibility of which is precisely what the critique of ideology denies. If, on the other hand, it renounces a rational justification, then the dispute of reason with dogmatism itself remains a matter of dogmatic opinion: the impossibility of resolving dogmatism would be admitted at the outset. Behind this dilemma there lies, it seems to me, the problem that the critique of ideology must tacitly presuppose as its own motivation just what it attacks as dogmatic, namely, the convergence of reason and commitment – thus precisely an encompassing concept of rationality. To be sure, this hidden concept of a substantial rationality is conceived differently depending on whether the motivating reflection is persuaded solely on the value of scientific techniques, or also of the significance of scientific emancipation for adult autonomy; thus whether the critique of ideology is motivated on the level of understanding by an interest in the empirical sciences' increase in technical knowledge, or is motivated on the level of reason by an interest in enlightenment as such. Positivism is as little capable of distinguishing between these two concepts of rationality as it is capable, altogether, of being conscious that it itself implies just what it seeks to oppose externally – committed reason. But on this, or the proper distinction between these two forms, depends the relation of theory and praxis in a scientific civilization.

The partisanship of the critique of ideology in favor of technological rationality

No matter how much it insists on a separation of theory and commitment in its opposition to dogmatism, positivism's critique of ideology itself remains a form of committed reason: *nolens volens* it takes a partisan position in favor of progressive rationalization. In the case which we will analyze to begin with, its concern, without reservation, is for the extension and dissemination of technical knowledge. In its conflict with dogmatism, as understood by positivism, this critique removes traditionalistic barriers, and ideological barriers of any sort, which can inhibit the progress of the analytic-empirical sciences and the unlimited process of their utilization. This critique is not a value-neutral analysis; its underlying premise is the value of empirical science theories, and this not simply hypothetically, but normatively. For with its first analytic step it already presupposes, normatively, that behaving in accordance with technical recommendations is not only desirable, but also "rational." This implicit concept of reason can, of course, not be clarified by means of the conceptual resources of positivism itself, even though this concept expresses its intention. By positivistic criteria, rationality of conduct is a value which we simply decide to accept or reject. At the same time, according to these same criteria, it can be demonstrated quite compellingly that rationality is a means for the realization of values, and therefore cannot itself be placed on the *same* level with all the other values. Indeed, the critique of ideology's preparation for rational conduct recommends rationality as the pre-ferred – if not exclusive – means for the realization of values, because it guarantees the "efficiency" or "economy" of procedures. Both of these terms betray the interest of knowledge guiding the empirical sciences to be a technical one. They reveal that from the outset rationalization is confined within the limits posed by the system of social labor, that what it refers to is exactly the making available of objective and objectified processes. And in this the power of technical control remains wholly indifferent with respect to the possible value-systems in the service of which it is to be exercised. Efficiency and economy, which are the definition of this rationality, cannot, in turn, be themselves conceived as values, and yet, within the framework of positivism's understanding of itself, they can only be justified as though they were values. A critique of ideology whose sole goal is to make technological rationality prevail cannot escape from this dilemma: it desires rationality as a value, because it has the advantage over all the other values of being implicit in the rational modes of procedure themselves. Because this value can be legitimized by pointing to the process of scientific investigation and its technical application, and does not have to be justified in terms of pure commitment alone, it has a preferential status as against all other values. The experience of the controlled success enjoyed by rational conduct exercises a rationally demonstrated compulsion toward the acceptance of such norms of conduct; thus even this limited rationality implies a decision in favor of rationality. In the critique of ideology, which at least tacitly realizes this, a particle of committed reason therefore remains active – in contradiction to the criteria by which it criticizes dogmatism. Because, no matter how perverted, it still remains of a piece with committed reason; it also entails consequences which violate its alleged neutrality toward any value-systems whatsoever. On the contrary, the concept of rationality which it seeks to make prevail in its commitment ultimately implies an entire organization of society: one in which a technology become autonomous dictates a value-system – namely, its own – to the domains of praxis it has usurped – and all in the name of value-freedom.

I wish to distinguish four levels of rationalization, on which we extend our technical powers of control qualitatively. On the first two levels, technologies demand an exclusion of normative elements from the process of scientific argumentation; on the two subsequent levels, however, this elimination changes into its opposite in the subordination of values, which have first been pronounced irrational, to technological procedures, which then establish themselves as values.

The *first* level of rationalization depends on the methodological state of the empirical sciences. The mass of corroborated lawlike hypotheses determines the extent of possible rational conduct. In this is involved technological rationality in the strict sense: we employ techniques placed at our disposal by science for the realization of goals. If, however, there is a choice between actions of equal technical appropriateness, a rationalization on the *second* level is required. The translation of technical recommendations into praxis – thus the technical utilization of theories of the empirical sciences – is also to be subject to the conditions of technological rationality. But the information furnished by empirical science is not sufficient for a rational choice between means which are functionally equivalent, given concrete goals, and which are to be realized within the framework of a value-system. Thus instead, this relation between alternative techniques and given goals, on the one hand, and value-systems and maxims for reaching decisions, on the other, is clarified by decision theory. It analyzes the possible decisions normatively in accordance with a rationality of choice defined as "economical" or "efficient." But in so doing, rationality refers solely to the form of the decisions, and not to objective situations and actual results.

On the first two levels, the rationality of conduct enforces an isolation of values, which are removed from any and every cogent discussion, and can only be related to given techniques and concrete goals in the form of hypothetically entertained imperatives; these relations are accessible to rational calculation because they remain external to the values rendered irrational as such. "What is designated as a value system here is thus a system of rules which prescribe how the consequences described by the information system are to be evaluated *on the basis of the value perceptions [Wertempfindungen] of the actor.*"[4] The subjectivistic reduction of the interests which are decisive in the orientation for action to "sentiments" or "perceptions," which cannot be rationalized beyond that, is a precise expression for the fact that the value freedom central to the technological concept of rationality functions within the system of social labor, and that all the other interests of the praxis of life are subordinated for the benefit of the sole interest in efficiency and economy in the utilization of means. The competing perspectives of interest, hypostatized to values, are excluded from discussion. Revealingly enough, according to the criteria of technological rationality, agreement on a collective value-system can never be achieved by means of enlightened discussion carried on in public politics, thus by way of a consensus rationally arrived at, but only by summation or compromise – values are in principle beyond discussion. Naturally, the decision-theoretical assumption of "autonomous" value-systems is not tenable in practice. The institution of formal rationality of choice, thus an extension of technological thinking to the selection of scientific techniques, changes the previously given value-systems themselves. By this I mean not only the systematization of value-conceptions required by this decision-theoretical analysis; I mean above all the reformulation or even total devaluation of traditional norms, which fail to function as principles of orientation for a technical realization of concrete goals. The dialectical relation between values which originate in specific configurations of interest and techniques for the satisfaction of value-oriented needs is evident: just as values become depreciated as ideological and then become extinct, when they have lost their connection with a technically adequate satisfaction of real needs over a longer period, so inversely new techniques can form new value-systems within changed configurations of interest. As is well known, Dewey was able to derive from the interconnection of values with technical knowledge the expectation that the deployment of continually multiplied and improved techniques would not remain bound solely to the [existing] orientation of values, but also would subject the values themselves indirectly to a pragmatic test of their viability. Only because this interrelationship between traditional values and scientific techniques, which decision theory neglects, exists can Dewey ask: "How shall we employ what we know to direct our practical behavior so as to test these beliefs and make possible better ones? The question is seen as it has always been empirically: What shall we do to make objects having value more secure in existence?"[5] This question can be answered in the sense of a reason which is interested in enlightenment; in any case, that is the sense in which Dewey posed it. Meanwhile, we first have to deal with the alternative answer, which subjects even the formation of value-systems to technological rationality. With that we reach the *third* level of rationalization.

The latter extends to strategic situations, in which rational conduct in the face of an opponent who also acts rationally is to be calculated. Both adversaries pursue competing interests; in the case of a strictly competitive situation, they evaluate the same consequences according to inverse series of preferences, no matter whether the value-systems correspond or not. Such a situation demands a far-reaching rationalization. Those acting do not only wish to gain control technically over a specific field of events by means of scientific prediction, but also to gain the same control over situations of rational indeterminacy; they cannot inform themselves about the conduct of the opponent empirically in the same manner as about processes of nature, by means of lawlike hypotheses; their information remains incomplete, not merely to a degree but in principle, because the opponent also has a choice of alternative strategies and thus is not confined to unambiguously deter-mined reactions. What interests us, however, is not the game-theoretical solution of the problem posed, but the peculiar technical compulsion which, in addition, such strategic situations exercise on value-systems. A basic value also enters into the technical task itself, namely, successful self-assertion against an opponent, the securing of survival. The orig-inally invested values, that is, those value-systems with which decision theory initially is solely occupied, are then relativized in terms of this strategic value, by which the game or the conflict is given its orientation.

As soon as the game theory's assumption concerning strategic situ-ations is generalized to cover all decision-making situations, decision-making processes can be analyzed under political conditions on all occasions – here I use "political" in the sense of the tradition from Hobbes to Carl Schmitt, in the sense of existential self-assertion. Then ultimately it is sufficient to reduce all value-systems to a, as it were, biological basic value, and to pose the problem of decision-making generally, in the following form: How must the systems by which decisions are made – whether by individuals or groups, specific insti-tutions or entire societies – be organized in order to meet the basic value of survival in a given situation and to avoid risks? The goal functions, which together with the initially invested values furnished the program, here disappear in favor of formalized goal variables, such as stability or adaptability, which are bound solely to a quasi-biological basic requirement of the system, that of reproducing life. To be sure, this self-programming of feedback systems only becomes possible on the *fourth* level of rationalization, as soon as it becomes possible to turn over the decision-making effort to a machine. Even if today there is a large class of problems for which machines can be utilized successfully in order to simulate the real case, still this last stage of rationalization as yet remains largely a fiction. However, it does reveal for the first time in its entirety the intention of a technological rationality extended over all the domains of praxis, and thereby the substantial concept of rationality, which the positivistic critique presupposes as its premise, and yet at the same time suppresses. Learning machines as cybernetic mechanisms for social organization can in principle take over such decision-making processes under political conditions. As soon as this threshold had been passed, the value-systems excluded from the process of rationalization at a lower level would themselves also be rendered interchangeable in accordance with the criteria of rational behavior; indeed, these values could only enter, as a liquid mass, into the adaptive procedures of a machine which stabilizes its own equilibrium and programs itself because the values had previously been rendered irrational qua values.

In a manuscript on the scientific and political significance of decision theory, Horst Rittel has drawn unmistakable conclusions for the fourth level of rationalization:

> Value systems can no longer be regarded as stable over a longer period. What can be desired depends on what can be made possible, and what can be made possible depends on what one desires. Goals and utility functions are not independent variables. They are in reciprocal interaction with the scope of decision-making. Within broad limits conceptions of value can be directed. In the face of the uncertainty which marks the alternatives of future development, there is no prospect for seeking to set up rigid models of decision-making and to offer strategies for longer time periods.... It proves more meaningful to view the problem of decision-making in a more general way and to look into the suitability of decision-making systems. How must an organization be constituted so that it will be equal to the uncertainty introduced by innovation and political vicissitudes? ... Instead of assuming a specific decision-making system and a value system as definitely given, the suitability of this system for fulfilling its tasks must be investigated. What feedback mechanisms to its object system are necessary? What data about the object system are needed and to what degree of precision? What devices are necessary for the preparation of this data? What value systems are at all consistent and guarantee chances for adaptation and therefore for "survival"?[6]

The negative utopia of technical control over history would be fulfilled if one were to set up a learning automaton as a central system of societal control which would answer these questions cybernetically, thus by "itself."

The critique of ideology, which for the sake of resolving dogmatism and asserting technologically rational behavior insistently separates reason from decisions of commitment, in the end automates the decisions according to the laws of the rationality thus made dominant. Critique, however, cannot maintain this separation and only finds its own rationality in its partisanship for rationality, no matter how restricted. That is why even the type of rationalization developed on these four levels is not tolerant, to say nothing of indifferent, toward values. For from this concept of rationality the ultimate decisions concerning the acceptance or rejection of norms are not excluded after all. Even these decisions ultimately are incorporated into the self-regulating process of adaptation of a learning automaton according to the laws of rational behavior – connected to a process of knowledge oriented toward technical control. The substantive rationality suppressed in the innocent partisanship for formal rationality reveals, in the anticipated concept of a cybernetically self-regulated organization of society, a tacit philosophy of history. This is based on the questionable thesis that human beings control their destinies rationally to the degree to which social techniques are applied, and that human destiny is capable of being rationally guided in proportion to the extent of cybernetic control and the application of these techniques. But such a rational administration of the world is not simply identical with the solution of the practical problems posed by history. There is no reason for assuming that a continuum of rationality exists extending from the capacity of technical control over objectified processes to the practical mastery of historical processes. The root of the irrationality of history is that we "make" it, without, however, having been able until now to make it consciously. A rationalization of history cannot therefore be furthered by an extended power of control on the part of manipulative human beings, but only by a higher stage of reflection, a consciousness of acting human beings moving forward in the direction of emancipation.

On the self-reflection of rationalistic "faith"

Now, even in its positivistic form the critique of ideology can pursue an interest in adult autonomy; as the example of Popper shows, it need not stop at an adherence to the technical interest of knowledge. Certainly, Popper was one of the first to insist on the demarcation rigidly drawn by the logic of science between knowing and valuing. He too identifies the knowledge of empirical science conforming to the rules of a cogent universal methodology with science as such; he too simply accepts the residual definition of thought, which is purged of the components of rational volition, and does not ask whether perhaps the monopolizing of all possible knowledge by a technical interest of knowledge does not itself create the norms, measured by which everything that does not comply takes on the fetishistic guise of valuing, commitment, or mere faith. But Popper's critique of the configurations of dogmatism, as positivistically defined, does not share the tacit metaphysics to which the partisans of technological rationality are committed. His motive is that of enlightenment, with the prior reservation, however, that he can only justify rationalism as his professed faith. If scientific insight purged of the interest of reason is devoid of all immanent reference to praxis, and if, inversely, every normative content is detached nominalistically from insights into its real relation to life – as Popper presupposes undialectically – then indeed the dilemma must be conceded: that I cannot rationally compel anyone to support his assumptions with arguments and evidence from experience. And just as little can I justify compellingly, with the aid of arguments and experiential evidence, why I should be resolved to pursue this conduct. I must simply decide to commit myself to a rationalistic attitude. Even here the problem consists "not in a choice between knowing and believing, but in the choice between two kinds of faith."[7] What is at issue here for Popper is not the recommendation to accept technological rationality as a value. Rather, the rationalism in which he believes desires to obligate society, by means of the enlightened consciousness of its citizens, to a sociotechnically correct behavior. These citizens will act rationally, in the sense which already points beyond technological rationality, when they establish or change social norms and institutions with a knowledge of the scientific information at their disposal. For precisely that dualism of facts and commitments, with the implicit assumption that history can have meaning just as little as nature can, appears as the premise for the practical effectiveness of a rationalism adopted as commitment. It presupposes that, in the dimension of historical facts, by virtue of commitment and due to our theoretical knowledge of factual laws of nature, we can realize a "meaning" sociotechnically which is inherently alien to history. Popper's concept of rationality, too, at first preserves the semblance of a purely formal concept, no matter how much his category of meaning otherwise exceeds the criteria of economy and efficiency required by the system of social labor; this meaning itself, for the realization of which specific procedures are provided, remains undefined and open to concretization in terms of the requirements of accepted value-systems. The material shaping of given situations cannot already be prejudiced from the start by the obligation to apply rational procedures – for then even in this other case a substantial concept of rationality would be presupposed which would deprive the rationalistic faith of its character of pure decision.

Rationalism in Popper's positivistically delimited sense initially demands only that as many individuals as possible assume a rationalistic attitude. This attitude, no matter whether it determines comportment in the process of inquiry or in social praxis, conforms to the rules of scientific methodology. It accepts the customary norms of scientific discussion, is instructed especially concerning the duality of fact and commitment, and knows the limits of intersubjectively valid knowledge. Therefore it resists dogmatism, as the positivists understand it, and obligates itself in its judgment of value-systems, and in general of social norms, to conform to critical principles which specify the relationship of theory to praxis. First, the absolute validity of all social norms is denied; instead, they are considered to be open to critical investigation and possible revision at any time. Second, norms are accepted only after their effects in given social life-contexts have been tested and evaluated on the basis of available scientific information. Finally, every politically relevant action will seek to exhaust the reserves of technical knowledge and will employ all means of prediction, in order to avoid uncontrolled secondary consequences. All levels of this rationalization always refer back to the communication of the citizens carrying on discussion with a rationalistic attitude – and this distinguishes them from the four levels of technology enumerated above. For Popper has fictitiously extended methodology to the principles of political discussion, and thus has also extended the forum of scientific researchers examining methods and discussing empirical-theoretical questions to embrace the political public sphere as a whole.

The sociopolitical extrapolation of methodology into social policy represents more than merely the form of a rational realization of meaning. Indeed, it unfolds a specific meaning, and even the intention of a specific order of society, namely, the liberal order of the "open society." From the formal assumption of a rationalistic attitude Popper draws maxims for the decision of practical questions, which, if they were followed on an order of magnitude which is politically relevant, would have to intervene profoundly in the "natural" structure of the existing society. That process of scientifically enlightened communication, to be institutionalized in the political public sphere, would set into motion a sociotechnical dissolution of all substantial forms of domination – and would maintain this dissolution itself in the permanent reflection of the citizens, for the sake of their emancipation. It is not without reason, therefore, that Popper expects a reduction of repression from such a liberalism in the formation of political will, reconstituted on the level of the modern sciences, and, as a consequence of this, the growing emancipation of human beings: the reduction of collective and individual suffering within the limits of a non-compulsive consensus concerning the bases of general welfare and peace. Just as in the Enlightenment of the eighteenth century, lack of rationality once again coincides with freedom denied and deprivation of happiness.

If, however, a well-founded interconnection actually existed between the canon of scientifically cogent communication, extrapolated into the sociopolitical domain, and such practical consequences, then a positivism which reflected on itself could no longer detach reason's interest in emancipation from its concept of rationality. Now, however, that interconnection exists because in rational discussion as such a tendency is inherent, irrevocably, which is precisely a decisive commitment entailed by rationality itself, and which therefore does not require the commitment [*Dezision*] of pure faith. But rationalism would revoke [sublate] itself to become the positivistic version of blind faith if the comprehensive rationality of unconstrained dialogue between communicating human beings – which Popper tacitly requires from the outset – were merely to be subjected once again to the limited rationality of social labor.

Popper's discussion of methodological questions, as David Pole pointed out against him quite correctly,[8] presupposes the prior understanding of a rationality that is not as yet divested of its normative elements: methodological decisions can only be discussed on a rational basis if prior to that we have formed a concept of a "good" theory, a "satisfactory" argument, a "true" consensus, and a perspective that is hermeneutically "fruitful;" in such a concept, descriptive and normative contents are still not separated. Popper, on the other hand, must deny the rationality of such decisions, because it is they which determine to begin with the rules according to which the empirical analysis can be carried out in a value-free manner. And what is cut off especially is a discussion which would have to develop the objective implications of methodical decisions within the social context of the process of research, but which cannot do so owing to an undialectical separation of questions of genesis from those of validity.

This precarious inhibition of rationality is revealed still more distinctly in the discussion of practical questions as envisioned by Popper. Value-systems, too, are to be subjected to rational tests of validity that are just as rigorous as those of scientific theory, even if they are conducted in a different manner. According to the criteria for this validity, just as in the sciences, decisions would have to be reached methodologically. By means of such criteria, the factual consequences that value-systems have for social life could be tested in given situations on analogy with the information content of empirical science theories. In this connection, Hans Albert makes the utilitarian suggestion:

> to place in the foreground . . . in the establishment of a criterion for the validity of ethical systems, the satisfaction of human needs, the fulfillment of human desires, the avoidance of unnecessary human suffering. Such a criterion would have to be discovered and established, just as this is true for the criteria of scientific thought. The social rules of the game and also institutions, which to a certain degree are embodiments of ethical ideas that could be tested with the aid of such a criterion, are based on human invention. It is not to be expected that such a criterion would simply be accepted without further argument . . . but a rational discussion of a usable criterion is possible without any difficulties.[9]

Now, however, the establishment of such criteria is withdrawn from empirical scientific control, in view of the methodologically presupposed dualism of matters of fact and of moral decision. Precisely the desire for a far-reaching rationalization involuntarily renders visible the positivistic limits: questions of fact are prejudged in the form of methodological decisions, and the practical consequences flowing from the application of such criteria are excluded from reflection. Instead, a hermeneutic clarification of the need and the need satisfaction historically appropriate to the developmental state of society would be required, as well as a concept of suffering and "unnecessary" suffering valid for the epoch. Above all, the criterion selected would have to be derived as such from the objective complex of underlying interests and justified in terms of these. That in turn already presupposes a comprehensive concept of rationality, and especially one that does not hesitate to reflect on its own interrelationship with the historical stage of development attained by the knowing subjects. As soon as argument with rational warrants is carried on at the methodological – the so-called metatheoretical and metaethical – level, the threshold to the dimension of comprehensive rationality has already been breached. The proponents of positivistic enlightenment, who have confidence in their rationalism only as an article of faith, cannot reflect on what they thus presuppose *as* reason, as an interest identical with that of reason, for although they themselves have only been infected with the dogmatism of the technologists, they cannot see through it.

Only a reason which is fully aware of the interest in the progress of reflection toward adult autonomy, which is indestructibly at work in every rational discussion, will be able to gain transcendent power from the awareness of its own materialistic involvements. It alone will be able to begin reflecting on the positivistic domination of the technical interest of knowledge, growing out of the interrelationships of an industrial society that integrates science within it as a productive force, and which thus protects itself as a whole from critical insight. It alone can dispense with sacrificing the attained dialectical rationality of language to the deeply irrational criteria of a technologically con-strained rationality of labor. Only it can seriously intervene in the complex of compulsive interrelations of history, which remains dialetical as long as it is not liberated so that the dialogue of mature, autonomous human beings can take place. Today the convergence of reason and commitment, which the philosophy of the great tradition considered to be intimately linked, must be regained, reflected, and reasserted on the level of positive science, and that means carried on through the separation which is necessarily and correctly drawn on the level of technological rationality, the dichotomy of reason and commitment. Science as a productive force can work in a salutary way when it is suffused by science as an emancipatory force, to the same extent as it becomes disastrous as soon as it seeks to subject the domain of praxis, which is outside the sphere of technical disposition, to its *exclusive* control. The demythification which does not break the mythic spell but merely seeks to evade it will only bring forth new witch doctors. The enlightenment which does not break the spell dialectically, but instead winds the veil of a halfway rationalization only more tightly around us, makes the world divested of deities itself into a myth.

Schelling's romantic dictum about reason as controlled insanity gains an oppressively acute sense under technological domination over a praxis, which for that reason alone is detached from theory. The motive of reason was already central and determining in myth, religion, and philosophy; there it had the function of laying the foundation, within the manifold of shapeless phenomena, for the unity and coherence of a world; this motive lives on in a perverted manner in insanity. When the sciences, within the flux of phenomena in principle devoid of world, seek to wrest from contingency that which is empirically uniform, they are positivistically purged of insanity. They control but they do not control insanity; and therefore insanity must remain ungoverned and uncontrolled. Reason would have to rule in both domains; but this way, reason falls between two stools. Accordingly, the danger of an exclusively technical civilization, which is devoid of the interconnection between theory and praxis, can be clearly grasped; it is threatened by the splitting of its consciousness, and by the splitting of human beings into two classes – the social engineers and the inmates of closed institutions.

Theory and Practice, pp. 253–82.

Notes

1 With the exception of the values immanent to science which are specified by the logical and methodological rules.
2 Ontological doctrines fall under this as well as dialectical ones, classical natural law as well as modern philosophies of history. It is not accidental that Popper places Plato in the ranks of the great dogmatists next to Hegel and Marx – as so-called historicists.
3 E. Topitsch, *Sozialphilosophie zwischen Ideologie und Wissenschaft* (Neuwied: Luchterhand, 1962), p. 279.
4 See G. Gäfgen, *Theorie der wissenschaftlichen Entscheidung* (Tübingen: 1963), p. 99.
5 John Dewey, *The Quest for Certainty* (New York: 1960), p. 43.
6 H. Rittel, "Überlegungen zur wissenschaftlichen und politischen Bedeutung der Entscheidungstheorien," Studiengruppe für Systemforschung, Heidelberg, MS, pp. 29f.
7 K.R. Popper, *The Open Society and its Enemies* (Princeton, N.J.: 1950).
8 D. Pole, *Conditions of Rational Inquiry* (London: 1961), pp. 30ff.
9 H. Albert, "Ethik und Metaethik," *Archiv für Philosophie*, 2, 1961: 59ff.

Knowledge and Human Interests: A General Perspective

II

[. . .] There is a real connection between the positivistic self-understanding of the sciences and traditional ontology. The *empirical-analytic* sciences develop their theories in a self-understanding that automatically generates continuity with the beginnings of philosophical thought. For both are committed to a theoretical attitude that frees those who take it from dogmatic association with the natural interests of life and their irritating influence; and both share the cosmological intention of describing the universe theoretically in its lawlike order, just as it is. In contrast, the *historical-hermeneutic* sciences, which are concerned with the sphere of transitory things and mere opinion, cannot be linked up so smoothly with this tradition – they have nothing to do with cosmology. But they, too, comprise a *scientistic consciousness*, based on the model of science. For even the symbolic meanings of tradition seem capable of being brought together in a cosmos of facts in ideal simultaneity. Much as the cultural sciences may comprehend their facts through understanding and little though they may be concerned with discovering general laws, they nevertheless share with the empirical-analytic sciences the methodological consciousness of describing a structured reality within the horizon of the theoretical attitude. Historicism has become the positivism of the cultural and social sciences.

Positivism has also permeated the self-understanding of the *social sciences*, whether they obey the methodological demands of an empirical-analytic behavioral science or orient themselves to the pattern of normative-analytic sciences, based on presuppositions about maxims of action. In this field of inquiry, which is so close to practice, the concept of value-freedom (or ethical neutrality) has simply reaffirmed the ethos that modern science owes to the beginnings of theoretical thought in Greek philosophy: psychologically an unconditional commitment to theory and epistemologically the severance of knowledge from interest.

This is represented in logic by the distinction between descriptive and prescriptive statements, which makes grammatically obligatory the filtering out of merely emotive from cognitive contents.

Yet the very term "value-freedom' reminds us that the postulates associated with it no longer correspond to the classical meaning of theory. To dissociate values from facts means counterposing an abstract "ought" to pure being. Values are the nominalistic by-products of a centuries-long critique of the emphatic concept of being to which theory was once exclusively oriented. The very term "values," which neo-Kantianism* brought into philosophical currency, and in relation to which science is supposed to preserve neutrality, renounces the connection between the two that theory originally intended.

Thus, although the sciences share the concept of theory with the major tradition of philosophy, they destroy its classical claim. They borrow two elements from the philosophical heritage: the methodological meanings of the theoretical attitude and the basic ontological assumption of a structure of the world independent of the knower. On the other hand, however, they have abandoned the connection of *theoria* and *kosmos*, of *mimesis* and *bios theoretikos* that was assumed from Plato through Husserl. What was once supposed to comprise the practical efficacy of theory has now fallen prey to methodological prohibitions. The conception of theory as a process of cultivation of the person has become apocryphal. Today it appears to us that the mimetic conformity of the soul to the proportions of the universe, which seemed accessible to contemplation, had only taken theoretical knowledge into the service of the internalization of norms and thus estranged it from its legitimate task. [. . .]

IV

[. . .] With Husserl we shall designate as objectivistic an attitude that naïvely correlates theoretical propositions with matters of fact. This attitude presumes that the relations between empirical variables represented in theoretical propositions are self-existent. At the same time, it suppresses the transcendental framework that is the precondition of the meaning of the validity of such propositions. As soon as these statements are understood in relation to the prior frame of reference to which they are affixed, the objectivist illusion dissolves and makes visible a knowledge-constitutive interest.

There are three categories of processes of inquiry for which a specific connection between logical-methodological rules and knowledge-constitutive interests can be demonstrated. This demonstration is the task of a critical philosophy of science that escapes the snares of positivism. The approach of the empirical-analytic sciences incorporates a *technical* cognitive interest; that of the historical-hermeneutic sciences incorporates a *practical* one; and the approach of critically oriented sciences incorporates the *emancipatory* cognitive interest that, as we saw, was at the root of traditional theories. I should like to clarify this thesis by means of a few examples.

V

In the *empirical-analytic sciences* the frame of reference that prejudges the meaning of possible statements establishes rules both for the construction of theories and for their critical testing. Theories comprise hypothetico-deductive connections of propositions, which permit the deduction of lawlike hypotheses with empirical content. The latter can be interpreted as statements about the covariance of observable events; given a set of initial conditions, they make predictions possible. Empirical-analytic knowledge is thus possible predictive knowledge. However, the *meaning* of such predictions, that is, their technical exploitability, is established only by the rules according to which we apply theories to reality.

In controlled observation, which often takes the form of an experiment, we generate initial conditions and measure the results of operations carried out under these conditions. Empiricism attempts to ground the objectivist illusion in observations expressed in basic statements. These observations are supposed to be reliable in providing immediate evidence without the admixture of subjectivity. In reality basic statements are not simple representations of facts in themselves, but express the success or failure of our operations. We can say that facts and the relations between them are apprehended descriptively. But this way of talking must not conceal that as such the facts relevant to the empirical sciences are first constituted through an a priori organization of our experience in the behavioral system of instrumental action.

Taken together, these two factors, that is, the logical structure of admissible systems of propositions and the types of condition for corroboration, suggest that theories of the empirical sciences disclose reality subject to the constitutive interest in the possible securing and expansion, through information, of feedback-monitored action. This is the cognitive interest in technical control over objectified processes.

The *historical-hermeneutic sciences* gain knowledge in a different methodological framework. Here the meaning of the validity of propositions is not constituted in the frame of reference of technical control. The levels of formalized language and objectified experience have not yet been divorced. For theories are not constructed deductively and experience is not organized with regard to the success of operations. Access to the facts is provided by the understanding of meaning, not observation. The verification of lawlike hypotheses in the empirical-analytic sciences has its counterpart here in the interpretation of texts. Thus the rules of hermeneutics determine the possible meaning of the validity of statements of the cultural sciences.

Historicism has taken the understanding of meaning, in which mental facts are supposed to be given in direct evidence, and grafted onto it the objectivist illusion of pure theory. It appears as though the interpreter transposes himself into the horizon of the world or language from which a text derives its meaning. But here, too, the facts are first constituted in relation to the standards that establish them. Just as positivist self-understanding does not take into account explicitly the connection between measurement operations and feedback control, so it eliminates from consideration the interpreter's pre-understanding. Hermeneutic knowledge is always mediated through this pre-understanding, which is derived from the interpreter's initial situation. The world of traditional meaning discloses itself to the interpreter only to the extent that his own world becomes clarified at the same time. The subject of understanding establishes communication between both worlds. He comprehends the substantive content of tradition by *applying* tradition to himself and his situation.

If, however, methodological rules unite interpretation and application in this way, then this suggests that hermeneutic inquiry discloses reality subject to a constitutive interest in the preservation and expansion of the intersubjectivity of possible action-orienting mutual understanding. The understanding of meaning is directed in its very structure toward the attainment of possible consensus among actors in the framework of a self-understanding derived from tradition. This we shall call the *practical* cognitive interest, in contrast to the technical.

The systematic *sciences of social action*, that is, economics, sociology, and political science, have the goal, as do the empirical-analytic sciences, of producing nomological knowledge. A critical social science, however, will not remain satisfied with this. It is concerned with going beyond this goal to determine when theoretical statements grasp invariant regularities of social action as such and when they express ideologically frozen relations of dependence that can in principle be transformed. To the extent that this is the case, the *critique of ideology*, as well, moreover, as *psychoanalysis*, take into account that information about lawlike connections sets off a process of reflection in the consciousness of those whom the laws are about. Thus the level of unreflected consciousness, which is one of the initial conditions of such laws, can be transformed. Of course, to this end a critically mediated knowledge of laws cannot through reflection alone render a law itself inoperative, but it can render it inapplicable.

The methodological framework that determines the meaning of the validity of critical propositions of this category is established by the concept of *self-reflection*. The latter releases the subject from dependence on hypostatized powers. Self-reflection is determined by an emancipatory cognitive interest. Critically oriented sciences share this interest with philosophy.

However, as long as philosophy remains caught in ontology, it is itself subject to an objectivism that disguises the connection of its knowledge with the human interest in autonomy and responsibility [*Mündigkeit*]. There is only one way in which it can acquire the power that it vainly claims for itself in virtue of its seeming freedom from presuppositions: by acknowledging its dependence on this interest and turning against its own illusion of pure theory the critique it directs at the objectivism of the sciences.

VI

The concept of knowledge-constitutive human interests already conjoins the two elements whose relation still has to be explained: knowledge and interest. From everyday experience we know that ideas serve often enough to furnish our actions with justifying motives in place of the real ones. What is called rationalization at this level is called ideology at the level of collective action. In both cases the manifest content of statements is falsified by consciousness's unreflected tie to interests, despite its illusion of autonomy. The discipline of trained thought thus correctly aims at excluding such interests. In all the sciences routines have been developed that guard against the subjectivity of opinion, and a new discipline, the sociology of knowledge, has emerged to counter the uncontrolled influence of interests on a deeper level, which derive less from the individual than from the objective situation of social groups. But this accounts for only one side of the problem. Because science must secure the objectivity of its statements against the pressure and seduction of particular interests, it deludes itself about the fundamental interests to which it owes not only its impetus but *the conditions of possible objectivity* themselves.

Orientation toward technical control, toward mutual understanding in the conduct of life, and toward emancipation from seemingly "natural" constraint establish the specific viewpoints from which we can apprehend reality as such in any way whatsoever. By becoming aware of the impossibility of getting beyond these transcendental limits, a part of nature acquires, through us, autonomy in nature. If knowledge could ever outwit its innate human interest, it would be by comprehending that the mediation of subject and object that philosophical consciousness attributes exclusively to *its own* synthesis is produced originally by interests. The mind can become aware of this natural basis reflexively. Nevertheless, its power extends into the very logic of inquiry.

Representations and descriptions are never independent of standards. And the choice of these standards is based on attitudes that require critical consideration by means of arguments, because they cannot be either logically deduced or empirically demonstrated. Fundamental methodological decisions, for example such basic distinctions as those between categorial and non-categorial being, between analytic and synthetic statements, or between descriptive and emotive meaning, have the singular character of being neither arbitrary nor compelling. They prove appropriate or inappropriate. For their criterion is the metalogical necessity of interests that we can neither prescribe nor represent, but with which we must instead *come to terms.* Therefore my *first thesis* is this: *The achievements of the transcendental subject have their basis in the natural history of the human species.*

Taken by itself this thesis could lead to the misunderstanding that reason is an organ of adaptation for men just as claws and teeth are for animals. True, it does serve this function. But the human interests that have emerged in man's natural history, to which we have traced back the three knowledge-constitutive interests, derive both from nature and *from the cultural break* with nature. Along with the tendency to realize natural drives they have incorporated the tendency toward release from the constraint of nature. Even the interest in self-preservation, natural as it seems, is represented by a social system that compensates for the lacks in man's organic equipment and secures his historical existence *against* the force of nature threatening from without. But society is not only a system of self-preservation. An enticing natural force, present in the individual as libido, has detached itself from the behavioral system of self-preservation and urges toward utopian fulfillment. These individual demands, which do not initially accord with the requirement of collective self-preservation, are also absorbed by the social system. That is why the cognitive processes to which social life is indissolubly linked function not only as means to the reproduction of life; for in equal measure they themselves determine the definitions of this life. What may appear as naked survival is always in its roots a historical phenomenon. For it is subject to the criterion of what a society intends for itself as *the good life.* My *second thesis* is thus that *knowledge equally serves as an instrument and transcends mere self-preservation.*

The specific viewpoints from which, with transcendental necessity, we apprehend reality ground three categories of possible knowledge: information that expands our power of technical control; interpretations that make possible the orientation of action within common traditions; and analyses that free consciousness from its dependence on hypostatized powers. These viewpoints originate in the interest structure of a species that is linked in its roots to definite means of social organization: work, language, and power. The human species secures its existence in systems of social labor and self-assertion through violence, through tradition-bound social life in ordinary-language communication, and with the aid of ego identities that at every level of individuation reconsolidate the consciousness of the individual in relation to the norms of the group. Accordingly the interests constitutive of knowledge

are linked to the functions of an ego that adapts itself to its external
conditions through learning processes, is initiated into the communication system of a social lifeworld by means of self-formative processes,
and constructs an identity in the conflict between instinctual aims and
social constraints. In turn these achievements become part of the
productive forces accumulated by a society, the cultural tradition
through which a society interprets itself, and the legitimations that a
society accepts or criticizes. My *third thesis* is thus that *knowledge-
constitutive interests take form in the medium of work, language, and
power.*

However, the configuration of knowledge and interest is not the same
in all categories. It is true that at this level it is always illusory to
suppose an autonomy, free of presuppositions, in which knowing first
grasps reality theoretically, only to be taken subsequently into the
service of interests alien to it. But the mind can always reflect back
upon the interest structure that joins subject and object a priori: this is
reserved to self-reflection. If the latter cannot cancel out interest, it can
to a certain extent make up for it.

It is no accident that the standards of self-reflection are exempted
from the singular state of suspension in which those of all other
cognitive processes require critical evaluation. They possess theoretical
certainty. The human interest in autonomy and responsibility is not
mere fancy, for it can be apprehended a priori. What raises us out of
nature is the only thing whose nature we can know: *language*. Through
its structure, autonomy and responsibility are posited for us. Our first
sentence expresses unequivocally the intention of universal and unconstrained consensus. Taken together, autonomy and responsibility constitute the only idea that we possess a priori in the sense of the
philosophical tradition. Perhaps that is why the language of German
idealism, according to which "reason" contains both will and consciousness as its elements, is not quite obsolete. Reason also means the will to
reason. In self-reflection knowledge for the sake of knowledge attains
congruence with the interest in autonomy and responsibility. The
emancipatory cognitive interest aims at the pursuit of reflection as such.
My *fourth thesis* is thus that *in the power of self-reflection, knowledge
and interest are one.*

However, only in an emancipated society, whose members' autonomy
and responsibility had been realized, would communication have developed into the non-authoritarian and universally practiced dialogue from
which both our model of reciprocally constituted ego identity and our
idea of true consensus are always implicitly derived. To this extent the
truth of statements is based on anticipating the realization of the good
life. The ontological illusion of pure theory behind which knowledge-
constitutive interests become invisible promotes the fiction that Socratic
dialogue is possible everywhere and at any time. From the beginning
philosophy has presumed that the autonomy and responsibility posited

with the structure of language are not only anticipated but real. It is pure theory, wanting to derive everything from itself, that succumbs to unacknowledged external conditions and becomes ideological. Only when philosophy discovers in the dialectical course of history the traces of violence that deform repeated attempts at dialogue and recurrently close off the path to unconstrained communication does it further the process whose suspension it otherwise legitimates: mankind's evolution toward autonomy and responsibility. My *fifth thesis* is thus that *the unity of knowledge and interest proves itself in a dialectic that takes historical traces of suppressed dialogue and reconstructs what has been suppressed.*

VII

The sciences have retained one characteristic of philosophy: the illusion of pure theory. This illusion does not determine the practice of scientific research but only its self-understanding. And to the extent that this self-understanding reacts back upon scientific practice, it even has its point.

The glory of the sciences is their unswerving application of their methods without reflecting on knowledge-constitutive interests. From knowing not what they do methodologically, they are that much surer of their discipline, that is of methodical progress within an unproblematic framework. False consciousness has a protective function. For the sciences lack the means of dealing with the risks that appear once the connection of knowledge and human interest has been comprehended on the level of self-reflection. It was possible for fascism to give birth to the freak of a national physics and Stalinism to that of a Soviet Marxist genetics (which deserves to be taken more seriously than the former) only because the illusion of objectivism was lacking. It would have been able to provide immunity against the more dangerous bewitchments of misguided reflection.

But the praise of objectivism has its limits. Husserl's critique was right to attack it, if not with the right means. As soon as the objectivist illusion is turned into an affirmative *Weltanschauung*, methodologically unconscious necessity is perverted to the dubious virtue of a scientistic profession of faith. Objectivism in no way prevents the sciences from intervening in the conduct of life, as Husserl thought it did. They are integrated into it in any case. But they do not of themselves develop their practical efficacy in the direction of a growing rationality of action.

Instead, the positivist self-understanding of the *nomological sciences* lends countenance to the substitution of technology for enlightened action. It directs the utilization of scientific information from an illusory viewpoint, namely that the practical mastery of history can be reduced to technical control of objectified processes. The objectivist self-understanding of the *hermeneutic sciences* is of no lesser consequence. It defends sterilized knowledge against the reflected appropriation of active traditions and locks up history in a museum. Guided by the objectivist attitude of theory as the image of facts, the nomological and hermeneutical sciences reinforce each other with regard to their practical consequences. The latter displace our connection with tradition into the realm of the arbitrary, while the former, on the levelled-off basis of the repression of history, squeeze the conduct of life into the behavorial system of instrumental action. The dimension in which acting subjects could arrive rationally at agreement about goals and purposes is surrendered to the obscure area of mere decision among reified value-systems and irrational beliefs. When this dimension, abandoned by all men of good will, is subjected to reflection that relates to history objectivistically, as did the philosophical tradition, then positivism triumphs at the highest level of thought, as with Comte. This happens when critique uncritically abdicates its own connection with the emancipatory knowledge-constitutive interest in favor of pure theory. This sort of high-flown critique projects the undecided process of the evolution of the human species into the level of a philosophy of history that dogmatically issues instructions for action. *A delusive philosophy of history, however, is only the obverse of deluded decisionism.* Bureaucratically prescribed partisanship goes only too well with contemplatively misunderstood value-freedom.

These practical consequences of a restricted, scientistic consciousness of the sciences can be countered by a critique that destroys the illusion of objectivism. Contrary to Husserl's expectations, objectivism is eliminated not through the power of renewed *theoria* but through demonstrating what it conceals: the connection of knowledge and interest. Philosophy remains true to its classic tradition by renouncing it. The insight that the truth of statements is linked in the last analysis to the intention of the good and true life can be preserved today only on the ruins of ontology. However, even this philosophy remains a specialty alongside of the sciences and outside public consciousness as long as the heritage that it has critically abandoned lives on in the positivistic self-understanding of the sciences.

Knowledge and Human Interests, pp. 302–17.

9

The Dualism of the Natural and Cultural Sciences

The once lively discussion initiated by neo-Kantianism concerning the methodological distinctions between natural-scientific and social-scientific inquiry has been forgotten; the problems that gave rise to it no longer seem to be of contemporary relevance. Scientistic consciousness obscures fundamental and persistent differences in the methodological approaches of the sciences. The positivistic self-understanding prevalent among scientists has adopted the thesis of the unity of sciences; from the positivist perspective, the dualism of science, which was considered to be grounded in the logic of scientific inquiry, shrinks to a distinction between levels of development. At the same time, the strategy based on the program of a unified science has led to indisputable successes. The nomological sciences, whose aim it is to formulate and verify hypotheses concerning the laws governing empirical regularities, have extended themselves far beyond the sphere of the theoretical natural sciences, into psychology and economics, sociology and political science. On the other hand, the historical-hermeneutic sciences, which appropriate and analyze meaningful cultural entities handed down by tradition, continue uninterrupted along the paths they have been following since the nineteenth century. There is no serious indication that their methods can be integrated into the model of the strict empirical sciences. Every university catalog provides evidence of this actual division between the sciences; it is unimportant only in the textbooks of the positivists.

This continuing dualism, which we take for granted in the *practice* of science, is no longer discussed in terms of the *logic* of science. Instead of being addressed at the level of the philosophy of science, it simply finds expression in the coexistence of two distinct frames of reference. Depending upon the type of science with which it is concerned, the philosophy of science takes the form either of a general methodology of the empirical sciences or of a general hermeneutics of the cultural and historical sciences. At this time the work of K.R. Popper and H.G. Gadamer can be taken as representative of state-of-the-art formulations of this specifically restricted self-reflection of the sciences. Neither analytic philosophy of science nor philosophical hermeneutics take any notice of the other; only seldom do their discussions step outside the boundaries of their respective realms, which are both terminologically and substantively distinct.[1] The analytic school dismisses the hermeneutic disciplines as pre-scientific, while the hermeneutic school considers the nomological sciences as characterized by a limited pre-understanding.

The mutually uncomprehending coexistence of analytical philosophy of science and philosophical hermeneutics troubles the rigid self-consciousness of neither of the two parties. Occasional attempts to bridge the gap have remained no more than good intentions. There would be no reason to touch on the well-buried issue of the dualism of science if it did not in one area continually produce symptoms that demand analytic resolution: in the social sciences, heterogeneous aims and approaches conflict and intermingle with one another. To be sure, the current state of the various social-scientific disciplines indicates a lack of even development; for this reason it is easy to ascribe unclarified methodological issues and unresolved controversies to a confusion that can be remedied through logical clarification and a program of unified science. Hence the positivists do not hesitate to start from scratch. According to their postulates, a general and, in principle, unified *empirical-analytic behavioral science*, not different in structure from the theoretical natural sciences, can be produced from the purified corpus of the traditional social sciences. Steps in this direction have been taken in psychology and social psychology. Economics, with the exception of econometrics, is organized on the model of a *normative-analytic science* that presupposes hypothetical maxims of action. Sociological research is carried out primarily within the *structural-functional framework* of a theory of action that can neither be reduced to observable behavior nor reconstructed on the model of purposive-rational action. Finally, much research in sociology and political science is historically oriented, without any intentional link to general theories.

As I shall demonstrate, all three of these theoretical approaches can lay claim to a relative legitimacy. Contrary to what positivism assumes, they are not based on faulty or unclear methodological presuppositions. Nor can the more complex of these approaches be reduced, without damage, to the platform of a general science of behavior. Only at first glance does the confusion seem capable of being eliminated through clear-cut distinctions. Rather, the competing approaches that have been developed within the social sciences are negatively interrelated, in that they all stem from the fact that the apparatus of general theories cannot be applied to society in the same way as to objectified natural processes. Whereas the natural and the cultural or hermeneutic sciences are capable of living in a mutually indifferent, albeit more hostile than peaceful, coexistence, the social sciences must bear the tension of divergent approaches under one roof, for in them the very practice of research compels reflection on the relationship between analytic and hermeneutic methodologies.

1 A historical reconstruction

Max Weber was not interested in the relationship between the natural and cultural sciences from an epistemological point of view, as were Rickert* and Cassirer.* He was not troubled by the implications that the recently arisen *Geisteswissenschaften* might have had for the extension of the critique of pure reason to historical reason. From the philosophical investigations that, since Dilthey, had been concerned with this question, he took only what he needed to clarify his own research practice. He conceptualized the new social sciences as cultural sciences with a systematic intent. Clearly they combine methodological principles that philosophers had found in opposing types of science: the social sciences have the task of bringing the heterogeneous methods, aims, and presuppositions of the natural and cultural sciences into balance. Above all, Weber analyzed the combination of explanation [*Erklären*] and understanding [*Verstehen*]. The connection between explanation and understanding involves quite different rules, however, depending on whether we are concerned with methods, with aims, or with presuppositions. Weber's intricate philosophy of science becomes easier to understand when one distinguishes among these cases.

The definition of sociology that Weber gives in the first paragraphs of *Economy and Society* applies to *method*: "Sociology is a science concerning itself with the interpretive understanding of social action and thereby with a causal explanation of its course and consequences." We may consider this sentence as an answer to the question, How are general theories of social action possible? General theories allow us to derive assumptions about empirical regularities in the form of hypotheses that serve the purpose of explanation. At the same time, and in contradistinction to natural processes, regularities of social action have the property of being understandable. Social action belongs to the class of intentional actions, which we grasp by reconstructing their meaning. Social facts can be understood in terms of motivations. Optimal intelligibility of social behavior under given conditions is not, of course, of itself proof of the hypothesis that a lawlike connection does in fact exist. Such a hypothesis must also prove true independently of the plausibility of an interpretation in terms of motivation. Thus the logical relationship of understanding and explanation can be reduced to the general relationship between hypothesis and empirical confirmation. Through understanding, I may interpolate a rationally pursued goal as sufficient motivation for an observed behavior. But only when the resulting assumption of a behavioral regularity occurring under given circumstances has been empirically substantiated can we say that our understanding of motivation has led to an explanation of a social action.

This logical connection also makes clear why Weber accorded methodological primacy to purposive-rational action. As a rule, the interpretively interpolated goal, the assumed intention, will lead to an empirically convincing explanation only if the goal provides a factually sufficient motive for the action. This is the case when the action is guided by the intention to achieve a result to be realized through means chosen in a purposive-rational manner, thus in the type of purposive-rational action that is oriented in the choice of adequate means to achieve an end grasped with subjective clarity. Theories that admit only this type of action proceed, like pure economics, normative-analytically. They can lead to substantive empirical hypotheses only within the very narrow limits in which social processes actually correspond to the methodological principle of purposive-rationality. Thus the discussion leads inevitably to the question how it is possible to form the systematic assumptions about actions that are understandable but irrational in relation to ends. Only theories of this kind would combine understanding and explanation within an empirical-analytic framework.

Weber himself believed that, in an interpretive sociology, behavior that was not purposive-rational could be investigated only as a "deviation" from a model of purposive-rational behavior constructed for the sake of comparison. In view of these difficulties, the question emerged whether the social sciences should consider the intentionality of action at all. The problematic of understanding, insofar as it relates to methodology, would be resolved if the assumptions concerning lawlike regularities were restricted to connections among descriptive behavioral variables, whether or not these assumptions could be rendered perspicuous through the interpretation of motivation as well. Weber, too, reckoned with the possibility that "future research might discover noninterpretable uniformities underlying what has appeared to be specifically meaningful action."[2] It would adequately explain social action without fulfilling the requirement of adequate meaningfulness. But Weber excluded such laws from the domain of the social sciences on principle. Otherwise the social sciences would have the status of *natural* sciences of social action, whereas, since they are oriented toward intentional action, they can only be nomological sciences of *mind and culture.*

In his essays on the philosophy of science, Weber often remarks that sociology must both understand social facts in their cultural significance and explain them as culturally determined. Here the relationship between explanation and understanding applies to the *aims* of the social sciences. Weber's statements are ambivalent, for two opposing intentions are involved.

On the one hand, Weber always emphasizes the empirical-analytic task of using proven lawlike hypotheses to explain social action and make conditional predictions. From this point of view, the social sciences, like all nomological sciences, yield information that can be translated into technical recommendations for the rational choice of means. They supply "knowledge of the technique by which one masters life – external things as well as human action – through calculation."[3] Technically exploitable knowledge of this kind is based on knowledge of empirical uniformities; such knowledge is the basis for causal explanations that make possible technical control over objective processes by means of conditional predictions. A social-scientific knowledge guided by this interest would have to develop and apply its instruments with the sole purpose of discovering reliable general rules of social behavior. Insofar as the subject at hand demands it, such an analysis can be mediated by an understanding of the meaning of social action. Nonetheless, the intention of understanding subjective meaning can do no more than open the way to the social facts. These are known only when the analysis proceeds beyond the propaedeutic understanding and grasps their lawlike connection in causal terms. In the controversy over value-judgments Weber adopted this position, which gives a methodologically subordinate status to the hermeneutic intention of understanding meaning. But he also had another scientific aim in view.

For Weber, as a pupil of Rickert, a cultural science cannot exhaust its interest in the study of empirical regularities. Thus, in other contexts in Weber's work, the derivation and verification of lawlike hypotheses from which technical recommendations can be made is considered a preparatory work that does not, as such, lead to "the knowledge which we are seeking." The overarching interest by which this work is guided is defined hermeneutically: "Analyzing and ordering a particular, historically given and individual grouping of those factors and their concrete and uniquely significant interaction, and, especially, making the basis and nature of this significance understandable, is the next task, one to be solved through the use of that preparatory work, certainly, but completely new and autonomous in relation to it."[4]

In this schema for the progress of social-scientific knowledge, causal-analytic and interpretive methods alternate. But in each case the knowledge terminates in the explication of a meaning that has practical significance for life, thus in "making something understandable." With this goal in mind, it is the procedure of explanation rather than that of the interpretive understanding of meaning that is relegated to a subordinate methodological status.

Weber did not expressly link these two conflicting intentions. He was the more easily deceived about their ambivalent character in that he had not sufficiently clarified the categories of meaning [*Sinn*] and significance [*Bedeutung*] in their respective usages. Weber did not distinguish consistently enough between the understanding of motivation, which reconstructs the subjectively intended meaning [*Sinn*] of a social action, and the hermeneutic understanding of meaning that appropriates the significance [*Bedeutung*] objectivated in works or events.

The understanding of motivation can be contained within the framework of an empirical-analytic science as a methodological step leading to a knowledge of laws that is not hermeneutically intelligible, that is, that has no relation to meaning. Two conflicting cognitive intentions arise in the social sciences only because there the knowing subjects are intuitively linked with their object domain. The social lifework is just as much an intentional structure as is social-scientific knowledge itself. Indeed, it is precisely this relationship that was invoked by transcendental philosophy's interpretation of the cultural sciences. Nomological knowledge of social processes can enter hermeneutically into the explication of the self-understanding of knowing subjects and their social reference groups, just as it can be translated into conditional predictions and used in the control of the administered domains of society. The controversial relationship between the methodological framework of research and the pragmatic function of applying the results of research can be clarified only when the knowledge-orienting interests invested in the methodological approaches have been made conscious. Only then will there be a precise answer to the question of when the social sciences in their internal structure are pursuing the intention of planning and administering, and when they are pursuing the intention of self-understanding and enlightenment. Weber neither clarifies nor completely suppresses his ambivalence of aims. In any case, he did not, as did his positivist successors, exempt the social sciences from the repeatedly announced task of interpreting the cultural significance of social relations as a basis for making the contemporary social situation understandable.[5]

The problematic relationship of explanation and understanding concerns not only the methods and aims of the social sciences but also their epistemological *presuppositions*. Are the social sciences, like all cultural sciences, bound in the methodological delimitation of their object domain to an implicit pre-understanding of their subject matter? Weber adopts the category of value-relation introduced by Rickert and uses it in its strict transcendental-logical sense. Value-relation applies primarily not to the selection of scientific problems but to the constitution of possible objects of the experience that is relevant to inquiry in the cultural sciences. The cultural scientist does not communicate with these objects with the naked eye, so to speak. Rather, he inevitably places them in the value-relations in which his own cultural situation is set. Thus he has to mediate the methodologically determinant value-relations with those that are already realized in the preconstituted object. Rickert had failed to recognize his mediation as a hermeneutic problem.[6] Weber analyzes it partially and then counters it with the postulate of value-freedom.

In the natural sciences, the theoretical framework of an investigation is subjected to control by the outcome of the investigation itself. Either it proves heuristically fruitful or it contributes nothing to the derivation of usable hypotheses. In contrast, the value-relations that determine method are transcendent to research in the cultural sciences; they cannot be corrected by the outcome of an investigation. When the light shed by value-ideas on important problems shifts, the cultural sciences likewise prepare to shift their standpoint and their conceptual apparatus and "follow those stars that alone can give their work meaning and direction."[7] In the social sciences, theories are dependent upon general interpretations that can be neither confirmed nor refuted by criteria immanent to the empirical sciences. Value-relations are methodologically unavoidable, but they are not objectively binding. Social sciences are thus obligated to declare the dependence of their basic theoretical assumptions on normative presuppositions of this sort. Hence the postulate of value-freedom.

In contrast to this position, the current view is that theory formation is subject to the same rules in all the nomological sciences. Value-freedom is assured through the logical separation of descriptive and normative statements; only the initial selection of problems is dependent on values. In this narrower formulation, the postulate of value-freedom attains the status of a political value; according to it, the only theories that are admissible as scientific are those whose basic assumptions are free of any historical pre-understanding that would require hermeneutic clarification. Such theories could thus be introduced by convention. Weber's formulation of the issue is excluded by definition. For he denied that underlying theoretical suppositions with no relationship to values, thus without ties to historical contexts, are possible at all in the social sciences. Not only the selection of problems but also the choice of the theoretical framework within which they will be analyzed is, according to Weber, determined by historically prevailing value-relations.

Once one has become convinced, as Weber was, of the methodologically significant interdependence of social-scientific inquiry and the objective content to which it is directed and in which it itself stands, a further question necessarily arises. Could these value-relations, which are methodologically determining, themselves be open to social-scientific analysis as a real context operating on the transcendental level? Could the empirical content of the fundamental decisions shaping the choice of a theoretical principle itself be elucidated in the context of social processes? It seems to me that it is precisely in Weber's theory of science that one can demonstrate the connection between methodology and a sociological analysis of the present.[8] Weber himself, however, like the neo-Kantians in general, was enough of a positivist to forbid himself this type of reflection.

On the Logic of the Social Sciences, pp. 1–16.

Notes

1 Exceptions are, among others, H. Skjervheim, *Objectivism and the Study of Man* (Oslo: 1959), and K.O. Apel, *Analytic Philosophy of Language and the Geisteswissenschaften* (Dordrecht: Reidel, 1967).
2 M. Weber, *Economy and Society*, eds G. Roth and C. Wittich (New York: 1968), vol. I, pp. 7–8.
3 M. Weber, "Science as a Vocation," in H.H. Gerth and C.W. Mills (eds), *From Max Weber* (New York: 1946), pp. 129–56; here p. 150.
4 "Objectivity in Social Science and Social Policy," in M. Weber, *The Methodology of the Social Sciences* (New York: 1949), pp. 49–112; here pp. 75–6.
5 Ibid., p. 72.
6 H. Rickert *De Grenzen der naturwissenschaftlichen Begriffsbildung* (Tübingen: Mohr, 1929), pp. 693ff.
7 Weber, *Methodology*, p. 112.
8 Cf. my contribution to the discussion in *Max Weber and Sociology Today*, pp. 59ff, in which I developed points of view from the older Weber scholarship: K. Löwith, *Max Weber and Karl Marx* (London: Allen and Unwin, 1982); S. Landshut, *Kritik der Soziologie* (Leipzig: 1928); H. Freyer, *Soziologie als Wirklichkeitswissenschaft* (Berlin: 1930). For more recent literature on Weber see R. Bendix, *Max Weber* (New York: 1960) and E. Baumgarten, *Max Weber* (Tübingen: J.C.B. Mohr, 1964).

PART IV

Language and Communication

Introduction

Working at the Starnberg research institute in the 1970s, Habermas developed the theories of language, ethics, social evolution, sociopolitical crisis, and modernity which he brought together in 1981 in the two volumes of The Theory of Communicative Action. Having dropped his initial leitmotiv of a practically oriented philosophy of history, he now felt that the model of critical reflection advanced in Knowledge and Human Interests also needed to be developed in a more differentiated way. After completing Knowledge and Human Interests, he realized that the term "reflection" is traditionally used to refer both to a subject's reflection on what makes it possible for him or her to perform certain actions and to a more critical insight into the distortions built into these and other processes. The first of these processes Habermas now calls "rational reconstruction," where what is reconstructed is the pretheoretical knowledge (knowing how, in Gilbert Ryle's* sense) of actors. Reconstructions, such as Noam Chomsky's linguistic theory, do not necessarily affect our practice. As for reflection in the second sense, Habermas reformulates in a somewhat more cautious way the analogies he had drawn between psychoanalysis and "collective processes of political enlightenment;" the latter must in turn be distinguished from "the organization of action."[1]

Habermas was initially attracted by the idea of providing a linguistic foundation for sociology and the other social sciences, as indicated in the title of the Gauss lectures which he gave in the United States in 1970–1 ("Vorlesungen zu einer sprachtheoretischen Grundlegung der Soziologie," in Vorstudien und Ergänzungen). As he came to abandon this idea,[2] his initial focus on linguistic communication, which parallelled, as he notes, what Karl-Otto Apel had called the "transformation of philosophy,"[3] broadens out into a substantive theory of communicative action, action oriented to the attainment and reproduction of mutual understanding. This may be a conversation, a political debate, or a decision-making process. Thus in The Theory of Communicative Action the analysis of communication in the narrower sense is embedded, as in the extracts selected below as readings 11–14, in a broader context of social theory, in *which communicative action is distinguished from the mere giving of orders and from instrumental or strategic action only concerned to produce effects desired by the actor.* Habermas's basic aims in The Theory of Communicative Action, *as he indicates at the end of reading 12 on "The Problem of Understanding Meaning in the Social Sciences," are to present his model of communicative rationality and then to relate it to one of the principal themes of traditional social theory: the analysis of what Max Weber called social rationalization. Habermas describes this as a "somewhat less demanding" approach than a more direct attempt to ground his model in a developmental history of individuals or of the human species as a whole, or, a third possibility, in the analysis of systematic distortions of communication of the kind identified by psycho-analysis. His strategy amounts, however, to an ambitious reworking of the tradition of Western Marxism against the background of a theory of communication which he identifies in the work of the American pragmatist philosopher George Herbert Mead* and of the French sociologist Émile Durkheim. The point of beginning the book as he does, with an analysis of the concept of rationality, is not just that it is a central concept in the social sciences. More specifically, Habermas wishes to show that Western Marxism from Marx himself through to Horkheimer and Adorno analyzes rationality in too subjectivistic a manner – as the accomplishment of an individual or collective subject rather than as an emergent property of forms of human life and communication. Readers who find Habermas's model excessively rationalistic, as just another reworking of Western enlightenment reason, should bear in mind that his work also contains a strong element of critique of that tradition – albeit a critique which aims to re-present it in a more adequate form. The extracts from* The Theory of Communicative Action *in this part (readings 11–14) and in parts VII and VIII should give a sense of the basic argument of the book; they are preceded by an essay of 1976 (reading 10), "What is Universal Pragmatics?"*

In reading 10, Habermas outlines the main features of his model, including a useful diagrammatic representation of the types of action which he is concerned to distinguish. This model is further specified in the first extract from The Theory of Communicative Action *(reading 11). Here he uses the concept of world-relations, drawn from phenomenological philosophy and philosophical anthropology, and contrasts it with Karl Popper's distinction between the three "worlds" of physical objects, mental states, and cultural products. In Popper's model, this sentence exists in all three worlds: first, as a set of black marks on the white page of your book; second, as something previously present in my brain and/or mind, to be transferred into written form; and finally as a symbolic construction which exists independently of its physical embodiment in this particular copy of the book or in my or my computer's memory. Habermas draws on a modified version of this model in specifying the world-relations involved in his various types of action. Here and in the rest of his recent work, he makes substantial use of the concept of the lifeworld, now construing it less as a cognitive structure or horizon and more as a complex world of practices and customs as well as ideas.*

The second extract (reading 12), "The Problem of Understanding Meaning in the Social Sciences," follows on from this, drawing together the rationality theme with the typology of action and explicating it via a detailed discussion (omitted here) of interpretive social science. The final section of this extract outlines the strategy of the book as a whole, in contrast to various alternative avenues which Habermas leaves open for possible future work. (Readers who turn from this Reader *to* The Theory of Communicative Action *itself are advised to refer again to these pages at the start.)*

The final two extracts clarify more systematically the concept of communicative action. In reading 13, Habermas sets up his model in contrast to Max Weber's concept of purposive-rational action. Reading 14, taken from volume 2, briefly restates the communicative action model in a way which sets the scene for Habermas's discourse ethics, the subject of the following part of this Reader.

Notes

1 *Theory and Practice*, p. 33.
2 Cf. *The Theory of Communicative Action*, vol. 1, Preface, p. xxxix.
3 *Vorstudien und Ergänzungen*, p. 7.

Further Reading

J.B. Thompson and D. Held (eds), *Habermas: Critical Debates* (London: Macmillan, 1982), esp. John Thompson, "Universal Pragmatics," ch. 6; Arie Brand, *The Force of Reason: An Introduction to Habermas' Theory of Communicative Action* (Sydney: Allen and Unwin, 1990); Axel Honneth and Hans Joas (eds), *Communicative Action* (Cambridge: Polity, 1991).

10

What is Universal Pragmatics?

The task of universal pragmatics is to identify and reconstruct universal conditions of possible understanding [*Verständigung*].[1] In other contexts one also speaks of "general presuppositions of communication," but I prefer to speak of general presuppositions of communicative action because I take the type of action aimed at reaching understanding to be fundamental. Thus I start from the assumption (without undertaking to demonstrate it here) that other forms of social action – for example, conflict, competition, strategic action in general – are derivatives of action oriented to reaching understanding [*verständigungsorientiert*]. Furthermore, as language is the specific medium of understanding at the sociocultural stage of evolution, I want to go a step further and single out explicit speech actions from other forms of communicative action. I shall ignore non-verbalized actions and bodily expressions.[2]

The validity basis of speech

Karl-Otto Apel proposes the following formulation in regard to the general presuppositions of consensual speech actions: to identify such presuppositions we must, he thinks, leave the perspective of the observer of behavioral facts and call to mind "what we must necessarily always already presuppose in regard to ourselves and others as normative conditions of the possibility of understanding; and in this sense, what we must necessarily always already have accepted."[3] Apel uses the aprioristic perfect [*immer schon*: always already] and adds the mode of necessity to express the transcendental constraint to which we, as speakers, are subject as soon as we perform or understand or respond to a speech act. In or after the performance of this act, we can become aware that we have involuntarily made certain assumptions, which Apel calls "normative conditions of the possibility of understanding." The addition "normative" may give rise to misunderstanding. Indeed one can say that the general and unavoidable – in this sense transcendental

– conditions of possible understanding have a normative content when one has in mind not only the binding character of norms of action or even the binding character of rules in general, but the validity basis of speech across its entire spectrum. To begin, I want to indicate briefly what I mean by "the validity basis of speech."

I shall develop the thesis that anyone acting communicatively must, in performing any speech action, raise universal validity-claims and suppose that they can be vindicated [or redeemed: *einlösen*]. Insofar as he wants to participate in a process of reaching understanding, he cannot avoid raising the following – and indeed precisely the following – validity-claims. He claims to be:

1 *uttering* something understandably;
2 giving [the hearer] *something* to understand;
3 making *himself* thereby understandable; and
4 coming to an understanding *with another person*.

The speaker must choose a comprehensible [*verständlich*] expression so that speaker and hearer can understand one another. The speaker must have the intention of communicating a true [*wahr*] proposition (or a propositional content, the existential presuppositions of which are satisfied) so that the hearer can share the knowledge of the speaker. The speaker must want to express his intentions truthfully [*wahrhaftig*] so that the hearer can believe the utterance of the speaker (can trust him). Finally, the speaker must choose an utterance that is right [*richtig*] so that the hearer can accept the utterance and speaker and hearer can agree with one another in the utterance with respect to a recognized normative background. Moreover, communicative action can continue undisturbed only as long as participants suppose that the validity claims they reciprocally raise are justified.

The goal of coming to an understanding [*Verständigung*] is to bring about an agreement [*Einverständnis*] that terminates in the intersubjective mutuality of reciprocal understanding, shared knowledge, mutual trust, and accord with one another. Agreement is based on recognition of the corresponding validity-claims of comprehensibility, truth, truthfulness, and rightness. We can see that the word *understanding* is ambiguous. In its minimal meaning it indicates that two subjects understand a linguistic expression in the same way; its maximal meaning is that between the two there exists an accord concerning the rightness of an utterance in relation to a mutually recognized normative background. In addition, two participants in communication can come to an understanding about something in the world, and they can make their intentions understandable to one another.

If full agreement, embracing all four of these components, were a normal state of linguistic communication, it would not be necessary to analyze the process of understanding from the dynamic perspective of *bringing about* an agreement. The typical states are in the gray areas in between: on the one hand, incomprehension and misunderstanding, intentional and involuntary untruthfulness, concealed and open discord; and, on the other hand, pre-existing or achieved consensus. Coming to an understanding is the process of bringing about an agreement on the presupposed basis of validity-claims that can be mutually recognized. In everyday life we start from a background consensus pertaining to those interpretations taken for granted among participants. As soon as this consensus is shaken, and the presupposition that certain validity-claims are satisfied (or could be vindicated) is suspended, the task of mutual interpretation is to achieve a new definition of the situation which all participants can share. If their attempt fails, communicative action cannot be continued. One is then basically confronted with the alternatives of switching to strategic action, breaking off communication altogether, or recommencing action oriented to reaching understanding at a different level, the level of argumentative speech (for purposes of discursively examining the problematic validity-claims, which are now regarded as hypothetical). In what follows, I shall take into consideration only consensual speech actions, leaving aside both discourse and strategic action.

In communicative action participants presuppose that they know what mutual recognition of reciprocally raised validity-claims means. If in addition they can rely on a shared definition of the situation and thereupon act consensually, the background consensus includes the following:

1 Speaker and hearer know implicitly that each of them has to raise the aforementioned validity-claims if there is to be communication at all (in the sense of action oriented to reaching understanding).
2 Both suppose that they actually do satisfy these presuppositions of communication, that is, that they could justify their validity-claims.
3 Thus there is a common conviction that any validity-claims raised either are – as in the case of the comprehensibility of the sentences uttered – already vindicated or – as in the case of truth, truthfulness, and rightness – could be vindicated because the sentences, propositions, expressed intentions, and utterances satisfy corresponding adequacy conditions.

Thus I distinguish (1) the *conditions* for the validity of a grammatical sentence, true proposition, truthful intentional expression, or normatively correct utterance suitable to its context, from (2) the *claims* with which speakers demand intersubjective recognition of the well-formedness of a sentence, truth of a proposition, truthfulness of an intentional expression, and rightness of a speech act, and from (3) the *vindication or redemption* of justified validity-claims. Vindication means that the proponent, whether through appeal to intuitions and experiences or through argumentation and action consequences, grounds the claim's worthiness to be recognized [or acknowledged: *Anerkennungswürdig-keit*] and brings about a suprasubjective recognition of its validity. In accepting a validity-claim raised by the speaker, the hearer acknowledges the validity of symbolic structures; that is, he acknowledges that a sentence is grammatical, a statement true, an intentional expression truthful, or an utterance correct. The validity of these symbolic structures is grounded in the fact that they satisfy certain adequacy conditions; but the meaning of the validity consists in worthiness to be recognized, that is, in the guarantee that intersubjective recognition can be brought about under suitable conditions.

I have proposed the name *universal pragmatics* for the research program aimed at reconstructing the universal validity basis of speech. I would like not to delimit the theme of this research program in a preliminary way. Thus before passing on (in part II) to the theory of speech acts, I shall prefix a few directorial remarks dealing with (1) a first delimitation of the object domain of the universal pragmatics called for; (2) an elucidation of the procedure of rational reconstruction, in contrast to empirical-analytic procedure in the narrower sense; (3) a few methodological difficulties resulting from the fact that linguistics claims the status of a reconstructive science; and finally (4) the question of whether the universal pragmatics proposed assumes the position of a transcendental reflective theory or that of a reconstructive science with empirical content. I shall restrict myself to directorial remarks because, while these questions are fundamental and deserve to be examined independently, they form only the context of the theme I shall treat and thus must remain in the background. [. . .]

A remark on the procedure of rational reconstruction

I have been employing the expression *formal analysis* in opposition to *empirical-analytic procedures* (in the narrower sense) without providing a detailed explanation. This is at least misleading. I am not using formal analysis in a sense that refers, say, to the standard predicate logic or to any specific logic. The tolerant sense in which I understand formal analysis can best be characterized through the methodological attitude we adopt in the rational reconstruction of concepts, criteria, rules, and schemata. Thus we speak of the explication of meanings and concepts, of the analysis of presuppositions and rules. Of course, reconstructive procedures are also important for empirical-analytic research, for example, for explicating frameworks of basic concepts, for formalizing assumptions intially formulated in ordinary language, for clarifying deductive relations among particular hypotheses, for interpreting results of measurement, and so on. Nonetheless, reconstructive procedures are not characteristic of sciences that develop nomological hypotheses about domains of observable events; rather, these procedures are characteristic of *sciences that systematically reconstruct the intuitive knowledge of competent subjects.*

I would like to begin (clarifying the distinction between empirical-analytic and reconstructive sciences) with the distinction between sensory experience or *observation* and communicative experience or *understanding* [*Verstehen*]. Observation is directed to perceptible things and events (or states); understanding is directed to the meaning of utterances.[4] In experiencing, the observer is in principle alone, even if the categorial net in which experiences are organized with a claim to objectivity is already shared by several (or even all) individuals. In contrast, the interpreter who understands meaning is experiencing fundamentally as a participant in communication, on the basis of a symbolically established intersubjective relationship with other individuals, even if he is actually alone with a book, a document, or a work of art. I shall not here analyze the complex relationship between observation and understanding any further; but I would like to direct attention to one aspect – the difference in level between perceptible reality and the understandable meaning of a symbolic formation. Sensory experience is related to sectors of reality immediately, communicative experience only mediately, as illustrated in the diagram below.

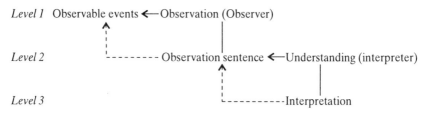

Figure 10.1

This diagram represents three different relationships:
1 Epistemic relations between experiential acts and their objects. In this sense, the act of understanding relates to the symbolic expression (here of the observation sentence), as does the act of observation to the events observed.
2 Relations of representing an aspect of reality in a propositional sentence. In this sense, the interpretation represents the semantic content (here of the observation sentence), as the observation sentence in turn represents certain events.
3 Relations of expressing intentional acts. In this sense, the understanding (here of the observation sentence) is expressed in the propositional content of the interpretation, just as the observation is expressed in the propositional content of the observation sentence.

Apart from the fact that all three types of relation point to fundamental problems, there is an additional difficulty in specifying the precise differences between the epistemic relations of the observer and the interpreter to their respective objects and between the representational relation of the observation sentence to reality, on the one hand, and that of the interpretation sentence to *symbolically prestructured* reality, on the other. This specification would require a comparison between observation and interpretation, between description and explication. For the time being, the diagram merely illustrates the two levels of reality to which sensory and communicative experience relate. The difference in level between perceptible and symbolically prestructured reality is reflected in the gap between direct access through observation of reality and communicatively mediated access through understanding an utterance referring to events.

The two pairs of concepts – perceptible reality versus symbolically prestructured reality and observation versus understanding – can be correlated with the concepts of description versus explication. By using a sentence that reports an observation, I can describe the observed aspect of reality. By using a sentence that renders an interpretation of the meaning of a symbolic formation, I can explicate the meaning of such an utterance. Naturally only when the meaning of the symbolic formation is unclear does the explication need to be set off as an independent analytic step. In regard to sentences with which we describe events, there can be questions at different levels. If the phenomenon described needs explanation, we demand a causal description that makes clear how the phenomenon in question comes to pass. If, by contrast, the description itself is incomprehensible, we demand an explication that makes clear what the observer meant by his utterance and how the symbolic expression in need of elucidation comes about. In the first case, a satisfactory answer will have the form of an explanation we undertake with the aid of a causal hypothesis. In the second case, we speak of explication of meaning. (Of course, explications of meaning need not be limited to descriptive sentences; any meaningfully structured formation can be subjected to the operation of meaning explication.)

Descriptions and explications have different ranges; they can begin on the surface and push through to underlying structures. We are familiar with this fact in regard to the explanation of natural phenomena – theories can be more or less general. The same is true of meaning explications. Of course, the range of explication does not depend on the level of generality of theoretical knowledge about structures of an external reality accessible to observation but on knowledge of the deep structures of a reality accessible to understanding, the reality of symbolic formations produced according to rules. The explanation of natural phenomena pushes in a different direction from the explication of the meaning of expressions.

I want to distinguish two levels of explication of meaning. If the meaning of a written sentence, action, gesture, work of art, tool, theory, commodity, transmitted document, and so on is unclear, the explication of meaning is directed first to the semantic content of the symbolic formation. In trying to understand its content, we take up the same position as the "author" adopted when he wrote the sentence, performed the gesture, used the tool, applied the theory, and so forth. Often too we must go beyond what was meant and intended by the author and take into consideration a context of which he was not conscious.[5] Typically, however, the *understanding of content* pursues connections that link the surface structures of the incomprehensible formation with the surface structures of other, familiar formations. Thus, linguistic expressions can be explicated through paraphrase in the same language or through translation into expressions of another language; in both cases, competent speakers draw on intuitively known meaning relations that obtain within the lexicon of one language or between those of two languages.

If he cannot attain his end in this way, the interpreter may find it necessary to alter his attitude. He then exchanges the attitude of understanding content – in which he looks, as it were, through symbolic formations to the world about which something is uttered – for an attitude in which he directs himself to the generative structures of the expressions themselves. The interpreter then attempts to explicate the meaning of a symbolic formation in terms of the rules according to which the author must have brought it forth. In normal paraphrase and translation, the interpreter draws on semantic meaning relations (for instance, between the different words of a language) in an ad hoc manner, in that he simply applies a knowledge shared with competent speakers of that language. In this sense, the role of interpreter can (under suitable conditions) be attributed to the author himself. The attitude changes, however, as soon as the interpreter tries not only to *apply* this intuitive knowledge but to *reconstruct* it. He then turns away from the surface structure of the symbolic formation; he no longer looks through it *intentione recta* to the world. He attempts instead to peer through the surface, as it were, and into the symbolic formation to discover the rules according to which the latter was produced (in our example, the rules according to which the lexicon of a language is constructed). The object of understanding is no longer the content of a symbolic expression or what specific authors meant by it in specific situations but the intuitive rule consciousness that a competent speaker has of his own language [. . .]

The bond into which the speaker is willing to enter with the performance of an illocutionary act means a guarantee that, in consequence of his utterance, he will fulfill certain conditions – for example, regard a question as settled when a satisfactory answer is given; drop an assertion when it proves to be false; follow his own advice when he finds himself in the same situation as the hearer; stress a request when it is not complied with; act in accordance with an intention disclosed by avowal, and so on. *Thus the illocutionary force of an acceptable speech act consists in the fact that it can move a hearer to rely on the speech-act-typical commitments of the speaker.* But if illocutionary force has more than a suggestive influence, what can motivate the hearer to base his action on the premise that the speaker seriously intends the engagement he indicates? When it is a question of institutionally bound speech actions, he can perhaps rely on the binding force of an established norm of action. In the case of institutionally unbound speech acts, however, illocutionary force cannot be traced back directly to the binding force of the normative context. The illocutionary force with which the speaker, in carrying out his speech act, influences the hearer, can be understood only if we take into consideration sequences of speech actions that are connected with one another on the basis of a reciprocal recognition of validity-claims.

With their illocutionary acts, speaker and hearer raise validity-claims and demand they be recognized. But this recognition need not follow irrationally, since the validity-claims have a cognitive character and can be checked. I would like, therefore, to defend the following thesis: *In the final analysis, the speaker can illocutionarily influence the hearer and vice versa, because speech-act-typical commitments are connected with cognitively testable validity-claims* – that is, because the reciprocal bonds have a rational basis. The engaged speaker normally connects the specific sense in which he would like to take up an interpersonal relationship with a thematically stressed validity-claim and thereby chooses a specific mode of communication.

Thus assertions, descriptions, classifications, estimates, predictions, objections, and the like have different specific meanings; but the claim put forward in these different interpersonal relationships is, or is based on, the truth of corresponding propositions or on the ability of a subject to have cognitions. Correspondingly, requests, orders, admonitions, promises, agreements, excuses, admissions, and the like have different specific meanings; but the claim put forward in these different interpersonal relationships is, or refers to, the rightness of norms or to the ability of a subject to assume responsibility. We might say that in different speech acts the content of the speaker's engagement is *determined by different ways of appealing to the same, thematically stressed, universal validity-claim.* And since as a result of this appeal to universal validity-claims, the speech-act-typical commitments take on the character of obligations to provide grounds or to prove trustworthy, the hearer can be rationally motivated by the speaker's signaled engagement to accept the latter's offer. I would like to elucidate this for each of the three modes of communication.

In the cognitive use of language, the speaker proffers a speech-act-immanent *obligation to provide grounds [Bergründungsverpflichtung].*

Constative speech acts contain the offer to recur if necessary to the *experiential source* from which the speaker draws the *certainty* that his statement is true. If this immediate grounding does not dispel an ad hoc doubt, the persistingly problematic truth claim can become the subject of a theoretical discourse. In the interactive use of language, the speaker proffers a speech-act-immanent *obligation to provide justification* [*Recht-fertigungsverpflichtung*]. Of course, regulative speech acts contain only the offer to indicate, if necessary, the *normative context* that gives the speaker the *conviction* that his utterance is right. Again, if this immediate justification does not dispel an ad hoc doubt, we can pass over to the level of discourse, in this case of practical discourse. In such a discourse, however, the subject of discursive examination is not the rightness claim directly connected with the speech act, but the validity-claim of the underlying norm. Finally, in the expressive use of language the speaker also enters into a speech-act-immanent obligation, namely, the *obligation to prove trustworthy* [*Bewährungsverpflichtung*], to show in the consequences of his action that he has expressed just that intention which actually guides his behavior. In case the immediate *assurance* expressing what is *evident* to the speaker himself cannot dispel ad hoc doubts, the truthfulness of the utterance can only be checked against the consistency of his subsequent behavior.

Every speech-act-immanent obligation can be made good at two levels, namely immediately, in the context of utterance – whether through recourse to an experiential base, through indicating a corresponding normative context, or through affirmation of what is evident to oneself – and mediately, in discourse or in subsequent actions. But only in the case of the obligations to ground and to prove trustworthy, into which we enter with constative and with expressive speech acts, do we refer to the *same* truth or truthfulness claim. The obligation to justify, into which we enter with regulative speech acts, refers immediately to the claim that the speech action performed fits an existing normative background; whereas with the entrance into practical discourse the topic of discussion is the validity of the very norm from which the rightness claim of the speaker is merely borrowed.

Our reflections have led to the following provisional results:

1 A speech act succeeds, that is, it brings about the interpersonal relation that *S* intends with it, if it is
   (a) comprehensible and acceptable, and
   (b) accepted by the hearer.
2 The acceptability of a speech act depends on (among other things) the fulfillment of two pragmatic presuppositions:
   (a) the existence of speech-act-typically restricted contexts (preparatory rule); and
   (b) a recognizable engagement of the speaker to enter into certain speech-act-typical obligations (essential rule, sincerity rule).

3 The illocutionary force of a speech act consists in its capacity to move a hearer to act under the premises that the engagement signaled by the speaker is seriously meant:
   (a) in the case of institutionally bound speech acts, the speaker can borrow this force from the binding force of existing norms;
   (b) in the case of institutionally unbound speech acts, the speaker can develop this force by inducing the recognition of validity-claims.
4 Speaker and hearer can reciprocally motivate one another to recognize validity-claims because the content of the speaker's engagement is determined by a specific reference to a thematically stressed validity-claim, whereby the speaker, in a cognitively testable way, assumes
   (a) with a truth claim, obligations to provide grounds,
   (b) with a rightness claim, obligations to provide justification, and
   (c) with a truthfulness claim, obligations to prove trustworthy.

Model of linguistic communication

The analysis of what Austin* called the illocutionary force of an utterance has led us back to the validity basis of speech. Institutionally unbound speech acts owe their illocutionary force to a cluster of validity-claims that speakers and hearers have to raise and recognize as justified if grammatical (and thus comprehensible) sentences are to be employed in such a way as to result in successful communication. A participant in communication acts with an orientation to reaching understanding only under the condition that, in employing comprehensible sentences in his speech acts, he raises three validity-claims in an acceptable way. He claims truth for a stated propositional content or for the existential presuppositions of a mentioned propositional content. He claims rightness (or appropriateness) for norms (or values), which, in a given context, justify an interpersonal relation that is to be performatively established. Finally, he claims truthfulness for the intentions expressed. Of course, individual validity-claims can be thematically stressed, whereby the truth of the propositional content comes to the fore in the cognitive use of language, the rightness (or appropriateness) of the interpersonal relation in the interactive, and the truthfulness of the speaker in the expressive. But in every instance of communicative action the system of all validity-claims comes into play; they must always be raised simultaneously, although they cannot all be thematic at the same time.

The universality of the validity-claims inherent in the structure of speech can perhaps be elucidated with reference to the systematic place of language. Language is the medium through which speakers and hearers realize certain fundamental demarcations. The subject demar-cates himself: (1) from an environment that he objectifies in the third-person attitude of an observer; (2) from an environment that he conforms to or deviates from in the ego–alter attitude of a participant; (3) from his own subjectivity that he expresses or conceals in a first-person attitude; and finally (4) from the medium of language itself. For these domains of reality I have proposed the somewhat arbitrarily chosen terms: *external nature, society, internal nature,* and *language.* The validity-claims unavoidably implied in speech oriented to reaching understanding show that these four regions must always simultaneously appear. I shall characterize the way in which these regions appear with a few phenomenological indications.

By *external nature* I mean the objectivated segment of reality that the adult subject is able (even if only mediately) to perceive and manipulate. One can, of course, adopt an objectivating attitude not only toward inanimate nature but toward all objects and states of affairs that are directly or indirectly accessible to sensory experience. *Society* designates that symbolically prestructured segment of reality that the adult subject can understand in a non-objectivating attitude, that is, as one acting communicatively (as a participant in a system of communication). Legitimate interpersonal relations belong here, as do institutions, traditions, cultural values, etc. We can replace this performative attitude with an objectivating attitude toward society; conversely, we can switch to a performative attitude in domains in which (today) we normally behave objectivatingly – for example, in relations to animals and plants. I class as *internal nature* all wishes, feelings, intentions, etc., to which an "I" has privileged access and can express as its own experiences before a public. It is precisely in this expressive attitude that the "I" knows itself not only as subjectivity but also as something that has always already transcended the bounds of mere subjectivity, in cognition, language, and interaction simultaneously. To be sure, if the subject adopts an objectivating attitude toward himself, this alters the sense in which intentions can be expressed.

Finally, I introduced the linguistic medium of our utterances as a special region; precisely because *language* (including non-propositional symbol systems) remains in a peculiar half-transcendence in the performance of our communicative actions and expressions, it presents itself to the speaker and the actor (pre-consciously) as a segment of reality sui generis. Again, this does not preclude our being able to adopt, in regard to linguistic utterances or systems of symbols, an objectivating attitude directed to the sounds or signs.

The model intuitively introduced here is that of a communication in which grammatical sentences are embedded, by way of universal validity-claims, in three relations to reality, thereby assuming the corresponding pragmatic functions of representing facts, establishing legitimate interpersonal relations, and expressing one's own subjectivity. According to this model, language can be conceived as the medium of interrelating three worlds; for every successful communicative action there exists a threefold relation between the utterance and (1) "the external world" as the totality of existing states of affairs, (2) "our social world" as the totality of all normatively regulated interpersonal relations that count as legitimate in a given society, and (3) "a particular inner world" (of the speaker) as the totality of his intentional experiences.

We can examine every utterance to see whether it is true or untrue, justified or unjustified, truthful or untruthful, because in speech, no matter what the emphasis, grammatical sentences are embedded in relations to reality in such a way that in an acceptable speech action segments of external nature, society, and internal nature always come into appearance together. Language itself also appears in speech, for speech is a medium in which the linguistic means that are employed instrumentally are also reflected. In speech, speech sets itself off from the regions of external nature, society, and internal nature, as a reality sui generis, as soon as the sign-substrate, meaning, and denotation of a linguistic utterance can be distinguished.

[Table 10.1] represents the correlations that obtain for:

1 the domains of reality to which every speech action takes up relation;
2 the attitude of the speaker prevailing in particular modes of communication;
3 the validity-claims under which the relations to reality are established;
4 the general functions that grammatical sentences assume in their relations to reality.

Communication and the Evolution of Society, pp. 1–68

Notes

1 Hitherto the term "pragmatics" has been employed to refer to the analysis of particular contexts of language use and not to the reconstruction of universal features of using language (or of employing sentences in utterances). To mark this contrast, I introduced a distinction between "empirical" and "universal" pragmatics". I am no longer happy with this terminology; the term "formal pragmatics" – as an extension of "formal semantics" – would serve better.

2 I shall focus on an idealized case of communicative action, viz. "consensual interaction," in which participants share a tradition and their orientations are normatively integrated to such an extent that they start from the same definition of the situation and do not disagree about the claims to validity that they reciprocally raise. The [...] schema [in Figure 10.2] locates the extreme case of consensual interaction in a system of different types of social action. Underlying this typology is the question of which categories of validity-claims participants are supposed to raise and to react to.

Figure 10.2

These action types can be distinguished by virtue of their relations to the validity basis of speech:

(i) *Communicative vs. strategic action.* In communicative action a basis of mutually recognized validity-claims is presupposed; this is not the case in strategic action. In the communicative attitude it is possible to reach a direct understanding oriented to validity-claims; in the strategic attitude, by contrast, only an indirect understanding via determinative indicators is possible.

(ii) *Action oriented to reaching understanding vs. consensual action.* In consensual action agreement about implicitly raised validity-claims can be *presupposed* as a background consensus by reason of common definitions of the situations; such agreement is supposed to be *arrived at* in action oriented to reaching understanding. In the latter case strategic elements may be employed under the proviso that they are meant to lead to a direct understanding.

(iii) *Action vs. discourse.* In communicative action it is naïvely supposed that implicitly raised validity-claims can be vindicated (or made immediately plausible by way of question and answer). In discourse, by contrast, the validity-claims raised for statements and norms are hypothetically bracketed and thematically examined. As in communicative action, the participants in discourse retain a cooperative attitude.

(iv) *Manipulative action vs. systematically distorted communication.* Whereas in systematically distorted communication at least one of the participants deceives *himself* about the fact that the basis of consensual action is only apparently being maintained, the manipulator deceives at least one of the *other* participants about his own strategic attitude, in which he *deliberately* behaves in a pseudo-consensual manner.

3 K.-O. Apel, "Sprechakttheorie und transzendentale Sprachpragmatik – zur Frage ethischer Normen," in K. O. Apel (ed.) *Sprachpragmatik und Philosophie* (Frankfurt, 1976), pp. 10–173.
4 J. Habermas, *On the Logic of the Social Sciences*, Section III, pp. 184ff.
5 H.G. Gadamer emphasizes this in *Truth and Method* (New York: Sheed and Ward, 1975).

Table 10.1

Domains of reality	Modes of communication: basic attitudes	Validity-claims	General functions of speech
"The" world of external nature	Cognitive: objectivating attitude	Truth	Representation of facts
"Our" world of society	Interactive: performative attitude	Rightness	Establishment of legitimate interpersonal relations
"My" world of internal nature	Expressive: expressive attitude	Truthfulness	Disclosure of speaker's subjectivity
Language	——	Comprehensibility	——

11

Relations to the World and Aspects of Rationality in Four Sociological Concepts of Action

The concept of communicative rationality that emerged from our provisional analysis of the use of the linguistic expression "rational" and from our review of the anthropological debate concerning the status of the modern understanding of the world is in need of a more precise explication. I shall pursue this task only indirectly, by way of a formal-pragmatic clarification of the concept of communicative action, and only within the limits of a systematic look at certain positions in the history of social theory. We can begin with the claim that the concept of communicative rationality has to be analyzed in connection with achieving understanding in language. The concept of reaching an understanding suggests a rationally motivated agreement among participants that is measured against criticizable validity-claims. The validity-claims (propositional truth, normative rightness, and subjective truthfulness) characterize different categories of a knowledge embodied in symbolic expressions. These expressions can be more closely analyzed in two ways – with respect to how they can be defended and with respect to how actors relate through them to something in a world. The concept of communicative rationality points, on the one side, to different forms of discursively redeeming validity-claims (thus Wellmer speaks also of discursive rationality); on the other side, it points to relations to the world that communicative actors take up in raising validity-claims for their expressions. Thus the decentration of our understanding of the world proved to be the most important dimension of the development of world-views. I shall pursue no further the discussion of the theory of argumentation. However, if we return to the thesis introduced at the outset – that every sociology with theoretical pretensions faces the problem of rationality on both the metatheoretical and methodological planes – we come upon the path of examining formal concepts of the world. [. . .]

To begin with, I would like to replace the ontological concept of "world" with one derived from the phenomenological tradition and to adopt the pair of concepts "world" and "lifeworld." Sociated subjects, when participating in cooperative processes of interpretation, themselves employ the concept of the world in an implicit way. Cultural tradition, which Popper introduces under the catchphrase "products of the human mind," plays different roles depending on whether it functions from behind as a cultural stock of knowledge from which the participants in interaction draw their interpretations or is itself made the topic of intellectual endeavor. *In the first case*, the cultural tradition shared by a community is constitutive of the lifeworld which the individual member finds already interpreted. This intersubjectively shared *lifeworld* forms the background for communicative action. Thus phenomenologists like Alfred Schutz speak of the lifeworld as the unthematically given horizon within which participants in communication move in common when they refer thematically to something in the *world*. *In the second case*, individual elements of the cultural tradition are themselves made thematic. The participants must thereby adopt a reflective attitude toward cultural patterns of interpretation that ordinarily *make possible* their interpretive accomplishments. This change in attitude means that the validity of the thematized interpretive pattern is suspended and the corresponding knowledge rendered problematic; at the same time, the problematic element of the cultural tradition is brought under the category of a state of affairs to which one can refer in an objectivating manner. Popper's theory of the third world explains how cultural semantic contents and symbolic objects can be understood as something in the world, and can at the same time be distinguished as higher-level objects from (observable) physical and (experienciable) mental episodes.

[. . .] Further, I would like to replace the one-sidedly cognitivistic interpretation of the concept "objective mind" with a concept of cultural knowledge differentiated according to several validity-claims. Popper's third world encompasses higher-level entities, which are accessible in a reflective attitude and which retain a relative autonomy in relation to subjective mind because they form, on the basis of their relation to truth, a network of problem complexes open to investigation. We could say in the language of neo-Kantianism that the third world enjoys the independence of a sphere of validity. The entities of this world that admit of truth stand in a peculiar relation to the first world. The problems, theories, and arguments attributed to the third world serve in the final analysis to describe and explain events and persons within the first world. And both are mediated in turn through the world of subjective mind, through acts of knowing and doing. The non-cognitive elements of culture thereby slip into a peculiar marginal position. But precisely these elements are of significance for a sociological theory of action. From the perspective of action theory, the activities of the

human mind are not easily limited to the cognitive-instrumental confrontation with external nature; social actions are oriented to cultural
values and these do not have a truth relation. Thus we are faced with
the following alternative: either we deny to the non-cognitive elements
of the cultural tradition the status that third world entities occupy by
virtue of being embedded in a sphere of validity connections, and
classify them in an empiricist manner as forms of expression of
subjective mind, or we seek equivalents for the missing truth relation.

As we shall see, Max Weber chose the second way. He distinguishes
several cultural spheres of value – science and technology, law and
technology, law and morality, as well as art and criticism. The non-
cognitive spheres of value are also spheres of validity. Legal and moral
representations can be criticized and analyzed from the standpoint of
normative rightness and works of art from that of authenticity (or
beauty); that is, they can be treated as autonomous problem domains.
Weber understands cultural tradition *in toto* as a store of knowledge
out of which special spheres of value and systems of knowledge are
formed under different validity-claims. He would thus include in the
third world the evaluative and expressive components of culture as well
as the cognitive-instrumental. If one adopts this alternative, one must
of course explain what "validity" and "knowledge" can mean in regard
to the non-cognitive components of culture. They cannot be correlated
in the same way as theories and statements with entities of the first
world. Cultural values do not fulfill a representational function.

[. . .] These shifts provide us with an opportunity to rid the concept of
world from its narrow ontological connotations. Popper introduces
different world concepts to demarcate regions of being *within* the one
objective world. In his later works he deems it important to speak not
of different worlds, but of *one* world with the indices "1," "2," and "3."[1]
I would like, on the contrary, to continue speaking of three worlds
(which are in turn to be distinguished from the lifeworld). Of these,
only one, namely the objective world, can be understood as the correlate
of the totality of true propositions; only this concept retains the strictly
ontological significance of a totality of entities. On the other hand,
taken together the worlds form a reference system that is mutually
presupposed in communication processes. With this reference system
participants lay down what there can possibly be understanding about
at all. Participants in communication who are seeking to come to an
understanding with one another about something do not take up a
relation only to the one objective world, as is suggested by the pre-
communicative model dominant in empiricism. They by no means refer
only to things that happen or could happen or could be made to happen
in the objective world, but to things in the social and subjective worlds
as well. Speakers and hearers operate with a *system* of several equally
primordial worlds. That is, with propositionally differentiated speech
they have mastered not only a level on which they can describe states

of affairs – as is suggested by Popper's classification into lower and higher functions of language; rather, all three functions – the "descriptive," the "signaling," and the "self-expressive" – lie in one and the same evolutionary plane.

[. . .] With the choice of a specific sociological concept of action we generally make specific "ontological" assumptions. And the aspects of possible rationality of an agent's actions depend, in turn, on the world relations that we thereby impute to him. The profusion of action concepts employed (for the most part, implicitly) in social-scientific theories can be reduced in essence to four basic, analytically distinguishable concepts.

Since Aristotle the concept of *teleological action* has been at the center of the philosophical theory of action. The actor attains an end or brings about the occurrence of a desired state by choosing means that have promise of being successful in the given situation and applying them in a suitable manner. The central concept is that of a *decision* among alternative courses of action, with a view to the realization of an end, guided by maxims, and based on an interpretation of the situation.

The teleological model of action is expanded to a *strategic* model when there can enter into the agent's calculation of success the anticipation of decisions on the part of at least one additional goal-directed actor. This model is often interpreted in utilitarian terms; the actor is supposed to choose and calculate means and ends from the standpoint of maximizing utility or expectations of utility. It is this model of action that lies behind decision-theoretic and game-theoretic approaches in economics, sociology, and social psychology.[2]

The concept of *normatively regulated action* does not refer to the behavior of basically solitary actors who come upon other actors in their environment, but to members of a social group who orient their action to common values. The individual actor complies with (or violates) a norm when in a given situation the conditions are present to which the norm has application. Norms express an agreement that obtains in a social group. All members of a group for whom a given norm has validity may expect of one another that in certain situations they will carry out (or abstain from) the actions commanded (or proscribed). The central concept of *complying with a norm* means fulfilling a generalized expectation of behavior. The latter does not have the cognitive sense of expecting a predicted event, but the normative sense that members are *entitled* to expect a certain behavior. This normative model of action lies behind the role theory that is widespread in sociology.[3]

The concept of *dramaturgical action* refers primarily neither to the solitary actor nor to the member of a social group, but to participants in interaction constituting a public for one another, before whom they present themselves. The actor evokes in his public a certain image, an impression of himself, by more or less purposefully disclosing his subjectivity. Each agent can monitor public access to the system of his own intentions, thoughts, attitudes, desires, feelings, and the like, to which only he has privileged access. In dramaturgical action, participants make use of this and steer their interactions through regulating mutual access to their own subjectivities. Thus the central concept of *presentation of self* does not signify spontaneous expressive behavior but stylizing the expression of one's own experiences with a view to the audience. The dramaturgical model of action is used primarily in phenomenologically oriented descriptions of interaction; but it has not yet been developed into a theoretically generalizing approach.[4]

Finally the concept of *communicative action* refers to the interaction of at least two subjects capable of speech and action who establish interpersonal relations (whether by verbal or by extra-verbal means). The actors seek to reach an understanding about the action situation and their plans of action in order to coordinate their actions by way of agreement. The central concept of *interpretation* refers in the first instance to negotiating definitions of the situation which admit of consensus. As we shall see, language is given a prominent place in this model.

The teleological concept of action was first rendered fruitful for an economic theory of choice by the founders of neo-classical economics, and then for a theory of strategic games by Von Neumann and Morgenstern. The concept of normatively regulated action gained paradigmatic significance for theory formation in the social sciences through Durkheim and Parsons, that of dramaturgical action through Goffman,* that of communicative action through Mead and later Garfinkel.* I cannot carry out a detailed explication of these concepts here. My concern is rather with the rationality implications of the corresponding conceptual strategies. At first glance, only the teleological concept of action seems to open up an aspect of the rationality of action. Action represented as purposeful activity can be viewed under the aspect of purposive-rationality. This is a point of view from which actions can be more or less rationally planned and carried out, or can be judged by a third person to be more or less rational. In elementary cases of purposeful activity the plan of action can be represented in the form of a practical syllogism.[5] The other three models of action appear at first not to place action in the perspective of rationality and possible rationalization. That this appearance is deceiving becomes evident when we represent to ourselves the "ontological" – in the broad sense – presuppositions that are, as a matter of conceptual necessity, connected with these models of action. In the sequence teleological, normative, dramaturgical, the presuppositions not only become increasingly complex; they reveal at the same time stronger and stronger implications for rationality.

(1) The concept of teleological action presupposes relations between an actor and a world of existing states of affairs. This objective world is

defined as the totality of states of affairs that either obtain or could arise or could be brought about by purposeful intervention. The model equips the agent with a "cognitive-volitional complex," so that he can, on the one hand, form *beliefs* about existing states of affairs through the medium of perception, and can, on the other hand, develop *intentions* with the aim of bringing desired states of affairs into existence. At the semantic level such states of affairs are represented as propositional contents of sentences expressing beliefs or intentions. Through his beliefs and intentions the actor can take up basically two types of rational relation to the world. I call these relations rational because they are open to objective appraisal depending on the "direction of fit."[6] In one direction the question arises whether the actor has succeeded in bringing his perceptions and beliefs into agreement with what is the case in the world; in the other direction the question is whether he succeeds in bringing what is the case in the world into agreement with his desires and intentions. In both instances the actor can produce expressions susceptible of being judged by a third person in respect to "fit and misfit;" he can make assertions that are *true* or *false* and carry out goal-directed interventions that succeed or fail, that *achieve* or *fail to achieve* the intended effect in the world. These relations between actor and world allow then for expressions that can be judged according to criteria of *truth* and *efficacy*.

With regard to ontological presuppositions, we can classify *teleological* action as a concept that presupposes *one* world, namely the objective world. The same holds for the concept of *strategic action*. Here we start with at least two goal-directed acting subjects who achieve their ends by way of an orientation to, and influence on, the decisions of other actors. Success in action is also dependent on other actors, each of whom is oriented to his own success and behaves cooperatively only to the degree that this fits with his egocentric calculus of utility. Thus strategically acting subjects must be cognitively so equipped that for them not only physical objects but decision-making systems can appear in the world. They must expand their conceptual apparatus for what can be the case; but they do not need any richer *ontological presuppositions*. The concept of the objective world does not itself become more complex with the growing complexity of inner-world entities. Even purposeful activity differentiated to include strategic action remains, as regards its ontological presuppositions, a *one-world concept*.

(2) By contrast, the concept of normatively regulated action presupposes relations between an actor and exactly two worlds. Besides the objective world of existing states of affairs there is the social world to which the actor belongs as a role-playing subject, as do additional actors who can take up normatively regulated interactions among themselves. A social world consists of a normative context that lays down which interactions belong to the totality of legitimate interpersonal relations.

And all actors for whom the corresponding norms have force (by whom they are accepted as valid) belong to the same social world. As the meaning of the objective world can be elucidated with reference to the existence [*Existieren*] of states of affairs, the meaning of the social world can be elucidated with reference to the "existence" [*Bestehen*] of norms. It is important here that we do *not* understand the "existence" of norms in the sense of existence sentences stating that there are social facts of the type: normative regulations. The sentence "It is the case that *q* is commanded" obviously has a different meaning than the sentence "It is commanded that *q*." The latter sentence expresses a norm or a specific command when it is uttered in suitable form with the claim to normative rightness, that is, such that it claims *validity* for a circle of addressees. And we say that a norm exists, is in force, or enjoys social currency [*Geltung*] when it is recognized as valid [*gültig*] or justified by those to whom it is addressed. Existing states of affairs are represented by true statements, existing norms by general ought-sentences or commands that count as justified among the addressees. That a norm is ideally *valid* means that it *deserves* the assent of all those affected because it regulates problems of action in their common interest. That a norm is de facto *established* means by contrast that the validity-claim with which it appears is recognized by those affected, and this intersubjective recognition grounds the *social force or currency* of the norm.

We do not attach such a normative validity-claim to cultural values; but values are candidates for embodiment in norms – they *can* attain a general binding force with respect to a matter requiring regulation. In the light of cultural values the needs [*Bedürfnisse*] of an individual appear as plausible to other individuals standing in the same tradition. However, plausibly interpreted needs are transformed into legitimate motives of action only when the corresponding values become, for a circle of those affected, normatively binding in regulating specific problem situations. Members can then expect of one another that in corresponding situations each of them will orient his action to values normatively prescribed for all concerned.

This consideration is meant to make comprehensible the fact that the normative model of action equips the agent not only with a "cognitive" but also with a "motivational complex" that makes norm-conformative behavior possible. Moreover, this model of action is connected with a learning model of value internalization.[7] According to this model, existing norms gain action-motivating force to the degree that the values embodied in them represent the standards according to which, in the circle of addressees, needs are interpreted and developed through learning processes into need dispositions.

Under these presuppositions the actor can again take up relations to the world, here to the social world, which are open to objective evaluation according to the "direction of fit." In one direction the question is whether the motives and actions of an agent are in accord with existing norms or deviate from these. In the other direction the question is whether the existing norms themselves embody values that, in a particular problem situation, give expression to generalizable interests of those affected and thus deserve the assent of those to whom they are addressed. In the one case, actions are judged according to whether they are in accord with or deviate from an existing normative context, that is, whether or not they are right with respect to a normative context recognized as legitimate. In the other case, norms are judged according to whether they can be justified, that is, whether they deserve to be recognized as legitimate.[8]

With regard to its ontological – in the broad sense – presuppositions, we can classify *normatively regulated action* as a concept that presupposes *two worlds*, the objective world and a social world. Norm-conformative action presupposes that the agent can distinguish the factual from the normative elements of an action situation, that is, conditions and means from values. The point of departure for the normative model of action is that participants can simultaneously adopt both an objectivating attitude to something that is or is not the case, and a norm-conformative attitude to something that is commanded (whether rightly or not). But as in the teleological model, action is represented *primarily* as a relation between the actor and a world – there, as a relation to the objective world over against which the actor as knower stands and in which he can goal-directly intervene; here, as a relation to the social world to which the actor in his role as a norm-addressee belongs and in which he can take up legitimately regulated interpersonal relations. Neither here nor there is the actor *himself* presupposed as a world toward which he can behave reflectively. It is the concept of dramaturgical action that requires the additional presupposition of a subjective world to which the actor relates when in acting he puts himself "on stage."

(3) The concept of dramaturgical action is less clearly developed in social-science literature than are those of teleological and normatively guided action. Goffman first explicitly introduced it in 1956 in his investigation of "the presentation of self in everyday life."[9] From the perspective of dramaturgical action we understand social action as an encounter in which participants form a visible public for each other and perform for one another. "Encounter" and "performance" are the key concepts. The performance of a troop before the eyes of third persons is only a special case. A performance enables the actor to present himself to his audience in a certain way; in bringing something of his subjectivity to appearance, he would like to be seen by his public in a particular way.

The dramaturgical qualities of action are in a certain way parasitic; they rest on a structure of goal-directed action:

> For certain purposes people control the style of their actions ... and superimpose this upon other activities. For instance work may be done in a manner in accordance with the principles of dramatic performance in order to project a certain impression of the people working to an inspector or manager ... In fact what people are doing is rarely properly described as *just* eating, or *just* working, but has stylistic features which have certain conventional meanings associated with recognized types of personae.[10]

Of course, there are special roles tailored to virtuoso self-staging: "The roles of prizefighters, surgeons, violinists, and policemen are cases in point. These activities allow so much dramatic self-expression that exemplary practitioners – whether real or fictional – become famous and are given special places in the commercially organized fantasies of the nation."[11] The trait that is here stylized into an element of the professional role, namely, the reflective character of self-presentation before others, is, however, constitutive for social interactions in general insofar as they are regarded only under the aspect of persons encountering one another.

In dramaturgical action the actor, in presenting a view of himself, has to behave towards his own subjective world. I have defined this as the totality of subjective experiences to which the actor has, in relation to others, a privileged access. To be sure, this domain of subjectivity deserves to be called a "world" only if the significance of the subjective world can be explicated in a way similar to that in which I explained the significance of the social world, through referring to an "existence" of norms analogous to the existence of states of affairs. Perhaps one can say that the subject is represented by truthfully uttered experiential sentences in nearly the same way as are existing states of affairs by true statements and valid norms by justified ought-sentences. We should not understand subjective experiences as mental states or inner episodes, for we would thereby assimilate them to entities, to elements of the objective world. We can comprehend having subjective experiences as something analogous to the existence of states of affairs without assimilating the one to the other. A subject capable of expression does not "have" or "possess" desires and feelings in the same sense as an observable object has extension, weight, color, and similar properties. An actor has desires and feelings in the sense that he can at will express these experiences before a public, and indeed in such a way that this public, if it trusts the actor's expressive utterances, attributes to him, as something subjective, the desires and feelings expressed.

Desires and feelings have a paradigmatic status in this connection. Of course, cognitions, beliefs, and intentions also belong to the subjective world; but they stand in internal relation to the objective world. Beliefs and intentions come to consciousness *as* subjective only when there is in the objective world no corresponding state of affairs that exists or is brought to exist. It becomes a question of "mere," that is, "mistaken" belief as soon as the corresponding statement turns out to be untrue. It is a matter merely of "good," that is, of "ineffectual" intentions as soon as it turns out that the corresponding action was either left undone or failed. In a similar way, feelings of, say, obligation, shame, or guilt stand in internal relation to the social world. But in general feelings and desires can *only* be expressed as something subjective. They cannot be expressed *otherwise*, cannot enter into relation with the external world, whether the objective or the social. For this reason the expression of desires and feelings is measured only against the reflexive relation of the speaker to his inner world.

Desires and feelings are two aspects of a partiality rooted in needs.[12] Needs have two faces. They are differentiated on the volitional side into inclinations and desires; and on the other side, the intuitive, into feelings and moods. Desires are directed toward situations of need satisfaction; feelings "perceive" situations in the light of possible need satisfaction. Needs are, as it were, the background of a partiality that determines our subjective attitudes in relation to the external world. Such predilections express themselves both in the active striving for goods and in the affective perception of situations (so long as the latter are not objectivated into something in the world and thus lose their situational character). The partiality of desires and feelings is expressed at the level of language in the interpretation of needs, that is, in evaluations for which evaluative expressions are available. One can gain clarity about the meaning of value-judgments by examining the dual, descriptive-prescriptive content of these evaluative, need-interpreting expressions. They serve to make predilection understandable. This component of justification[13] is the bridge between the subjectivity of experience and that intersubjective transparency that experience gains in being truthfully expressed and, on this basis, attributed to an actor by onlookers. For example, in characterizing an object or a situation as splendid, ample, elevating, auspicious, dangerous, forbidding, dreadful, and so forth, we are trying to express a predilection and at the same time to justify it, in the sense of making it plausible by appeal to general standards of evaluation that are widespread at least in our own culture. Evaluative expressions or standards of value have justificatory force when they characterize a need in such a way that addressees can, in the framework of a common cultural heritage, recognize in these interpretations their own needs. This explains why attributes of style, aesthetic expression, formal qualities in general, have such great weight in dramaturgical action.

In the case of dramaturgical action the relation between actor and world is also open to objective appraisal. As the actor is oriented to his own subjective world in the presence of his public, there can be *one* direction of fit: in regard to a self-presentation, there is the question whether at the proper moment the actor is expressing the experiences he has, whether he *means* what he *says*, or whether he is merely feigning the experiences he expresses. So long as we are dealing here with beliefs or intentions, that is, with cognitive acts, the question of whether someone says what he means is clearly a question of truthfulness or sincerity. With desires and feelings this is not always the case. In situations in which accuracy of expression is important, it is sometimes difficult to separate questions of sincerity from those of authenticity. Often we lack the words to say what we feel; and this in turn places the feelings themselves in a questionable light.

According to the dramaturgical model of action, a participant can adopt an attitude to his own subjectivity in the role of an actor and to the expressive utterances of another in the role of a public, but only in the awareness that the ego's inner world is bounded by an external world. In this external world the actor can certainly distinguish between normative and non-normative elements of the action situation; but Goffman's model of action does not provide for his behaving toward the social world in a norm-conformative attitude. He takes legitimately regulated interpersonal relations into account only as social facts. Thus it seems to me correct also to classify *dramaturgical action* as a concept that presupposes *two worlds*, the internal world and the external. Expressive utterances present subjectivity in demarcation from the external world; the actor can in principle adopt only an objectivating attitude toward the latter. And in contrast to the case of normatively regulated action, this holds not only for physical but for social objects as well.

In virtue of this option, dramaturgical action can take on latently strategic qualities to the degree that the actor treats his audience as *opponents* rather than as a public. The scale of self-presentations ranges from sincere communication of one's own intentions, desires, moods, etc. to cynical management of the impressions the actor arouses in others.

> At one extreme, one finds that the performer can be fully taken in by his own act; he can be sincerely convinced that the impression of reality which he stages is the real reality. When his audience is also convinced in this way about the show he puts on – and this seems to be the typical case – then for the moment at least, only the sociologist or the socially disgruntled will have doubts about the "realness" of what is presented. At the other extreme ... the performer may be moved to guide the conviction of his audience only as a means to other ends, having no ultimate concern with the beliefs of his audience; we may call him cynical, reserving the term "sincere" for individuals who believe in the impression fostered by their own performance.[14]

The manipulative production of false impressions – Goffman investigates techniques of "impression management," from harmless segmentation to long-term information control – is by no means identical with strategic action. It too remains dependent on a public that takes itself to be present at a performance and fails to recognize its strategic character. Even a strategically intended self-presentation has to be capable of being understood as an expression that appears with the claim to subjective truthfulness. As soon as it is judged only according to criteria of success by the audience as well, it no longer falls under the description of dramaturgical action. We then have a case of strategic interaction in which participants have conceptually enriched their objective world in such a way that opponents can appear in it who are capable not only of purposive-rational action but of subjective expressions as well.

[...] With the concept of communicative action there comes into play the additional presupposition of a *linguistic medium* that reflects the actor's relations to the world as such. At this level of concept formation the rationality problematic, which until now has arisen only for the social scientist, moves into the perspective of the agent himself. We have to make clear in what sense achieving understanding in language is thereby introduced as a mechanism for coordinating action. Even the strategic model of action *can* be understood in such a way that participants' actions, directed through egocentric calculations of utility and coordinated through interest situations, are mediated through speech acts. In the cases of normatively regulated and dramaturgical action we even *have to* suppose a consensus formation among participants that is in principle of a linguistic nature. Nevertheless, in these three models of action language is conceived *one-sidedly* in different respects.

The teleological model of action takes language as one of several media through which speakers oriented to their own success can influence one another in order to bring opponents to form or to grasp beliefs and intentions that are in the speakers' own interest. This concept of language – developed from the limit case of indirect communication aimed at *getting* someone to form a belief, an intention, or the like – is, for instance, basic to intentionalist semantics. The normative model of action presupposes a consensus that is merely reproduced with each additional act of understanding. This culturalist concept of language is widespread in cultural anthropology and content-oriented linguistics.[15] The dramaturgical model of action presupposes language as a medium of self-presentation; the cognitive significance of the propositional components and the interpersonal significance of the illocutionary components are thereby played down in favor of the expressive functions of speech acts. Language is assimilated to stylistic and aesthetic forms of expression.[16] Only the communicative model of action presupposes language as a medium of uncurtailed communication whereby speakers and hearers, out of the context of their pre-interpreted lifeworld, refer simultaneously to things in the objective, social, and subjective worlds in order to negotiate common definitions of the situation. This interpretive concept of language lies behind the various efforts to develop a formal pragmatics.

The one-sidedness of the first three concepts of language can be seen in the fact that the corresponding types of communication singled out by them prove to be limited cases of communicative action: *first*, the indirect communication of those who have only the realization of their own ends in view; *second*, the consensual action of those who simply actualize an already existing normative agreement; and *third*, presentation of self in relation to an audience. In each case only one function of language is thematized: the release of perlocutionary effects, the establishment of interpersonal relations, and the expression of subjective experiences. By contrast, the communicative model of action, which defines the traditions of social science connected with Mead's symbolic interactionism, Wittgenstein's concept of language games, Austin's theory of speech acts, and Gadamer's hermeneutics, takes all the functions of language equally into consideration. As can be seen in the ethnomethodological and hermeneutic approaches, there is a danger here of reducing social *action* to the interpretive accomplishments of participants in communication, of assimilating action to speech, interaction to conversation. In the present context I can introduce this concept of communicative action only in a provisional way. I shall restrict myself to remarks concerning: (1) the character of independent actions; and (2) the reflective relation to the world of actors in processes of understanding.

(1) In order to avoid mislocating the concept of communicative action from the start, I would like to characterize the level of complexity of speech acts that simultaneously express a propositional content, the offer of an interpersonal relationship, and the intention of the speaker. In the course of the analysis it will become evident how much this concept owes to investigations in the philosophy of language stemming from Wittgenstein. Precisely for this reason it might be well to point out that the concept of following a rule with which analytic philosophy of language begins does not go far enough. If one grasps linguistic conventions only from the perspective of rule following, and explains them by means of a concept of intentions based on rule consciousness, one loses that aspect of the *threefold relation to the world* of communicative agents that is important to me.

I shall use the term "action" only for those symbolic expressions with which the actor takes up a relation to at least one world (but always to the objective world *as well*) – as is the case in the previously examined models of teleological, normatively regulated, and dramaturgical action. I shall distinguish from actions the bodily movements and operations that are *concomitantly executed* and can acquire the independence of actions only *secondarily*, through being *embedded, for instance, in play or teaching* practices. This can easily be shown through the example of bodily movements. Under the aspect of observable events in the world, actions appear as bodily movements of an organism. Controled by the central nervous system, these movements are the substratum in which actions are carried out. With his actions the agent changes something in the world. We can, of course, distinguish the movements with which a subject intervenes in the world (acts instrumentally) from those with which a subject embodies a meaning (expresses himself communicatively). In both cases the bodily movements bring about a physical change in the world; in the one case this is of causal relevance, in the other of semantic relevance. Examples of causally relevant bodily movements are straightening the body, spreading the hand, lifting the arm, bending the leg, and so forth. Examples of semantically relevant bodily movements are movements of the larynx, tongue, lips, etc., in the generation of phonetic sounds; nodding the head; shrugging the shoulders; finger movements while playing the piano; hand movements while writing, drawing; and so on.

Arthur Danto has analyzed these movements as "basic actions."[17] This has given rise to a broad discussion which is biased by the idea that bodily movements do not represent the substratum through which actions enter into the world but are themselves primitive actions. In this view, a complex action is characterized by the fact that it is performed "through" carrying out another action: "through" flicking the light switch I turn on the light; "through" raising my right arm I greet someone; "through" forcefully kicking a ball I score a goal. These are examples of actions performed "through" a basic action. A basic action is characterized in turn by the fact that it cannot be performed by means of an additional act. I regard this conceptual strategy as misleading. In a certain sense, actions are realized through movements of the body, but only in such a way that the actor, in following a technical or social rule, *concomitantly executes* these movements. Concomitant execution means that the actor intends an action but not the bodily movements with the help of which he realizes it.[18] *A bodily movement is an element of an action but not an action.*

As far as their status as non-independent actions is concerned, *bodily* movements are similar to just those *operations* from which Wittgenstein developed his concepts of rules and rule following. Operations of thought and speech are always only executed concomitantly in *other* actions. If need be, they can be *rendered independent* within the framework of a training exercise – for instance, when a Latin teacher, in the course of a lesson, demonstrates the passive transformation with a sample sentence formed in the active voice. This explains the special heuristic utility of the model of social games. Wittgenstein preferred to elucidate operational rules with reference to chess. He did not see that this model has only limited value. We can certainly understand speaking or doing sums as practices constituted by the grammar of a particular language or the rules of arithmetic, in a way similar to that in which chess playing is constituted by the familiar rules of the game. But the two cases are as distinct as is the concomitantly executed arm movement from the gymnastic exercise that is carried out by means of the same movement. In applying arithmetical or grammatical rules we generate symbolic objects such as sums or sentences; but they do not lead an independent existence. We normally carry out *other* actions by means of sums and sentences – for example, schoolwork or commands. Operatively generated structures can, taken by themselves, be judged as more or less correct, in conformity with a rule, or well formed; but they are not, as are actions, open to criticism from the standpoints of truth, efficacy, rightness, or sincerity, for they acquire relations to the world only as the infrastructure of other actions. *Operations do not concern the world.*

This can be seen in the fact that operational rules can serve to identify an operatively generated structure as more or less well formed, that is, to make it *comprehensible* but not to *explain* its appearance. They permit an answer to the question of whether certain scrawled-out symbols are sentences, measurements, computations, etc,; and if they are, say, a computation, just which one it is. To show that someone has calculated, and indeed correctly, does not, however, explain *why* he carried out this computation. If we wish to answer *this* question, we must have recourse to a rule of *action*; for example, to the fact that a pupil used this sheet of paper to solve a mathematical problem. With the help of arithmetic rules, we can, it is true, state the reason why he continues the number series 1, 3, 6, 10, 15 ... with 21, 28, 36, and so forth; but we cannot *explain* why he writes this series on a piece of paper. We are explicating the meaning of a symbolic structure and not giving a rational explanation for its coming to be. Operational rules do not have explanatory power; following them does not mean, as does following rules of action, that the actor is relating to something in the world and is thereby oriented to validity-claims connected with action-motivating reasons.

(2) This should make clear why we cannot analyze communicative utterances in the same way as we do the grammatical sentences with the help of which we carry them out. For the communicative model of action, language is relevant only from the pragmatic viewpoint that speakers, in employing sentences with an orientation to reaching understanding, take up relations to the world, not only directly as in teleological, normatively regulated, or dramaturgical action, but in a reflective way. Speakers integrate the three formal world-concepts, which appear in the other models of action either singly or in pairs, into a system and presuppose this system in common as a framework of interpretation within which they can reach an understanding. They no longer relate *straightaway* to something in the objective, social, or

subjective worlds; instead they relativize their utterances against the possibility that their validity will be contested by other actors. Reaching an understanding functions as a mechanism for coordinating actions only through the participants in interaction coming to an agreement concerning the claimed *validity* of their utterances, that is, through intersubjectively recognizing the *validity-claims* they reciprocally raise. A speaker puts forward a criticizable claim in relating with his utterance to at least one "world;" he thereby uses the fact that this relation between actor and world is in principle open to objective appraisal in order to call upon his opposite number to take a rationally motivated position. The concept of communicative action presupposes language as the medium for a kind of reaching understanding, in the course of which participants, through relating to a world, reciprocally raise validity-claims that can be accepted or contested.

With this model of action we are supposing that participants in interaction can now mobilize the rationality potential – which according to our previous analysis resides in the actor's three relations to the world – expressly for the cooperatively pursued goal of reaching understanding. If we leave to one side the well-formedness of the symbolic expressions employed, an actor who is oriented to understanding in this sense must raise at least three validity-claims with his utterance, namely:

(a) that the statement made is true (or that the existential presuppositions of the propositional content mentioned are in fact satisfied);
(b) that the speech act is right with respect to the existing normative context (or that the normative context that it is supposed to satisfy is itself legitimate); and
(c) that the manifest intention of the speaker is meant as it is expressed.

Thus the speaker claims truth for statements or existential presuppositions, rightness for legitimately regulated actions and their normative context, and truthfulness or sincerity for the manifestation of subjective experiences. We can easily recognize therein the three relations of actor to world presupposed *by the social scientist* in the previously analyzed concepts of action; but in the concept of communicative action they are ascribed to the perspective of *the speakers and hearers themselves*. It is the actors themselves who seek consensus and measure it against truth, rightness, and sincerity, that is, against the "fit" or "misfit" between the speech act, on the one hand, and the three worlds to which the actor takes up relations with his utterance, on the other. Such relations hold between an utterance and:

(a) the objective world (as the totality of all entities about which true statements are possible);

(b) the social world (as the totality of all legitimately regulated interpersonal relations);
(c) the subjective world (as the totality of the experiences of the
speaker to which he has privileged access).

Every process of reaching understanding takes place against the
background of a culturally ingrained pre-understanding. This background knowledge remains unproblematic as a whole; only that part of
the stock of knowledge that participants make use of and thematize at
a given time is put to the test. To the extent that definitions of situations
are negotiated by participants *themselves*, this thematic segment of the
lifeworld is at their disposal with the negotiation of each new definition
of the situation.

A definition of the situation establishes an order. Through it, participants in communication assign the various elements of an action
situation to one of the three worlds and thereby incorporate the actual
action situation into their pre-interpreted lifeworld. A definition of the
situation by another party that prima facie diverges from one's own
presents a problem of a peculiar sort; for in cooperative processes of
interpretation no participant has a monopoly on correct interpretation.
For both parties the interpretive task consists in incorporating the
other's interpretation of the situation into one's own in such a way that
in the revised version "his" external world and "my" external world can
– against the background of "our" lifeworld – be relativized in relation
to "the" world, and the divergent situation definitions can be brought
to coincide sufficiently. Naturally this does not mean that interpretation
must lead in every case to a stable and unambiguously differentiated
assignment. Stability and absence of ambiguity are rather the exception
in the communicative practice of everyday life. A more realistic picture
is that drawn by ethnomethodologists – of a diffuse, fragile, continuously
revised and only momentarily successful communication in which
participants rely on problematic and unclarified presuppositions and
feel their way from one occasional commonality to the next.

To avoid misunderstanding I would like to repeat that the communicative model of action does not equate action with communication.
Language is a medium of communication that serves understanding,
whereas actors, in coming to an understanding with one another so as
to coordinate their actions, pursue their particular aims. In this respect
the teleological structure is fundamental to *all* concepts of action.
Concepts of *social action* are distinguished, however, according to how
they specify the *coordination* among the goal-directed actions of different participants: as the interlacing of egocentric calculations of utility
(whereby the degree of conflict and cooperation varies with the given
interest positions); as a socially integrating agreement about values and
norms instilled through cultural tradition and socialization; as a consensual relation between players and their publics; or as reaching under-

standing in the sense of a cooperative process of interpretation. In all cases the teleological structure of action is presupposed, inasmuch as the capacity for goal-setting and goal-directed action is ascribed to actors, as well as an interest in carrying out their plans of action. But only the strategic model of action *rests content* with an explication of the features of action oriented directly to success; whereas the other models of action specify conditions under which the actor pursues his goals – conditions of legitimacy, of self-presentation, or of agreement arrived at in communication, under which alter can "link up" his actions with those of ego. In the case of communicative action the interpretive accomplishments on which cooperative processes of interpretation are based represent the mechanism for *coordinating* action; communicative action is *not exhausted* by the act of reaching understanding in an interpretive manner. If we take as our unit of analysis a simple speech act carried out by *S*, to which at least one participant in interaction can take up a "yes" or "no" position, we can clarify the conditions for the communicative coordination of action by stating what it means for a hearer to understand what is said. But communicative action designates a type of interaction that is *coordinated through* speech acts and does *not coincide with* them.

The Theory of Communicative Action, vol. 1, pp. 75, 82–101.

Notes

1 K.R. Popper, "Reply to My Critics," in P.A. Schilpp (ed.), *The Philosophy of Karl Popper* (La Salle, Ill, 1974), p. 1050. Popper takes this terminology from J.C. Eccles, *Facing Realities* (New York, 1970).
2 On decision theory, see H. Simon, *Models of Man* (New York, 1957); G. Gäfgen, *Theorie der wirtschaftlichen Entscheidung* (Tübingen, 1968). On game theory, see R.D. Luce and H. Raiffa, *Games and Decisions* (New York, 1957); M. Shubik, *Spieltheorie und Sozialwissenschaften* (Frankfurt, 1965). On exchange-theoretical approaches in social psychology, see P.P. Ekeh, *Social Exchange Theory* (London, 1964).
3 T.R. Sarbin, "Role Theory," in G. Lindsey (ed.), *Handbook of Social Psychology*, vol. 1 (Cambridge, Mass., 1954), pp. 223–58; Talcott Parsons, "Social Interaction," in *International Encyclopedia of Social Science*, 7:1429–41; Hans Joas, *Die gegenwärtige Lage der Rollentheorie* (Frankfurt, 1977), pp. 68ff.
4 G.J. McCall and J.L. Simmons, *Identity and Interactions* (New York, 1966); E. Goffman, *Frame Analysis* (Harmondsworth, 1975), *Relations in Public* (Harmondsworth, 1971), *Interaction Ritual* (Harmondsworth, 1957); R. Harré and P.F. Secord, *Explanation of Behavior* (Totowa, N.J., 1972); R. Harré, *Social Being* (Oxford, 1979).
5 G.H. von Wright, *Explanation and Understanding* (London, 1971), pp. 96ff. Von Wright's point of departure is G. E. M. Anscombe, *Intention* (Oxford, 1957).

6 J.L. Austin speaks of the "direction of fit" or the "onus of match," which Anthony Kenny elaborates as follows: "Any sentence whatever can be regarded as – *inter alia* – a description of a state of affairs ... Now let us suppose that the possible state of affairs described in the sentence does not, in fact, obtain. *Do we fault the sentence or do we fault the facts?* If the former, then we shall call the sentence assertoric, if the latter, let us call it for the moment imperative." *Will, Freedom and Power* (Oxford, 1975), p. 38. If we conceive of intention sentences as imperatives that a speaker addresses to himself, then assertoric and intention sentences represent the two possibilities of agreement between sentence and state of affairs that are open to objective appraisal.

7 H. Gerth and C.W. Mills, *Character and Social Structure* (New York, 1953).

8 This does not prejudge the question of whether we, as social scientists and philosophers, adopt a cognitive or a skeptical position in regard to moral-practical questions; that is, whether we hold a justification of action norms that is not relative to given ends to be possible. For example, Talcott Parsons shares with Weber a position of value skepticism; but when we use the concept of normatively regulated action we have to describe the actors *as if* they consider the legitimacy of action norms to be basically open to objective appraisal, no matter in which metaphysical, religious, or theoretical framework. Otherwise they would not take the concept of a world of legitimately regulated interpersonal relations as the basis of their action and could not orient themselves to valid norms but only to social facts. Acting in a norm-conformative attitude requires an intuitive understanding of normative validity; and this concept presupposes *some* possibility or other of normative grounding. It cannot be a priori excluded that this conceptual necessity is a deception embedded in linguistic meaning conventions and thus calls for enlightenment – for example, by reinterpreting the concept of normative validity in emotivist or decisionistic terms and redescribing it with the help of other concepts like expressions of feeling, appeals, or commands. But the action of agents to whom such categorially "purified" action orientations can be ascribed could no longer be described in concepts of normatively regulated action.

9 E. Goffman, *The Presentation of Self in Everyday Life* (New York, 1959).

10 Harré and Secord, *Explanation of Behavior*, pp. 215–16.

11 Goffman, *Presentation of Self*, p. 31.

12 Compare the analysis of desires and feelings by Charles Taylor, "Explaining Action," *Inquiry* 13, 1970:54–89.

13 Richard Norman, *Reasons for Actions*, pp. 65ff.

14 Goffman, *Presentation of Self*, pp. 17–18.

15 Benjamin Lee Whorf, *Language, Thought and Reality* (Cambridge, Mass., 1956).

16 Harré and Secord, *Explanation of Behavior*, pp. 215ff; see esp. Charles Taylor,* *Language and Human Nature* (Carleton, Montreal, 1978).

17 Arthur C. Danto, "Basic Actions," *American Philosophical Quarterly*, 2, 1965:141–48, and *Analytical Philosophy of Action* (Cambridge, 1973).

18 A.I. Goldmann, *A Theory of Action* (Englewood Cliffs, N.J., 1970).

12

The Problem of Understanding Meaning in the Social Sciences

The same rationality problematic that we encounter in examining sociological concepts of action appears in another light when we pursue the question: What does it mean to understand social actions? There is an interdependence between the basic concepts of social action and the methodology of understanding social actions. Different models of action presuppose different relations of actor to world; and these world-relations are constitutive not only for aspects of the rationality of action, but also for the rationality of interpretations of action by, say, social-scientific interpreters. With a formal world-concept an actor becomes involved in suppositions of commonality that, from his perspective, point beyond the circle of those immediately involved and claim to be valid for outside interpreters as well. This connection can easily be made clear in the case of teleological action. The concept of the objective world – in which the actor can intervene in a goal-directed manner – which is presupposed with this model of action must hold in the same way for the actor himself and for any other interpreter of his actions. Thus Max Weber could construct for teleological action the ideal type of purpose-rational action and set up the standard of the "rationality of objective correctness" for interpreting purposive-rational actions.[1] [. . .]

An action can be interpreted as more or less purposive-rational if there are standards of judgment which both the agent and his interpreter equally accept as valid, that is, as standards of an objective or impartial appraisal. In advancing what Weber calls a rational interpretation, the interpreter himself takes a position on the claim with which purposive-rational actions appear; he relinquishes the attitude of a third person for the performative attitude of a participant who is examining a problematic validity-claim and, if need be, criticizing it. Rational interpretations are undertaken in a performative attitude, since the interpreter presupposes a basis for judgment that is shared by all parties, including the actors.

The other two world-relations provide a similar basis. Normatively regulated and dramaturgical actions also admit of rational interpretation. Of course, in these cases the possibility of rationally reconstructing action orientations is not so evident, and in fact not so uncomplicated, as in the case of teleological action considered above.

In normatively regulated actions the actor, by entering into an interpersonal relation, takes up a relation to something in the social world. An actor's behavior is subjectively "right" (in the sense of normative rightness) if he sincerely believes himself to be following an existing norm of action; his behavior is objectively "right" if the norm in question is in fact regarded as justified among those to whom it applies. At this level the question of a rational interpretation does not yet arise, since an observer can ascertain descriptively whether an action accords with a given norm and whether or not the norm in turn enjoys social currency. According to the presuppositions of this model of action, however, an actor can comply with (or violate) only norms that he subjectively regards as valid or justified; and with this recognition of normative validity-claims he exposes himself to an objective judgment. He challenges the interpreter to examine not only the actual norm-*conformity* of his action, or the de facto currency of the norm in question, but the rightness of this norm itself. The interpreter can in turn accept the challenge or, from a standpoint skeptical of values, dismiss it as senseless.

If the interpreter adopts such a skeptical standpoint, he will explain, with the help of a non-cognitive variety of ethics, that the actor is deceiving himself in regard to the possibility of justifying norms, and that instead of reasons he could at best adduce empirical motives for the recognition of norms. Whoever argues in this way has to regard the concept of normatively regulated action as theoretically unsuitable; he will try to replace a description initially drawn in concepts of normatively regulated action with another one given, for example, in causal-behavioristic terms. On the other hand, if the interpreter is convinced of the theoretical fruitfulness of the normative model of action, he has to get involved in the suppositions of commonality that are accepted with the formal concept of the social world and allow for the possibility of testing the *worthiness* to be recognized of a norm held by an actor to be right. Such rational interpretation of normatively regulated action is based on comparing the social currency of a given normative context with its counterfactually constructed validity. I shall not here go into the methodological problems of a practical discourse carried out by the interpreter as a representative of action subjects (i.e., as their advocate).[2] The moral-practical appraisal of norms of actions certainly places an interpreter in even greater difficulties than monitoring the success of rules of purposive-rational action. At the moment, however, I am concerned only to show that normatively regulated actions, like teleological actions, can be rationally interpreted.

A similar consequence follows from the dramaturgical model of action. Here the actor, in revealing something of himself before a public, refers to something in his subjective world. Again, the formal world-concept provides a basis for judgment that is shared by the agent and his interpreter. An interpreter can interpret an action rationally in such a way that he thereby captures elements of deception or self-deception. He can expose the latently strategic character of a self-presentation by comparing the manifest content of the utterance, that is, what the actor says, with what the actor means. The interpreter can, furthermore, uncover the systematically distorted character of processes of understanding by showing how the participants express themselves in a subjectively truthful manner and yet objectively say something other than what they (also) mean (unbeknownst to themselves). The depth-hermeneutic procedure of interpreting unconscious motives again involves difficulties different from those connected with judging objectively ascribed interest positions in the role of advocate or with examining the empirical content of technical and strategic rules of action. Drawing on the example of therapeutic critique, however, we can make clear the possibility of rationally interpreting dramaturgical action.[3]

The procedures of rational interpretation enjoy a questionable status in the social sciences. The critique of "model-Platonism" in economics shows that some contest the empirical content and the explanatory fruitfulness of models of rational choice; objections to cognitivist approaches in ethics, and reservations with regard to the critique of ideology developed in the Hegelian-Marxist tradition, show that others doubt the possibility of providing moral-practical justification for norms of action and of setting off particular from generalizable interests; and the widespread critique of the scientific character of psychoanalysis shows that many regard as problematic the very *conception* of the unconscious, the concept of the latent/manifest double meaning of experiential expressions. In my view these objections are themselves based on empiricist assumptions that are open to question.[4] There is no need to go into this controversy here, as it is not my intention to demonstrate the "possibility" and theoretical fruitfulness of rational interpretations; I want rather to give reasons for the stronger claim that access to the object domain of social action through the understanding of meaning of itself makes the rationality problematic *unavoidable*. Communicative actions always require an interpretation that is rational in approach.

The relations of strategic, normatively regulated, and dramaturgical actors to the objective, social, and subjective worlds are in principle open to objective appraisal, both for the individual actor and for an observer. In communicative action, the very outcome of interaction is even made to depend on whether the participants can come to an agreement among themselves on an *intersubjectively valid* appraisal of their relations to the world. On this model of action, an interaction can succeed only if those involved arrive at a consensus among themselves, a consensus that depends on yes/no responses to claims potentially based on grounds. I shall be analyzing below this *rational infrastructure of action oriented to reaching understanding.* In the present context we are dealing with the question of whether, and if so how, this internal structure of the actors' understanding among themselves is represented in the understanding of an interpreter. Does not the task of describing complexes of communicative action consist only in giving as precise as possible an explication of the meaning of the symbolic expressions that make up the observed sequence? And is not this explication of meaning entirely independent of the (in principle testable) rationality of those opinions and attitudes that carry the interpersonal coordination of action? This would be the case only if the interpretation of action oriented to reaching understanding could allow a strict separation between questions of meaning and questions of validity; and this is precisely the problem. To be sure, we have to distinguish the interpretive accomplishments of an observer who wants to understand the meaning of a symbolic expression from those of participants in interaction who coordinate their actions through the mechanism of reaching understanding. Unlike those immediately involved, the interpreter is not striving for an interpretation on which there can be a consensus in order to harmonize his own action plans with those of other actors. But perhaps the interpretive accomplishments of observer and participant differ only in their function and not in their structure. The yes/no position of the interpreter, by which, as we have seen, rational interpretations of ideal-typically simplified courses of action are characterized, must enter incipiently even into the mere description, the semantic explication of a speech act. Communicative actions can only be interpreted "rationally" in a sense still to be explained. I would like to develop this disquieting thesis in connection with the problematic of *Sinnverstehen,* or understanding meaning, in the social sciences. I shall treat it first from the perspective of the theory of science, and then from that of the phenomenological, ethnomethodological, and hermeneutic schools of interpretive sociology.

[. . .] Our discussions of the basic concepts of action theory and of the methodology of *Verstehen* have shown that the rationality problematic does not come to sociology from the outside but breaks out within it. It is centered around a concept of reaching understanding that is basic from both a metatheoretical and a methodological point of view. This concept has been of interest to us both under the aspect of the coordination of action and under that of an interpretive access to the object domain. Processes of reaching understanding are aimed at a consensus that depends on the intersubjective access to the object domain. Processes of reaching understanding are aimed at a consensus that depends on the intersubjective recognition of validity-claims; and these claims can be reciprocally raised and fundamentally criticized by participants in communication. In the orientation to validity-claims the actors' world-relations are actualized. In referring with their utterances to something in one or another world, subjects presuppose formal commonalities that are constitutive for reaching any understanding at all. If this rationality problematic cannot be avoided in the basic concepts of social action and in the method of understanding meaning, how do things stand with respect to the substantial question of whether, and if so how, modernization processes can be viewed from the standpoint of rationalization?

Sociology, which arose as the theory of society, has occupied itself with this theme since its beginnings. This is a reflection of preferences which, as I mentioned above, have to do with the conditions under which this discipline arose; these preferences can be explained historically. Beyond this, however, there is an *internal* relation between sociology and the theory of rationalization. In the investigation that follows I shall introduce the theory of communicative action in connection with this theme.

If *some* concept of rationality is unavoidably built into the action-theoretic foundations of sociology, then theory formation is in danger of being limited from the start to a particular, culturally or historically bound perspective, unless fundamental concepts are constructed in such a way that the concept of rationality they implicitly posit is encompassing and general, that is, satisfies universalistic claims. The demand for such a concept of rationality also emerges from methodological considerations. If the understanding of meaning has to be understood as communicative experience, and if this is possible only in the performative attiude of a communicative actor, the experiential basis of an interpretive [*sinnverstehenden*] sociology is compatible with its claim to objectivity only if hermeneutic procedures can be based at least intuitively on general and encompassing structures of rationality. From both points of view, the metatheoretical and the methodological, we cannot expect objectivity in social-theoretical knowledge if the corresponding concepts of communicative action and interpretation express a merely particular perspective on rationality, one interwoven with a particular cultural tradition.[5]

We have, by way of anticipation, characterized the rational internal structure of processes of reaching understanding in terms of (1) the three world-relations of actors and the corresponding concepts of the objective, social, and subjective worlds; (2) the validity-claims of propositional truth, normative rightness, and sincerity or authenticity; (3) the concept of a rationally motivated agreement, that is, one based on the intersubjective recognition of criticizable validity-claims; and (4) the concept of reaching understanding as the cooperative negotiation of common definitions of the situation. If the requirement of objectivity is to be satisfied, this structure would have to be shown to be *universally valid* in a specific sense. This is a very strong requirement for someone who is operating without metaphysical support and is also no longer confident that a rigorous transcendental-pragmatic program, claiming to provide ultimate grounds, can be carried out.

It is, of course, obvious that the type of action oriented to reaching understanding, whose rational internal structure we sketched above in very rough outline, is by no means everywhere and always encountered as the normal case in everyday practice. I have myself pointed to contrasts between the mythical and the modern understandings of the world, to contrasts between action orientations that typically appear in archaic and in modern societies. In claiming universal validity – with however many qualifications – for *our* concept of rationality, without thereby adhering to a completely untenable belief in progress, we are taking on a sizable burden of proof. Its weight becomes completely clear when we pass from sharp and oversimplified contrasts supporting a superiority of modern thought to the less glaring oppositions disclosed by intercultural comparison of the modes of thought of the various world religions and world civilizations. Even if this multiplicity of systematized and highly differentiated world-views could still be placed in a hierarchical relation to the modern understanding of the world, we would encounter within the modern period, at the latest, a pluralism of belief systems from which it is not so easy to extract a universal core.

If one is at all still willing today to venture to expound the universality of the concept of communicative rationality, without falling back upon the guarantees of the great philosophical tradition, basically three ways present themselves. The *first* way is the formal-pragmatic development of the concept of communicative action introduced above in a propadeutic fashion. Linking up with formal semantics, speech-act theory, and other approaches to the pragmatics of language, this is an attempt at rationally reconstructing universal rules and necessary presuppositions of speech actions oriented to reaching understanding. Such a program aims at hypothetical reconstructions of that pre-theoretical knowledge that competent speakers bring to bear when they employ sentences in actions oriented to reaching understanding. This program holds out no prospect of an equivalent for a transcendental deduction of the communicative universals described. The hypothetical reconstructions must, however, be capable of being checked against speakers' intuitions, scattered across as broad a sociocultural spectrum as possible. While the universalistic claim of formal pragmatics cannot be conclusively redeemed (in the sense of transcendental philosophy) by way of rationally reconstructing natural intuitions, it can be rendered plausible in this way.

Second, we can try to assess the empirical usefulness of formal-pragmatic insights. For this purpose, there are above all three relevant areas of research: the explanation of pathological patterns of communication, the evolution of the foundations of sociocultural forms of life, and the ontogenesis of capabilities for action.

1 If formal pragmatics reconstructs universal and necessary conditions of communicative action, it must be possible to obtain from this reconstruction non-naturalistic standards for normal, that is, undisturbed communication. Disturbances in communication could then be traced back to violations of normalcy conditions marked out by formal pragmatics. Hypotheses of this type could be examined in the light of the material concerning patterns of systematically distorted communication that heretofore has been gathered primarily in pathogenic families from clinical points of view and evaluated in terms of the theory of socialization.
2 Anthropogenesis should also be capable of throwing light on whether the universalistic claims of formal pragmatics can be taken seriously. We would have to be able to find the formal-pragmatically described structures of action oriented to success and to understanding in the emergent properties that appear in the course of hominization and that characterize the form of life of socioculturally sociated individuals.
3 Finally, the universalistic claims of formal pragmatics can be examined in the light of the material that developmental psychology presents in regard to the acquisition of communicative and interactive capabilities. The reconstruction of action oriented to reaching understanding would have to be suitable for describing the competences whose ontogenesis has already been investigated from universalistic points of view in the Piagetian tradition.

It would obviously require a great effort to fill in these three research perspectives, even if only through secondary evaluation of the empirical research in these areas. A *third*, somewhat less demanding way would be to work up the sociological approaches to a theory of societal rationalization. Here we could link up with a well-developed tradition of social theory. This is the path I shall follow – not with the intention of carrying out historical investigations; rather, I shall take up conceptual strategies, assumptions, and lines of argument from Weber to Parsons with the systematic aim of laying out the problems that can be solved by means of a theory of rationalization developed in terms of the basic concept of communicative action. What can lead us to this goal is not a history of ideas but a history of theory with a systemic intent. I am hoping that the flexible exploration and deliberate exploitation of important theories constructed for explanatory purposes will allow us to proceed in a fruitful, problem-oriented way. [. . .]

The path of a history of theory with a systemic intent recommends itself not by reason of a false convenience that always creeps in when we cannot yet deal with a problem frontally. In my view, this alternative

– escape into the history of theory versus systematic treatment – is based on a false assessment of the status of social theory, in two respects. For one thing, the competition of paradigms has a different significance in the social sciences than in modern physics. The originality of great social theorists like Marx, Weber, Durkheim, and Mead consists – as it does for Freud and Piaget – in their having introduced paradigms that, in a certain way, still compete on an equal footing today. These theorists have remained contemporaries; at any rate, they have not become "historical" in the same sense as Newton, Maxwell, Einstein, or Planck, who achieved advances in theoretically exploiting a single fundamental paradigm.[6] For another thing, social-scientific paradigms are internally connected with the social contexts in which they emerge and become influential. In them is reflected the world- and self-understanding of various collectives; mediately they serve the interpretation of social-interest situations, horizons of aspiration and expectation.[7] Thus for any social theory, linking up with the history of theory is also a kind of test; the more freely it can take up, explain, criticize, and carry on the intentions of earlier theory traditions, the more impervious it is to the danger that particular interests are being brought to bear unnoticed in its own theorectical perspective. Moreover, reconstructions of the history of theory have the advantage that we can move back and forth between basic action-theoretic concepts, theoretical assumptions, and the illustrative use of empirical evidence, and can at the same time hold fast to the fundamental problem that is our point of reference, namely the question of whether, and if so how, capitalist modernization can be conceived as a process of one-sided rationalization.

The Theory of Communicative Action, vol. 1, pp. 102–7, 136–40.

Notes

1 On the connection between Weber's ontological presuppositions and his theory of action and methodology of *Verstehen*, see Seyla Benhabib, "Rationality and Social Action," *Philosophical Forum*, XII 1981: 356–75.

2 Compare my remarks in *Legitimation Crisis* (Boston: Beacon Press, 1975), pp. 111ff.

3 J. Habermas, "The Hermeneutic Claim to Universality," in J. Bleicher (ed.), *Contemporary Hermeneutics* (London: Routledge, 1980), pp. 181–211.

4 Alasdair MacIntyre, *The Unconscious* (London, 1958).

5 Alasdair MacIntyre, "Rationality and the Explanation of Action," in MacIntyre, *Against the Self-Images of the Age* (London: Duckworth, 1991), pp. 244–58, gives a particularly clear statement of this thesis: "If I am correct in supposing rationality to be an inescapable sociological category, then once again the positivist account of sociology in terms of a logical dichotomy between facts and values must break down. For to characterize actions and institutionalised practices as rational or irrational is to evaluate them. Nor is

it the case that this evaluation is an element superadded to an original merely descriptive element. To call an argument fallacious is always at one to describe and to evaluate it. It is highly paradoxical that the impossibility of deducing evaluative conclusions from factual premises should have been advanced as a truth of logic, when logic is itself the science in which the coincidence of description and evaluation is most obvious. The social scientist is, if I am right, committed to the values of rationality in virtue of his explanatory projects in a stronger sense than the natural scientist is. For it is not only the case that his own procedures must be rational; but he cannot escape the use of the concept of rationality in his inquiries."

6 Alan Ryan, "Normal Science or Political Ideology?," in P. Laslett, W.G. Runciman, and Q. Skinner (eds), *Philosophy, Politics and Society*, vol. 4 (Cambridge, 1972).

7 Sheldon Wolin, "Paradigms and Political Theories," in P. King and B.C. Parekh (eds), *Politics and Experience* (Cambridge, Mass., 1968); Richard Bernstein, *The Restructuring of Social and Political Theory* (Philadelphia, 1978).

13

Social Action, Purposive Activity, and Communication

The model of purposive-rational action takes as its point of departure the view that the actor is primarily oriented to attaining an end (which has been rendered sufficiently precise in terms of purposes), that he selects means that seem to him appropriate in the given situation, and that he calculates other foreseeable consequences of action as secondary conditions of success. Success is defined as the appearance in the world of a desired state, which can, in a given situation, be causally produced through goal-oriented action or omission. The effects of action comprise the results of action (which the actor foresaw and intended, or made allowance for) and the side effects (which the actor did not foresee). We call an action oriented to success *instrumental* [Figure 13.1] when we consider it under the aspect of following technical rules of action and assess the efficiency of an intervention into a complex of circumstances and events. We call an action oriented to success *strategic* when we consider it under the aspect of following rules of rational choice and assess the efficacy of influencing the decisions of a rational opponent. Instrumental actions can be connected with and subordinated to social interactions of a different type – for example, as the "task elements" of social roles; strategic actions are social actions by themselves. By

Action orientation / Action situation	Oriented to success	Oriented to reaching understanding
Non-social	Instrumental action	–
Social	Strategic action	Communicative action

Figure 13.1 Types of action

contrast, I shall speak of *communicative* action whenever the actions of the agents involved are coordinated not through egocentric calculations of success but through acts of reaching understanding. In communicative action participants are not primarily oriented to their own individual successes; they pursue their individual goals under the condition that they can harmonize their plans of action on the basis of common situation definitions. In this respect the negotiation of definitions of the situation is an essential element of the interpretive accomplishments required for communicative action.

B Orientation to success versus orientation to reaching understanding

In identifying strategic action and communicative action as types, I am assuming that concrete actions can be classified from these points of view. I do not want to use the terms "strategic" and "communicative" only to designate two analytic aspects under which the same action could be described – on the one hand as a reciprocal influencing of one another by opponents acting in a purposive-rational manner and, on the other hand, as a process of reaching understanding among members of a lifeworld. Rather, social actions can be distinguished according to whether the participants adopt either a success-oriented attitude or one oriented to reaching understanding. And, under suitable conditions, these attitudes should be identifiable on the basis of the intuitive knowledge of the participants themselves.

In the framework of action theory, the conceptual analysis of the two attitudes cannot be understood as a psychological task. It is not my aim to characterize behavioral dispositions empirically, but to grasp structural properties of processes of reaching understanding, from which we can derive general pragmatic presuppositions of communicative action. To explain what I mean by "an attitude oriented to reaching understanding," I have to analyze the concept of "reaching understanding." This is not a question of the predicates an observer uses when describing processes of reaching understanding, but of the pre-theoretical knowledge of competent speakers, who can themselves distinguish situations in which they are causally exerting an influence *upon* others from those in which they are coming to an understanding *with* them, and who know when their attempts have failed. Once we are able to specify the standards on which these distinctions are implicitly based, we will be in a position to explain the concept of reaching understanding.

Reaching understanding [*Verständigung*] is considered to be a process of reaching agreement [*Einigung*] among speaking and acting subjects. Naturally, a group of persons can feel at one in a mood which is so diffuse that it is difficult to identify the propositional content or the intentional object to which it is directed. Such a collective like-mindedness [*Gleichgestimmtheit*] does not satisfy the conditions for the type of agreement [*Einverständnis*] in which attempts at reaching understanding terminate when they are successful. A communicatively achieved agreement, or one that is mutually presupposed in communicative action, is propositionally differentiated. Owing to this linguistic structure, it cannot be merely induced through outside influence; it has to be accepted or presupposed as valid by the participants. To this extent it can be distinguished from merely de facto accord [*Übereinstimmung*]. Processes of reaching understanding aim at an agreement that meets the conditions of rationally motivated assent [*Zustimmung*] to the content of an utterance. A communicatively achieved agreement has a rational basis; it cannot be imposed by either party, whether instrumentally through intervention in the situation directly or strategically through influencing the decisions of opponents. Agreement can indeed be objectively obtained by force; but what comes to pass manifestly through outside influence or the use of violence cannot count subjectively as agreement. Agreement rests on common *convictions*. The speech act of one person succeeds only if the other accepts the offer contained in it by taking (however implicitly) a "yes" or "no" position on a validity-claim that is in principle criticizable. Both ego, who raises a validity-claim with his utterance, and alter, who recognizes or rejects it, base their decisions on potential grounds or reasons.

If we were not in a position to refer to the model of speech, we could not even begin to analyze what it means for two subjects to come to an understanding with one another. Reaching understanding is the inherent telos of human speech. Naturally, speech and understanding are not related to one another as means to end. But we can explain the concept of reaching understanding only if we specify what it means to use sentences with a communicative intent. The concepts of speech and understanding reciprocally interpret one another. Thus we can analyze the formal-pragmatic features of the attitude oriented to reaching understanding in connection with the model of the attitude of participants in communication, one of whom – in the simplest case – carries out a speech act, to which the other takes a "yes" or "no" position (even though utterances in the communicative practice of everyday life usually do not have a standard linguistic form and often have no verbal form at all). [. . .]

Our classification of speech acts can serve to introduce three pure types – or better, *limit cases* – of communicative action: conversation, normatively regulated action, and dramaturgical action. If we further take into account the internal relation of strategic action to perlocutionary acts and imperatives, we get the classification of linguistically mediated interactions in Figure [13.2.]

Types of action \ Formal-pragmatic features	Characteristic speech acts	Functions of speech	Action orientations	Basic attitudes	Validity-claims	World-relations
Strategic action	Perlocutions Imperatives	Influencing one's opposite number	Oriented to success	Objectivating	(Effectiveness)	Objective world
Conversation	Constatives	Representation of state of affairs	Oriented to reaching understanding	Objectivating	Truth	Objective world
Normatively regulated action	Regulatives	Establishment of interpersonal relations	Oriented to reaching understanding	Norm-conformative	Rightness	Social world
Dramaturgical action	Expressives	Self-representation	Oriented to reaching understanding	Expressive	Truthfulness	Subjective world

Figure 13.2   Pure types of linguistically mediated interaction

F   Formal and empirical pragmatics

Even if the program I have outlined for a theory of speech acts were carried out, one might ask what would be gained for a useful sociological theory of action by such a formal-pragmatic approach. The question arises, why would not an empirical-pragmatic approach be better for this, an approach that did not dwell on the rational reconstruction of isolated, highly idealized speech acts but started at once with the communicative practice of everyday life? From the side of linguistics there are interesting contributions to the analysis of stories and texts,[1] from sociology contributions to conversational analysis,[2] from anthropology contributions to the ethnography of speech,[3] and from psychology investigations into the pragmatic variables of linguistic interaction.[4] By comparison, formal pragmatics – which, in its reconstructive intention (that is, in the sense of a theory of competence), is directed to the universal presuppositions of communicative action[5] – seems to be hopelessly removed from actual language use.[6] Under these circumstances, does it make any sense to insist on a formal-pragmatic grounding for an action theory?

I would like to respond to this question by first (1) enumerating the methodological steps through which formal pragmatics gains a connection to empirical pragmatics; then I shall (2) identify the problems that make it necessary to clarify the rational foundations of processes of reaching understanding; finally, I would like (3) to take up a strategically important argument about which empirical pragmatics has to learn from formal pragmatics if the problem of rationality is not to end up in the wrong place – that is, in the orientations for action, as it does in Max Weber's theory of action – but in the general structures of the lifeworld to which acting subjects belong.

(1) The pure types of linguistically mediated interaction can be brought progressively closer to the complexity of natural situations without sacrificing all theoretical perspectives for analyzing the coordination of interactions. This task consists in reversing step by step the strong idealizations by which we have built up the concept of communication action:

- In addition to the basic modes, we first admit the concretely shaped illocutionary forces that form the culture-specific net of possible interpersonal relations standardized in each individual language.
- In addition to the standard forms of speech acts, we admit other forms of linguistic realization of speech acts.
- In addition to explicit speech acts, we admit elliptically foreshortened, extra-verbally supplemented, implicit utterances, for understanding which the hearer is thrown back upon the knowledge of non-standardized, contingent contexts.
- In addition to direct speech acts, we admit indirect, transposed, and ambiguous expressions, the meaning of which has to be inferred from the context.
- The focus is enlarged from isolated acts of communication (and yes/no responses) to sequences of speech acts, to texts or conversations, so that conversational implications can come into view.
- In addition to the objectivating, norm-conformative, and expressive basic attitudes, we admit an overlapping performative attitude, to take account of the fact that with each speech act participants in communication relate simultaneously to something in the objective, social, and subjective worlds.
- In addition to the level of acts of communication (that is, speech), we bring in the level of communicative action (that is, the coordination of the plans of individual participants).
- Finally, in addition to communicative action, we include in our analysis the resources of the background knowledge (that is, lifeworlds) from which participants feed their interpretations.

These extensions amount to dropping the methodological provisions that we began with in introducing standard speech acts. In the standard case the literal meaning of the sentences uttered coincides with what the speaker means with his speech acts.[7] However, the more that what the speaker means with his utterance is made to depend on a background knowledge that remains implicit, the more the context-specific meaning of the utterance can diverge from the literal meaning of what is said.

When one drops the idealization of a complete and literal representation of the meaning of utterances, the resolution of another problem is also made easier – namely, distinguishing and identifying in natural situations actions oriented to understanding and actions oriented to success. Here we must take into consideration that not only do illocutions appear in strategic-action contexts, but perlocutions appear in contexts of communicative action as well. Cooperative interpretive processes run through different phases. In the initial phase participants are often handicapped by the fact that their interpretations do not overlap sufficiently for the purpose of coordinating actions. In this phase participants have either to shift to the level of metacommunication or to employ means of indirectly achieving understanding. Coming indirectly to an understanding proceeds according to the model of intentionalist semantics. Through perlocutionary effects, the speaker gives the hearer something to understand which he cannot (yet) directly communicate. In this phase, then, the perlocutionary acts have to be embedded in contexts of communicative action. These strategic *elements* within a use of language oriented to reaching understanding can be distinguished from strategic *actions* through the fact that the entire sequence of a stretch of talk stands – on the part of all participants – under the presuppositions of communicative action.

(2) An empirical pragmatics without a formal-pragmatic point of departure would not have the conceptual instruments needed to recognize the rational basis of linguistic communication in the confusing complexity of the everyday scenes observed. It is only in formal-pragmatic investigations that we can secure for ourselves an idea of reaching understanding that can guide empirical analysis into particular problems – such as the linguistic representation of different levels of reality, the manifestation of communication pathologies, or the development of a decentered understanding of the world.

The linguistic *demarcation of the levels of reality* of "play" and "seriousness," the linguistic construction of a fictive reality, wit and irony, transposed and paradoxical uses of language, allusions and the contradictory withdrawal of validity-claims at a metacommunicative level – all these accomplishments rest on intentionally confusing modalities of being. For clarifying the mechanisms of deception that a speaker has to master to do this, formal pragmatics can do more than even the most precise empirical description of the phenomena to be explained. With training in the basic modes of language use, the growing child gains the ability to demarcate the subjectivity of his own expressions from the objectivity of an external reality, from the normativity of

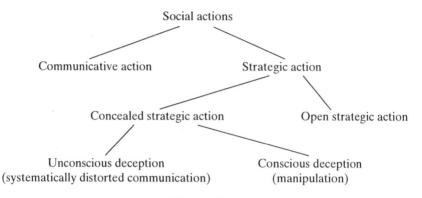

Figure 13.3

society, and from the intersubjectivity of the medium of language itself. In learning how to deal hypothetically with the corresponding validity-claims, he practices drawing the categorial "is" and "ought," sign and meaning. With these modalities of being he gets hold of the deceptive phenomena that first spring from the unwilling confusion between his own subjectivity, on the one hand, and the domains of the objective, the normative, and the intersubjective, on the other. He now knows how one can master the confusions, produce de-differentiations intentionally, and employ them in fiction, wit, irony, and the like.[8]

The situation is similar with manifestations of *systematically distorted communication*. Here too formal pragmatics can contribute to the explanation of phenomena that are first identified only on the basis of an intuitive understanding matured by clinical experience. Such communication pathologies can be conceived of as the result of a confusion between actions oriented to reaching understanding and actions oriented to success. In situations of concealed strategic action, at least one of the parties behaves with an orientation to success, but leaves others to believe that all the presuppositions of communicative action are satisfied. This is the case of manipulation which we mentioned in connection with perlocutionary acts. On the other hand, the kind of unconscious repression of conflicts that the psychoanalyst explains in terms of defense mechanisms leads to disturbances of communication on both the intrapsychic and interpersonal levels.[9] In such cases at least one of the parties is deceiving himself about the fact that he is acting with an attitude oriented to success and is only keeping up the appearance of communicative action. The place of systematically distorted communication within a framework of a theory of communicative action can be seen in Figure [13.3].

In the present context, the main advantage of a formal pragmatics is that it highlights, in the pure types of linguistically mediated interaction, precisely those aspects under which social actions embody different sorts of knowledge. The theory of communicative action can make good the weaknesses we found in Weber's action theory, inasmuch as it does not remain fixated on purposive rationality as the only aspect under which action can be criticized and improved. Drawing on the types of action introduced above, I would like now to comment briefly on the different aspects of the rationality of action.

Teleological actions can be judged under the aspect of effectiveness. The rules of action embody technically and strategically useful knowledge, which can be criticized in reference to truth claims and can be improved through a feedback relation with the growth of empirical-theoretical knowledge. This knowledge is stored in the form of technologies and strategies.

Constative speech acts, which not only embody knowledge but explicitly represent it and make conversations possible, can be criticized under the aspect of truth. In cases of more obstinate controversy concerning the truth of statements, theoretical discourse offers its services as a continuation, with different means, of action oriented to reaching understanding. When discursive examination loses its ad hoc character and empirical knowledge is systematically placed in question, when quasi-natural learning processes are guided through the sluices of argumentation, there results a cumulative effect – this knowledge is stored in the form of theories.

Normatively regulated speech acts embody moral-practical knowledge. They can be contested under the aspect of rightness. Like claims to truth, controversial claims to rightness can be made thematic and examined discursively. In cases of disturbance of the regulative use of language, practical discourse offers its services as a continuation of consensual action with other means. In moral-practical argumentation, participants can test both the rightness of a given action in relation to a given norm, and, at the next level, the rightness of such a norm itself. This knowledge is handed down in the form of legal and moral representations.

Dramaturgical actions embody a knowledge of the agent's own subjectivity. These expressions can be criticized as untruthful, that is, rejected as deceptions or self-deceptions. Self-deceptions can be dissolved in therapeutic dialogue by argumentative means. Expressive knowledge can be explicated in terms of those values that underlie need interpretations, the interpretations of desires and emotional attitudes. Value-standards are dependent in turn on innovations in the domain of evaluative expressions. These are reflected in an exemplary manner in works of art. The aspects of the rationality of action are summarized in Figure [13.4].

(3) This interconnection of action orientations, types of knowledge, and forms of argumentation is, of course, inspired by Weber's idea that

Types of action	Type of knowledge embodied	Form of argumentation	Model of transmitted knowledge
Teleological action: instrumental, strategic	Technically and strategically useful knowledge	Theoretical discourse	Technologies Strategies
Constative speech acts (conversation)	Empirical-theoretical knowledge	Theoretical discourse	Theories
Normatively regulated action	Moral-practical knowledge	Practical discourse	Legal and moral representations
Dramaturgical action	Aesthetic practical knowledge	Therapeutic and aesthetic critique	Works of art

Figure 13.4   Aspects of the rationality of action

in modern Europe, with the development of science, morals, and art, stores of explicit knowledge were differentiated out; these flowed into various domains of institutionalized everyday action and, as it were, put under the pressure of rationalization certain action orientations that had been determined in a traditionalist manner. The aspects of the rationality of action that we found in communicative action should now permit us to grasp processes of societal rationalization across their whole breadth, and no longer solely from the selective viewpoint of the rationalization of purposive-rational action.

In posing the problem in this way, the role of implicit knowledge is not given its due. We are not yet clear about the horizon of everyday action into which the explicit knowledge of cultural experts comes rushing, nor about how the communicative practice of everyday life actually changes with this influx. The concept of action oriented to reaching understanding has the additional – and quite different – advantage of throwing light on this background of implicit knowledge which enters *a tergo* into cooperative processes of interpretation. Communicative action takes place within a lifeworld that remains at the backs of participants in communication. It is present to them only in the pre-reflective form of taken-for-granted background assumptions and naïvely mastered skills.

The Theory of Communicative Action, vol. 1, pp. 285–8, 327–35.

Notes

1 W. Kummer, *Grundlagen der Texttheorie* (Hamburg, 1975); M. Halliday, *System and Function in Language: Selected Papers* (Oxford, 1976); K. Bach and R.M. Hanisch, *Linguistic Communication and Speech Acts* (Cambridge, 1979).

2 M. Coulthard, *An Introduction into Discourse Analysis* (London, 1977); L. Churchill, *Questioning Strategies in Sociolinguistics* (Rowley, Mass., 1978); J. Schenken (ed.), *Studies in the Organization of Conversational Interaction* (New York, 1978); S. Jacobs, "Recent Advances in Discourse Analysis," *Quarterly Journal of Speech*, 66, 1980: 450ff.

3 D. Hymes (ed.), *Language in Culture and Society* (New York, 1964) and "Models of the Interactions of Language and Social Life," in J. Gumperz and D. Hymes (eds), *Directions in Sociolinguistics* (New York, 1972), pp. 35ff.

4 R. Rommetveit, *On Message-Structure* (New York, 1974).

5 K.O. Apel, "Sprechakttheorie und transzendentale Sprachpragmatik," in Apel (ed.), *Sprachpragmatik und Philosophie* (Frankfurt, 1976), pp. 10ff; J. Habermas, "What is Universal Pragmatics?".

6 See the critical appraisal of the formal-pragmatic approaches of Allwood, Grice, and myself in Kreckel, *Communicative Acts*, pp. 14ff.

7 This is the methodological meaning of Searle's "principle of expressibility," *Speech Acts* (Cambridge, 1970), pp. 87–8. Compare T. Binkley, "The Principle of Expressibility," *Philosophy and Phenomenological Research*, 39, 1979: 307ff.

8 J. Habermas, "Universalpragmatische Hinweise auf das System der Ich-Abgrenzungen," in M. Auwärter, E. Kirsch, and M. Schröter (eds), *Kommunikation, Interaktion, Identität* (Frankfurt, 1976), pp. 332ff, and "Some Distinctions in Universal Pragmatics," *Theory and Society*, 3, 1976: 155–67.

9 J.M. Ruskin, "An Evaluative Review of Family Interaction Research," *Family Process*, 11, 1972: 365ff; J. H. Weakland, "The Double Bind Theory: A Reflexive Hindsight," *Family Process*, 13, 1974: 269ff; S. S. Kety, "From Rationalization to Reason," *American Journal of Psychiatry*, 131, 1974: 957ff; D. Reiss, "The Family and Schizophrenia," *American Journal of Psychiatry*, 133, 1976: 181ff.

14

The Three Roots of Communicative Action

We have distinguished three structural components of speech acts: the propositional, the illocutionary, and the expressive. If we take as our basis the normal form of a speech act ("I am telling you that p;" "I promise you that q;" "I admit to you that r"), we can say that the propositional component is represented by a dependent sentence with propositional content ("that p"). Each such sentence can be transformed into an assertoric sentence with descriptive content. The structure of the latter can be clarified in terms of an analysis of simple predicative sentences (e.g., "The ball is red"). The illocutionary component can be represented in normal form by a superordinated performative sentence that is constructed with the first-person pronoun (as the subject expression), a performative verb (with a predicative function), and a personal pronoun in the second person (as [indirect] object). The structure of such sentences can be clarified in terms of an analysis of the special case of institutionally bound speech acts with which an actor fulfills a single, well-circumscribed norm (e.g., betting, congratulating, marrying). The expressive component remains implicit in the normal form, but it can always be expanded into an expressive sentence. The latter is constructed with the first-person pronoun (as subject expression) and an intentional [in Husserl's sense] verb (with a predicative function), while the place of the logical object is occupied either by an object (e.g., "I love T") or by a nominalized state of affairs (e.g., "I fear that p"). The fact that each of these three structural components exhibits significant peculiarities speaks for their mutual independence. With each component there is connected *one* property that is constitutive for grammatically differentiated understanding in general. *Assertoric sentences* can be true or false. Truth-conditional semantics has singled them out to show the internal connection between meaning and validity. With *performative sentences* the speaker carries out an action in saying something. The theory of speech acts has used them to establish the internal connection between speaking and acting. Performative sentences are neither true nor false; the actions carried out with their help can be understood as complements to commands (such as,

"You should help *A*"). In comparison to assertoric sentences, *expressive sentences* have the peculiar feature that when they are meaningfully employed neither their objective reference nor their content can be contested – mistaken identification is excluded, as is criticism of a knowledge to which the speaker has privileged access. The internal connection between intention and meaning, between what is meant and what is said, can be demonstrated in connection with such first-person sentences. Furthermore, there is no logical continuum between assertoric, normative, and expressive sentences such that sentences of one category can be inferred from sentences of another category. The structural components of speech acts cannot be reduced to one another.

What interests us in the present context is the correlation of these three components of speech acts with cognitions, obligations, and expressions. If, for purposes of comparison, we bring in here the *prelinguistic correlates* familiar to us from behavioral research, we see how they are changed at the linguistic level. Perceptions and representations take on a propositional structure, as does adaptive behaviour. Ritually generated solidarity, obligations to the collectivity are split up at the level of normatively regulated action into intersubjective recognition of existing norms on the one hand, and norm-conformative motives for action on the other. Spontaneous expressions linked to the body lose their involuntary character when they are replaced with or interpreted by linguistic utterances. Expressive utterances serve communicative ends; they can be employed intentionally [in Husserl's sense].

When communicative acts take the shape of grammatical speech, the symbolic structure has penetrated *all* components of interaction; the cognitive-instrumental grasp of reality and the steering mechanism that attunes the behavior of different interaction partners to one another, as well as the actors and their behavior dispositions, get connected to linguistic communication and are symbolically restructured. At the same time, this transposition of cognitions, obligations, and expressions onto a linguistic basis makes it possible in turn for the means of communication to take on new functions – in addition to the function of *reaching understanding*, those of *coordinating action* and *socializing actors* as well. Under the aspect of reaching understanding, communicative acts serve the *transmission of culturally stored knowledge* – as shown above, cultural tradition reproduces itself through the medium of action oriented to reaching understanding. Under the aspect of coordinating action, the same communicative acts serve the *fulfillment of norms* appropriate to a given context; social integration also takes place via this medium. Under the aspect of socialization, finally, communicative acts serve the construction of internal controls on behavior, in general, the *formation of personality structures*; one of Mead's fundamental insights is that socialization processes take place via linguistically mediated interaction. [. . .]

The binding effect of illocutionary forces comes about, ironically, through the fact that participants can say "no" to speech-act offers. The critical character of this saying "no" distinguishes taking a position in this way from a reaction based solely on caprice. A hearer can be "bound" by speech-act offers because he is not permitted arbitarily to refuse them but only to say "no" to them, that is, to reject them for reasons. We are already familiar with two consequences for the structure of communication that flow from this "being able to say no."[1]

I am referring, *first* of all, to the stratification of action oriented to reaching understanding into naïve and reflexive forms of communication. Because communicative action demands an orientation to validity-claims, it points from the start to the possibility of settling disagreements by adducing reasons. From this can develop institutionalized forms of argumentative speech, in which validity-claims normally raised naïvely, and immediately affirmed or denied, can be made thematic as controversial validity-claims and discussed hypothetically. In the *second* place, I am referring to the demarcation of action oriented to understanding from action oriented to consequences. Generally, alter is moved to link up his actions with ego's actions by a complicated mix of empirical and rational motives. Because communicative action demands an orientation to validity-claims, it points from the start to the possibility that participants will distinguish more or less sharply between having an influence *upon* one another and reaching an understanding *with* one another. Thus, as we shall see, a generalized "willingness to accept" can develop along two lines: empirical ties forged by inducement and intimidation, on the one hand, and rational trust motivated by agreement based on reasons, on the other hand.

A *further* consequence of being able to say "no," which was merely suggested above, concerns the actors themselves. If one aims to reconstruct how participants learn to orient their actions explicitly to validity-claims, and wants to do so by means of the mechanism of taking the attitude of the other, the model of inner dialogue, which Mead used rather too unspecifically, turns out in fact to be helpful. In anticipating from alter a negative answer to his own speech act, and raising against himself an objection that alter might raise, ego understands what it means to make a *criticizable* validity-claim. As soon, then, as ego masters the orientation to validity-claims, he can repeat the internalization of discursive relations once more. Now alter already encounters him with the expectation that ego is not assuming the communicative role of the first person only in a naïve manner, but will expand it, if necessary, to the role of a proponent in argumentation. If ego makes *this* attitude of alter his own, that is to say, if he views himself through the eyes of an arguing opponent and considers how he will answer to his critique, he gains a reflective relation to himself. By internalizing the role of a participant in argumentation, ego becomes capable of self-criticism. It is the relation-to-self established by this model of self-criticism that we shall call "reflective." Knowing that one does not know has, since Socrates, rightly been regarded as the basis for self-knowledge.

The reflective relation-to-self takes on different shadings according to the modes of language use. Ego can take up a relation to himself by way of a critique of his own statement, his own action, or his own self-presentation. The self to which he then relates is not a mysterious something; it is familiar to him from the communicative practice of daily life; it is ego himself in the communicative role of the first person, as he asserts the existence of states of affairs in an objectivating attitude, or enters into an interpersonal relation regarded as legitimate in the norm-conformative attitude, or makes a subjective experience accessible to a public in an expressive attitude. Correspondingly, ego can relate to himself according to the model of self-criticism: as an *epistemic* subject who is capable of learning and has already acquired a certain knowledge in his cognitive-instrumental dealings with reality, or as a *practical* subject who is capable of acting and has already formed a certain character or a superego in interactions with his reference persons, or as an *affective* subject who is sensitive, "passionate" in Feuerbach's sense, and has already demarcated from the external world of facts and norms a special domain of subjectivity marked by privileged access and intuitive presence.

It is of course misleading to speak of three subjects. In the perspective of self-criticism, when ego adopts in relation to himself the role of a possible opponent in a debate about validity-claims he has raised naïvely, he encounters a self that is, naturally, one and the same under all three aspects. Indeed, it is one and the same from the very start, so to speak; there is no need at all for a subsequent identification of the three relations-to-self.

We have presupposed that ego can take up these different relations to himself only by confronting himself as a communicatively acting subject, by adopting toward himself the attitude of *another* participant in argumentation. He encounters himself just as he has adopted a performative attitude. It is this attitude of a first person toward a second that guarantees the unity in the changing modes of language use, the continuity in the transitions between objectivating, norm-conformative, and expressive attitudes that we continually make in communicative practice. From a genetic standpoint, the performative attitude can be understood, perhaps, as the result of a secularization and generalization of that emotionally ambivalent attitude toward sacred objects that originally secured the recognition of moral authority. This transformation becomes necessary to the degree that the illocutionary components of speech acts are released from their symbiotic entanglement with archaic institutions and differentiated so that assertoric and expressive sentences are also endowed with illocutionary forces, and in this way modalized and incorporated in communicative actions.

If it is the performative attitude that secures unity through changes in mode, then practical self-consciousness has a certain priority over epistemic and affective self-consciousness. The reflective relation-to-self is the ground of the actor's accountability. A responsible actor behaves self-critically not only in his directly moralizable actions but also in his cognitive and expressive utterances. Although accountability is at bottom a moral-practical category, it also extends to the cognitions and expressions included in the validity spectrum of action oriented to reaching understanding.

The Theory of Communicative Action, vol. 2, pp. 62–3, 73–6.

Notes

1 From Herder through Nietzsche to Heidegger and Gehlen, being able to say "no" has been repeatedly stressed as an anthropological monopoly of ours. The thesis put forward by Popper and Adorno in different versions, to the effect that reliable knowledge can only be gained through the negation of statements, is based on the same insight.

PART V

Ethics and Law

Introduction

Habermas's concept of validity-claims covers both the domain of factual truth and that of moral or expressive statements. Although the validity of norms or the sincerity (Wahrhaftigkeit) *of expressions of subjective feelings must not be confused with propositional truth, we do not do justice to the meaning of normative validity if we simply say that truth and falsity are not relevant to ethical statements: "rightness and truth come together in that both claims can only be vindicated discursively, by way of argumentation and a rational consensus."*[1]

Habermas's model thus contrasts with the more familiar ethical subjectivist position acording to which moral prescriptions are constrained only by requirements of consistency and practicability. Habermas notes that a discourse ethic, which he sees as one of the reconstructive sciences,[2] *is based on the claim "that (a) normative validity claims have a cognitive meaning and can be treated like truth claims, and that (b) the grounding of norms and prescriptions demands the carrying-through of an actual dialogue and in the last instance is not possible monologically, in the form of an argumentation process hypothetically run through in the mind."*[3]

Habermas starts from a principle of universalization related to, but also importantly different from, that of Kant. As McCarthy puts it, "The emphasis shifts from what each can will without contradiction to be a universal law to what all can will in agreement to be a universal norm."[4] *This discourse ethic is, Habermas concedes, necessarily somewhat formal. It is based on a procedure, that of practical discourse, rather than specific ethical prescriptions.*[5] *It draws a sharp distinction between questions of justice and questions of the "good life;" the latter can only be addressed in the context of diverse cultures or forms of life or of individual life-projects.*[6] *On the other hand, a universalistic morality can bridge the division between morality and law, in that both are based, in varying ways, on a relation to discourse. As he had put it much earlier, in* Legitimation Crisis, *"the validity of all norms is tied to discursive will-formation."*[7]

Habermas makes two related claims for his discourse ethic, as pre-

sented here in readings 15–17. First, it expresses our moral intuitions, at least as these bear on the process of discursive justification of norms.[8] Second, this focus on normative consensus as opposed to abstract universalizability means that a discourse ethic, unlike Kant's, can go beyond a pure concept of justice to include the more universal structural aspects of ways of life which relate to communicative action itself.[9] Thus even a moral philosophy which confines itself to justifying and elucidating the "moral point of view," and avoids pre-empting the concrete moral decisions of social actors, includes a kind of vision of the good life as one which embodies these forms of moral-political reasoning.

Habermas's and Apel's discourse ethics has attracted very substantial discussion. Their position falls squarely on the battle-lines between those who uphold an essentially Kantian notion of universalizability, such as R.M. Hare and, in a related application to social justice, John Rawls,* and the "contextualists" or "communitarians" who stress the embeddedness of moral principles in cultures and ways of life, where these are themselves seen as objects as well as sources of moral value.[10] This ongoing controversy is in many ways a replay of the opposition between Hegel and Kant. Habermas addresses this issue in the final extract from Moral Consciousness and Communicative Action (reading 17): his strategy is essentially to socialize Kant's individualistic moral theory in such a way as to meet Hegelian objections, or at least to point in the direction of their resolution.

Readings 18–20 are taken from Habermas's most recent book, Between Norms and Values, in which he develops the implications of this model for a theory of law and the democratic state. A variant of the same discourse principle on which he had based his ethical theory also forms a foundation for a legitimate political order, and it can thus be shown, he suggests, that democracy is a condition for genuine legality.

Notes

1 *The Theory of Communicative Action*, vol. I, p. 109
2 *Moral Consciousness and Communicative Action*, p. 116
3 Ibid. p. 68; below, p. 186.
4 T. McCarthy, *The Critical Theory of Jürgen Habermas* (Cambridge: Polity, 1978), p.326.
5 *Moral Consciousness and Communicative Action*, p. 103.
6 Ibid. p. 108
7 *Legitimation Crisis*, p. 87.
8 *Moral Consciousness and Communicative Action*, p. 180.
9 Ibid.
10 See S. Benhabib and F. Dallmayr (eds), *The Communicative Ethics Controversy* (Cambridge, Mass.: MIT Press, 1990) Kenneth Baynes, *The Normative Grounds of Social Criticism: Kant, Rawls, and Habermas* (Albany N.Y.: State University of New York, 1992).

Further Reading

Stephen White, *The Recent Work of Jürgen Habermas: Reason, Justice and Modernity* (Cambridge: Cambridge University Press, 1988); Benhabib and Dallmayr, *The Communicative Ethics Controversy*; Baynes, *The Normative Grounds of Social Criticism.*

15

Discourse Ethics

When employing normative utterances in everyday life, we raise claims to validity that we are prepared to defend against criticism. When we discuss moral-practical questions of the form "What ought I to do?" we presuppose that the answers need not be arbitrary; we trust our ability to distinguish in principle between right norms or commands and wrong ones. But if normative sentences do not admit of truth in the narrow sense of the word "true," that is, *in the same sense* in which descriptive statements can be true or false, we will have to formulate the task of explaining the meaning of "moral truth" or, if that expression is already misleading, the meaning of "normative rightness" in such a way that we are not tempted to assimilate the one type of sentence to the other. We will have to proceed on a weaker assumption, namely, that normative claims to validity are *analogous to truth claims.* We will have to return to Toulmin's* formulation of the basic question of ethics: "What kind of argument, of reasoning is it proper for us to accept in support of moral decisions?"[1] Toulmin abandons the semantic analysis of expressions and sentences, focussing instead on the issue of the mode in which normative propositions are justified, the *form of the arguments* adduced in defending or rejecting norms and commands, and the criteria for good reasons that motivate us, by dint of insight, to recognize demands as moral obligations. "What kind of things make a conclusion worthy of belief?"[2] With this query Toulmin makes the transition to the level of a theory of argumentation.

[...] The attempt to ground ethics in the form of a logic of moral argumentation has no chance of success unless we can identify a special type of validity-claim connected with commands and norms and can identify it on the level on which moral dilemmas initially emerge: within the horizon of the lifeworld. [...]

On the face of it, *assertoric statements* used in *constative speech acts* appear to be related to *facts* as *normative statements* used in *regulative speech acts* are related to *legitimately ordered interpersonal relations.* The *truth* of propositions seems to signify the *existence* of states of affairs in much the same way as the *rightness* of actions signifies the *observance* of norms. If we look at the matter more closely, however, we notice some interesting differences. The relation of speech acts to norms is not the same as the relation of speech acts to facts. Let us look at the case of moral norms that can be formulated in terms of universal "ought" sentences of commandments:

(a) One ought not to kill anybody.
(a′) It is commanded not to kill anybody.

We make reference to norms of action of the above kind in regulative speech acts, and we do so in a variety of ways: by giving orders, making contracts, opening meetings, issuing warnings, granting exceptions, giving advice, etc. A moral norm, however, lays claim to meaning and validity regardless of whether it is promulgated or made use of in a specific way. A norm may be formulated in a statement like (a), but this act of formulating it, i.e., of writing a sentence, *need not* itself be conceived of as a speech act, that is, as something other than the impersonal expression of the norm. Statements such as (a) are commands that we can address *secondarily* in one way or another through speech acts. This has no equivalent in the domain of facts. There are no assertoric propositions that have an existence independent of speech acts, as norms do. If such assertoric statements are to have pragmatic meaning at all, they *must* be used in a speech act. Unlike sentences (a) and (a′), descriptive statements such as "Iron is magnetic" or "It is the case that iron is magnetic" cannot be expressed or used independently of the illocutionary role of a certain type of speech act if they are to retain their assertoric power.

We can account for this asymmetry by saying that claims to truth reside *only* in speech acts, whereas the locus of normative claims to validity is primarily in norms and only derivatively in speech acts.[3] To use an ontological mode of expression, we might say that this asymmetry is due to the fact that the orders of society, which we either conform to or deviate from, are not constituted *independently of validity*, as are the orders of nature, toward which we can assume an objectivating attitude. The social reality that we address in our regulative speech acts has by its very nature an *intrinsic* link to normative validity-claims. Claims to truth, on the other hand, have no such intrinsic link to entities; they are inherently related only to the constative speech acts by which we refer to entities when we use fact-stating locutions to represent states of affairs.

Owing to the fact that normative validity-claims are built into the universe of norms, the latter reveals a peculiar kind of objectivity vis-à-vis regulative speech acts, an objectivity that the universe of facts does not possess vis-à-vis constative speech acts. To be sure, "objectivity" in this connection refers only to the independence of "objective spirit," for entities and facts are, of course, independent in a completely different sense than is everything we consider part of the social world when we take a norm-conformative attitude. For example, norms are dependent upon the continual re-establishment of legitimately ordered interpersonal relationships. They would assume a utopian character in the negative sense and lose their very meaning if we did not *complement* them, at least in our minds, with actors who might follow them and actions that might fulfill them. States of affairs, for their part, must be assumed to exist independently of whether we formulate them by means of true propositions or not.

Normative claims to validity, then, *mediate a mutual dependence* of language and the social world that does not exist for the relation of language to the objective world. This interlocking of claims to validity that reside in norms and claims to validity raised in regulative speech acts is also connected with the *ambiguous nature* of *normative validity*. While there is an unequivocal relation between existing states of affairs and true propositions about them, the "existence" or social currency of norms says nothing about whether the norms are valid. We must distinguish between the social fact that a norm is intersubjectively recognized and its worthiness to be recognized. There may be good reasons to consider the validity-claim raised in a socially accepted norm to be unjustified. Conversely, a norm whose claim to validity is in fact redeemable does not necessarily meet with actual recognition or approval. Gaining acceptance on the part of a norm is encoded in a twofold fashion because our motives for recognizing normative claims to validity are rooted both in convictions and in sanctions, that is, they derive from a complex mixture of rational insight and force. Typically, rationally motivated assent will be combined with empirical *acquiescence*, effected by weapons or goods, to form a belief in legitimacy whose component parts are difficult to isolate. Such alloys are interesting in that they indicate that a positivistic enactment of norms is not sufficient to secure their *lasting* social acceptance. Enduring acceptance of a norm *also* depends on whether, in a given context of tradition, reasons for obedience can be mobilized, reasons that suffice to make the corresponding validity-claim at least appear justified in the eyes of those concerned. Applied to modern societies, this means that there is no mass loyalty without legitimacy.[4]

But if in the long run the social currency of a norm depends on its being accepted as valid in the group to which it is addressed and if this recognition is based in turn on the expectation that the corresponding claim to validity can be redeemed with reasons, it follows that there is a connection between the "existence" of norms and the anticipated justifiability of the corresponding "ought" statements, a connection for which there is no parallel in the ontic sphere; while there is an internal connection between the existence of states of affairs and the *expectation*, held by a certain group of people, that such statements can be justified.

This difference may also explain why, when we ask what makes valid moral judgments possible, we are compelled to proceed *directly* to a logic of practical discourse, whereas determining the conditions for the validity of empirical judgments requires analysis in terms of epistemology and the philosophy of science, an analysis that is, at least initially, independent of a logic of theoretical discourse.

4 The moral principle, or the criterion for generalizing maxims of action

Following Toulmin,[5] I have recently set forth the outlines of a theory of argumentation.[6] I will not discuss that here. In what follows, I presuppose that a theory of argumentation must take the form of an "informal logic," because it is impossible to *force* agreement on theoretical and moral-practical issues either by means of deduction or on the basis of empirical evidence. To the degree to which arguments are deductively valid, i.e., compelling in terms of logical inference, they reveal nothing substantively new. To the degree to which arguments do have substantive content, they are based on experiences and needs/wants that are open to various interpretations in light of changing theories using changing systems of description. Such experiences and needs/wants thus fail to offer an *ultimate* basis for argumentation.

In theoretical discourse the gap between particular observations and general hypotheses is bridged by some canon or other of induction. An analogous bridging principle is needed for practical discourse.[7] Accordingly, all studies of the logic of moral argumentation end up having to introduce a moral principle as a rule of argumentation that has a function equivalent to the principle of induction in the discourse of the empirical sciences.

Interestingly enough, in trying to identify such a moral principle, philosophers of diverse backgrounds always come up with principles whose basic idea is the same. *All* variants of cognitivist ethics take their bearings from the basic intuition contained in Kant's categorical imperative. What I am concerned with here is not the diversity of Kantian formulations but their underlying idea, which is designed to take into account the impersonal or general character of valid universal commands. The moral principle is so conceived as to exclude as invalid any norm that could not meet with the qualified assent of all who are or might be affected by it. This bridging principle, which makes consensus possible, ensures that only those norms are accepted as valid that express a *general will*. As Kant noted time and again, moral norms must be suitable for expression as "universal laws." The categorical imperative can be understood as a principle that requires the universalizability of *modes of action* and *maxims*, or of the *interests* furthered by them (that is, those embodied in the norms of action). Kant wants to eliminate as invalid all those norms that "contradict" this requirement. He focuses on "that inner contradiction which promptly arises for an agent's maxim when his behavior can lead to its desired goal only upon the condition that it is not universally followed."[8] Admittedly, this and similar versions of the bridging principle imply a requirement of consistency which has led to *formalistic misunderstandings* and *selective interpretations*.

The principle of universalization is by no means exhausted by the requirement that moral norms must take the *form* of unconditionally universal "ought" statements. The *grammatical form* of normative statements alone, which does not permit such sentences to refer to or be addressed to particular groups or individuals, is not a sufficient condition for valid moral commands, for we could give such universal form to commands that are plainly immoral. What is more, in some respects the requirement of formal universality may well be too restrictive; it may make sense to submit non-moral norms of action (whose range of jurisdiction is socially and spatiotemporally limited) to a practical discourse (restricted in this case to those affected and hence relative), and to test them for generalizability.

Other philosophers subscribe to a less formalistic view of the consistency required by the principle of universality. Their aim is to avoid the contradictions that occur when equal cases are treated unequally and unequal ones equally. R.M. Hare has given this requirement the form of a semantic postulate. As we do when we attribute descriptive predicates ("is red"), so we should attribute normative predicates ("is of value," "is good," "is right") in *conformity with a rule*, using the same linguistic expression in all cases that are the same in the respects relevant to the particular case. Applied to moral norms, Hare's consistency postulate comes to this: every individual, before making a particular norm the basis for his moral judgment, should test whether he can advocate or "will" the adoption of this norm by every other individual in a comparable situation. This or another similar postulate is suitable to serve as a moral principle only if it is conceived as a warrant of impartiality in the process of judging. But one can hardly derive the meaning of impartiality from the notion of consistent language use.

Kurt Baier[9] and Bernard Gert[10] come closer to this meaning of the principle of universalization when they argue that valid moral norms must be generally teachable and publicly defendable. The same is true of Marcus Singer when he proposes the requirement that norms are valid only if they ensure equality of treatment.[11] Yet just as an impartial process of judging is not guaranteed by an empirical check to see that allowance for disagreement has been made, so a norm cannot be considered the expression of the common interest of all who might be affected simply because it seems acceptable to some of them under the condition that it be applied in a non-discriminatory fashion. The intuition expressed in the idea of the generalizability of maxims intends something more than this, namely, that valid norms must *deserve* recognition by *all* concerned. It is not sufficient, therefore, for *one person* to test whether he can will the adoption of a contested norm after considering the consequences and the side effects that would occur if all persons followed that norm or whether every other person in an identical position could will the adoption of such a norm. In both cases the process of judging is relative to the vantage point and perspective of *some* and not *all* concerned. True impartiality pertains only to that standpoint from which one can generalize precisely those norms that can count on universal assent because they perceptibly embody an interest common to all affected. It is these norms that deserve intersubjective recognition. Thus the impartiality of judgment is expressed in a principle that constrains *all* affected to adopt the perspectives of *all others* in the balancing of interests. The principle of universalization is intended to compel the *universal exchange of roles* that G. H. Mead called "ideal role taking" or "universal discourse."[12] Thus every valid norm has to fulfill the following condition:

> U   *All* affected can accept the consequences and the side effects its *general* observance can be anticipated to have for the satisfaction of *everyone's* interests (and these consequences are preferred to those of known alternative possibilities for regulation).

We should not mistake this principle of universalization (U) for the following principle, which already contains the distinctive idea of an ethics of discourse:

> D   Only those norms can claim to be valid that meet (or could meet) with the approval of all affected in their capacity *as participants in a practical discourse.*

This principle of discourse ethics (D), to which I will return after offering my justification for (U), already *presupposes* that we *can* justify our choice of a norm. At this point in my argument, that presupposition is what is at issue. I have introduced (U) as a rule of argumentation that makes agreement in practical discourses possible whenever matters of concern to all are open to regulation in the equal interest of everyone. Once this bridging principle has been justified, we will be able to make the transition to discourse ethics. I have formulated (U) in a way that precludes a monological application of the principle. First, (U) regulates only argumentation among a plurality of participants; second, it suggests the perspective of real-life argumentation, in which all affected are admitted as participants. [. . .]

If we keep in mind the action-coordinating function that normative validity-claims play in the communicative practice of everyday life, we see why the problems to be resolved in moral argumentation cannot be handled monologically but require a cooperative effort. By entering into a process of moral argumentation, the participants continue their communicative action in a reflexive attitude with the aim of restoring a consensus that has been disrupted. Moral argumentation thus serves to settle conflicts of action by consensual means. Conflicts in the domain of norm-guided interactions can be traced directly to some disruption of a normative consensus. Repairing a disrupted consensus can mean one of two things: restoring intersubjective recognition of a validity-claim after it has become controversial or assuring intersubjective recognition for a new validity-claim that is a substitute for the old one. Agreement of this kind expresses a *common will*. If moral argumentation is to produce this kind of agreement, however, it is not enough for the individual to reflect on whether he can assent to a norm. It is not even enough for each individual to reflect in this way and then to register his vote. What is needed is a "real" process of argumentation in which the individuals concerned cooperate. Only an intersubjective process of reaching understanding can produce an agreement that is reflexive in nature; only it can give the participants the knowledge that they have collectively become convinced of something.

From this viewpoint, the categorical imperative needs to be reformulated as follows: "Rather than ascribing as valid to all others any maxim that I can will to be a universal law, I must submit my maxim to all others for purposes of discursively testing its claim to universality. The emphasis shifts from what each can will without contradiction to be a general law, to what all can will in agreement to be a universal norm."[13] This version of the universality principle does in fact entail the idea of a cooperative process of argumentation. For one thing, nothing better prevents others from perspectivally distorting one's own interests than actual participation. It is in this pragmatic sense that the individual is the last court of appeal for judging what is in his best interest. On the other hand, the descriptive terms in which each individual perceives his interests must be open to criticism by others. Needs and wants are interpreted in the light of cultural values. Since cultural values are always components of intersubjectively shared traditions, the revision of the values used to interpret needs and wants cannot be a matter for individuals to handle monologically.[14]

5   Argumentation versus participation

Discourse ethics, then, stands or falls with two assumptions: (1) that normative claims to validity have cognitive meaning and can be treated *like* claims to truth and (2) that the justification of norms and commands requires that a real discourse be carried out and thus cannot occur in a strictly monological form, i.e., in the form of a hypothetical process of argumentation occurring in the individual mind. [. . .]

(1) The principle of discourse ethics (D) makes reference to a *procedure*, namely, the discursive redemption of normative claims to validity. To that extent discourse ethics can properly be characterized as *formal*, for it provides no substantive guidelines but only a procedure: practical discourse. Practical discourse is not a procedure for generating justified norms but a procedure for testing the validity of norms that are being proposed and hypothetically considered for adoption. That means that practical discourses depend on content brought to them from outside. It would be utterly pointless to engage in a practical discourse without a horizon provided by the lifeworld of a specific social group and without real conflicts in a concrete situation in which the actors consider it incumbent upon them to reach a consensual means of regulating some controversial social matter. Practical discourses are always related to the concrete point of departure of a disturbed normative agreement. These antecedent disruptions determine the topics that are up for discussion. This procedure, then, is not formal in the sense that it abstracts from content. Quite the contrary, in its openness, practical discourse is dependent upon contingent content being fed into it from outside. In discourse this content is subjected to a process in which particular values are ultimately discarded as being not susceptible to consensus. The question now arises as to whether this very selectivity might not make the procedure unsuitable for resolving practical questions.

(2) If we define practical issues as issues of the good life, which invariably deal with the totality of a particular form of life or the totality of an individual life-history, then ethical formalism is incisive in the literal sense: the universalization principle acts like a knife that makes razor-sharp cuts between evaluative statements and strictly normative ones, between the good and the just. While cultural values may imply a claim to intersubjective acceptance, they are so inextricably intertwined with the totality of a particular form of life that they cannot be said to claim normative validity in the strict sense. By their very nature, cultural values are at best *candidates* for embodiment in norms that are designed to express a general interest.

Participants can distance themselves from norms and normative systems that have been set off from the totality of social life only to the extent necessary to assume a hypothetical attitude toward them. Individuals who have been socialized cannot take a hypothetical attitude toward the form of life and the personal life-history that have shaped their own identity. We are now in a position to define the scope of application of a deontological ethics: it covers only practical questions that can be debated rationally, i.e., those that hold out the prospect of consensus. It deals not with value preferences but with the normative validity of norms of action.

(3) It remains for us to deal with the hermeneutic objection that the discourse-ethical procedure for justifying norms is based on an extravagant idea whose practical consequences may even be dangerous. The principle of discourse ethics, like other principles, cannot regulate problems concerning its own application. The application of rules requires a practical prudence that is *prior to* the practical reason that discourse ethics explicates. Prudence itself is not subject to rules of discourse. If that is so, the principle of discourse ethics can be effective only if it makes use of a faculty that links it with the local conventions of a hermeneutic point of departure and draws it back within the provincialism of a particular historical horizon.

This objection cannot be disputed as long as problems of application are viewed from a *third-person perspective*. The hermeneuticist's reflective insight, however, does not undercut the claim of the principle of discourse ethics to transcend all local conventions. No participant in argumentation can escape this claim as long as he takes a *performative attitude*, confronts normative claims to validity seriously, and does not objectify norms as social facts, i.e., avoids reducing them to something that is simply found in the world. The transcending force of validity-claims that are dealt with in a straightforward manner has an empirical impact as well, and the hermeneuticist's reflective insight cannot catch up with it. The history of human rights in modern constitutional states offers a wealth of examples showing that once principles have been recognized, their application does not fluctuate wildly from one situation to another but tends to have a *stable direction*. Through the reflecting mirror of different interest positions, the universal content of these norms itself makes those concerned aware of the partiality and selectivity of applications. Applications can distort the meaning of the norm itself; we can operate in a more or less biased way in the dimension of prudent application. *Learning processes* are possible in this dimension too.[15]

(4) In the face of foundationalist programs one must stress the fact that practical discourses are in fact subject to limitations. What these are has been shown with consummate clarity by Albrecht Wellmer in his unpublished manuscript "Reason and the Limits of Rational Discourse."

- Practical discourses – which must address, among other things, the question of how adequately needs are interpreted – are intimately linked with two other forms of argumentation: aesthetic and therapeutic criticism. These two forms of argumentation are not subject to the premise we posit for strict discourses, namely that *in principle* a rationally motivated agreement must always be reachable, where the phrase "in principle" signifies the counterfactual reservation "if argumentation were conducted openly and continued long enough."

But if in the last analysis forms of argumentation make up a system and cannot be isolated from one another, the fact that practical discourse, with its stricter claim, is related (along with theoretical and explicative discourse) to forms of argumentation with more lenient criteria represents a liability for the former, a liability that originates in the sociohistorical situatedness of reason.

- Practical discourses cannot be relieved of the burden of social conflicts to the degree that theoretical and explicative discourses can. They are less free of the burdens of action because contested norms tend to upset the balance of relations of intersubjective recognition. Even if it is conducted with discursive means, a dispute about norms is still rooted in the struggle for recognition.

- Like all argumentation, practical discourses resemble islands threatened with inundation in a sea of practice where the pattern of consensual conflict resolution is by no means the dominant one. The means of reaching agreement are repeatedly thrust aside by the instruments of force. Hence, action that is oriented toward ethical principles has to accommodate itself to imperatives that flow not from principles but from strategic necessities. On the one hand, the problem posed by an ethics of responsibility that is mindful of the temporal dimension is in essence trivial, since the perspective that an ethics of responsibility would use for a future-oriented assessment of the indirect effects of collective action can be derived from discourse ethics itself. On the other hand, these problems do give rise to questions of a political ethics that deals with the aporias of a political practice whose goal is radical emancipation and that must take up those themes that were once part of Marxian revolutionary theory.

These limitations of practical discourses testify to the power history has over the transcending claims and interests of reason. The skeptic for his part tends to give an overdrawn account of these limits. The key to understanding the problem is that moral judgments, which provide demotivated answers to decontextualized questions, require an offsetting *compensation*. If we are clear about the feats of abstraction to which universalist moralities owe their superiority to conventional ones, the old problem of the relationship between morality and ethical life appears in a different, rather trivial light.

For the hypothesis-testing participant in a discourse, the relevance of the experiential context of his lifeworld tends to pale. To him, the normativity of existing institutions seems just as open to question as the objectivity of things and events. In a discursive framework we perceive the lived world of the communicative practice of everyday life from an artificial, retrospective point of view: as we hypothetically consider claims to validity, the world of institutionally ordered relations becomes *moralized*, just as the world of existing states of affairs becomes *theoretized*. Facts and norms that had previously gone unquestioned can now be true or false, valid or invalid. Moreover, in the realm of subjectivity, modern art inaugurated a comparable thrust toward problematization. The world of lived experiences is aestheticized, that is, freed of the routines of *everyday perception* and the conventions of everyday action. For this reason we do well to look at the relationship of morality and ethical life as part of a more complex whole.

According to Max Weber, one of the features of Western rationalism is the creation in Europe of expert cultures that deal with cultural traditions reflectively and in so doing isolate the cognitive, aesthetic-expressive, and moral-practical components from one another. These cultures specialize in questions of truth, questions of taste, or questions of justice. With the internal differentiation into what Weber calls "spheres of value" (i.e., scientific production, art and art criticism, and law and morality), the elements that make up an almost indissoluble syndrome in the lifeworld are dissociated at the cultural level. It is only with these value-spheres that reflective perspectives emerge, perspectives from which the lifeworld appears as practice with which theory is to be mediated, as life with which art is to be reconciled (in line with the surrealist credo), or ethical life to which morality must be related.

From the viewpoint of a participant in moral argumentation, the lifeworld that he has put at a distance, a world in which unproblematic cultural givens of cognitive, expressive, or moral origin are interwoven with one another, appears as the sphere of ethical life. In this sphere, duties are so inextricably tied to concrete habitual behavior that they derive their self-evident quality from background convictions. In the sphere of ethical life, questions of justice are posed only within the horizon of questions concerning the good life, questions which have *always already been answered.* Under the unrelenting moralizing gaze of the participant in discourse this totality has lost its quality of naive acceptance, and the normative power of the factual has weakened. Familiar institutions can be transformed into so many instances of problematic justice. Under this gaze the store of traditional norms has disintegrated into those norms that can be justified in terms of principles and those that operate only de facto. The fusion of validity and social acceptance that characterizes the lifeworld has disintegrated. With this, the practice of everyday life separates into the component of the practical (into norms and values that can be subjected to the demands of strict moral justification) and into another component that cannot be moralized (a component that comprises the particular value-orientations integrated to form individual and collective modes of life).

To be sure, cultural values too transcend de facto behavior. They congeal into historical and biographical syndromes of value-orientations through which subjects can distinguish the good life from the reproduction of mere life. But ideas of the good life are not something we hold before us as an abstract "ought." Rather, they shape the identities of groups and individuals in such a way that they form an intrinsic part of culture or personality. Thus the development of the moral point of view goes hand in hand with a differentiation within the practical into *moral questions* and *evaluative questions*. Moral questions can in principle be decided rationally, i.e., in terms of *justice* or the generalizability of interests. Evaluative questions present themselves at the most general level as issues of the *good life* (or of self-realization); they are accessible to rational discussion only *within* the unproblematic horizon of a concrete historical form of life or the conduct of an individual life.

If we consider the abstraction achieved by morality, two things become clear: (1) the increase in rationality achieved when we isolate issues of justice and (2) the problems of mediating morality and ethical life that arise therefrom. Within the horizon of the lifeworld, practical judgments derive both their concreteness and their power to motivate action from their inner connection to unquestioningly accepted ideas of the good life, in short, from their connection to ethical life and its institutions. Under these conditions, problematization can never be so profound as to risk all the assets of the existing ethical substance. But the abstractive achievements required by the moral point of view do precisely that. This is why Kohlberg* speaks of a transition to the *postconventional* stage of moral consciousness. At this stage, moral judgment becomes dissociated from the local conventions and historical coloration of a particular form of life. It can no longer appeal to the naïve validity of the context of the lifeworld. Moral answers retain only the rationally motivating force of insights. Along with the naïve self-certainty of their lifeworld background they lose the thrust and efficacy of empirical motives for action. To become effective in practice, every universalist morality has to make up for this loss of concrete ethical substance, which is initially accepted because of the cognitive advantages attending it. Universalist moralities are dependent on forms of life that are rationalized in that they make possible the prudent application of universal moral insights and support motivations for translating insights into moral action. Only those forms of life that meet universalist moralities halfway in this sense fulfill the conditions necessary to reverse the abstractive achievements of decontextualization and demotivation.

Moral Consciousness and Communicative Action, pp. 56–68, 103–109.

Notes

1 S. Toulmin, *An Examination of the Place of Reason in Ethics* (Cambridge, 1970), p. 64.
2 Ibid., p. 74.
3 At most we can compare theories, as higher-level systems of propositions, with norms. But it is debatable whether theories can be said to be true or false in the same sense as the descriptions, predictions, and explanations that

we derive from them, whereas norms for their part are right or wrong in the same sense as the actions that satisfy or violate them.

4 J. Habermas, "Legitimation Problems in the Modern State," in *Communication and the Evolution of Society* (London: Heinemann, 1979), pp. 178ff.

5 S. Toulmin, *The Uses of Argument* (Cambridge, 1958).

6 J. Habermas, "Wahrheitstheorien," in H. Fahrenbach (ed.), *Festschrift für W. Schulz* (Pfullingen, 1973), pp. 211ff and *The Theory of Communicative Action*, vol. II (Boston, 1984), pp. 22ff.

7 On the logic of practical discourse, see T. McCarthy, *The Critical Theory of Jürgen Habermas* (Cambridge, Mass., 1978), pp. 310ff.

8 G. Patzig, *Tatsachen, Normen, Sätze* (Stuttgart, 1980), p. 162.

9 Kurt Baier, *The Moral Point of View* (London, 1958).

10 Bernard Gert, *Moral Rules* (New York, 1976).

11 Marcus Singer, *Generalization in Ethics* (New York, 1961).

12 G.H. Mead, "Fragments on Ethics," in *Mind, Self, and Society* Chicago, 1934), pp. 379ff. See also H. Joas, *G. H. Mead: A Contemporary Reexamination of his Thought* (Cambridge. Mass., 1985), and J. Habermas, *The Theory of Communicative Action*, vol. 2 (Boston, 1987), pp. 92ff.

13 McCarthy, *Critical Theory*, p. 326.

14 S. Benhabib, "The Methodological Illusions of Modern Political Theory: The Case of Rawls and Habermas," *Neue Hefte für Philosophie*, 21, 1982: 47ff.

15 I am referring to Tugendhat's concept of "normative learning" as presented in G. Frankenberg and U. Rödel, *Von der Volkssouveränität zum Minderheitenschutz* (Frankfurt, 1981).

16

Remarks on Discourse Ethics

Generally the problem of which moral actions can be reasonably enjoined first arises with the transition from moral to legal theory. Modern rational law makes the transition from morality to law by way of specific reflections on the reasonableness of imposing obligations. Norms are judged to be valid in the light of the moral principle only under the presupposition – explicitly stated in (U) – of *general* observance of norms. If this precondition is not met, norms cannot be reasonably imposed, regardless of whether they are valid. Kant uses this fact to justify the state monopoly on the exercise of legal coercion. Legal institutionalization alone can ensure general adherence to morally valid norms. That amounts to a moral reason for law in general. Conversely, there are moral considerations relevant to the justification of particular legal norms that the democratic legislative process must take into account. Since problems of application must be distinguished from problems of justification also in the case of legal norms, there arises the additional demand for institutionalization of discourses of application in the shape of an independent judiciary. In this way, the contours of a constitutional state, which Kant consistent with these determinations treated in his doctrine of law, became discernible; here the moral point of view is no longer applied *directly* to modes of action but to legal and political institutions. Finally, this normative approach can be pursued to the point where the classic problem of the limits of obedience to the law, and hence the preconditions for civil disobedience, legitimate resistance, and a "right to revolt" is raised. Then it is a question of the conditions under which a politically motivated violation of positive law would be morally justified or legitimate.[1]

[. . .] By contrast, a discourse theory of law *grounded in* discourse ethics holds fast to the discourse model. It explains the difference between the normative validity-claim of moral rules and the claim to legitimacy of legal norms in terms of the fact that not just moral (and ethical) considerations enter into a presumptively rational process of political will formation of a legislator, but, in the first instance, programs and goals that are the result of more or less fair compromises, as well as information and predictions resulting from more or less controversial discussions among experts. A process of collective will formation along these lines would have the presumption of rationality in its favor to the extent that it could be realized in general in forms of discourse. The idea of the constitutional state can then be understood in terms of the endeavor to institutionalize the demanding communicative presuppositions and procedures of a network of forms of argumentation and negotiation differentiated in terms of the problem areas, for the political power employed in executing the requirements of the principle of discourse must itself be tamed through discourse.

[...] The more that principles of equality gain a foothold in social practice, the more sharply do forms of life and life-projects become differentiated from one another. And the greater this diversity is, the more abstract are the rules and principles that protect the integrity and egalitarian coexistence of subjects who are becoming increasingly unfamiliar with one another in their difference and otherness. To be sure, the sphere of questions that can be answered rationally from the moral point of view shrinks in the course of the development toward multiculturalism within particular societies and toward a world society at the international level. But finding a solution to these few more sharply focussed questions becomes all the more critical to coexistence, and even survival, in a more populous world. It remains an empirical question how far the sphere of strictly generalizable interests extends. Only if it could be shown in principle that moral discourses must prove *unfruitful* despite the growing consensus concerning human rights and democracy – for example, because common interests *can no longer even* be identified in incommensurable languages – would the deontological endeavor to uncouple questions of justice from context-dependent questions of the good life have failed.

These reflections bring us back to a theme already broached in discussing Taylor's universalistic ethics of the good. The priority of the right over the good is also the main bone of contention in the disputes between communitarians and liberals.[2] The *socio-ontological* aspects of this involved debate need not concern us here, since the objections raised by communitarians against individualistic concepts of the person or instrumentalist concepts of society do not apply to the basic concepts of discourse ethics derived from the theory of communicative action. Discourse ethics occupies an intermediate position, sharing with the "liberals" a deontological understanding of freedom, morality, and law that stems from the Kantian tradition and with the communitarians an intersubjective understanding of individuation as a product of socialization that stems from the Hegelian tradition.[3] But the priority of the right over the good is disputed primarily on epistemological grounds. In this respect discourse ethics is as vulnerable as liberal theories of justice to objections that appeal to the contextuality and the rootedness in tradition of *all* conceptions of justice and practical reason, including the procedural. The contextualists insist that behind the allegedly general and neutral explanations of the moral point of view and the perspective of justice there are *always* concealed particular world interpretations informed by specific evaluative languages and traditions. This context dependency contradicts the asserted independence of the general from the particular and the consequent priority of the right over the good. [. . .]

Even in exemplary instances of intercultural understanding where not just rival conceptions but conflicting standards of rationality clash, unprejudiced communication between "us" and "them" nevertheless necessitates a *symmetrical relation*. The fusion of interpretive horizons at which, on Gadamer's account, every communicative process aims should not be understood in terms of the false alternative between an assimilation "to us" and a conversion "to them." It is more properly described as a convergence between "our" perspective and "theirs" guided by learning processes, regardless of whether "they" or "we" or both sides must reform the practices of justification thus far accepted as valid. Concepts such as truth, rationality, and justification play the *same* role in *every* language community, even if they are interpreted differently and applied in accordance with different criteria. And this fact is sufficient to anchor the same universalistic concepts of morality and justice in different, even competing, forms of life and show that they are compatible with different conceptions of the good – on the assumption that the "comprehensive doctrines" and "strong traditions" enter into unrestricted dialogue with one another instead of persisting in their claims to exclusivity in a fundamentalistic manner. In this sense Rawls' concept of an overlapping consensus represents one possible interpretation of the principle that the general and the particular reciprocally presuppose each other.[4]

Justification and Application, pp. 87–92, 104–5.

Notes

1 Cf. my remarks on the issue of civil disobedience in *The New Conservatism* (Cambridge: Polity, 1989), pp. 77-9.

2 Cf. Charles Taylor, "The Liberal-Communitarian Debate," in N. Rosenblum (ed.), *Liberalism and the Moral Life* (Cambridge, Mass., 1989).

3 Seyla Benhabib, "Autonomy, Modernity and Community," in A. Honneth, T. McCarthy, C. Offe, and A. Wellmer (eds), *Cultural-Political Interventions in the Unfinished Project of Enlightenment* (Cambridge, Mass., 1992), pp. 39–59, and "In the Shadow of Aristotle and Hegel: Communicative Ethics and the Current Controversy in Practical Philosophy," *Philosophical Forum*, 21, 1989/ 90: 1–31; Kenneth Baynes, "The Liberal-Communitarian Controversy and Communicative Ethics," *Philosophy and Social Criticism*, 14, 1988: 293–315.

4 John Rawls, "Justice as Fairness: A Briefer Restatement" (ms., 1989). Cf. also Rawls, "Justice as Fairness," *Philosophy and Public Affairs*, 14, 1985: 223–51.

17

Morality and Ethical Life

What moral intuitions does discourse ethics conceptualize?

How can it be argued that the *procedural* explanation discourse ethics gives of the moral point of view – in other words, of the impartiality of moral judgment – constitutes an adequate account of moral intuitions, which are after all *substantive* in kind? This is an open question that needs to be addressed.

Moral intuitions are intuitions that instruct us on how best to behave in situations where it is in our power to counteract the extreme vulnerability of others by being thoughtful and considerate. In anthropological terms, morality is a safety device compensating for a vulnerability built into the sociocultural form of life. The basic facts are the following: Creatures that are individuated only through socialization are vulnerable and morally in need of considerateness. Linguistically and behaviorally competent subjects are constituted as individuals by growing into an intersubjectively shared lifeworld, and the lifeworld of a language community is reproduced in turn through the communicative actions of its members. This explains why the identity of the individual and that of the collective are interdependent; they form and maintain themselves together. Built into the consensus-oriented language use of social interaction is an inconspicuous necessity for participants to become more and more individuated. Conversely, everyday language is also the medium by which the intersubjectivity of a shared world is maintained.[1] Thus, the more differentiated the structures of the lifeworld become, the easier it is to discern the simultaneous growth of the autonomous individual subject and his dependence on interpersonal relationships and social ties. The more the subject becomes individuated, the more he becomes entangled in a densely woven fabric of mutual recognition, that is, of reciprocal exposedness and vulnerability. Unless the subject externalizes himself by participating in interpersonal relations through language, he is unable to form that inner center that is his personal identity. This explains the almost constitutional insecurity and chronic fragility of personal identity – an insecurity that is antecedent to cruder threats to the integrity of life and limb.

Moral philosophies of sympathy and compassion (Schopenhauer) have discovered that this profound vulnerability calls for some guarantee of mutual consideration.[2] This considerateness has the twofold objective of defending the integrity of the individual and of preserving the vital fabric of ties of mutual recognition through which individuals *reciprocally* stabilize their fragile identities. No one can maintain his identity by himself. Consider suicide, for example. Notwithstanding the Stoic view that held that this final, desperate act reflects the imperious self-determination of the lone individual, the responsibility for suicide can never be attributed to the individual alone. This seemingly loneliest of deeds actually enacts a fate for which others collectively must take some of the blame, the fate of ostracism from an intersubjectively shared lifeworld.

Since moralities are tailored to suit the fragility of human beings individuated through socialization, they must always solve *two* tasks at *once*. They must emphasize the inviolability of the individual by postulating equal respect for the dignity of each individual. But they must also protect the web of intersubjective relations of mutual recognition by which these individuals survive as members of a community. To these two complementary aspects correspond the principles of justice and solidarity respectively. The first postulates equal respect and equal rights for the individual, whereas the second postulates empathy and concern for the well-being of one's neighbor. Justice in the modern sense of the term refers to the subjective freedom of inalienable individuality. Solidarity refers to the well-being of associated members of a community who intersubjectively share the same lifeworld. Frankena distinguishes a principle of justice or equal treatment from a principle of beneficence, which commands us to advance the common weal, to avert harm, and to do good.[3] In my view, it is important to see that both principles have one and the same root: the specific vulnerability of the human species, which individuates itself through sociation. Morality thus cannot protect the one without the other. It cannot protect the rights of the individual without also protecting the well-being of the community to which he belongs.

The fundamental motif of an ethics of compassion can be pushed to the point where the link between the two moral principles becomes clear. In the past these principles have served as core elements of two contrary traditions in moral philosophy. Theories of duty have always centered on the principle of justice, whereas theories of the good have always emphasized the common weal. Hegel was the first to argue that we misperceive the basic moral phenomenon if we isolate the two aspects, assigning opposite principles to each. His concept of ethical life [*Sittlichkeit*] is an implicit criticism of two kinds of one-sidedness, one the mirror image of the other. Hegel opposes the abstract universality of justice manifesting itself in the individualist approaches of the modern age, in rational natural right theory, and in Kantian moral philosophy. No less vigorous is his opposition to the concrete particularism of the common good that pervades Aristotle and Thomas Aquinas. The ethics of discourse picks up this basic Hegelian aspiration to redeem it with Kantian means.

This idea is not so remarkable if one keeps in mind that discourses, treating as they do problematic validity-claims as hypotheses, represent a reflective form of communicative action. To put it another way, the normative content of the pragmatic presuppositions of argumentation is borrowed from that of communicative action, onto which discourses are superimposed. This is why all moralities coincide in one respect: the same medium, linguistically mediated interaction, is both the reason for the vulnerability of socialized individuals and the key resource they possess to compensate for that vulnerability. Every morality revolves around equality of respect, solidarity, and the common good. Fundamental ideas like these can be reduced to the relations of symmetry and reciprocity presupposed in communicative action. In other words, the common core of all kinds of morality can be traced back to the reciprocal imputations and shared presuppositions actors make when they seek understanding in everyday situations.[4] Admittedly, their range in everyday practice is limited. While equal respect and solidarity are present in the mutual recognition of subjects who orient their actions to validity-claims, normative obligations usually do not transcend the boundaries of a concrete lifeworld, be it that of a family, a neighborhood, a city, or a state. There is only one reason why discourse ethics, which presumes to derive the substance of a universalistic morality from the general presuppositions of argumentation, is a promising strategy: discourse or argumentation is a more exacting type of communication, going beyond any particular form of life. Discourse generalizes, abstracts, and stretches the presuppositions of context-bound communicative actions by extending their range to include competent subjects beyond the provincial limits of their own particular form of life.

These considerations address the issues of whether and why discourse ethics, though organized around a concept of procedure, can be expected to say something relevant about substance as well and, more important perhaps, about the hidden link between justice and the common good, which have traditionally been divorced, giving rise to separate ethics of duty and the good. On the strength of its improbably pragmatic features, practical discourse, or moral argumentation, serves as a warrant of insightful will-formation, insuring that the interests of individuals are given their due without cutting the social bonds that intersubjectively unite them.[5]

In his capacity as a participant in argumentation, everyone is on his own and yet embedded in a communication context. This is what Apel means by an "ideal community of communication." In discourse the social bond of belonging is left intact despite the fact that the consensus required of all concerned transcends the limits of any actual community. The agreement made possible by discourse depends on two things: the individual's inalienable right to say "yes" or "no" and his overcoming of his egocentric viewpoint. Without the individual's uninfringeable freedom to respond with a "yes" or "no" to criticizable validity-claims, consent is merely factual rather than truly universal. Conversely, without empathetic sensitivity by each person to everyone else, no solution deserving universal consent will result from the deliberation. These two aspects – the autonomy of inalienable individuals and their embeddedness in an intersubjectively shared web of relations – are internally connected, and it is this link that the procedure of discursive decision-making takes into account. The equal rights of individuals and the equal respect for the personal dignity of each depend upon a network of interpersonal relations and a system of mutual recognition. On the other hand, while the degree of solidarity and the growth of welfare are indicators of the quality of communal life, they are not the only ones. Just as important is that *equal* consideration be given to the interests of every individual in defining the general interest. Going beyond Kant, discourse ethics extends the deontological concept of justice by including in it those structural aspects of the good life that can be distinguished from the concrete totality of specific forms of life. [. . .]

III

In sum, I argue that Hegel's objections apply less to the reformulation of Kantian ethics itself than to a number of resulting problems that discourse ethics cannot be expected to resolve with a single stroke. Any ethics that is at once deontological, cognitivist, formalist, and universalist ends up with a relatively narrow conception of morality that is uncompromisingly abstract. This raises the problem of whether issues of justice can be isolated from particular contexts of the good life. This problem, I believe, can be solved. But a second difficulty makes its appearance, namely, whether practical reason may be forced to abdicate in favor of a faculty of judgment when it comes to applying justified norms to specific cases. Discourse ethics, I think, can handle this difficulty too. A third problem is whether it is reasonable to hope that the insights of a universalist morality are susceptible to translation into practice. Surely the incidence of such a morality is contingent upon a complementary form of life. This by no means exhausts the list of consequent problems. I mention only one more: How can political action be morally justified when the social conditions in which practical discourses can be carried on and moral insight can be generated and transformed do not exist but have to be created? I have so far not addressed two other problems that flow from the self-limitation of every non-metaphysical point of view.

Discourse ethics does not see fit to resort to an objective teleology, least of all to a countervailing force that tries to negate dialectically the irreversible succession of historical events – as was the case, for instance, with the redeeming judgment of the Christian God on the last day. But how can we live up to the principle of discourse ethics, which postulates the consent of *all*, if we cannot make restitution for the injustice and pain suffered by previous generations or if we cannot at least promise an equivalent to the day of judgment and its power of redemption? Is it not obscene for present-day beneficiaries of past injustices to expect the posthumous consent of slain and degraded victims to norms that appear justified to us in light of our own expectations regarding the future?[6] It is just as difficult to answer the basic objection of ecological ethics: How does discourse ethics, which is limited to subjects capable of speech and action, respond to the fact that mute creatures are also vulnerable? Compassion for tortured animals and the pain caused by the destruction of biotopes are surely manifestations of moral intuitions that cannot be fully satisfied by the collective narcissism of what in the final analysis is an anthropocentric way of looking at things.

At this point I want to draw only one conclusion from these skeptical considerations. Since the concept of morality is limited, the self-perception of moral theory should be correspondingly modest. It is incumbent on moral theory to explain and ground the moral point of view. What moral *theory* can do and should be trusted to do is to clarify the universal core of our moral intuitions and thereby to refute value skepticism. What it cannot do is make any kind of substantive contribution. By singling out a procedure of decision-making, it seeks to make room for those involved, who must then find answers on their own to the moral-practical issues that come at them, or are imposed upon them, with objective historical force. Moral philosophy does not have privileged access to particular moral truths. In view of the four big moral-political liabilities of our time – hunger and poverty in the third world, torture and continuous violations of human dignity in autocratic regimes, increasing unemployment and disparities of social wealth in Western industrial nations, and finally the self-destructive risks of the nuclear arms race – my modest opinion about what philosophy can and cannot accomplish may come as a disappointment. Be that as it may, philosophy cannot absolve anyone of moral responsibility. And that includes philosophers, for like everyone else, they face moral-practical issues of great complexity, and the first thing they might profitably do is to get a clearer view of the situation they find themselves in. The historical and social sciences can be of greater help in this endeavor than philosophy. On this note I want to end with a quote from Max Horkheimer from the year 1933: "What is needed to get beyond the utopian character of Kant's idea of a perfect constitution of humankind, is a materialist theory of society."[7]

Moral Consciousness and Communicative Action, pp. 199–203, 210–11.

Notes

1 J. Habermas, *The Theory of Communicative Action. Vol. 2, Lifeworld and System* (Boston, 1987), pp. 58ff.
2 Compare my critique of Arnold Gehlen: "The profound vulnerability that makes necessary an ethical regulation of behavior as its counterpoise is rooted, not in the biological weaknesses of humans, not in the newborn infant's lack of organic faculties and not in the risks of a disproportionately long rearing period, but in the cultural systems that are constructed as compensation. The fundamental problem of ethics is guaranteeing mutual consideration and respect in a way that is effective in actual conduct. That is the core of truth in any ethics of compassion." J. Habermas, "Imitation Substantiality," in *Philosophical-Political Profiles* (Cambridge, Mass., 1983), p. 120.
3 W. Frankena, *Ethics* (Englewood Cliffs, N.J., 1973). pp. 45ff.
4 This is an old topic of action theory. See A. Gouldner, "The Norm of Reciprocity," *American Sociological Review*, 25, 1960: 161–78.
5 Michael Sandel has justly criticized Rawls for saddling his construct of an original position with the atomistic legacy of contract theory. Rawls envisions isolated, independent individuals who, prior to any sociation, possess the ability to pursue their interests rationally and to posit their objectives monologically. Accordingly, Rawls views the basic covenant not so much in terms of an agreement based on argumentation as in terms of an act of free will. His vision of a just society boils down to a solution of the Kantian problem of how the individual will can be free in the presence of other individual wills. Sandel's own anti-individualist conception is not without problems either, in that it further deepens the separation between an ethics of duty and an ethics of the good. Over against Rawls's pre-social individual, he posits an individual who is the product of his community; over against the rational covenant of autonomous individuals, he posits a reflective awareness of prior social bonds; over against Rawls's idea of equal rights, he posits the ideal of mutual solidarity; over against equal respect for the dignity of the individual, he posits the advancement of the common good. With these traditional juxtapositions Sandel blocks the way to an intersubjectivist extension of Rawls's ethics of justice. He roundly rejects the deontological approach and instead returns to a teleological conception that presupposes an objective notion of community. "For a society to be a community in the strong sense, community must be constitutive of the shared self-understandings of the participants and embodied in their institutional arrangements, not simply an attribute of certain of the participants' plans of life." M.J. Sandel, *Liberalism and the Limits of Justice* (Cambridge, 1982), p. 173. Clearly, totalitarian (i.e., forcibly integrated) societies do not fit this description, which is why Sandel would have to explicate carefully the normative content of such key notions as community, embodied, and shared self-understanding. He

does not do so. If he did, he would realize just how onerous the burden of proof is that neo-Aristotelian approaches must bear, as in the case of A. MacIntyre in *After Virtue* (London, 1981). They must demonstrate how an objective moral order can be grounded without recourse to metaphysical premises.

6 See H. Peukert, *Science, Action, and Fundamental Theology* (Cambridge, Mass., 1984), and C. Lenhardt, "Anamnestic Solidarity," *Telos*, 25, 1975.

7 M. Horkheimer, "Materialismus und Moral," *Zeitschrift für Sozialforschung*, 2, 1933: 175. English translation, 'Materialism and Morality," *Telos*, 69, 1986: 85–118.

18

Law and Morality

Autonomous morality and the enacted law that depends on justification stand in a *complementary relationship*. From a sociological point of view, both of these emerged simultaneously from that encompassing social ethos in which traditional law and a conventional ethic were still intertwined with each other. Once the sacred foundations of this network of law, morality, and ethical life were shaken, processes of differentiation set in. At the level of cultural knowledge, legal questions separated from moral and ethical questions [...]. At the institutional level, positive law separated from the customs and habits that were devalued to mere conventions. To be sure, moral and legal questions refer to the same problems: how interpersonal relationships can be legitimately ordered and actions coordinated with one another through justified norms, how action conflicts can be consensually resolved against the background of intersubjectively recognized normative principles and rules. But they refer to these same problems in different ways. Despite the common reference point, morality and law differ prima facie inasmuch as post-traditional morality only represents a form of cultural *knowledge*, whereas law has, in addition to this, a binding character at the institutional level. Law is not only a symbolic system but an action system as well.

The empirically informed view that modern legal orders are a coeval complement of autonomous morality no longer fits with the platonistic notion that law and morality are related by a kind of imitation – as if the same geometric figure were simply projected upon a different level of presentation. Hence we must not understand basic rights of *Grundrechte*, which take the shape of constitutional norms, as mere imitations of moral rights, and we must not take political autonomy as a mere copy of moral autonomy. Rather, norms of action *branch out* into moral and legal rules. From a normative point of view this corresponds to the assumption that moral and civic autonomy are co-original and can be explained with the help of a parsimonious discourse principle that merely expresses the meaning of postconventional requirements of justification. Like the postconventional level of justification itself – the level at which substantial ethical life dissolves into its elements – this principle certainly has a normative content inasmuch as it explicates the meaning of impartiality in practical judgments. However, despite its normative content it lies at a level of abstraction that is *still neutral* with respect to morality and law, for it refers to action norms in general:

> (D) Just those action norms are valid to which all possibly affected persons could agree as participants in rational discourses.

This formulation contains some basic terms that require elucidation. The predicate "valid" [*gültig*] pertains to action norms and all the general normative propositions that express the meaning of such norms; it expresses normative validity in a non-specific sense that is still indifferent to the distinction between morality and legitimacy. I understand "active norms" as temporally, socially, and substantively generalized behavioral expectations. I include among "those affected" (or involved) anyone whose interests are touched by the foreseeable consequences of a general practice regulated by the norms at issue. And "rational discourse" should include *any* attempt to reach an understanding over problematic validity-claims insofar as this takes place under conditions of communication that enable the free processing of topics and contributions, information and reasons in the public space constituted by illocutionary obligations. The expression also refers indirectly to bargaining processes insofar as these are regulated by discursively grounded procedures.

Naturally, to conceive (D) with sufficient abstraction, it is important that we do not limit a fortiori the kinds of theme and contribution and the sorts of reason that "count" in each case. The moral principle first results when one specifies the general discourse principle for those norms that can be justified if and *only* if equal consideration is given to the interests of all those who are possibly involved. The principle of democracy results from a corresponding specification for those action norms that appear in legal form. Such norms can be justified by calling on pragmatic, ethical-political, and moral reasons – here justification is not restricted to moral reasons alone. [. . .] The required kinds of reason result from the logic of the question at issue in each case. With moral questions, humanity or a presupposed republic of world citizens constitute the reference system for justifying regulations that lie in the equal interest of all. In principle, the decisive reasons must be acceptable to each and everyone. With ethical-political questions, the form of life of the political community that is "in each case our own" constitutes the reference system for justifying decisions that are supposed to express an authentic collective self-understanding. In principle, the decisive reasons must be acceptable to all members sharing "our" traditions and strong evaluations. Oppositions between interests require a rational balancing of competing value-orientations and interest positions. Here the totality of social or subcultural groups that are directly involved constitute the reference system for negotiating compromises. Insofar as these compromises come about under fair bargaining conditions, they must be acceptable in principle to all parties, even if on the basis of respectively different reasons.

In my previous publications on discourse ethics I have not sufficiently distinguished between the discourse principle and the moral principle. The discourse principle is only intended to explain the point of view from which norms of action can be *impartially justified*; I assume that the principle itself reflects those symmetrical relations of recognition built into communicatively structured forms of life in general. Now, to introduce such a discourse principle already presupposes that practical questions can be judged impartially and decided rationally. This is not a trivial supposition; its justification is incumbent on a theory of argumentation [. . .]. This investigation leads one to distinguish various types of discourse (and their corresponding sorts of reason) according to the logic of the question at issue; it also leads to a distinction between discourse and procedurally regulated bargaining. Specifically, one must show for each type which rules would allow pragmatic, ethical, and moral questions to be answered.[1] We might say that these various rules of argumentation are so many ways of operationalizing the discourse principle. For the justification of moral norms, the discourse principle takes the form of a universalization principle. To this extent the moral principle functions as a rule of argumentation. Starting with the general presuppositions of argumentation – as the reflective form of communicative action – one can attempt to elucidate this principle in a formal-pragmatic fashion.[2] I cannot go into this here. For the application of moral norms to particular cases, the universalization principle is replaced by a principle of appropriateness. We will deal with this later in regard to legal discourses of application.[3] The two principles express different aspects of the same moral principle, which requires that the interests of each person be given equal consideration. In the present context, however, I am primarily concerned with the ways in which one can distinguish the principle of democracy from that of morality.

Caution is necessary here. At this juncture one must not succumb to the ingrained prejudice suggesting that morality pertains only to social relationships for which one is personally responsible, while law and political justice extend to institutionally mediated spheres of interaction.[4] Discourse theory conceives of morality as an authority that crosses the boundaries between private and public spheres; these boundaries vary throughout history anyhow, depending on social structure. If we construe the universalist claim of the moral principle intersubjectively, then we must relocate ideal role taking, which according to Kant each individual undertakes privately, to a public practice implemented by all persons in common. Besides, allocating the jurisdictions of morality and law according to private and public spheres of action is counterintuitive in any event, for the simple reason that the will-formation of the political legislator has to include the moral aspects of the matter in need of regulation. Indeed, in complex societies morality can become effective beyond the local level only by being translated into the legal code.

To obtain sufficiently selective criteria for the distinction between the principles of democracy and morality, I start with the fact that the principle of democracy should establish a procedure of legitimate law-making. Specifically, the democratic principle states that only those statutes may claim legitimacy that can meet with the assent of all citizens in a discursive process of legislation that in turn has been legally constituted. In other words, this principle explains the performative meaning of the practice of self-determination on the part of legal consociates who recognize one another as free and equal members of an association they have joined voluntarily. Thus the principle of democracy lies at *another level* than the moral principle.

Whereas the moral principle functions as a rule of argumentation for deciding moral questions rationally, the principle of democracy already presupposes the possibility of valid moral judgments. Indeed, it presupposes the possibility of *all* the types of practical judgment and discourse that supply laws with their legitimacy. The principle of democracy thus does not answer the question whether and how political affairs in general can be handled discursively; that is for a theory of argumentation to answer. On the premise that rational political opinion- and will-formation is at all possible, the principle of democracy only tells us how this can be institutionalized – namely, through a system of rights that secures for each person an equal participation in a process of legislation whose communicative presuppositions are guaranteed to begin with. Whereas the moral principle operates at the level at which a specific form of argumentation is *internally* constituted, the democratic principle refers to the level at which interpenetrating forms of argumentation are *externally* institutionalized. At this latter level, provisions are made for an effective participation in discursive processes of opinion- and will-formation, which take place in forms of communication that are themselves legally guaranteed.

One way we can distinguish the principles of democracy and morality is by their different levels of reference. The other is by the difference between legal norms and other action norms. While the moral principle extends to any norm for whose justification moral arguments are both necessary and sufficient, the democratic principle is tailored to legal norms. These rules differ from the simple, more or less quasi-natural norms of interaction we find in everyday life. The legal form in which these norms are clad is a relatively recent product of social evolution. In contrast to naturally emergent rules, whose validity can be judged solely from the moral point of view, legal norms have an artificial character – they comprise an intentionally produced layer of action norms that are reflexive in the sense of being applicable to themselves.

Hence the principle of democracy must not only establish a procedure of legitimate law-making, it must also *steer the production of the legal medium itself.* The democractic principle must specify – in accordance with the discourse principle – the conditions to be satisfied by individual rights in general, that is, by any rights suitable for the constitution of a legal community and capable of providing the medium for this community's self-organization. Thus, along with the system of rights one must also create the *language* in which a community can understand itself as a voluntary association of free and equal consociates *under law.*

Corresponding to the two ways in which we have distinguished the principles of democracy and morality, then, are two tasks the required system of rights is supposed to solve. It should institutionalize the communicative framework for a rational political will-formation; and it should ensure the very medium in which alone this will-formation can express itself as the common will of freely associated legal persons. To specify this second task we must precisely define the formal characteristics of the medium of law.

2

In what follows I want to elucidate the formal characteristics of law by means of the complementary relation between law and morality. This elucidation is part of a *functional* explanation and not a normative justification of law. For the legal form is in no way a principle one could "ground," either epistemically or normatively. [. . .] Kant characterized the legality or juridical form of ways of acting through three abstractions referring to the addressees, and not the authors, of law. Law abstracts, first, from the capacity of the addressees to bind their will of their own accord, since it assumes that *free choice* is a sufficient source of law-abiding behavior. Further, the law abstracts from the complexities that action plans owe to their lifeworld contexts; it restricts itself to the *external relation* of interactive influence that typical social actors exert upon one another. Finally, we have already seen that law abstracts from the *kind of motivation*; it is satisfied with action that outwardly conforms to rules, however such conformity may arise.

The specifically limited status of the legal person corresponds to these modes of action constrained by law in this way. Moral norms regulate interpersonal relationships and conflicts between natural persons who are supposed to recognize one another both as members of a concrete community and as irreplaceable individuals. Such norms are addressed to persons who are individualized through their life histories. By contrast, legal norms regulate interpersonal relationships and conflicts between actors who recognize one another as consociates in an abstract community first produced by legal norms themselves. Although they too are addressed to individual subjects, these subjects are individualized not through personal identifies developed over a lifetime but through the capacity to occupy the position of typical members of a legally constituted community. From the perspective of the addressee, then, one abstracts in a legal relation from the person's capacity to bind her will through normative insights as such; it is sufficient to expect that she have the capacity for making purposive-rational decisions, i.e., the capacity for freedom of choice.[5] The further aspects of legality issue from this reduction of the free (and authentic) will of a morally (and ethically) accountable person to the free choice of a legal subject oriented toward her own preferences. Only matters pertaining to external relations can be legally regulated at all. For rule-conformative behavior must, if necessary, be enforced. This explains in turn why the legal form has an atomizing effect, which naturally does not negate the intersubjective bases of law as such.

Up to this point, Kant's concept of legality is a helpful guide to analyzing the formal characteristics of law. However, we must not follow him in conceiving the aspects of legality as limitations of morality. I suggest instead that we explain these aspects in terms of the complementary relation between law and morality. This is suggested by a sociological approach as well: the constitution of the legal form became necessary to offset deficits arising with the collapse of traditional ethical life. From that point on, an autonomous morality supported by reason alone is concerned only with correct judgments. With the transition to a postconventional level of justification, moral consciousness detaches itself from customary practices, while the encompassing social ethos shrinks to mere convention, to habit and customary law.

A principled, postconventional morality takes a critical approach that challenges all quasi-natural, received action orientations backed by institutions and motivationally anchored through patterns of socialization. As soon as the possible options along with their normative background are exposed to the searching gaze of such a morality, they fall into the whirlpool of problematization. Specialized for questions of justice, a principled morality views *everything* through the powerful but narrow lens of universalizability. Its telos consists in the impartial judgment of morally relevant action conflicts, and hence it facilitates a knowledge that is meant to orient one's action but does not thereby *dispose* one to act rightly. Sublimated into knowledge, this morality is, like all knowledge, represented at the cultural level. It exists in the first instance only as the meaning content of cultural symbols that can be understood and interpreted, handed down and critically developed. Naturally, this type of cultural knowledge also refers to *possible* actions; but of itself it no longer maintains any contact, so to speak, with the motivations that lend moral judgments their practical thrust, nor with the institutions that ensure that justified moral expectations are actually fulfilled. A morality thus withdrawn into the cultural system maintains only a virtual relation to action as long as it is not actualized by motivated actors *themselves*. The latter must be disposed to act according to conscience. A principled morality thus depends on socialization processes that meet it halfway by engendering the corresponding agencies of conscience, namely the correlative superego formations. Besides the weak motivating force of good reasons, such a morality becomes effective for action only through the internalization of moral principles in the personality system.

The move from knowledge to action remains uncertain – on account of the vulnerability of the moral actor's precarious, highly abstract system of self-control, and in general on account of the vicissitudes of socialization processes that promote such demanding competences. A morality that depends on the accommodating substrate of propitious personality structures would have a limited effectiveness if it could not engage the actor's motives in *another* way besides internalization, i.e., precisely by way of an institutionalized legal system that *supplements* postconventional morality in a manner effective for action. Law is two things at the same time: a system of knowledge and a system of action. We can understand it just as much as a text comprised of normative propositions and interpretations as we can view it as an institution, i.e., as a complex of normatively regulated action. Because motivations and value-orientations are interwoven with each other in law as an action system, legal norms have the immediate effectiveness for action that moral judgments as such lack. At the same time, legal institutions differ from naturally emergent institutional orders in virtue of their comparatively high degree of rationality; for they give firm shape to a system of knowledge that has been doctrinally refined and coupled with a principled morality. Because law is simultaneously established this way at the levels of culture and society, it can *offset* the weaknesses of a morality that exists primarily as knowledge.

The person who judges and acts morally must independently appropriate this moral knowledge, assimilate it, and put it into practice. She is subject to unprecedented (1) cognitive, (2) motivational, and (3) organizational demands, from which the person as legal subject is *unburdened.*

(1) Postconventional morality provides no more than a procedure for impartially judging disputed questions. It cannot pick out a catalog of duties, or even designate a list of hierarchically ordered norms, but expects subjects to form their own judgments. Moreover, the communicative freedom they enjoy in moral discourses leads only to fallible insights in the contest of interpretations. Problems of norm justification are not those that present the real difficulties. Normally the basic principles themselves – entailing such duties as equal respect for each person, distributive justice, benevolence toward the needy, loyalty, sincerity, etc. – are not disputed. Rather, the abstractness of these highly generalized norms leads to problems of application as soon as a

conflict reaches beyond the routine interactions in familiar contexts. Complex operations are required to reach a decision in cases of this sort. On the one hand, one must uncover and describe the relevant features of the situation in light of competing but somewhat indeterminate norm candidates; on the other hand, one must select, interpret, and apply the norm most appropriate to the present case in light of a description of the situation that is as complete as possible. Thus, problems of justification and application in complex issues often overtax the individual's analytical capacity. This *cognitive indeterminacy* is absorbed by the facticity of the genesis of law. The political legislature decides which norms count as law, and the courts settle contests of interpretation over the application of valid but interpretable norms in a manner at once judicious and definitive for all sides. The legal system deprives legal persons in their role of addressees of the power to define the criteria for judging between lawful and unlawful. Parliamentary legislative procedures, judicial decision-making, and the doctrinal jurisprudence that precisely defines rules and systematizes decisions represent different ways that law complements morality by relieving the individual of the cognitive burdens of forming her own moral judgments.

(2) However, a principled morality encumbers the individual not only with the problem of deciding action conflicts but also with expectations [*Erwartungen*] regarding her strength of will. On the one hand, in conflict situations she is supposed to be willing to seek a consensual solution, i.e., to enter discourses or to carry out imaginary discourses in an advocatory fashion. On the other hand, she is supposed to find the strength to act according to moral insights, if necessary against her own immediate interests, and hence reconcile duty and inclination. The actor is supposed to achieve harmony between herself as author of moral "oughts" and herself as their addressee. In addition to the cognitive indeterminacy of principled judgment, then, there is the *motivational uncertainty* about action guided by known principles. This is absorbed by the facticity of the law's enforcement. To the extent that moral cognition is not sufficiently anchored in the motives and attitudes of its addressees, it must be supplemented by a law that enforces norm-conformative behavior while leaving motives and attitudes open. Coercive law overlays normative expectations with threats of sanctions in such a way that addressees may restrict themselves to the prudential calculation of consequences.

The problem of weakness of will also gives rise to the further problem of what can be reasonably expected [*Zumutbarkeit*]. A principled morality directs individuals to examine the validity of norms under the presupposition that everyone in fact observes, or at least externally complies with, valid norms. However, if precisely those norms are valid that deserve the rationally motivated agreement of all under the condition that actual compliance with the norm is *universal*, then no one *can reasonably be expected* to abide by valid norms insofar as this condition is not fulfilled. Each must be able to expect [*erwarten*] that everyone will observe valid norms. Valid norms represent reasonable expectations only if they can be actually enforced against deviant behavior.

(3) A third problem, that of the imputability of obligations, or account-ability, results from the universalistic character of postconventional morality. This problem arises especially in regard to positive duties, which often – and increasingly so, as a society becomes more complex – require cooperation or organization. For example, the unmistakable duty to preserve even anonymous neighbors from starvation conspicu-ously contrasts with the fact that millions of inhabitants of the first world allow hundreds of thousands in poverty-stricken areas of the third world to perish. Even charitable aid can only be transmitted along organized paths; the convoluted route taken by food, medicine, clothing, and infrastructures exceeds by far the initiative and range of individual action. As many studies have shown, a structural improvement would require no less than a new economic world-order. Similar problems that can only be managed by institutions arise in one's own region, and even in one's very neighborhood. The more that moral consciousness attunes itself to universalistic value-orientations, the greater are the discrepan-cies between uncontested moral demands, on the one hand, and organizational constraints and resistances to change, on the other. Thus the moral demands that can be fulfilled only through anonymous networks and organizations first find clear addressees only within a system of rules that can be reflexively applied to itself. Law alone is reflexive *in its own right*; it contains secondary rules that serve the production of primary rules for guiding behavior. It can define jurisdic-tional powers and found organizations – in short, produce a system of accountabilities that refers not only to natural legal persons but to fictive legal subjects such as corporations and public agencies.

Similar to the problems of reasonable expectability, weakness of will, and decidability, the question of the moral division of labor[6] announces the limits of a postconventional morality, the point where supplemen-tation by law becomes functionally necessary. A further problem results from the fact that the postconventional level of justification removes the foundation for traditional modes of legitimating institutions. As soon as the more demanding moral standards can no longer be naïvely established, an impulse to raise questions arises, putting pressure on devalued traditional institutions to justify themselves. But the morality that supplies the criteria for the disillusioning assessment of existing institutions does not itself offer any *operative* means for their recon-struction. To this end, positive law stands in reserve as an action system able to take the place of other institutions.

To be sure, the law recommends itself not only for the reconstruction of quasi-natural institutional complexes that have fallen into disrepair as a result of their loss of legitimation. In the course of social modernization a *new* kind of organizational need arises, which can only be managed constructively. Traditional spheres of interaction such as the family or school are *refashioned* at their institutional base, while formally organized action systems such as markets, businesses, and administrations are first *created* through legal regulation. The capitalist economy or bureaucratic agencies first come to exist in the legal medium in which they are institutionalized.

Despite what the previously examined problems might suggest, of course, the need of morality for compensation is not enough to explain the specific achievements of the legal code that are required to answer the growing need for regulation and organization in increasingly complex societies. The real proportions only become evident when one turns things around and also views morality from the vantage point of the legal system. A principled morality whose effectiveness was based solely on socialization processes and individual conscience would remain restricted to a narrow radius of action. Through a legal system with which it remains internally coupled, however, morality can spread to *all* spheres of action, including those systemically independent spheres of media-steered interactions that unburden actors of all moral expectations besides that of a general obedience to law. In less complex societies, socially integrating force inheres in the ethos of a form of life, inasmuch as this integral ethical life binds all the components of the lifeworld together, attuning concrete duties to institutions and linking them with motivations. Under conditions of high complexity, moral contents can spread throughout a society along the channels of legal regulation.

Between Facts and Norms, ch. 3, p. 106–118.

Notes

1 J. Habermas, "On the Pragmatic, the Ethical, and the Moral Employments of Practical Reason," in *Justification and Application*, pp. 1–17.
2 Cf. W. Rehg, "Discourse and the Moral Point of View: Deriving a Dialogical Principle of Universalization," *Inquiry*, 34, 1991: 27–48, also his *Insight and Solidarity: A Study in the Discourse Ethics of Jürgen Habermas* (Berkeley, Cal.: University of California Press, 1994).
3 Habermas, *Moral Consciousness and Communicative Action*, also *Justification and Application*; K. Günther, *The Sense of Appropriateness*, tr. J. Farrell(Albany, N.Y.: State University of New York Press, 1993).
4 Albrecht Wellmer does just this when he contrasts the privately applicable moral principle with a principle of justice that regulates common political will-formation; A. Wellmer, "Ethics and Dialogue: Elements of Moral

Judgement in Kant and Discourse Ethics," in *The Persistence of Modernity*, tr. D. Midgley (Cambridge, Mass.: MIT Press, 1991), pp. 113–231.

5 The character of this abstraction is such that it secures freedom; the status of the legal person protects the sphere in which real persons who both are morally responsible and follow their ethical conceptions of the good life can freely develop. Insofar as the legal guarantee of individual liberties secures the space for an authentic and autonomous conduct of life, it makes sense even from a moral and ethical standpoint to reduce the legal person to a bearer of rights who is individuated by freedom of choice. Law is held up as a "protective mask" (Hannah Arendt) over the physiognomy of persons individuated through their life-histories, persons who want to live conscientiously and authentically; on this, see R. Forst, *Kontexte der Gerechtigkeit* (Frankfurt, 1994).

6 H. Shue, "Mediating Duties," *Ethics*, 98, 1988: 687–704.

19

The Constitutional State

From a reconstructive standpoint we have seen that constitutional rights and principles merely explicate the performative character of the self-constitution of a society of free and equal citizens. The organizational forms of the constitutional state make this practice permanent. Every historical example of a democratic constitution has a double temporal reference: as a historic document it recalls the foundational act that it interprets – it marks a beginning in time. At the same time, its normative character means that the task of interpreting and elaborating the system of rights poses itself *anew* for each generation – as the project of a just society, a constitution articulates the horizon of expectation opening on an ever-present future. From this perspective, as an *ongoing* process of constitution-framing set up for the long haul, the democratic procedure of legitimate law-making acquires a privileged status. This leads to the pressing question of whether such a demanding procedure can be implemented in complex societies like our own and, if it can, how this can be done effectively, so that a constitutionally regulated circulation of power actually prevails in the political system. The answers to this question in turn inform our own paradigmatic understanding of law. I would like to note the following points for elucidating such an historically situated understanding of the constitution.

(1) The constitutionally organized political system is, on the one hand, specialized for generating collectively binding decisions. To this extent, it represents only one of several subsystems. On the other hand, in virtue of its internal relation to law, politics is responsible for problems that concern society as a whole. It must be possible to interpret collectively binding decisions as a realization of rights such that the structures of recognition built into communicative action are trans-ferred, via the medium of law, from the level of simple interactions to the abstract and anonymous relationships among strangers. In pursuing what in each case are particular collective goals and in regulating specific conflicts, politics simultaneously deals with general problems of integration. Because it is constituted in a legal form, a politics whose

mode of operation is functionally specified still refers to society-wide problems: it carries on the tasks of social integration at a reflexive level when other action systems are no longer up to the job.

(2) This asymmetrical position explains the fact that the political system is subject to constraints on two sides – and that corresponding standards govern its achievements and decisions. As a functionally specified action system, it is limited by other functional systems that obey their own logic and, to this extent, bar direct political interventions. On this side the political system encounters limits on the effectiveness of administrative power (including legal and fiscal instruments). On the other side, as a constitutionally regulated action system politics is connected with the public sphere and depends on lifeworld sources of communicative power. Here the political system is not subject to the external constraints of a social environment, but rather experiences its internal dependence on enabling conditions. For the conditions that make the production of legitimate law possible are ultimately not at the disposition of politics.

(3) The political system is vulnerable on both sides to disturbances that can reduce the *effectiveness* of its achievements and the *legitimacy* of its decisions, respectively. The regulatory competence of the political system fails if the implemented legal programs remain ineffective or if regulatory activity gives rise to disintegrating effects in the action systems that require regulation. Failure also occurs if the instruments deployed overtax the legal medium itself and strain the normative composition of the political system. As steering problems become more complex, irrelevance, misguided regulations, and self-destruction can accumulate to the point where a "regulatory trilemma" results. On the other side, the political system fails as a guardian of social integration if its decisions, even though effective, can no longer be traced back to legitimate law. The constitutionally regulated circulation of power is nullified if the administrative system becomes independent of communicatively generated power, if the social power of functional systems and large organizations (including the mass media) is converted into illegitimate power, or if the lifeworld resources for spontaneous public communication no longer suffice to guarantee an uncoerced articulation of social interests. The independence of illegitimate power, together with the weakness of civil society and the public sphere, can deteriorate into a "legitimation dilemma," which in certain circumstances can combine with the steering trilemma and develop into a vicious circle. Then the political system is pulled into the whirlpool of legitimation deficits and steering deficits that mutually reinforce one another.

(4) Such crises can at most be explained historically. They are not built into the structures of functionally differentiated societies in such a way

that they would intrinsically compromise the project of self-empowerment undertaken by a society of free and equal subjects who bind themselves by law. However, they are symptomatic of the peculiar position of political systems as asymmetrically embedded in highly complex circulation processes. Actors must form an image of this context whenever, adopting the performative attitude, they want to engage successfully as citizens, representatives, judges, or officials in realizing the system of rights. Because these rights must be interpreted in various ways under changing social circumstances, the light they throw on this context is refracted into a spectrum of changing legal paradigms. Historical constitutions can be seen as so many ways of construing one and the *same* practice – the practice of self-determination on the part of free and equal citizens; but like every practice this too is situated in history. Those involved must start with their *own current* practice if they want to achieve clarity about what such a practice means *in general*.

Between Facts and Norms, pp. 384–387.

20

Discourse Theory and the Public Sphere

The social substratum for the realization of the system of rights consists neither in spontaneous market forces nor in the deliberate measures of the welfare state but in the currents of communication and public opinion that, emerging from civil society* and the public sphere, are converted into communicative power through democratic procedures. The fostering of autonomous public spheres, an expanded citizen participation, curbs on the power of the media, and the mediating function of political parties that are not simply elements of the state are of central significance for this. The well-known proposals to insert plebiscitary elements into the constitution (direct popular vote, petitions for a referendum, etc.), as well as the proposals to introduce democratic procedures at a grass-roots level (in the nomination of candidates, will-formation inside the party, etc.), are meant to counteract the subversion of *the political public sphere* by power. The attempts at a stronger constitutional regulation of the *power of the media* have the same intent. The mass media must be kept free from the pressure of political and other functional elites; they must be capable of raising and maintaining the discursive level of public opinion-formation without constraining the communicative freedom of critical audiences. In the proceduralist legal paradigm, the political public sphere is not conceived simply as the backroom of the parliamentary complex, but as the impulse-generating periphery that *surrounds* the political center: in cultivating normative reasons it has an effect on all parts of the political system without intending to conquer it. Passing through the channels of general elections and various forms of participation, public opinions are converted into a communicative power that authorizes the legislature and legitimates regulatory agencies, while a publicly mobilized critique of judicial rulings imposes more intense justificatory obligations on a judiciary engaged in further developing the law.

The criticism of the assimilation of *political parties* into the state apparatus is primarily directed against an established practice that reduces the competition of party platforms for voters' approval to an instrument for personnel recruitment and the distribution of public offices. This criticism objects to a conflation of two different functions that, for good reasons, parties exercise simultaneously. As catalysts of public opinion they are called to collaborate in political will-formation and political education (with the goal of promoting the qualifications required for citizenship). At the same time, as recruiting machines they select personnel and dispatch leadership groups into the political system. To the extent that the parties have themselves become an integral part of this very system the two functions are no longer kept separate. For in the eyes of power-holders inside the administrative system, parties do not exercise their privileges in collaboration with civil society but treat the political public sphere as the system's environment, from which they extract mass loyalty. In contrast to this, the public of citizens should have the opportunity to recognize itself, not in the person of a chancellor or president, i.e., the chief administrator, but in democratic party leaders. The latter would have to define themselves in the contest over the appropriate interpretation of needs and promotion of relevant issues, in the dispute over the correct description of problems and the best proposals for their solution. As long as democratic competition provides them with no higher reputation than the bonus of an office post awarded to holders of administrative power, politics has not yet laid aside its false appearance of sanctity. For in a constitutional democracy, as the dwelling of a self-organizing legal community, the symbolic location of discursively fluid sovereignty remains *empty*.

3

Under the conditions of postmetaphysical thinking – for which no plausible alternatives exist, despite fundamentalist reactions against the losses incurred by modernization – the state has lost its sacred substance. This secularization of the spiritual bases of government authority, by now long underway, suffers from a deficit in implementation that is overdue. If this deficit is not met by more extensive democratization, the constitutional state itself will be endangered. We could gather further evidence for this thesis if we were to go beyond our limited focus on national societies and, as an epoch of decolonization draws to a close, broaden our view to take in the international order of the world society. The legitimations enlisted by the allies for the Gulf War provide evidence of a progressive denationalization of international law.[1] This example reflects the trends toward the dissolution of the sovereignty of the nation-state. Against the horizon of an emerging global public sphere, such trends could signal the beginning of a new universalist world-order.[. . .]this is naturally no more than a hope – indeed a hope born of desperation.

If one counters such reformist perspectives with the usual arguments referring to complexity, then one conflates legitimacy and efficiency. Moreover, one fails to realize that the institutions of government by law were always already set up not only to reduce complexity, but also to maintain it through countersteering so as to stabilize the tension inherent in law between facticity and validity. At the same time, when I infer from the proceduralist legal paradigm certain consequences for understanding the "crisis of the constitutional state," I am certainly not offering anything original at the level of particular details. But this paradigm can provide a certain coherence to the reform efforts that are either under discussion or already underway.

If a utopia is equivalent to the ideal projection [*Entwurf*] of a concrete form of life, then the constitution taken as a project [*Projekt*] is neither a social utopia nor a substitute for such. This project is, in fact, just the "opposite to a utopia in which collective reason and secularized omnipotence are unified and institutionalized in the state: rather, it implies the idea of civil society and its capacity to regulate itself in discursive processes and through clever institutionalization."[2] Ulrich Preuß defines "constitution" as the establishment of a fallible learning process through which a society gradually overcomes its inability to engage in normative reflection on itself: "A society is constituted when it is confronted with itself in suitable institutional forms and normatively guided processes of adjustment, resistance, and self-correction."[3] The procedural paradigm is not distinguished from the two earlier paradigms by its being "formal" in the sense of "empty" or "poor in content." For in pointing to civil society and the political public sphere, it forcefully singles out points of reference from which the democratic process acquires a different weight and a role previously neglected in the realization of the system of rights. In complex societies, the scarcest resources are neither the productivity of a market economy nor the regulatory capacity of the public administration. It is above all the resources of an exhausted economy of nature and of a disintegrating social solidarity that require a nurturing approach. The forces of social solidarity can be regenerated in complex societies only in the forms of communicative practices of self-determination.

The project of realizing the system of rights – a project specifically designed for the conditions of our society, and hence for a particular, historically emergent society – cannot be merely formal. Nevertheless, this paradigm of law – unlike the liberal and social-welfare models – no longer favors a particular ideal of society, a particular vision of the good life, or even a particular political option. It is "formal" in the sense that it merely states the necessary conditions under which legal subjects in their role of enfranchised citizens can reach an understanding with one another about what their problems are and how they are to be solved. The procedural paradigm is certainly connected with the self-referential expectation of shaping not only the self-understanding of elites that deal with law as experts, but that of *all* participants. But this expectation does not aim at indoctrination and has nothing totalitarian about it – to anticipate an objection that, though far-fetched, is leveled against discourse theory again and again. For the new paradigm is up for discussion under its own conditions: to the extent that it would shape the horizon of a pre-understanding within which everyone could take part in the interpretation of the constitution, each sharing the labor in his or her own way, every perceived historical change in the social context would have to be conceived as a challenge to re-examine the legal paradigm itself. Certainly this understanding, like the rule of law itself, retains a dogmatic core: the idea of autonomy according to which human beings act as free subjects only insofar as they obey just those laws they give themselves in accordance with insights they have acquired intersubjectively. This is "dogmatic" only in a harmless sense. For this idea expresses a tension between facticity and validity, a tension that is "given" with the fact of the symbolic infrastructure of sociocultural forms of life, which is to say that *for us*, who have developed our identity in such a form of life, it cannot be circumvented.

Between Facts and Norms, pp. 442–446.

Notes

1 *The Past as Future* (Cambridge: Polity, 1994), pp. 5–31.
2 Preuß, "Verfassungstheoretische Überlegungen zur normativen Begründung des Wohlfahrtstaates', in C. Sachße et al. (eds.), *Sicherheit und Freiheit* (Frankfurt, 1990)," p. 64.
3 Ibid., p. 73.

PART VI

Evolution and Legitimation

Introduction

In the extracts which make up this part, Habermas puts his theory of communicative action and communicative or discourse ethics in the context of an ambitious theory of the evolution of human societies. In English-speaking countries, explicitly evolutionary theories of history have generally been regarded with suspicion since the rise of functionalist social anthropology in the middle years of the twentieth century. German social theorists, by contrast, have been more favorably disposed to models of social development and social learning. In Habermas's view, we can "reconstruct" the underlying developmental logic of social learning processes – the way societies learn to cope with problems of their physical environment (irrigation, agricultural techniques, industrialism, etc.) and of their own internal organization (bureaucratic administration, codified law) along the lines of the reconstruction of individual learning by developmental psychologists such as Jean Piaget and Lawrence Kohlberg. In each case, we are dealing with "the realization of an ordered sequence of structural possibilities".[1]

This does not mean that the details of human history can be shoehorned into a deterministic sequence, merely that we can identify the underlying potentials and trends. A person who learns English as his or her first language could as easily, in appropriate circumstances, have learned Korean or Urdu instead. Similarly, some societies industrialized in a relatively uncoordinated manner, others through state action. Some European regions developed into nation-states in the early modern period, others only in the twentieth century. When and where such processes occur, if they occur at all, depends on historical contingencies, but there are certain common features to do with the handling of natural resources, boundaries, minorities, and so on.

Habermas's outline reconstruction of historical development as a learning process was also conceived as a reconstruction of historical materialism, which he took to be the best available theory of these processes. It needed, however, to be extended and developed: it concentrates, in Habermas's terms, too much on the domain of "work" and not enough on that of "interaction." And it also, despite Marx's break with *traditional German idealist philosophy, takes over too much from that tradition: in particular, the idea of a unified collective subject of history.*

For Habermas, as for Marx, the reconstruction of evolutionary sequences does not yield a smooth, unbroken pattern of advance, and Habermas's work of the 1970s is also substantially concerned with reconceptualizing Marxist and other accounts of crisis. Once again, he expands Marx's focus. Whereas Marx concentrates on the economic crisis tendencies which lead to other social transformations, Habermas concentrates on the displacement of these tendencies into other social spheres – notably the political domain of legitimation. Reading 20 in part V contains a reformulation of the model sketched out in Legitimation Crisis, *from which a short extract is provided here as reading 22. "Legitimation Problems in the Modern State," based on a conference paper of 1974 and reproduced here as reading 23, is a useful summary of the argument of that book.*

Notes

1 Johann Arnason, "A Review of Jürgen Habermas, *Zur Rekonstruktion des historischen Materialismus," Telos*, 39, 1979: 215.

Further Reading

Tom Rockmore, *Habermas on Historical Materialism* (Bloomington and Indianapolis: Indiana University Press, 1989); Piet Strydom, "The Ontogenetic Fallacy: The Immanent Critique of Habermas' Developmental Logical Theory of Evolution," *Theory, Culture and Society*, 9, 3, 1992: 65–93.

21

Historical Materialism and the Development of Normative Structures

I

[In recent years I have made] various attempts to develop a theoretical program that I understand as a reconstruction of historical materialism. The word *restoration* signifies the return to an initial situation that had meanwhile been corrupted; but my interest in Marx and Engels is not dogmatic, nor is it historical-philological. *Renaissance* signifies the renewal of a tradition that has been buried for some time; but Marxism is in no need of this. In the present connection, *reconstruction* signifies taking a theory apart and putting it back together again in a new form in order to attain more fully the goal it has set for itself. This is the normal way (in my opinion normal for Marxists too) of dealing with a theory that needs revision in many respects but whose potential for stimulation has still not been exhausted.

Not by chance [during the same period] I have been working on a theory of communicative action. Although the theory of communication is intended to solve problems that are rather of a philosophical nature – problems concerning the foundations of the social sciences – I see a close connection with questions relating to a theory of social evolution. This assertion might appear somewhat off the track; I would like, therefore, to begin by recalling the following circumstances:

(1) In the theoretical tradition going back to Marx the danger of slipping into bad philosophy was always especially great when there was an inclination to suppress philosophical questions in favor of a scientistic understanding of science. Even in Marx himself the heritage of the philosophy of history sometimes came rather unreflectedly into play.[1] This historical objectivism took effect above all in the evolutionary theories of the Second International – for example, in Kautsky and "Diamat." Thus special care is called for if we are today to take up once again the basic assumptions of historical materialism in regard to social

evolution. This effort cannot consist in borrowing a list of prohibitions from a methodology developed with physics as the model, prohibitions that bar the way to social-scientific theories of development which pursue a research program suggested by Freud, Mead, Piaget, and Chomsky. But care is called for in the choice of the basic concepts that determine the object domain of communicative action, for by this step, the kind of knowledge with which historical materialism may credit itself is decided.

(2) From the beginning there was a lack of clarity concerning the normative foundation of Marxian social theory. This theory was not meant to renew the ontological claims of classical natural law, nor to vindicate the descriptive claims of nomological sciences; it was supposed to be "critical" social theory but only to the extent that it could avoid the naturalistic fallacies of implicitly evaluative theories. Marx believed he had solved this problem with a *coup de main*, namely with a declaredly materialistic appropriation of the Hegelian logic. Of course, he did not have to occupy himself especially with this task; for his practical research purposes he could be content to take at its word, and to criticize immanently, the normative content of the ruling bourgeois theories of modern natural law and political economy – a content that was, moreover, incorporated into the revolutionary bourgeois constitutions of the time. In the meantime, bourgeois consciousness has become cynical; as the social sciences – especially legal positivism, neo-classical economics, and recent political theory – show, it has been thoroughly emptied of binding normative contents. However, if (as becomes even more apparent in times of recession) the bourgeois ideals have gone into retirement, there are no norms and values to which an immanent critique might appeal with [the expectation of] agreement. On the other hand, the melodies of ethical socialism have been played through without result. A philosophical ethics not restricted to meta-ethical statements is possible today only if we can reconstruct general presuppositions of communication and procedures for justifying norms and values.

In practical discourse we thematize one of the validity-claims that underlie speech as its *validity-basis*. In action oriented to reaching understanding, validity-claims (to the comprehensibility of the symbolic expression, the truth of the propositional content, the truthfulness of the intentional expression, and the rightness of the speech act with respect to existing norms and values) are set in the general structures of possible communication. In these validity-claims communication theory can locate a gentle but obstinate, a never silent although seldom redeemed claim to reason, a claim that must be recognized de facto whenever and wherever there is to be consensual action. If this is idealism, then idealism belongs in a most natural way to the conditions of reproduction of a species that must preserve its life through labor and interaction, that is, *also* by virtue of propositions that can be true and norms that are in need of justification.

(3) Not only are there connections between the theory of communicative action and the foundations of historical materialism; in examining individual assumptions of evolutionary theory, we run up against problems that make communications-theoretical reflections necessary. Whereas Marx localized the learning processes important for evolution in the dimension of objectivating thought – of technical and organizational knowledge, of instrumental and strategic action, in short, of *productive forces* – there are good reasons meanwhile for assuming that learning processes also take place in the dimension of moral insight, practical knowledge, communicative action, and the consensual regulation of action conflicts – learning processes that are deposited in more mature forms of social integration, in new *productive relations*, and that in turn first make possible the introduction of new productive forces. The rationality structures that find expression in world-views, moral representations, and identity formations, that become practically effective in social movements and are finally embodied in institutional systems, thereby gain a strategically important position from a theoretical point of view. The systematically reconstructible patterns of development of normative structures are now of particular interest. These structural patterns depict a *developmental logic* inherent in cultural traditions and institutional change. This logic says nothing about the *mechanisms* of development; it says something only about the range of variations within which cultural values, moral representations, norms, and the like – at a given level of social organization – can be changed and can find different historical expression. In its developmental *dynamics*, the change of normative structures remains dependent on evolutionary challenges posed by unresolved, economically conditioned, system problems and on learning processes that are a response to them. In other words, culture remains a superstructural phenomenon, even if it does seem to play a more prominent role in the transition to new developmental levels than many Marxists have heretofore supposed. This prominence explains the contribution that communication theory can, in my view, make to a renewed historical materialism. In the following pages I would like to at least suggest wherein this contribution could consist.

II

The structures of linguistically established intersubjectivity – which can be examined prototypically in connection with elementary speech actions – are conditions of both social and personality systems. Social systems can be viewed as networks of communicative actions; person-

ality systems can be regarded under the aspect of the ability to speak
and act. If one examines social institutions and the action competences
of socialized individuals for general characteristics, one encounters the
same structures of consciousness. This can be shown in connection with
those arrangements and orientations that specialize in maintaining the
endangered intersubjectivity of understanding in cases of action conflicts
– law and morality. When the background consensus of habitual daily
routine breaks down, consensual regulation of action conflicts (accomplished under the renunciation of force) provides for the continuation
of communicative action with other means. To this extent, law and
morality mark the core domain of interaction. One can see here the
identity of the conscious structures that are, on the one hand, embodied
in the institutions of law and morality and that are, on the other hand,
expressed in the moral judgment and actions of the individuals. Cognitive developmental psychology has shown that in ontogenesis there are
different stages of moral consciousness, stages that can be described in
particular as pre-conventional and postconventional patterns of problem solving.[2] The same patterns turn up again in the social evolution of
moral and legal representations.

The ontogenetic models are certainly better analyzed and better
corroborated than their social-evolutionary counterparts. But it should
not surprise us that there are homologous structures of consciousness in
the history of the species, if we consider that linguistically established
intersubjectivity of understanding marks that innovation in the history
of the species which first made possible the level of sociocultural
learning. At this level the reproduction of society and the socialization
of its members are two aspects of the same process; they are dependent
on the same structures.

The homologous structures of consciousness in the histories of the
individual and the species [are not restricted to the domain of law and
morality]. The success of the theoretical approach programmatically
presented here also requires an investigation of rationality structures in
domains that have heretofore been scarcely examined, either conceptually or empirically – in the domain of ego development and the
evolution of world-views on the one hand, and in the domain of ego
and group identities on the other. [. . .]

The continuity-guaranteeing character of role identities is based on
the intersubjective validity and temporal stability of behavioral expectations. If the development of moral consciousness leads beyond this
conventional stage, role identity is shattered because the ego then
withdraws behind all particular roles. An ego expected to judge any
given norm in the light of internalized principles, that is, to consider
them hypothetically and to provide justifications, can no longer tie its
identity to particular pre-given roles and sets of norms. Now continuity
can be established only through the ego's own integrating accomplishment. This ability is paradigmatically exercised when the growing child

gives up its early identities, which are tied to familial roles, in favor of more and more abstract identities secured finally to the institutions and traditions of the political community. To the extent that the ego generalizes this ability to overcome an old identity and to construct a new one and learns to resolve identity crises by re-establishing at a higher level the disturbed balance between itself and a changed social reality, role identity is replaced by ego identity. The ego can then maintain his identity in relation to others, expressing in all relevant role games the paradoxical relationship of being like and yet being absolutely different from the other, and represent himself as the one who organizes his interactions in an unmistakable complex of life-history.

In modern society this ego identity could be supported by individual-istic vocational roles. The vocational role, understood in Weber's sense, was the most significant vehicle for projecting a unifying life-historical career. Today this vehicle seems more and more to be slipping away. Thus feminism is an example of an emancipatory movement that (under the catchword of self-realization) searches for paradigmatic solutions to the problem of stabilizing ego identity under conditions that render problematic – especially for women – recourse to the vocational role as the crystallizing nucleus of life-history.

In looking for homologies between patterns of identity development and the historical articulation of collective identities, we have to avoid, again, drawing hasty parallels. The provisos I mentioned above hold here as well; and I would like to add three special ones.

1 The collective identity of a group or a society secures continuity and recognizability. For this reason it varies with the temporal concepts in terms of which the society can specify the requirements for remaining the same. The individual lifetime too is schematized on different levels of cognitive development; but it is objectively bounded, at least, by birth and death. There are no comparable objective cut-off points for the historical existence of a society, with its overreaching generations and, often, epochs.

2 Furthermore, collective identity determines how a society demar-cates itself from its natural and social environments. In this respect too, clear analogies [to individual life] are lacking. A personal lifeworld is bounded by the horizon of all possible experiences and actions that can be attributed to the individual in his exchange with his social environ-ment. By contrast, the symbolic boundaries of a society are formed primarily as the horizon of the actions that members reciprocally attribute to themselves internally.

3 The third feature is all the more important – collective identity regulates the membership of individuals in the society (and exclusion therefrom). In this respect there is a complementary relation between ego and group identity, because the unity of the person is formed through relations to other persons of the same group; and as I

mentioned above, identity development is characterized by the fact that early identification with concrete and less complex groups (the family) is weakened and subordinated to identification with more encompassing and more abstract units (city, state). This suggests that we can infer from the ontogenetic stages of ego development the complementary social structures of the tribal group, the state, and, finally, global forms of intercourse. Elsewhere I advanced certain conjectures to that effect; but I see now that I underestimated the complexity of the connection of collective identities with world-views and systems of norms. Following Parsons, we can distinguish cultural values, action systems in which values are institutionalized, and collectives that act in these systems. Only *a certain segment* of the culture and action system is important for the identity of a collective – namely the taken-for-granted, consensual, basic values and institutions that enjoy a kind of fundamental validity in the group. Individual members of the group perforce experience the destruction or violation of this normative core as a threat to their own identity. The different forms of collective identity can be found only in such normative cores, in which individual members "know themselves as one" with each other.

In *neolithic societies* collective identity was secured through the fact that individuals traced their descent to the figure of a common ancestor and thus, in the framework of their mythological world-view, assured themselves of a common cosmogonic origin. On the other hand, the personal identity of the individual developed through identification with a tribal group, which was in turn perceived as part of a nature interpreted in interaction categories. As social reality was not yet clearly distinguished from natural reality, the boundaries of the social world merged into those of the world in general. Without clearly defined boundaries of the social system there was no natural or social environment in the strict sense; contacts with alien tribes were interpreted in accord with the familiar kinship connection. On the other hand, encounters with civilizations that (unlike alien tribes) could no longer be assimilated to their own world represented a danger for the collective identity of societies organized along kinship lines (independently of the real danger of colonial conquest).

The transition to *societies organized through a state* required the relativization of tribal identities and the construction of a more abstract identity that no longer based the membership of individuals on common descent but on belonging in common to a territorial organization. This took place first through identification with the figure of a ruler who could claim a close connection and privileged access to the mythological originary powers. In the framework of mythological world-views the integration of different tribal traditions was accomplished through a large-scale, syncretistic expansion of the world of the gods – a solution that proved to be rather unstable. For this reason, imperially developed civilizations had to secure their collective identity in a way that presupposed a break with mythological thought. The universalistic world-interpretations of the great founders of religions and of the great philosophers grounded a commonality of conviction mediated through a teaching tradition and permitting only abstract objects of identification. As members of universal communities of faith, citizens could recognize their ruler and the order represented by him so long as it was possible to render political domination plausible in some sense as the legacy of an order of the world and of salvation that was believed in and posited absolutely.

In contrast to archaic tribal societies, the *great empires* had to demarcate themselves from a desocialized outer nature as well as from the social environment of those alien to the empire. But since collective identity could now be secured only by way of doctrines with a universal claim, the political order also had to be in accord with this claim – the empires were not universal in name alone. Their peripheries were fluid; they consisted of allies and dependents. In addition there were barbarians, whom one attempted either to conquer or to convert – aliens who were potential members but who, so long as they had not the status of citizen, did not count as fully human. Only the reality of other empires was incompatible with this definition of the boundaries and social environment of an empire. Despite the existence of trade relations, and despite the diffusion of innovations, the empires shielded themselves from this danger; among themselves they maintained no diplomatic relations in the sense of an institutionalized foreign policy. In any case, their political existence was not dependent on a system of reciprocal recognition.

The limits of this identity formation manifested themselves inwardly as well. In societies organized along kinship lines collective identity was correlated, in most cases, with individual role identities established through kinship structures. Within the framework of mythological world-views there was no stimulus to develop identity beyond this stage; individual discrepancies could easily be accommodated in the roles of priest and shaman. In highly stratified civilizations, on the other hand, the integrating power of the identity of the empire had to confirm itself precisely in unifying the evolutionarily non-synchronous structures of consciousness of the country, the aristocracy, city tradesmen, priests, and officials, and in binding them to the same political order. A broad spectrum of belief attitudes toward the same tradition was permitted; what was for one something like a myth that could still be connected with magical practices was for others a tradition of faith, however supported by ritual. The dogmatic organization of doctrinal knowledge often displaced even the weight of tradition with the weight of arguments and replaced an attitude of faith based on the authority of a doctrine with a theoretical attitude. But this universalistic potential could not be released on a large scale if the particularity of domination and of the citizen's status, which was merely concealed by the empire's claim to universality, was to remain imperceptible and not lead to significant discrepancies.

Such discrepancies turned up again and again in the ancient empires; but only with the transition to *the modern world* did they become unavoidable. The capitalist principle of organization meant the differentiation of a depoliticized and market-regulated economic system. This domain of decentralized individual decisions was organized on universalistic principles in the framework of bourgeois civil law. It was thereby supposed that the private, autonomous, legal subjects pursued their interests in this morally neutralized domain of intercourse in a purposive-rational manner, in accord with general maxims. From this conversion of the productive sphere to universalistic orientations there proceeded a strong structural compulsion for the development of personality structures that replaced conventional role identity with ego identity. In fact, emancipated members of bourgeois society, whose conventional identity had been shattered, could know themselves as one with their fellow citizens in their character as (1) free and equal subjects of civil law (the citizen as private commodity owner), (2) morally free subjects (the citizen as private person), and (3) politically free subjects (the citizen as democratic citizen of the state). Thus the collective identity of bourgeois society developed under the highly abstract viewpoints of legality, morality, and sovereignty; at least it expressed itself in this way in modern natural-law constructions and in formalist ethics.

However, these abstract determinations are best suited to the identity of world citizens, not to that of citizens of a particular state that has to maintain itself against other states. The modern state arose in the sixteenth century as a member of a system of states; the sovereignty of one found its limits in the sovereignty of all other states; indeed its sovereignty was only constituted in this system based on reciprocal recognition. Even if the system could have defined away, as peripheral, the non-European world with which it was economically involved from the start, it still could not have represented itself as a universal unity in the style of a grand empire. This was excluded by the international relations between the sovereign states – relations based in the final analysis on the threat of military force. Moreover, the modern state was more reliant than the state in tribal societies on the loyalty and willingness to sacrifice of a population made economically and socially mobile. The identity of world citizens obviously is not strong enough to establish universal conscription. A symptom of this can be seen in the double identity of the citizen of the modern state – he is *homme* and *citoyen* in one.[3]

This competition between two group identities was temporarily silenced through membership in nations: the nation is the modern identity formation that defused and made bearable the contradiction between the intrastate universalism of bourgeois law and morality, on the one hand, and the particularism of individual states, on the other. Today there are a number of indications that this historically significant solution is no longer stable. The Federal Republic of Germany has the first army expected by the responsible minister to maintain fighting readiness without an image of the enemy. Conflicts that are ignited below the threshold of national identity are breaking out everywhere, in connection with questions of race, creed, language, regional differences, and other subcultures.

One alternative to the presently disintegrating national identity was the European working-class movement. Taking the bourgeois philosophy of history as its point of departure, historical materialism projected a collective identity compatible with universalistic ego structures. What the eighteenth century had thought of under the rubric of cosmopolitanism was now conceived of as socialism; but this identity was projected into the future and thus made a task for political practice. This was the first example of an identity that had become reflective, of a collective identity no longer tied retrospectively to specific doctrines and forms of life but prospectively to programs and rules for bringing about something. Until now identity formation of this type could be maintained only in social movements; whether societies in a normal state could develop such a fluid identity is questionable. It would have to adjust itself to high mobility, not only in regard to productive resources, but also in regard to processes of norm and value formation. For the time being only China is experimenting with such arrangements.

This sketch can at best suggest how to use the identity development of the individual as a key to the change of collective identities. In both dimensions identity projections apparently become more and more general and abstract, until finally the projection mechanism as such becomes conscious, and identity formation takes on a reflective form, in the knowledge that to a certain extent individuals and societies themselves establish their identities.

IV

The [preceding] two excurses were meant to make plausible the search for homologous structures of consciousness in ego development and social evolution in two areas [viz. world-views and collective identities] that are not nearly as well researched as the structures of legal and moral representations. All three complexes lead back to structures of linguistically established intersubjectivity. (1) Law and morality serve to regulate action conflicts consensually and thus to maintain an endangered intersubjectivity of understanding among speaking and acting subjects. (2) The demarcation of different universal object domains – one of which appears in the propositional attitude of the observer as external nature, a second in the performative attitude of the participant in interaction as normative social reality, and a third in the expressive attitude of one who expresses an intention as his own subjective nature – makes possible the differentiation (and if necessary thematization) of those validity-claims (truth, rightness, truthfulness) that we implicitly tie to all speech actions. (3) Finally, the construction of personal and corresponding collective identities is a necessary presupposition for taking on the general communicative roles, which are provided for in every speaking and acting situation and which find their expression in the employment of personal pronouns.

To be sure, the communication theory I have in mind is not yet developed to a point at which we could adequately analyze the symbolic structures that underlie law and morality, an intersubjectively consti-tuted world, and the identities of persons and collectives. And we are really far from being able to provide convincing reconstructions of the patterns of development of these structures in the spheres of ontogene-sis and species history. The very concept of a developmental logic requires additional sharpening before we can say formally what it means to describe the direction of development in ontogenesis and in the history of the species by means of such concepts as universalization and individualization, decentration, autonomization, and becoming reflec-tive. If I stick to this theme in spite of the (for the time being) unsatisfactory degree of explication, it is because I am convinced that normative structures do not simply follow the path of development of reproductive processes and do not simply respond to the pattern of system problems, but that they have instead an *internal history*. In earlier investigations I have tried to argue that holistic concepts such as productive activity and *praxis* have to be resolved into the basic concepts of communicative action and purposive-rational action in order to avoid confusing the two rationalization processes that deter-mine social evolution; the rationalization of action takes effect not only on productive forces but also, and independently, on normative structures.

Purposive-rational actions can be regarded under two different aspects – the empirical efficiency of technical means and the consistency of choice between suitable means. Actions and action systems can be rationalized in both respects. The rationality of means requires techni-cally utilizable, empirical knowledge; the rationality of decisions requires the explication and inner consistency of value-systems and decision maxims, as well as the correct derivation of acts of choice. I shall speak of strategic action in the case of competing opponents insofar as they are determined by the intention of influencing each others' decisions in a purposive-rational way, that is, in a way oriented only to each's own success.

In contexts of social action, the rationalization of means and the choice of means signifies a *heightening of productive forces*, that is, a socially significant implementation of knowledge, with the help of which we can improve the technical outfitting, organizational deployment, and qualifications of available labor power. Marx saw in this process the motor of social development. It is of course necessary to distinguish more precisely among (1) the rationality structures and (if appropriate) developmental logic of the knowledge that can be transposed into technologies, into strategies or organizations, and into qualifications; (2) the mechanisms that can explain the acquisition of this knowledge, the corresponding learning processes; and (3) the boundary conditions under which available knowledge can be implemented in a socially significant way. Only these three complexes of conditions together can explain rationalization processes in the sense of the development of productive forces. However, there is now the further question of whether *other* rationalization processes are just as important or even more important for the explanation of social evolution. In addition to the development of the forces of production, Marx regarded social movements as important. But in conceiving of the organized struggle of oppressed classes as itself a productive force, he established between the two motors of social development – technical-organizational pro-gress on the one hand and class struggle on the other – a confusing, in any event an inadequately analyzed, connection.

In contradistinction to purposive-rational action, *communicative action* is, among other things, oriented to observing intersubjectively valid norms that link reciprocal expectations. In communicative action, the validity-basis of speech is presupposed. The universal validity-claims (truth, rightness, truthfulness), which participants at least implicitly raise and reciprocally recognize, make possible the consensus that carries action in common. In strategic action, this background consensus is lacking; the truthfulness of expressed intentions is not expected, and the norm-conformity of an utterance (or the rightness of the norm itself) is presupposed in a different sense than in communicative action – namely, contingently. One who repeatedly makes senseless moves in playing chess disqualifies himself as a chess player; and one who follows rules other than those constitutive of chess is not playing chess. Strategic action remains indifferent with respect to its motivational conditions, whereas the consensual presuppositions of communicative action can secure motivations. Thus strategic actions must be institutionalized, that is, embedded in intersubjectively binding norms that guarantee the fulfillment of the motivational conditions. Even then we can distinguish the aspect of purposive-rational action – in Parsons's terminology, the task aspect – from the framework of normatively guided communicative action. In purposive-rational action it is supposed only that each subject is following preferences and decision maxims that he has determined for himself – that is, monologically, regardless of whether or not he agrees therein with other subjects. When, therefore, a strategic action system (e.g., war) makes it necessary for several subjects to agree in certain preferences (and to the extent that this agreement is not guaranteed in fact by the interest situations), purposive-rational action has somehow to be bound or institutionalized (e.g., in the framework of the Hague Convention). Institutionalization again means the organization of consensual action resting on intersubjectively recognized validity claims.

Communicative action can be rationalized neither under the technical aspect of the means selected nor under the strategic aspect of the selection of means but only under the moral-practical aspect of the responsibility of the acting subject and the justifiability of the action norm. Whereas the rationalization of purposive-rational action depends on the accumulation of true (empirically or analytically true) knowledge, the rationalizable aspect of communicative action has nothing to do with propositional truth; but it has everything to do with the truthfulness of intentional expressions and with the rightness of norms. The rationality of action oriented to reaching understanding is measured against:

1 whether a subject truthfully expresses his intentions in his actions (or whether he deceives himself and others because the norm of action is so little in accord with his needs that conflicts arise that have to be defended against unconsciously, through setting up internal barriers to communications);
2 whether the validity-claims connected with norms of action, and recognized in fact, are legitimate (or whether the existing normative context does not express generalizable or compromisable interests, and thus can be stabilized in its de facto validity only so long as those affected can be prevented by inconspicuous restrictions on communication from discursively examining the normative validity-claim).

Rationalization here means extirpating those relations of force that are inconspicuously set in the very structures of communication and that prevent conscious settlement of conflicts, and consensual regulation of conflicts, by means of intrapsychic as well as interpersonal communicative barriers. Rationalization means overcoming such systematically distorted communication in which the action-supporting consensus concerning the reciprocally raised validity claims – especially the consensus concerning the truthfulness of intentional expressions and the rightness of underlying norms – can be sustained in appearance only, that is, counterfactually. The stages of law and morality, of ego demarcations and world-views, of individual and collective identity formations, are stages in this process. Their progress cannot be measured against the choice of correct strategies, but rather against the intersubjectivity of understanding achieved without force, that is, against the expansion of the domain of consensual action together with the re-establishment of undistorted communication.

The categorial distinction between purposive-rational and communicative action thus permits us to separate the aspects under which action can be rationalized. As learning processes take place not only in the dimension of objectivating thought but also in the dimension of moral-practical insight, the rationalization of action is deposited not only in forces of production, but also – mediated through the dynamics of social movements – in forms of social integration. Rationality structures are embodied not only in amplifications of purposive-rational action – that is, in technologies, strategies, organizations, and qualifications – but also in mediations of communicative action – in the mechanisms for regulating conflict, in world-views, and in identity formations. I would even defend the thesis that the development of these normative structures is the pacemaker of social evolution, for new principles of social organization mean new forms of social integration; and the latter, in turn, first make it possible to implement available productive forces or to generate new ones, as well as making possible a heightening of social complexity.

The prominent place I have given to normative structures in the framework of social evolution could lead to several misunderstandings – one, that the dynamics of species history is to be explained through an internal history of spirit; and another, that a developmental logic is once again to take the place of historical contingencies. Behind the first misunderstanding lies the suspicion that I am quietly dropping the materialist assumptions regarding the motor of social development; the second suspects another logification of history – and philosophical mystifications instead of empirical-scientific analysis. As indicated, I consider these to be misunderstandings.

Let us assume for a moment that developmental patterns for the normative structures of a certain society can be reconstructed and corroborated. (I am not talking here of any arbitrarily selected classification of stages but of developmental logics in Piaget's sense, which must satisfy rather improbable conditions.) Such rationally reconstructible patterns then represent *rules for possible problem-solving*, that is, only formal restrictions and not mechanisms that could explain individual problem-solving processes, not to mention the acquisition of general problem-solving abilities. The *learning mechanisms* have to be sought first on the psychological level. If that succeeds, with the help of cognitive developmental psychology, there is need for additional empirical assumptions that might explain sociologically how individual learning processes find their way into a society's collectively accessible store of knowledge. *Individually acquired learning abilities* and information must be latently available in world-views before they can be used in a socially significant way, that is, before they can be transposed into *societal learning processes*.

Since the cognitive development of the individual takes place under social boundary conditions, there is a circular process between societal and individual learning. To be sure, one could argue for a primacy of social over individual structures of consciousness on the grounds that the rationality structures embodied in the family have first to be absorbed by the child in the development of his interactive competence (as he passes out of the pre-conventional stage). On the other hand, the initial state of archaic societies – characterized by a conventional kinship organization, a pre-conventional stage of law, and an egocentric interpretive system – could itself be changed only by constructive learning on the part of socialized individuals. It is only in a derivative sense that societies "learn." I shall assume two series of initial conditions for evolutionary learning processes of society: on the one hand, unresolved system problems that represent challenges; on the other, new levels of learning that have already been achieved in world-views and are latently available but not yet incorporated into action systems and thus remain institutionally inoperative.

System problems express themselves as disturbances of the reproduction process of a society that is normatively fixed in its identity. Whether problems arise which overload the adaptive capacity of a society is a contingent matter; when problems of this type do arise, the reproduction of the society is placed in question – unless it takes up the evolutionary challenge and alters the established form of social integration that limits the employment and development of resources. *Whether* this alteration – which Marx describes as an overthrow of the relations of production – is actually possible, and *how* it is developmental-logically possible, cannot be read off the system problems; it is rather a question of access to a new learning level. The solution to the problems producing the crisis requires (1) attempts to loosen up the existing form of social integration by embodying in new institutions the rationality structures already developed in world-views, and (2) a milieu favorable to the stabilization of successful attempts. Every economic advance can be characterized in terms of institutions in which rationality structures of the next higher stage of development are embodied – for example, the royal courts of justice, which, early in the development of civilization, permitted administration of justice at the *conventional* level of moral consciousness; or the capitalist firm, rational administration of the state, and bourgeois norms of civil law, which, at the beginning of the modern period, organized morally neutral domains of strategic action according to *universalistic* principles. Previously sociologists talked only of an "institutionalization of values," through which certain value-orientations receive binding force for actors. When I now attempt to grasp evolutionary learning processes with the aid of the concept of "the institutional embodiment of structures of rationality," it is no longer a question of making orienting *contents* binding but of opening up *structural possibilities for the rationalization of action.*

Looking now at this explanatory strategy (which has proven itself in Klaus Eder's investigation of the rise of societies organized around a state),[4] we can see that the objections mentioned above are pointless. The analysis of developmental dynamics is "materialist" insofar as it makes reference to crisis-producing system problems in the domain of production and reproduction; and it remains "historically" oriented insofar as it has to seek the causes of evolutionary changes in the whole range of those contingent circumstances under which (1) new structures are acquired in the individual consciousness and transposed into structures of world-views; (2) system problems arise, which overload the steering capacity of a society; (3) the institutional embodiment of new rationality structures can be tried and stabilized; and (4) the new latitude for the mobilization of resources can be utilized. Only after rationalization processes (which require explanations that are both historical and materialist) have been historically completed can we specify the patterns of development for the normative structures of society. These developmental logics betoken the independence – and to this extent the internal history – of the spirit.

Communication and the Evolution of Society, pp. 95–123.

Notes

1 A. Wellmer, *Critical Theory of Society* (New York: Seaburg, 1971), and "Communication and Emancipation: Reflections on the Linguistic Turn in Critical Theory," in John O'Neill (ed.), *On Critical Theory* (New York, 1976), pp. 321–63; and J. Habermas, "Uber das Subjekt der Geschichte," in *Kultur und Kritik* (Frankfurt: Suhrkamp, 1973), pp. 389–98.

2 J. Piaget, *The Moral Judgment of the Child* (New York, 1965); and L. Kohlberg, "Stage and Sequence," in D. Goslin (ed.), *Handbook of Socialization Theory and Research* (Chicago, 1969), and "From is to Ought," in T. Mischel (ed.), *Cognitive Development and Epistemology* (New York, 1971), pp. 151–236.

3 Marx analyzed this double identity – with reference naturally to Rousseau – in "On the Jewish Question," *Writings of the Young Marx on Philosophy and Society*, L.D. Easton and K.H. Guddat (eds. and trans.) (New York, 1967), pp. 216–48.

4 Klaus Eder, *Die Enstehung staatlich organisierter Gesellschaften. Ein Beitrag zu einer Theorie sozialer Evolution*. Frankfurt: Suhrkamp, 1976.

22

Social Principles of Organization

I think it meaningful to distinguish four social formations: primitive [*vorhochkulturelle*], traditional, capitalist, postcapitalist.[1] Except for primitive societies, we are dealing with class societies. (I designate state-socialist societies – in view of their political-elitist disposition of the means of production – as "postcapitalist class societies.")

Social formations

	Primitive
Class societies {	Civilizations
	Traditional
	Modern
	Capitalist
	Liberal-capitalist
	Organized or advanced capitalist
	Postcapitalist
	Postmodern

The interest behind the examination of crisis tendencies in late-[capitalist] and postcapitalist class societies is in exploring the possibilities of a "postmodern" society – that is, a historically new principle of organization and not a different name for the surprising vigor of an aged capitalism.[2] I would like to illustrate what is meant by social principles of organization and how definite types of crisis can be derived from them in terms of three social formations. These loose remarks are intended neither to stimulate nor to substitute for a theory of social evolution. They serve solely to introduce a concept by way of examples. For each of the three social formations I shall sketch the determining principle of organization, indicate the possibilities it opens to social evolution, and infer the type of crisis it allows. Without a theory of social evolution to rely on, principles of organization cannot be grasped abstractly, but only picked out inductively and elaborated with reference to the institutional sphere (kinship system, political system, economic system) that possesses functional primacy for a given stage of development.

Primitive social formation

The primary roles of age and sex form *the organizational principle* of primitive societies.[3] The institutional core is the *kinship system*, which at this stage of development represents a total institution; family structures determine the totality of social intercourse. They simultaneously secure social and system integration. World-views and norms are scarcely differentiated from one another; both are built around rituals and taboos that require no independent sanctions. This principle of organization is compatible only with familial and tribal morals. Vertical or horizontal social relations that overstep the bounds of the kinship system are not possible. In societies organized along kinship lines, the forces of production cannot be augmented through exploitation of labor power (raising the rate of exploitation through physical force). The learning mechanism, which is built into the behavioral system of instrumental action [*Funktionskreis instrumentalen Handelns*],[4] leads, over long periods, to a seemingly ordered sequence of less fundamental innovations.[5] At the stage of development of primitive society, there seems to be no systematic motive for producing more goods than are necessary to satisfy basic needs, even though the state of the productive forces may permit a surplus.[6] Since no contradictory imperatives follow from this principle of organization, it is external change that overloads the narrowly limited steering capacity of societies organized along kinship lines and undermines the familial and tribal identities. The usual source of change is demographic growth in connection with ecological factors – above all, interethnic dependency as a result of economic exchange, war, and conquest.[7]

Traditional social formation

The *principle of organization* is *class domination* [*Klassenherrschaft*] in political form.[8] With the rise of a bureaucratic apparatus of authority, a control centre is differentiated out of the kinship system. This allows the transference of the production and distribution of social wealth from familial forms of organization to ownership of the means of production. The kinship system is no longer the institutional nucleus of the whole system; it surrenders the central functions of power and control to the state. This is the beginning of a functional specification and autonomization, in the course of which the family loses all of its economic functions and some of its socializing functions. At this stage of development, subsystems arise that serve predominantly either system or social integration. At their point of intersection lies the legal order that regulates the privilege of disposition of the means of production and the strategic exercise of power, which, in turn, requires legitimation. To the differentiation between the authority apparatus and the legal order on the one side, and the counterfactual justifications and moral systems on the other, there corresponds the institutional separation of secular and sacred powers.

The new organizational principle permits a significant strengthening of system autonomy. It presupposes functional differentiation and makes possible the formation of generalized media (power and money) as well as reflexive mechanisms (positive law). But this latitude for growth in steering capacity is developed at the cost of a fundamentally unstable class structure. With private ownership of the means of production, a power relationship is institutionalized in class societies, which in the long run threatens social integration;[9] for the opposition of interests established in the class relationship represents a conflict potential. Of course, within the framework of a legitimate order of authority, the opposition of interests can be kept latent and integrated for a certain time. This is the achievement of legitimating world-views or ideologies. They remove the counterfactual validity-claims of normative structures from the sphere of public thematization and testing. The order of authority is justified by falling back on traditional world-views and a conventional civic ethic.

In spite of considerable vertical differentiation, the new organizational principle holds horizontal social relations through unpolitical exchange relations (local markets, city – country) within narrow limits. The political class rule requires a mediation of tribal morals through civic ethics that remain dependent on tradition – that is, particularistic. It is incompatible with universalistic forms of intercourse. In a class system of social labor, the forces of production can be augmented through raising the rate of exploitation, that is, through organized forced labor. Thus a socially produced surplus product arises that is appropriated according to privilege. The enhancing of the productive force has its limits, to be sure, in the persistence of unplanned, nature-like development [*Naturwüchsigkeit*] of technical innovations. (Technically utilizable knowledge is not extended through reflexive learning.)[10]

In traditional societies the type of crisis that arises proceeds from internal contradictions. The contradiction exists between validity-claims of systems of norms and justifications that cannot explicitly permit exploitation, and a class structure in which privileged appropriation of socially produced wealth is the rule. The problem of how socially produced wealth may be inequitably, and yet legitimately, distributed is temporarily solved through the ideological protection of counterfactual validity-claims. In critical situations, traditional societies extend the scope of their control through heightened exploitation of labor power; that is, they augment power either directly through heightened physical force (of which the history of penal law gives good indicators), or indirectly through generalization of forced payments (in the sequence of work-, product-, and money-rents). Consequently, crises as a rule issue from steering problems that necessitate a strengthening of system autonomy through heightened repression. The latter leads in turn to legitimation losses, which for their part result in class struggles (often in connection with foreign conflicts). Class struggles finally threaten social integration and can lead to an overthrow of the political system and to new foundations of legitimation – that is, to a new group identity.

Liberal-capitalist social formation

The *principle of organization* is the *relationship of wage labor and capital*, which is anchored in the system of bourgeois civil law. With the rise of a sphere, free of the state, of commerce between private autonomous owners of commodities – that is, with the institutionalization in independent states of goods-, capital-, and labor-markets and the establishment of world trade – "civil society" [*bürgerliche Gesellschaft*] is differentiated out of the political-economic system. This signifies a depoliticization of the class relationship and an anonymization of class domination. The state and the politically constituted system of social labor are no longer the institutional nucleus of the system as a whole. Instead, the modern rational state – whose prototype Max Weber analyzed – becomes the complementary arrangement to self-regulative market commerce. Externally, the state still insures by political means the territorial integrity and the competitiveness of the domestic economy. Internally, the previously dominant medium of control, legitimate power, serves above all to maintain the general conditions of production, which make possible the market-regulated process of capital realization. Economic exchange becomes the dominant steering medium. After the capitalist mode of production has been established, the exercise of the state's power within the social system can be limited: (1) to the protection of bourgeois commerce in accord with civil law (police and administration of justice); (2) to the shielding of the market mechanism from self-destructive side effects (for example, legislation for the protection of labor); (3) to the satisfaction of the prerequisites of production in the economy as a whole (public school education, transportation, and communication); and (4) to the adaptation of the system of civil law to needs that arise from the process of accumulation (tax, banking, and business law). By fulfiling these four classes of tasks, the state secures the structural prerequisites of the reproduction process as capitalistic.

Although in traditional societies an institutional differentiation between spheres of system integration and social integration had already set in, the economic system remained dependent on the supply of legitimation from the sociocultural system. Only the relative uncoupling of the economic system from the political permits a sphere to arise in bourgeois society that is free from the traditional ties and given over to the strategic-utilitarian action orientations of market participants. Competing entrepreneurs then make their decisions according to maxims of profit-oriented competition and replace value-oriented with interest-guided action.

The new organizational principle opens a broad scope for the development of productive forces and of normative structures. With the imperatives of the self-realization of capital, the mode of production sets in motion an expanded reproduction that is tied to the mechanism of innovations that enhance labor productivity. As soon as the limits of physical exploitation – that is, of raising the absolute surplus value – are reached, the accumulation of capital necessitates development of technical productive forces and, in this way, coupling of technically utilizable knowledge to reflexive learning processes. On the other hand, the now autonomous economic exchange relieves the political order of the pressures of legitimation. Self-regulative market commerce requires supplementation, not only through rational state administration and abstract law, but through a strategic-utilitarian morality in the sphere of social labor, which in the private domain is equally compatible with a "Protestant" or a "formalistic" ethic. Bourgeois ideologies can assume a universalistic structure and appeal to generalizable interests because the property order has shed its political form and been converted into a relation of production that, it seems, can legitimate itself. The institution of the market can be founded on the justice inherent in the exchange of equivalents; and, for this reason, the bourgeois constitutional state finds its justification in the legitimate relations of production. This is the message of rational natural law since Locke. The relations of production can do without a traditional authority legitimated from above.

Of course, the socially integrative effect of the value form may be restricted, by and large, to the bourgeois class. The loyalty and subordination of members of the new urban proletariat, recruited mainly from the ranks of the peasants, are certainly maintained more through a mixture of traditionalistic ties, fatalistic willingness to follow, lack of perspective, and naked repression than through the convincing force of bourgeois ideologies. This does not diminish the socially integrative significance of this new type of ideology in a society that no longer recognizes political domination in personal form.

With the political anonymization of class rule, the socially dominant class must convince itself that it no longer rules. Universalistic bourgeois ideologies can fulfill this task insofar as they (1) are founded "scientifically" on the critique of tradition and (2) possess the character of a model, that is, anticipate a state of society whose possibility need not from the start be denied by a dynamically growing economic society. All the more sensitively, however, must bourgeois society react to the evident contradiction between idea and reality. For this reason the critique of bourgeois society could take the form of an unmasking of bourgeois ideologies themselves by confronting idea and reality. The achievement of the capitalist principle of organization is nevertheless extraordinary. It not only frees the economic system, uncoupled from the political system, from the legitimations of the socially integrative subsystems, but enables it, along with its system integrative tasks, to make a contribution to social integration. With these achievements, the susceptibility of the social system to crisis certainly grows, as steering problems can now become *directly* threatening to identity. In this sense I would like to speak of *system crises*.

In an unplanned, nature-like [*naturwüchsig*] movement of economic development, the organizational principle sets no limits to the development of productive forces. The normative structures also obtain a broad scope for development, for the new principle of organization permits (for the first time) universalistic value-systems. It is, of course, incompatible with a communicative ethic, which requires not only generality of norms but a discursively attained consensus about the *generalizability* of the normatively prescribed interests. The principle of organization transposes the conflict potential of class opposition into the steering dimension, where it expresses itself in the form of economic crises. For liberal capitalism, the fluctuation of prosperity, crisis, and depression is typical. The opposition of interests, which is grounded in the relation of wage labor and capital, comes to light, not directly in class conflicts, but in the interruption of the process of accumulation, that is, in the form of steering problems. A general concept of system crisis can be gained from the logic of this economic crisis.

[Table 22.1] sums up the connections between the organizational principles introduced as examples and the corresponding types of crisis.

In determining the possibilities for evolution in each of the three developmental dimensions (production, steering, and socialization), the principle of organization determines whether, and if so, (1) how system and social integration can be functionally differentiated; (2) when dangers to system integration must result in dangers to social integration, that is crises; and (3) in what way steering problems are transformed into dangers to identity, that is, what type of crisis predominates.

Legitimation Crisis, pp. 17–24.

Table 22.1

Social formations	Principle of organization	Social and system Integration	Type of crisis
Primitive	Kinship relations: primary roles (age, sex)	No differentiation between social and system integration	Externally induced identity crisis
Traditional	Political class rule: state power and socioeconomic classes	Functional differentiation between social and system integration	Internally determined identity crisis
Liberal-capitalist	Unpolitical class rule: wage labor and capital	System-integrative economic system also takes over socially integrative tasks	System crisis

Notes

1 [Translator's Note] Habermas uses the term *vorhochkulturell* to designate social formations that do not generally meet the criteria of civilizations (*Hochkulturen*). (For a brief characterization of these criteria see *Toward a Rational Society* (Boston: Beacon Press, 1970), p. 94ff.) Included in the class of "pre-civilizations" are the more primitive societies characteristic of the "long initial phase until the end of the Mesolithic period," as well as the "first settled cultures based on the domestication of animals and the cultivation of plants" (*Toward a Rational Society*, p. 114). There is, to my knowledge, no exactly corresponding term in English anthropological literature. "Pre-civilization" seems unnecessarily cumbersome. The characteristics of such societies stressed by Habermas in what follows are those generally associated with "primitive" societies. I have therefore, with Habermas's agreement, employed this more usual terminology.
2 D. Bell, "The Post-Industrial Society: The Evolution of an Idea," *Survey* 1971: 102ff.
3 T. Parsons, *Societies: Evolutionary and Comparative Perspectives* (Englewood Cliffs, N.J., 1966); G. Lenski, *Power and Privilege* (New York, 1966); Sahlins, *Service, Evolution and Culture* (Ann Arbor, 1968); further literature in K. Eder, *Mechanismen der sozialen Evolution*.
4 [Translator's Note] For an elucidation of the concept of instrumental action see Habermas, *Toward a Rational Society*, pp. 91–4, and *Knowledge and Human Interests*.
5 C. Lévi-Strauss, *The Savage Mind* (Chicago, 1966).
6 R.L. Caneiro, "A Theory of the Origin of the State," *Science*: 733ff.
7 Ibid., pp. 736ff.

8 [Translator's note] *Herrschaft,* literally "lordship," can be employed with various nuances in German social thought and has, for this reason, no adequate English equivalent. Parsons translates the term as "imperative co-ordination" and "authority" in his edition of Weber's *Theory of Social and Economic Organization* (New York, 1947), pp. 152ff, 342ff. This translation reflects Parsons' interpretation of Weber's position on value-neutrality in social science. Whatever the merits of his case (see G. Roth and C. Wittich (eds.), *Economy and Society,* 3 vols. (New York, 1968) for a critique of his translation), Habermas certainly wishes to retain the valuational nuances associated with the term. Thus, "domination" seems the more appropriate translation in many contexts. I have used both "authority" and "domination," and less frequently "rule," according to the context.

9 I am using the expression "private" here, not in the sense of modern bourgeois civil law [*Privatrecht*], but in the sense of a "privileged" disposition.

10 [Translator's note] Unfortunately, there is no English equivalent for the important term *Naturwüchsigkeit.* The suffix -*wüchsig* (from *wachsen,* to grow) means literally "growing." *Naturwüchsig* is used by critical theorists to refer to structures that develop spontaneously, without reflection or plan. It is employed by way of contrast to consciously directed processes, to structures that are the result of human will and determination. I have translated *Naturwüchsigkeit* here – somewhat awkwardly – as "unplanned, nature-like development."

23

Legitimation Problems in the Modern State

I

Legitimacy means that there are good arguments for a political order's claim to be recognized as right and just; a legitimate order deserves recognition. *Legitimacy means a political order's worthiness to be recognized.* This definition highlights the fact that legitimacy is a contestable validity-claim; the stability of the order of domination (also) depends on its (at least) de facto recognition. Thus, historically as well as analytically, the concept is used above all in situations in which the legitimacy of an order is disputed, in which, as we say, legitimation problems arise. One side denies, the other asserts legitimacy. This is a *process* – Talleyrand endeavored to *legitimize* the House of Bourbon. Processes of this kind were rendered less dramatic in the modern constitutional state (with the institutionalization of an opposition); that is, they were defused and normalized. For this reason it is realistic to speak today of legitimation as a permanent problem. Of course, in this framework too, legitimation conflicts flare up only over questions of principle ... Such conflicts can lead to a temporary withdrawal of legitimacy; and this can in certain circumstances have consequences that threaten the continued existence of a regime. If the outcome of such legitimation crises is connected with a change of the basic institutions not only of the state but of the society as a whole, we speak of revolutions [. . .]

Less trivial is the *domain of application* of the concept of legitimacy. Only political orders can have and lose legitimacy; only they need legitimation. Multinational corporations or the world market are not capable of legitimation. This is true also of pre-state, so-called primitive, societies that are organized according to kinship relations. To be sure, in these societies there are myths that interpret the natural and social order. They fix membership in the tribal group (and its limits) and thus secure a collective identity. Mythological world-views here have a constitutive significance rather than a subsequent legitimating significance.

We first speak of legitimacy in relation to political orders. Historically political domination crystallized around the function of the royal judge, around the nucleus of conflict regulation on the basis of recognized legal norms (and no longer only through the force of arbitration). The administration of justice at this level establishes a position that owes its authority to disposition over a legal system's force of sanction and no longer only to kinship status (and to the mediator role of the arbitrator). The legitimate power of the judge can become the nucleus of a system of domination to which the society gives over the function of intervening when its integrity is threatened. The state does not, it is true, itself establish the collective identity of the society; nor can it itself carry out social integration through values and norms, which are not at its disposition. But inasmuch as the state assumes the guarantee to prevent social disintegration by way of binding decisions, the exercise of state power is tied to the claim of maintaining society in its normatively determined identity. The legitimacy of state power is then measured against this; and it must be recognized as legitimate if it is to last.

In more recent theories of political development, which attempt to explain the emergence of the modern state, securing identity, procuring legitimation, and social integration are listed as general system problems. Of course, the systems-theoretic reformulation of these concepts conceals the connection that is constitutive for political domination. The political subsystem takes on the task of protecting society from disintegration; but it cannot freely dispose of the capacities of social integration or of the definitional power through which the identity of the society is fixed. At the evolutionary stage of societies organized through a state, different forms of identity have developed: the empire, the city state, the nation-state. These are, to be sure, only compatible with certain types of political domination, but they do not coincide with them. A world empire, a polis, a medieval commune, a nation – these express the connection of different political orders with different forms of life (ethos). Thus modernization research is correct in taking state-building and nation-building as two different, if interdependent, processes.

[...] By *legitimacy* I understand the worthiness of a political order to be recognized. The *claim to legitimacy* is related to the social-integrative preservation of a normatively determined social identity. *Legitimations* serve to make good this claim, that is, to show how and why existing (or recommended) institutions are fit to employ political power in such a way that the values constitutive for the identity of the society will be realized. Whether legitimations are convincing, whether they are believed, depends naturally on empirical motives; but these motives are not formed independently of the (formally analyzable) justificatory force of the legitimations themselves. We can also say that they are not independent of the legitimation potential, of the *grounds or reasons*, that can be mobilized. What is accepted as reasons and have the power to produce consensus, and thereby to shape motives, depends on the *level of justification* required in a given situation. Since I would like to use the concept of legitimation in a reconstructive manner, I shall take up briefly the question of the internal structure of justifications.

II

P. von Kielmannsegg has provided clear criticisms of Weberian types of legitimacy and proposed that we understand traditionalism and charisma as states that *every* legitimate order can assume.[1] We can distinguish these aspects of the establishment and maintenance of legitimate power from the forms of legitimate power, the types of domination. Here again we can separate the *legitimating grounds* from the *institutionalizations of domination*. Certain systems of institutions are compatible with a given level of justification; others are not.

I cannot characterize the historically familiar levels of justification in terms of their formal properties (as would be necessary); instead I shall illustrate them with a few allusions. In early civilizations the ruling families justified themselves with the help of myths of origin. Thus the pharaohs represented themselves first as gods – for example, as the god Horus, son of Osiris. On this level narrative grounds are sufficient, viz. mythological stories. With the imperial development of the ancient civilizations the need for legitimation grew; now not only the person of the ruler had to be justified, but a political order (against which the ruler could transgress). This end was served by cosmologically grounded ethics, higher religions, and philosophies, which go back to the great founders: Confucius, Buddha, Socrates, the prophets of Israel, and Jesus. These rationalized world-views had the form of dogmatizable knowledge. Arguments took the place of narratives. There were to be sure ultimate grounds, unifying principles, which explained the world as a whole (the natural and human world). The ontological tradition of thought was also on this level. Finally, in modern times, especially since the rise of modern science, we learned to distinguish more strictly between theoretical and practical argumentation. The status of ultimate grounds became problematic. Classical natural law was reconstructed; the new theories of natural law that legitimated the emerging modern state claimed to be valid independently of cosmologies, religions, or ontologies.

With Rousseau and Kant this development led to the conclusion that the formal principle of reason replaced material principles like Nature or God in practical questions, questions concerning the justification of norms and actions. Here justifications are not based only on arguments – that was also the case in the framework of philosophically formed world-views. Since ultimate grounds can no longer be made plausible, *the formal conditions of justification themselves obtain legitimating force.*

The procedures and presuppositions of rational agreement themselves become principles. In contract theories, from Hobbes and Locke to John Rawls, the fiction of a state of nature or of an original position *also* has the meaning of specifying the conditions under which an agreement will express the common interest of all involved – and to this extent can count as rational. In transcendentally oriented theories, from Kant to Karl-Otto Apel, these conditions, as universal and unavoidable presuppositions of rational will-formation, are transposed either into the subject as such or into the ideal communication community. In both traditions, it is the formal conditions of possible consensus formation, rather than ultimate grounds, which possess legitimating force.

Thus, by *levels of justification* I mean formal conditions for the acceptability of grounds or reasons, conditions that lend to legitimations their efficacy, their power to produce consensus and shape motives. These levels can be ordered hierarchically. The legitimations of a superseded stage, no matter what their content, are depreciated with the transition to the next higher stage; it is not this or that reason which is no longer convincing but the *kind* of reason. Such depreciation of the legitimation potential of entire blocks of tradition occurred in civilizations with the retrenchment of mythological thought, and in modern times with the retrenchment of cosmological, religious, and ontological modes of thought. My conjecture is that these depreciatory shifts are connected with social-evolutionary transitions to new learning levels, learning levels that lay down the conditions of possibility for learning processes in the dimensions of both objectivating thought and practical insight. I cannot go into that here. In any case, for the legitimation problems of the modern period, what is decisive is that the level of justification has become reflective. The procedures and presuppositions of justification are themselves now the legitimating grounds on which the validity of legitimations is based. The idea of an agreement that comes to pass among all parties, as free and equal, determines the procedural type of legitimacy of modern times. (By contrast, the classical type of legitimacy was determined by the idea of teachable knowledge of an ordered world.) Corresponding to this is an alteration of the position of the subject. Myth was taken for true in a naïve attitude. The ordo-knowledge of God, the Cosmos, and the world of man was recognizable as the handed-down teachings of wise men or prophets. Those who make agreements under idealized conditions have taken the competence to interpret into their own hands.

The procedural type of legitimacy was first worked out by Rousseau. The *contrat social* that seals the break with nature means a new principle of regulating behavior: the social. It shows by what path "justice can replace instinct in (human) behavior." That situation in which every individual totally gives himself and all his quasi-natural rights over to the community sums up the conditions under which only those regulations count as legitimate which express a common interest, that is, the general will: "For if each gives himself over completely, the situation is the same for all; and if the situation is the same for all, no one has an interest in making it difficult for others."[2] Of course, Rousseau did not understand his ideal contract only as the definition of a level of justification; he mixed the introduction of a new principle of legitimation with proposals for institutionalizing a just rule. The *volonté générale* was supposed not only to explicate grounds of validity but also to mark the place of sovereignty. This has confused the discussion of democracy right up to the present day.

I am thinking for one thing of the discussion of council democracy. If one calls democracies precisely those political orders that satisfy the procedural type of legitimacy, then questions of democratization can be treated as what they are: as organizational questions. For it then depends on the concrete social and political conditions, on scopes of disposition, on information, and so forth, which types of organization and which mechanisms are in each case better suited to bring about procedurally legitimate decisions and institutions. Naturally one must think here in process categories. I can imagine the attempt to arrange a society democratically only as a self-controlled learning process. It is a question of finding arrangements which can ground the presumption that the basic institutions of the society and the basic political decisions would meet with the unforced agreement of all those involved, if they could participate, as free and equal, in discursive will-formation. Democratization cannot mean an a priori preference for a specific type of organization, for example, for so-called direct democracy.

The discussion between representatives of a normative theory of democracy on the one side and those of a "realistic" or empirical concept of democracy on the other has gone just as badly. If democracies are distinguished from other systems of domination by a rational principle of legitimation and not by types of organization marked out a priori, then the opposing critics are missing their targets. Schumpeter and his followers reduce democracy to a method for selecting elites. I find this questionable, but not because, say, this competition of elites is incompatible with forms of basic democracy – one could imagine initial situations in which competitive-democratic procedures would be most likely to produce institutions and decisions having a presumption of rational legitimacy. I find Schumpeter's concept questionable because it defines democracy by procedures that have nothing to do with the procedures and presuppositions of free agreement and discursive will-formation. The procedures of democratic domination by elites are understood in a decisionistic manner, so that they cannot be linked with the idea of justification on the basis of generalizable interests. On the other side, normative theories of democracy are not to be faulted for holding fast to this procedural legitimacy. But they expose themselves to justified criticism as soon as they confuse a level of justification of domination with procedures for the organization of domination. If these are not kept separate, one can easily object – what Rousseau already knew – that there never was and never will be a true democracy [. . .]

III

I would like now to take a brief look at the legitimation problems that emerge with the modern state. We characterize this state by features like the monopolization of legitimate power, centralized and rational (in Weber's sense) administration, territoriality, and so on. These features describe a structure of state organization that becomes visible only when we leave behind a narrowly political view fixated on the state and consider the emergence of capitalist society. This society requires a state organization different from that of the class societies of the great empires, which were constituted in an immediately political way (in ancient Egypt, China, and India, as well as in European feudalism). Let me separate the internal and external aspects of this process.

Internally the modern state can be understood as the result of the differentiation of an economic system which regulates the production process through the market – that is, in a decentralized and unpolitical manner. The state organizes the conditions under which the citizens, as competing and strategically acting private persons, carry on the production process. The state itself does not produce, except perhaps as a subsidiary to entrepreneurs for whom certain functionally necessary investments are not yet or no longer profitable. In other words, the state develops and guarantees bourgeois civil law, the monetary mechanism, and certain infrastructures – overall the prerequisites for the continued existence of a depoliticized economic process set free from moral norms and orientations to use value. Since the state does not itself engage in capitalist enterprise, it has to siphon off the resources for its ordering achievements from private incomes. The modern state is a state based on taxation (Schumpeter). From these determinations there results a constellation of state and civil society which the Marxist theory of the state has been continually concerned to analyze.

In comparison to the state of feudalism or the ancient empires, the modern state gains greater functional autonomy; the ability of the modern administration to assert itself vis-à-vis citizens and particular groups also grows in the framework of stronger functional specification. On the other hand, however, the complementary relationship to the economy into which the state now enters makes clear for the first time the economic limitation on the state's scope of disposition. "Because (the state) is excluded from capitalist production as well as simultaneously dependent on it . . . it is forced to create the formal and (increasingly) also the material conditions and presuppositions for carrying on production and accumulation and for ensuring that their continuity does not founder on the material, temporal, and social instabilities inherent in the anarchic adaptation of the capital process to society."[3] The pre-modern state also faced the task of protecting society from disintegration without being able freely to dispose of the capacities for social integration; but the modern state directs its ordering achievements to delimiting a subsystem from its domain of sovereignty, a subsystem that replaces (at least in part) the social integration accomplished through values and norms with a system integration operating through exchange relations.[4]

As to the *external aspect* of the new state structure, the modern state did not emerge in the singular but as a system of states. It took shape in the Europe of the sixteenth century, where traditional power structures were dissipated and cultural homogeneity was rather great, where secular and spiritual authority had parted ways, trade centers had developed, and so on.[5] Wallerstein has shown that the modern system of states emerged in the midst of a "European world economy," that is, of a world market dominated by the European states.[6] The power differential between the centers and the periphery did not mean, however, that any single state had gained the power to control the worldwide relations of exchange. This means that the modern state took shape not only together with an internal economic environment but with an external one as well. This also explains the peculiar form of state sovereignty that is defined by relation to the sovereignty of other states. The private autonomy of individual, strategically acting, economic subjects is based on a reciprocal recognition that is secured legally and can be regulated universalistically. The political autonomy of individual, strategically acting, state powers is based on a reciprocal recognition that is sanctioned by the threat of military force and thus, despite the agreement in international law, remains particular and quasi-natural. War and the mobilization of resources for building up standing armies and fleets are constitutive for the modern state system as it has existed for almost three hundred years since the Peace of Westphalia. The construction of a tax administration, of a central administrative apparatus in general, was at least as strongly shaped by this imperative as directly by the organizational needs of the capitalist economy.

If one keeps these two aspects of the state structure before one's eyes, it becomes clear that the process of state building had to react upon the form of collective identity. The great empires were characterized by the fact that, as complex unities with a claim to universality, they could demarcate themselves externally – from a periphery territorially not precisely determined – only through incorporation, tributary subjugation, and association. The identity of such empires had to be anchored internally in the consciousness of only a small elite; it could coexist with other loosely integrated, pre-state identities of archaic origin. The emergence of nations shows how this kind of collective identity was transformed under the pressure of the modern state structure. The nation is a (not yet adequately analyzed) structure of consciousness that satisfies at least two imperatives. First, it makes the formally egalitarian structures of bourgeois civil law (and later of political democracy) in internal relations subjectively compatible with the particularistic structures of self-assertion of sovereign states in external relations. Second, it makes possible a high degree of social mobilization of the population (for all share in the national consciousness). The French Revolution provides a model case for this; the nation emerged along with the bourgeois constitutional state and universal conscription.

I have recalled the structures of state and nation building because they can help decode the legitimation themes that accompanied the formation of the bourgeois state. If for the sake of simplicity we restrict ourselves to controversies concerning the theory of the state, we can (very roughly) distinguish five complexes. These thematic strata run through several centuries. The first two reflect the constitution of the new level of justification, the other three the structures of the modern state and the nation.

1 *Secularization.* With the functional specification of the tasks of public administration and government, there developed a concept of the political that called for politically immanent justification. Detaching the legitimation of state power from religious traditions thus became a controversy of the first order. So far as I can see, Marsilius of Padua (drawing on Aristotle in his *Defensor Pacis* of 1324) was one of the first, if not the first, to criticize the theory of *translatio imperii* and thereby all theological justification.[7] This controversy extended into the nineteenth century, when conservative theoreticians such as De Bonald and De Maistre once again sought to ground religiously the traditional powers of church, monarchy, and a society of estates.

2 *Rational law.* The great controversy between rational natural law and classical natural law, the effects of which also reached into the nineteenth century, focussed on working out a procedural type of legitimation. From Hobbes to Rousseau and Kant the leading ideas of rational agreement and self-determination were explicated to the extent that questions of justice and public welfare were stripped of all ontological connotations. This controversy dealt implicitly with the depreciation of a level of justification dependent on world-views.

3 *Abstract right and capitalist commodity exchange.* Rational natural law had, of course, not only a formal side but a material side as well. From Hobbes and Locke through the Scottish moral philosophers (Hume, Smith, Millar), the French Enlightenment philosophers (Helvetius, d'Holbach), and classical political economy to Hegel, there emerged a theory of civil society that explained the bourgeois system of civil law, the basic liberties of the citizen, and the capitalist economic process as an order that guaranteed freedom and maxi-

mized welfare. At the new level of justification only an order of state and society organized along universalistic lines could be defended. The controversy with the traditionalists concerned the historical price exacted by bourgeois ideals; it concerned, that is, the rights of the particular, the limits of rationality – from the perspective of the present, the "dialectic of enlightenment."

4 *Sovereignty*. The establishment of monarchic sovereignty within and without ignited a conflict that was carried out first along the fronts of the wars of religions. (See the political journalism of the Protestants after St Bartholomew's Night in 1572.) From Bodin to Hobbes the sovereignty question was then resolved in favor of absolutism. In the course of the eighteenth century there was an attempt to rethink princely sovereignty into sovereignty of the people, so that the external sovereignty of the state could be unified with political democracy. The sovereignty of the people was, of course, a diffuse battle cry, which was unfolded in the constitutional debates of the nineteenth century. In it various thought motifs flow together: the sovereign power of the state appears as the expression of a new principle of legitimation, of the domination of the third estate, and of national identity as well.

5 *Nation*. This last complex has a special place insofar as national consciousness developed inconspicuously in very differentiated cultures, often on the basis of a common language, before it was dramatized in independence movements. Actually national identity became a controversial theme (in the nineteenth century) only where modernization processes were delayed, as in the succession states of the empire dissolved in 1804. A nationalism that served, as in the Bismarckian empire, to separate out internal enemies – *Reichsfeinde* such as socialists, Poles, and Catholics – no longer reflected the legitimacy thematic of the bourgeois state in its formative period; rather it now reflected the legitimacy conflicts into which this state fell when it became clear that modern bourgeois society did not dissolve class structures but first gave them pure expression *as* socioeconomic class structures. This shock became permanent in the face of the threat to legitimacy represented, since the nineteenth century, by the international labor movement.

Up to this point we have discussed legitimation themes that emerged with the development of the capitalist mode of production and the establishment of the modern state. They are an expression of legitimation problems on a scale that remains hidden so long as one limits oneself, as Hennis does,[8] to the few parapets of the class struggle, the few historically significant legitimation crises, to the bourgeois revolutions. The extent of what has to be legitimated can be surmised only if one contemplates the vestiges of the centuries-long repressions, the great wars, the small insurrections and defeats, that lined the path to the modern state. I am thinking, for example, of the resistance to what modernization research calls "penetration" (the establishment of administrative power) – hunger revolts when the food supply broke down, tax revolts when public exploitation became unbearable, revolts against the conscription of recruits, and so forth. These local insurrections against the offshoots of the modern state trickled away in the nineteenth century. They were replaced by social confrontations of artisans, industrial workers, the rural proletariat. This dynamic produced new legitimation problems. The bourgeois state could not rely on the integrative power of national consciousness alone; it had to try to head off the conflicts inherent in the economic system and channel them into the political system as an institutionalized struggle over distribution. Where this succeeded, the modern state took on one of the forms of social welfare state-mass democracy.

IV

[. . .] In regard to the legitimation problems in developed capitalist societies, I would like to make only a few remarks concerning (1) a fundamental conflict which today gives rise to legitimation problems, (2) restrictive conditions on problem resolution, and (3) two stages of delegitimation.

(1) The expression "social welfare state-mass democracy" mentions two properties of the political system which are effective for legitimation. On the one hand, it tells us that the opposition to the system which emerged in the labor movement has been defused by regulated competition between political parties. Among other things, this has institutionalized oppositional roles, formalized and rendered permanent the process of legitimation, periodized variations in legitimation and canalized the withdrawal of legitimation in the form of changes of regime, and finally it has involved everyone in the legitimation process as voting citizens.

On the other hand, threats to legitimacy can be averted only if the state can credibly present itself as a social welfare state which intercepts the dysfunctional side effects of the economic process and renders them harmless for the individual – after the fact, through a system of social security which is supposed to mediate the basic risks connected with weak positions in the market, and before the fact, through a system of securing the conditions of life that is supposed to function primarily by way of equal-opportunity access to formal schooling. In mass democracies, fulfilling this social welfare state program is, if not the foundation, at least a necessary condition of legitimacy; it presupposes of course an economic system relatively free of disturbances. Thus the state programmatically assumes the responsibility to make good deficiencies in the functioning of the economic process. There is today no disagreement concerning the structural risks built into developed capitalist economies. These have to do primarily with interruptions of the accumulation process conditioned by the business cycle, the external costs of a private production that cannot adequately deal with the problem situations it itself creates, and a pattern of privilege whose core is a structurally conditioned unequal distribution of wealth and income.

The three great areas of responsibility against which the performance of the government is today measured are then: shaping a business policy that ensures growth, influencing the structure of production in a manner oriented to collective needs, and correcting the pattern of social inequality. The problem does not lie in the fact that such things are expected of the state and that the state has to take them up in a programmatic way. The conflict – in which, with Claus Offe,* we can see a source of legitimation problems – lies rather in the fact that the state is supposed to perform all these tasks without violating the functional conditions of a capitalist economy, and this means without violating the complementarity relations that exclude the state from the economic system and, at the same time, also make it dependent on the dynamic of the economy.

Viewed historically, the state was from the beginning supposed to protect a society determined normatively in its identity from disintegration, without ever having at its free disposal the capacities for social integration, without ever being able, as it were, to make itself master of social integration. The modern state at first fulfilled this function by guaranteeing the prerequisites for the continued existence of a private economic system free of the state. Disturbances and undesired side effects of the accumulation process did not have to result in the withdrawal of legitimation so long as the interests harmed could count as private interests and be segmented. To the extent, however, that the capitalist economic process penetrated ever broader areas of life and subjected them to its principle of societal adaptation, the systemic character of bourgeois society was consolidated. The interdependence of conditions in these once-private domains increased the susceptibility to disturbance and also gave these disturbances a politically relevant scale. Thus the dysfunctional side effects of the economic process could less and less be segmented from one another and neutralized in relation to the state. From this there grew *a general responsibility of the state for deficiencies* and a presumption of its competence to eliminate them. This places the state in a dilemma. On the one hand, the definitions of deficiencies and the criteria of success in dealing with them arise in the domain of political goal-settings that have to be legitimated; for the state has to deploy legitimate power if it takes on the catalog of tasks mentioned above. On the other hand, in this matter the state cannot deploy legitimate power in the usual way, to push through binding decisions, but only to manipulate the decisions of others, whose private autonomy may not be violated. Indirect control is the answer to the dilemma, and the limits to the effectiveness of indirect control signal the persistence of this dilemma.

The legitimation problem of the state today is not how to conceal the functional relations between state activity and the capitalist economy in favor of ideological definitions of the public welfare. This is no longer possible – at least not in times of economic crisis – and exposure by Marxism is no longer necessary. The problem consists rather in representing the accomplishments of the capitalist economy as, comparatively speaking, the best possible satisfaction of generalizable interests – or at least insinuating that this is so. The state thereby programmatically obligates itself to keep dysfunctional side effects within acceptable limits. In this assignment of roles, the state provides legitimating support to a social order claiming legitimacy.

(2) The state can prove itself as an aid to legitimation only if it successfully manages the tasks it has programmatically taken on; and to a considerable extent this can be checked. The legitimation theme that is today in the foreground can thus be located on the line between technocracy theories and participation models. I shall not go into this now. But I would like to mention a series of restrictive conditions under which the state today must deal with those of its tasks effective for legitimation.

(a) The complementarity relationship between state and economy results in a goal conflict, of which there is a broadly effective awareness, especially in downward phases of the business cycle; the conflict is between a policy of stability that has to adjust its measures to the independent, cyclical dynamic of the economic process and, on the other hand, a policy of reform meant to compensate for the social costs of capitalist growth, which policy requires investments irrespective of the business situation and of profit considerations.

(b) The development of the world market, the internationalization of capital and labor, has also placed external limits on the national state's latitude for action. The problems that arise for developing countries from international stratification can, it is true, be segmented to the point where they do not react back upon the legitimation process in developed countries. But the consequences of interlacing national economies with one another (e.g., the influence of multinational corporations) cannot be neutralized. The need for coordination at a supranational level cannot easily be satisfied as long as governments have to legitimate themselves exclusively in terms of national decisions and thus have to react to national developments that are extremely non-synchronous.

(c) Until the middle of this century, national identity in advanced European countries was so strongly developed that legitimation crises could be headed off by nationalistic means if in no other way. Today there are growing indications not only that exhaustion has set in where national consciousness has been overstimulated, but that a process of erosion is underway in all the older nations. The disproportion between worldwide mechanisms of system integration (world market, weapons systems, news media, personal communication) and the localized social integration of the state may be a contributing factor. Today it is no longer so easy to separate out internal and external enemies according to national characteristics. Characteristics relating to opposition to the system serve as a substitute (as, e.g., in the "Radicals Decree" [of 1972 in the Federal Republic of Germany]). Conversely, however, membership in the system cannot, it seems, be built up to a positive identifying characteristic.

(d) Nor are the sociostructural conditions particularly favorable for the "planning of ideology" (Luhmann). Horizontal and vertical expansion of the educational system does make it easier to exercise social control through the mass media. But the symbolic use of politics (in the sense of M. Edelman)* thereby also becomes more and more susceptible to exercises in self-contradiction [. . .]

(3) If under these restrictive conditions the state does not succeed in keeping the dysfunctional side effects of the capitalist economic process within bounds acceptable to the voting public, if it is also unsuccessful in lowering the threshold of acceptability itself, then manifestations of delegitimation are unavoidable. This is marked at first by symptoms of a sharpened struggle over distribution, which proceeds according to the rules of a zero-sum game between the state's share, the share of wages, and the rate of profit. The rate of inflation, the financial crisis of the state, and the rate of unemployment – which can be substituted for one another only within limits – are measures of failure in the tasks of securing stability; the breakdown of reform politics is a sign of failure in the task of altering undesirable structures of production and privilege. At the moment, some of these symptoms can be found in the Federal Republic of Germany; yet the repercussions in the political sphere are almost minimal. I do not have data at my disposal with which we might satisfactorily explain this situation, and which would allow us to make a correct estimate of the weight of particular factors – for example, the role of an ideological shift, initially emanating from the universities, which was consciously brought about through the mobilization of fear, much anthropological pessimism, adjuration of the virtues of subordination, and little argument.

Delegitimations on this level presuppose that the categories of rewards over which the distributional struggle is carried on are not themselves contested. One wants money, free time, and security. These "primary goods" are represented as neutral means for attaining an indefinite multiplicity of concrete ends selected according to values. These are certainly highly abstract means that can be employed for a number of purposes; nevertheless, these media lay down clearly circumscribed "opportunity structures." In them is reflected a form of life, the form of life of private commodity owners who bring their property – labor power, products, or means of payment – into exchange relations and thereby accommodate the capitalist form of mobilizing resources. I shall not go through the characteristics of this familial, vocational, and civil privatism in detail. Nor shall I criticize the form of life that has its crystallizing point in possessive individualism (Macpherson). I doubt, however, whether the form of life mirrored in system-conforming rewards can today – in light of the alternatives opened by capitalist development itself – still be as convincingly legitimated as it could in Hobbes's time. Of course, such questions relevant to legitimation need not even be allowed if the powers that be are successful in further redefining practical questions into technical questions, if they are successful in preventing questions that radicalize the value-universalism of bourgeois society from even arising.

Otherwise the "pursuit of happiness" might one day mean something different – for example, not accumulating material objects of which one disposes privately, but bringing about social relations in which mutuality predominates and satisfaction does not mean the triumph of one over the repressed needs of the other. In this connection it is important whether the educational system can again be coupled to the occupational system, and whether discursive desolidification of the (largely externally controlled or traditionally fixed) interpretations of our needs in homes, schools, churches, parliaments, planning administrations, bureaucracies, in culture production generally, can be avoided.

V

In closing I would like to return to the conceptual-analytic starting point of our reflections. What is the significance of the reconstructive concept I am using in analyzing legitimation problems?

The treatment of legitimation problems by social scientists, including Marxist theoreticians,[9] today moves in Max Weber's "sphere of influence." The legitimacy of an order of domination is measured against the *belief* in its legitimacy on the part of those subject to the domination. This is a question of the "belief that the structures, procedures, actions, decisions, policies, officials, or political leaders of a state possess the quality of rightness, of appropriateness, of the morally good, and ought to be recognized in virtue of this quality."[10] For systems theory (Parsons, Easton,* Luhmann) this poses the question: With the help of which mechanisms can an adequate supply of legitimation be created, or through which functional equivalents can missing legitimation be replaced? Learning theorists accommodate the question of the socio-psychological conditions under which a belief in legitimacy arises in a theory of the motivation for obedience. Thus the empiricist replacement of legitimacy with what is held to be such allows for meaningful sociological investigations (the value of which will be decided by the success of the systems-theoretic and behaviorist approaches generally).

But we may well want to ask what price the empiricist must pay for the redefinition of his object. If the object domain is conceived in such a way that not legitimate orders but only orders that are *held to be legitimate* can belong to it, then the connection between reasons and motives that exists in communicative action is screened out of the analysis. At least any independent evaluation of reasons is methodically excluded – the researcher himself refrains from any systematic judgment of the reasons on which the claim to legitimacy is based. Since the days of Max Weber this has been regarded as a virtue; however, even if one adopts this interpretation, the suspicion remains that legitimacy, the belief in legitimacy, and the willingness to comply with a legitimate order have something to do with motivation through "good reasons." But whether reasons are "good reasons" can be ascertained only in the performative attitude of a *participant* in argumentation, and not through the neutral *observation* of what this or that participant in a discourse holds to be good reasons. To be sure, the sociologist is concerned with the facticity of validity-claims – for example, with the fact that the claim to legitimacy raised on behalf of a political order is recognized with specific frequencies in specific populations. But can he ignore the fact that normative validity-claims meet with recognition because, among other reasons, they are held to be capable of discursive vindication, to be right, that is, to be well grounded? It is as with truth claims: the universality of this claim gives a sociologist the possibility of systematically checking the truth of an assertion independently of whether or not it is held to be true in a specific population. It can be decisive for an analysis to know whether a population acted on the basis of an accurate or a false opinion (e.g., to determine whether cognitive errors or other causes were principally responsible for observed failures). The case could be the same with the normative validity-claim of political institutions; for example, one might well want to know whether a certain party renounces obedience because the legitimacy of the state *is* empty, or whether other causes are at work. To make that judgment we have to be able to systematically evaluate legitimacy claims in a rational, intersubjectively testable way. Can we do this?

Hennis is apparently of the opinion that we can. He holds a "critical-normative demarcation of legitimacy from illegitimacy" to be absolutely necessary. But he does not specify the procedures or the criteria for this demarcation. He mentions legitimacy factors: personal esteem, efficiency in managing public tasks, approval of structures. But this personal authority is supposed to "spring from sources that can't be rationally grounded." What can count as efficient task management is measured against standards. These in turn are connected with those structures about whose legitimacy Hennis says only that they establish themselves in different national variants. He does not say what can count as a ground for the legitimacy of domination. To do so requires a concept of legitimacy with normative content. Hennis does not present us with such a concept, but he must have one, at least implicitly, in mind. The old-European style to his strategy of argumentation leads me to suspect connections with the classical doctrine of politics.

In this tradition (which goes back to Plato and Aristotle) stand important authors who still possess a substantial concept of morality, normative concepts of the good, of the public welfare, and so on. Neo-Aristotelianism in particular experienced a renaissance in the writings of Hannah Arendt, Leo Strauss, Joachim Ritter,* and others. [. . .] Today it is no longer easy to render the approach of this metaphysical mode of thought plausible. It is no wonder that the neo-Aristotelian writings do not contain systematic doctrines, but are works of high interpretive art that suggest the truth of classical texts through interpretation, rather than by grounding it. [. . .]

I have discussed two concepts of legitimation, the empiricist and the normativist. One can be employed in the social sciences but is unsatisfactory because it abstracts from the systematic weight of grounds for validity; the other would be satisfactory in this regard but is untenable because of the metaphysical context in which it is embedded. I would like, therefore, to propose a third concept of legitimation, which I shall call the "reconstructive."

I shall begin by assuming that the proposition: "Recommendation X is legitimate" has the same meaning as the proposition: "Recommendation X is in the general (or public) interest," where X can be an action as well as a norm of action or even a system of such norms (in the case we are considering, a system of domination). "X is the general interest" is to mean that the normative validity-claim connected with X counts as justified. The justifiability of competing validity-claims is decided by a system of possible justifications; a single justification is called a legitimation. The reconstruction of given legitimations can consist, first, in discovering the justificatory system, S, that allows for evaluating the given legitimations as valid or invalid in S. "Valid in S is to mean only that anyone who accepts S – a myth or a cosmology or a political theory – must also accept the grounds given in valid legitimations. This necessity expresses a consistency connection resulting from the internal relations of the justificatory system.

In taking a justification up to this threshold, we have interpreted a belief in legitimacy and tested its consistency. Along this hermeneutic path alone, however, we do not arrive at a judgment of the legitimacy that is believed in. Nor does comparison of the belief in legitimacy with the institutional system justified take us much further. Assuming that idea and reality do not split apart, what is needed is rather an evaluation of the reconstructed justificatory system itself. This brings us back to the fundamental question of practical philosophy. In modern times it has been taken up reflectively as a question of the procedures and presuppositions under which justifications can have the power to produce consensus. I have mentioned the theory of justice of John Rawls, who examines how the original situation would have to be constituted so that a rational consensus about the basic decisions and basic institutions of a society could come to pass. Paul Lorenzen* examines the methodic norms of the speech practice that makes rational consensus possible in such practical questions. Finally Karl-Otto Apel radicalizes this question with regard to the universal and necessary – that is, transcendental – presuppositions of practical discourse; the normative content of the universal presuppositions of communication is supposed thereby to form the core of a universal ethics of speech.[11] This is the point of convergence toward which the attempts to renew practical philosophy today seem to strive.

Even if we assent to this thesis, an objection comes readily to mind. Every general theory of justification remains peculiarly abstract in relation to the historical forms of legitimate domination. If one brings standards of discursive justification to bear on traditional societies, one behaves in an historically "unjust" manner. Is there an alternative to this historical injustice of general theories, on the one hand, and the standardlessness of mere historical understanding, on the other? The only promising program I can see is a theory that structurally clarifies the historically observable sequence of different levels of justification and reconstructs it as a developmental-logical nexus. Cognitive developmental psychology, which is well corroborated and which has reconstructed ontogenetic stages of moral consciousness in this way, can be understood at least as a heuristic guide and an encouragement.

Communication and the Evolution of Society, pp. 178–205.

Notes

1 P. von Kielmannsegg, "Legitimität als analytische Kategorie," *Politische Vierteljahresschrift*, 12, 1971: 367–401, esp. pp. 391ff.
2 Rousseau, *The Social Contract*, book I, chapter 6.
3 C. Offe, *Bildungsreform* (Frankfurt, 1975), pp. 24–5.
4 Cf. my concept of a "system crisis" in *Legitimation Crisis*, pp. 24–31.
5 C. Tilly, "Reflections on the History of European State-Making," in Tilly (ed.), *The Formation of National States in Western Europe* (Princeton, N.J., 1975), pp. 3–83.
6 I. Wallerstein, *The Modern World-System* (New York, 1974).
7 D. Sternberger, "Legitimacy," *International Encyclopedia of Social Science* (New York: Macmillan and Free Press, 1968), vol. 9, pp. 244–8.

8 Wilhelm Hennis had spoken before Habermas at the conference at which this paper was first delivered.
9 R. Miliband, *The State in Capitalist Society* (New York, 1969).
10 R.M. Merelman, "Learning and Legitimacy," *American Political Science Review*, 60, 1966: 548.
11 Cf. John Rawls, *A Theory of Justice* (Cambridge, Mass.: Harvard University Press), 1971; Paul Lorenzen, *Normative Logic and Ethics* (Mannheim, 1969); Karl-Otto Apel, "Sprechakttheorie und transzendentale Ethik," in Apel (ed.), *Sprachpragmatik und Philosophie* (Frankfurt: Suhrkamp, 1976), pp. 10–173.

PART VII

The Theory of Modernity

Introduction

As can be seen from reading 23 in part VI, Habermas's reconstructive theory of communicative action includes an account of the changing institutional forms which it takes in Europe and North America from around the eighteenth century. This is a two-sided process. On the one hand, more and more areas of social life are prised out of traditional contexts and subjected to rational examination and argument. On the other hand, the expansion of markets and administrative structures leads to what Habermas calls the colonization or hollowing-out of the lifeworld by autonomous subsystems which are removed from rational evaluation, except within their own highly circumscribed terms.

Habermas is thus following the tradition of analysis developed by Marx in his theory of alienation, by Max Weber in terms of rationalization and disenchantment (Entzauberung), and in Georg Lukács's concept of reification (Verdinglichung). In the early critical theorists' critique of instrumental rationality as something inevitably linked to domination, all these motifs come together.[1] In Habermas's view, however, all these models are insufficiently complex. Marx focusses too one-sidedly on the rationalization of the forces and relations of material production; Max Weber sees societal reationalization too narrowly in terms of patterns of individual purposive-rational action. One needs instead to differentiate between "the rationalization of action orientations and lifeworld structures" and "the expansion of the 'rationality,' that is, complexity of action systems."[2]

Habermas's strategy in The Theory of Communicative Action is to develop a broader concept of communicative action, with the aid of elements in the work of Durkheim and Mead, and then to reformulate the insights of Western Marxism by bringing together action theory and system theory.[3] Thus in the second volume of the book, from which the three extracts in this part are drawn, he returns to these classical themes of social theory in developing his own account of capitalist modernity.[4] Reading 24 provides a "look back" at Max Weber's theory of modernity in the context of his theory of action.

Since Talcott Parsons also attempted to incorporate his action theory *into a theory of social systems, Habermas contrasts his own theory, in the book as a whole and in the second extract provided here as reading 25, with that of Parsons and with the system theory developed more recently by his contemporary Niklas Luhmann. Habermas argues that his own theory, unlike these, is able not just to describe the processes of modern society, but to explain their pathological character. In Habermas's model, described in reading 25, the "uncoupling" of autonomous market and administrative systems means that the lifeworld becomes "one subsystem among others." As Max Weber realized, these subsystems become like machines, running independently of their original sources in the moral and political structures of the lifeworld: "economic and bureaucratic spheres emerge in which social relations are regulated only by money and power."*[5]

In a detailed discussion omitted from this extract, Habermas traces this process of the development of subsystems. Tribal societies, he claims, are almost coextensive with their lifeworlds; a society of this kind "reproduces itself as a whole in every single interaction."[6] *Hence, Habermas suggests, the plausibility of functionalism in social or cultural anthropology: "systemic interdependencies are directly mirrored in normative struc-tures."*[7] *Or in Marxist terms, "these societies consist of base and super-structure both in one."*[8] *It is only with capitalism and the development of the modern state that a clear differentiation between economic and political relations occurs, and class differentiation develops on a basis independent of kinship and defined by functional position, income, and way of life. The growth of formal law and its differentiation from morality "both [express] a rationalization of the lifeworld and [make] new levels of integration possible."*[9]

But in what Habermas ironically calls "the unresistable irony of the world-historical process of enlightenment,"[10] *the autonomous systems become dominant: "In the end, systemic mechanisms suppress forms of social integration even in those areas where a consensus-dependent coordination of action cannot be replaced, that is, where the symbolic reproduction of the lifeworld is at stake. In these areas, the mediatization of the lifeworld assumes the form of a colonization."*[11] *Examples of this process can be found, as Habermas indicates elsewhere, in the attempts by welfare-state systems to extend legal regulation and monetary calcula-tion right into the private sphere, at the cost of those traces of solidarity which remain; and solidarity is a resource which cannot be bought or constrained. These issues are addressed in the section of* The Theory of Communicative Action *from which reading 26 is taken, as well as in some of the essays in* The New Conservatism.

In reading 26, Habermas reformulates Marx's critique of capitalism in the categories of his own model of internal colonization. Marx's theory of value and his analysis of abstract labor capture essential aspects of what Habermas calls "the reification of communicatively structured domains of action."[12] *Marx "uses the theory of value to get from the lifeworld of concrete labor to the economic valorization of abstract labor" and can then examine the consequences for the lifeworld of this degradation of the work process.*[13] *But Marx's analysis is too undifferentiated; he lumps together processes of system differentiation such as the development of formal law, the economy, and the state, which have "intrinsic evolutionary value,"*[14] *with their pathological consequences under the specific conditions of a capitalist class society. As a result, he also cannot distinguish "the destruction of traditional forms of life from the reification of posttraditional lifeworlds."*[15] *Finally, Marx's focus on labour and his model of the purposive actor do not enable him to grasp the generality of the process of reification.*[16] *And these weaknesses have consequences for Marxist theories of advanced capitalism.*

Notes

1 *The Theory of Communicative Action*, vol. I, p. 144.
2 Ibid., p. 145n.
3 As I noted in the general introduction, the need for this recourse to system theory has been questioned, notably by Hans Joas and Thomas McCarthy in A. Honneth and H. Joas (eds), *Communicative Action* (Cambridge: Polity, 1986).
4 On the state socialist alternative, see, for example, Habermas's comments in *The Past as Future*.
5 *The Theory of Communicative Action*, vol. II, p. 154; here p. 279.
6 Ibid., p. 157.
7 Ibid., p. 164.
8 Ibid., p. 168.
9 Ibid., p. 179.
10 Ibid., p. 155.
11 Ibid., p. 196.
12 Ibid., p. 332.
13 Ibid., p. 338.
14 Ibid., p. 339.
15 Ibid., p. 340.
16 Ibid., p. 342; below, p. 283.

Further Reading

Habermas's *Die neue Unübersichtlichkeit*, translated as *The New Conservatism*, includes material on the practical problems of modern welfare democracies.

24

Weber's Theory of Modernity

(3) Weber characterized cultural modernity by the fact that the substantive reason expressed in religious and metaphysical world-views falls apart into moments that are held together only procedurally, that is, through the form of argumentative justification. As traditional problems are divided up under the specific viewpoints of truth, normative rightness, and authenticity or beauty, and are dealt with respectively as questions of knowledge, justice, or taste, there is a differentiation of the value-spheres of science, morality, and art. In the corresponding cultural action systems, scientific discourse, studies in moral and legal theory, and the production and criticism of art are all institutionalized as the affairs of experts. Professionalized treatment of cultural tradition under only *one* abstract aspect of validity *at a time* permits the inner logics of cognitive-instrumental, moral-practical, and aesthetic-expressive complexes of knowledge to manifest themselves. From this point on, there are also *internal histories* of science, of moral and legal theory, of art – not linear developments, to be sure, but learning processes nonetheless.

In consequence of this professionalization, the distance between expert cultures and the broader public grows greater. What accrues to a culture by virtue of specialized work and reflection does not come *as a matter of course* into the possession of everyday practice. Rather, cultural rationalization brings with it the danger that a lifeworld devalued in its traditional substance will become impoverished. This problem was first seen in all its acuteness in the eighteenth century; it called into being the project of the Enlightenment. Eighteenth-century philosophers still hoped to develop unflinchingly the objectivating sciences, universalistic foundations of morality and law, and art, each according to its own inner logic, and *at the same time* to free the cognitive potentials built up in this way from their esoteric forms and to use them in practice, that is, in rationally shaping the conditions of daily life. Enlighteners cast in the mold of a Condorcet[1] had the extravagant expectation that the arts and sciences would promote not only the control of natural forces, but also interpretations of the world and of ourselves, moral progress, the justice of social institutions, even the happiness of humankind.

The twentieth century has left little of this optimism intact; but now, as then, there is a difference of opinion as to whether we should hold fast to the intentions of the Enlightenment, in however refracted a form, or should give up the project of modernity as lost – whether, for instance, cognitive potentials that do not flow into technical progress, economic growth, and rational administration should be dammed up in the enclaves of their high-cultural forms so that habits dependent on blind tradition can remain untouched by them.

The processes of reaching understanding upon which the lifeworld is centered require a cultural tradition across the whole spectrum. In the communicative practice of everyday life, cognitive interpretations, moral expectations, expressions, and valuations have to interpenetrate and form a rational interconnectedness via the transfer of validity that is possible in the performative attitude. This communicative infrastructure is threatened by two interlocking, mutually reinforcing tendencies: *systemically induced reification* and *cultural impoverishment*.

The lifeworld is assimilated to juridified,* formally organized domains of action and simultaneously cut off from the influx of an intact cultural tradition. In the deformations of everyday practice, symptoms of rigidification combine with symptoms of desolation. The former, the one-sided rationalization of everyday communication, goes back to the growing autonomy of media-steered subsystems, which not only get objectified into a norm-free reality beyond the horizon of the lifeworld, but whose imperatives also penetrate into the core domains of the lifeworld. The latter, the dying out of vital traditions, goes back to a differentiation of science, morality, and art, which means not only an increasing autonomy of sectors dealt with by experts, but also a splitting-off from traditions; having lost their credibility, these traditions continue along on the basis of everyday hermeneutics as a kind of second nature that has lost its force.

Working Weber's diagnosis of the times into our interpretive framework has the advantage of elucidating, in terms of communication theory, the sense in which the phenomena he observed, when they appear with broad effect, should be regarded as pathologies, that is, as symptoms of a distorted everyday practice. This does not explain, however, why pathologies of this kind appear in the first place. Our reconstruction of Weber's paradox of societal rationalization is by no means complete. We have not explained, for instance, why the differentiation of economic and administrative systems of action at all pushes beyond the bounds of what is necessary for the institutionalization of money and power, why the subsystems build up irresistible internal dynamics and systematically undermine domains of action dependent upon social integration. Nor have we explained why cultural rationalization not only sets free the inner logics of cultural value-spheres, but also remains encapsulated in expert cultures; why modern science serves technical progress, capitalist growth, and rational administration, but not the understanding that communicating citizens have of themselves and the world; why, in general, the explosive contents of cultural modernity have been defused. In such matters, Weber himself had recourse only to the inner logics of cultural value-spheres and the effectiveness of new forms of organization.

But this does not explain why modernization follows a highly selective pattern that appears to exclude two things at once: building institutions of freedom that protect communicatively structured areas of the private and public spheres against the reifying inner dynamics of the economic and adminstrative systems,[2] and reconnecting modern culture to an everyday practice that, while dependent on meaning-bestowing traditions, has been impoverished with traditionalist left-overs.[3]

It is no mere accident that Parsons can base his rather too harmonious picture of modernity on Weber's analyses. In comparison to Parsons, Weber was, to be sure, sensitive to the price that the capitalist modernization of the lifeworld exacted for a new level of system differentiation, but he too failed to investigate the drive mechanism behind the autonomized expansion of the economic system and its governmental complement.

Perhaps an explanation of the Marxian type could help here. It points us in the direction of an economically constituted class domination, which withdraws into the anonymous internal dynamics of valorization processes uncoupled from orientations to use values. And this might explain why the imperatives Weber connected with the idea of "bureaucratization" penetrate into communicatively structured domains of action, so that the space opened up by the rationalization of the lifeworld for moral-practical will-formation, expressive self-presentation, and aesthetic satisfaction does not get utilized.

(4) If we appropriate Weber's diagnosis of the times from this Marxian perspective, the paradox of societal rationalization looks rather different. The rationalization of the lifeworld makes it possible to differentiate off autonomized subsystems and at the same time opens up the utopian horizon of a bourgeois society in which the formally organized spheres of action of the *bourgeois* (the economy and the state apparatus) form the foundation of the post-traditional lifeworld of the *homme* (the private sphere) and the *citoyen* (the public sphere). Since the eighteenth century, the features of a form of life in which the rational potential of action oriented to mutual understanding is set free have been reflected in the self-understanding of the humanistically imbued European middle classes – in their political theories and educational ideals, in their art and literature.[4] Metaphysical-religious world-views ceded the function of legitimating domination to the basic ideas of rational natural law, which offered justification for the modern state

from the perspective of a social order free of violence and centered on markets organized by private law. At the same time, bourgeois ideals penetrated private spheres of life; they stamped the individualism of relationships of love and friendship as well as the culture of morality and feeling in intensified family relations. From this point of view, the subject of private law, who was wholly absorbed by the functional interconnections of material reproduction, could be unceremoniously identified with the *human being* who was formed in the private sphere and realized himself there, and with the *private person* who, together with others, formed the *public* of citizens of the state.

To be sure, this *utopia of reason, formed in the Enlightenment*, was persistently contradicted by the realities of bourgeois life and shown to be a *bourgeois ideology*. But it was never a mere illusion; it was an objective illusion that arose from the structures of differentiated life-worlds which, while certainly limited in class-specific ways, were nonetheless rationalized. To the extent that culture, society, and personality separated off from one another as Mead and Durkheim said they did, and the validity-basis of communicative action replaced the sacred foundations of social integration, there was at least *an appearance of post-traditional everyday communication* suggested by the structures of the lifeworld. It was, so to speak, a transcendental apparition – determining bourgeois ideology, while yet surpassing it. In it, communication was represented as standing on its own feet, setting limits to the inner dynamics of autonomous subsystems, bursting encapsulated expert cultures, and thus as escaping the combined threat of reification and desolation.

The paradox, however, is that the rationalization of the lifeworld simultaneously gave rise to *both* the systemically induced reification of the lifeworld *and* the utopian perspective from which capitalist modernization has always appeared with the stain of dissolving traditional life-forms without salvaging their communicative substance. Capitalist modernization destroys these forms of life, but does not transform them in such a way that the intermeshing of cognitive-instrumental with moral-practical and expressive moments, which had obtained in everyday practice prior to its rationalization, could be retained at a higher level of differentiation. Against this background, images of traditional forms of life – of rural and peasant life, or the life of town dwellers and craftsmen, even the plebian way of life of the agricultural laborers and cottage-industry pieceworkers recently dragged into the accumulation process[5] – retained the melancholy charm of irretrievable past and the radiance of nostalgic remembrance of what had been sacrificed to modernization. But more than this, modernization processes have been followed, as if by a shadow, by what might be called an instinct formed by reason: the awareness that, with the one-sided canalization and destruction of possibilities for expression and communication in private and in public spheres, chances are fading that we can bring together again, in a post-traditional everyday practice, those moments that, in traditional forms of life, once composed a unity – a diffuse one surely, and one whose religious and metaphysical interpretations were certainly illusory.

In understanding Weber's paradox of societal rationalization in this way, we are making two decisive changes in his argument. Since its beginnings in the late eighteenth century, bourgeois cultural criticism has always wanted to attribute the pathologies of modernity to one of two causes: either to the fact that secularized world-views lose their socially integrating power, or to the fact that society's high level of complexity overtaxes the individual's power to integrate. Like an echo, bourgeois cultural apologetics has furnished two mirror-arguments maintaining that disenchantment and alienation are structurally necessary conditions of freedom (where the latter is always represented merely as individual choice among institutionally guaranteed possibilities). Weber tried to combine both pairs of arguments and counterarguments through the idea of a paradox built into Occidental development itself. His theses of the loss of meaning and freedom pick up on themes of bourgeois cultural criticism; he varies them, however, with the idea that it is precisely in these phenomena that the reason of Occidental rationalism establishes itself – and thus tries to meet apologetic needs.

The modifications I have made in Weber's thesis do not fit into this pattern of argumentation within bourgeois cultural theory. They run counter to the critical and apologetic lines of argument no less than their paradoxical combination. The deformations that interested Marx, Durkheim, and Weber – each in his own way – ought not to be attributed either to the rationalization of the lifeworld as such or to increasing system complexity as such. Neither the secularization of world-views nor the structural differentiation of society has unavoidable pathological side effects per se. It is not the differentiation and independent development of cultural value-spheres that lead to the cultural impoverishment of everyday communicative practice, but an elitist splitting-off of expert cultures from contexts of communicative action in daily life. It is not the uncoupling of media-steered subsystems and of their organizational forms from the lifeworld that leads to the one-sided rationalization or reification of everyday communicative practice, but only the penetration of forms of economic and administrative rationality into areas of action that resist being converted over to the media of money and power because they are specialized in cultural transmission, social integration, and child rearing, and remain dependent on mutual understanding as a mechanism for coordinating action. If we assume, further, that the phenomena of a loss of meaning and freedom do not turn up by chance but are structurally generated, we must try to explain why media-steered subsystems develop *irresistible inner dynamics* that *bring about* both the colonization of the lifeworld and its segmentation from science, morality, and art.

The Theory of Communicative Action, vol. 2, pp. 326–31.

Notes

1 Cf. M.J.A. Condorcet, *Esquisse d'un tableau historique des progrès de l'esprit humain* (1794).
2 This is the basic guiding intention of Hannah Arendt, *The Human Condition* (New York, 1958), and *The Life of the Mind*, vols 1 and 2 (New York, 1978). Cf. J. Habermas, "Hannah Arendt on the Concept of Power," in *Philosophical-Political Profiles*, pp. 171–87; J. T. Knauer, "Motive and Goal in Hannah Arendt's Concept of Political Action," *American Political Science Review*, 1980: 721ff.
3 On this basic intention of Benjamin's theory of art, see J. Habermas, "Consciousness-Raising or Rescuing Critique," in *Philosophical-Political Profiles*, pp. 129–63.
4 Theorists inspired by Marxism, such as Adorno, Bloch, Lukács, Lowenthal, and Hans Mayer, have worked up this utopian content in the classical works of bourgeois art and literature.
5 E.P. Thompson, *The Making of the English Working Class* (Harmondsworth: Penguin, 1968).

25

The Uncoupling of System and Lifeworld

The provisional concept of society proposed here is radically different in one respect from the Parsonian concept: the mature Parsons reinterpreted the structural components of the lifeworld – culture, society, personality – as action systems constituting environments for one another. Without much ado, he subsumed the concept of the lifeworld gained from an action-theoretical perspective under systems-theoretical concepts. As we shall see below, the structural components of the lifeworld become subsystems of a general system of action, to which the physical substratum of the lifeworld is reckoned along with the "behavior system." The proposal I am advancing here, by contrast, attempts to take into account the methodological differences between the internalist and the externalist viewpoints connected with the two conceptual strategies.

From the participant perspective of members of a lifeworld it looks as if sociology with a systems-theoretical orientation considers only one of the three components of the lifeworld, namely, the institutional system, for which culture and personality merely constitute complementary environments. From the observer perspective of systems theory, on the other hand, it looks as if lifeworld analysis confines itself to one societal subsystem specialized in maintaining structural patterns (pattern maintenance); in this view, the components of the lifeworld are merely internal differentiations of this subsystem, which specifies the parameters of societal self-maintenance. It is already evident on methodological grounds that a systems theory of society cannot be self-sufficient. The structures of the lifeworld, with their own inner logic placing internal constraints on system maintenance, have to be gotten at by a hermeneutic approach that picks up on members' pre-theoretical knowledge. Furthermore, the objective conditions under which the systems-theoretical objectification of the lifeworld becomes necessary have themselves only risen in the course of social evolution. And this calls for a type of explanation that does not already move within the system perspective.

I understand social evolution as a second-order process of differentiation: system and lifeworld are differentiated in the sense that the complexity of the one and the rationality of the other grow. But it is not only qua system and qua lifeworld that they are differentiated; they get differentiated from one another at the same time. It has become conventional for sociologists to distinguish the stages of social evolution as tribal societies, traditional societies or societies organized around a state, and modern societies (where the economic system has been differentiated out). From the system perspective, these stages are marked by the appearance of new systemic mechanisms and corresponding levels of complexity. On this plane of analysis, the uncoupling of system and lifeworld is depicted in such a way that the lifeworld, which is at first coextensive with a scarcely differentiated social system, gets cut down more and more to one subsystem among others. In the process, system mechanisms get further and further detached from the social structures through which social integration takes place. As we shall see, modern societies attain a level of system differentiation at which increasingly autonomous organizations are connected with one another via delinguistified media of communication: these systemic mechanisms – for example, money – steer a social intercourse that has been largely disconnected from norms and values, above all in those subsystems of purposive-rational economic and administrative action that, on Weber's diagnosis, have become independent of their moral-political foundations.

At the same time, the lifeworld remains the subsystem that defines the pattern of the social system as a whole. Thus, systemic mechanisms need to be anchored in the lifeworld: they have to be institutionalized. This institutionalization of new levels of system differentiation can also be perceived from the internal perspective of the lifeworld. Whereas system differentiation in tribal societies only leads to the increasing complexity of pre-given kinship systems, at higher levels of integration new social structures take shape, namely, the state and media-steered subsystems. In societies with a low degree of differentiation, systemic interconnections are tightly interwoven with mechanisms of social integration; in modern societies they are consolidated and objectified into norm-free structures. Members behave toward formally organized action systems, steered via processes of exchange and power, as toward a block of quasi-natural reality; within these media-steered subsystems society congeals into a second nature. Actors have always been able to sheer off from an orientation to mutual understanding, adopt a strategic attitude, and objectify normative contexts into something in the objective world, but in modern societies, economic and bureaucratic spheres emerge in which social relations are regulated only via money and power. Norm-conformative attitudes and identity-forming social memberships are neither necessary nor possible in these spheres; they are made peripheral instead.

[. . .] In tribal societies, system differentiation is linked to existing structures of interaction through the exchange of spouses and the formation of prestige; for this reason it does not yet make itself noticeable by intervening in the structures of the lifeworld. In politically stratified class societies, a new level of functional interconnection, in the form of the state, rises above the level of simple interactions. This difference in levels is reflected in the relation of the whole to its parts – a relation that is at the heart of classical political theory from the time of Aristotle, although the corresponding images of society as polity that arise in the spectrum from popular to high culture are considerably different. The new level of system differentiation has the form of a general political order that needs to be legitimated; this order can be brought into the lifeworld only at the cost of an illusory interpretation of class society, that is, through religious world-views taking on ideological functions. Finally, a third level of functional interconnection arises in modern societies with interchange processes that operate via media. These systemic interconnections, detached from normative contexts and rendered independent as subsystems, challenge the assimilative powers of an all-encompassing lifeworld. They congeal into the "second nature" of a norm-free sociality that can appear as something in the objective world, as an *objectified* context of life. The uncoupling of system and lifeworld is experienced in modern society as a particular kind of objectification: the social system definitively bursts out of the horizon of the lifeworld, escapes from the intuitive knowledge of everyday communicative practice, and is henceforth accessible only to the counterintuitive knowledge of the social sciences developing since the eighteenth century.

What we have already found in the system perspective seems to be confirmed from this internal perspective: the more complex social systems become, the more provincial lifeworlds become. In a differentiated social system the lifeworld seems to shrink to a subsystem. This should not be read causally, as if the structures of the lifeworld changed in dependence on increases in systemic complexity. The opposite is true: increases in complexity are dependent on the structural differentiation of the lifeworld. And however we may explain the dynamics of this structural transformation, it follows the inner logic of communicative rationalization. I have developed this thesis with reference to Mead and Durkheim and have carried it over to lifeworld analysis. Now I shall make systematic use of it.

As we have seen, the level of possible increases in complexity can be raised only by the introduction of a new system mechanism. Every new leading mechanism of system differentiation must, however, be anchored in the lifeworld; it must be *institutionalized* there via family status, the authority of office, or bourgeois private law. In the final analysis, social formations are distinguished by the institutional cores that define society's "base," in the Marxian sense. These basic institutions form a series of evolutionary innovations that can come about only if the lifeworld is sufficiently rationalized, above all only if law and morality have reached a corresponding stage of development. The institutionalization of a new level of system differentiation requires reconstruction in the core institutional domain of the moral-legal (i.e., consensual) regulation of conflicts.

[. . .] In subsystems differentiated out via steering media, systemic mechanisms create their own, norm-free social structures jutting out from the lifeworld. These structures do, of course, remain linked with everyday communicative practice via basic institutions of civil or public law. We cannot directly infer from the mere fact that system and social integration have been largely uncoupled to linear dependency in one direction or the other. Both are conceivable: the institutions that anchor steering mechanisms such as power and money in the lifeworld could serve as a channel *either* for the influence of the lifeworld on formally organized domains of action *or*, conversely, for the influence of the system on communicatively structured contexts of action. In the one case, they function as an institutional framework that subjects system maintenance to the normative restrictions of the lifeworld, in the other, as a base that subordinates the lifeworld to the systemic constraints of material reproduction and thereby "mediatizes" it.

In theories of the state and of society, both models have been played through. Modern natural law theories neglected the inner logic of a functionally stabilized civil society in relation to the state; the classics of political economy were concerned to show that systemic imperatives were fundamentally in harmony with the basic norms of a polity guaranteeing freedom and justice. Marx destroyed this practically very important illusion; he showed that the laws of capitalist commodity production have the latent function of sustaining a structure that makes a mockery of bourgeois ideals. The lifeworld of the capitalist carrier strata, which was expounded in rational natural law and in the ideals of bourgeois thought generally, was devalued by Marx to a sociocultural superstructure. In his picture of base and superstructure he was also raising the methodological demand that we exchange the internal perspective of the lifeworld for an observer's perspective, so that we might grasp the systemic imperatives of an independent economy as they act upon the bourgeois lifeworld *a tergo*. In his view, only in a socialist society could the spell cast upon the lifeworld by the system be broken, could the dependence of the superstructure on the base be lifted.

In one way, the most recent systems functionalism is an heir-successor to Marxism, which it radicalizes and defuses at the same time. On the one hand, systems theory adopts the view that the systemic constraints of material production, which it understands as imperatives of self-maintenance of the general social system, reach right through the symbolic structures of the lifeworld. On the other hand, it removes the critical sting from the base-superstructure thesis by reinterpreting what was intended to be an empirical diagnosis as a prior analytical distinction. Marx took over from bourgeois social theory a presupposition that we found again in Durkheim: it is not a matter of indifference to a society whether and to what extent forms of social integration dependent on consensus are repressed and replaced by anonymous forms of system-integrative sociation. A theoretical approach that presents the lifeworld merely as one of several anonymously steered subsystems undercuts this distinction. Systems theory treats accomplishments of social and system integration as functionally equivalent and thus deprives itself of the standard of communicative rationality. And without that standard, increases in complexity achieved *at the expense* of a rationalized lifeworld cannot be identified *as costs*. Systems theory lacks the analytic means to pursue the question that Marx (also) built into his base-superstructure metaphor and Weber renewed in his own way by inquiring into the paradox of societal rationalization. For us, this question takes on the form of whether the rationalization of the lifeworld does not become paradoxical with the transition to modern societies. The rationalization of the lifeworld makes possible the emergence and growth of subsystems whose independent imperatives turn back destructively upon the lifeworld itself. [. . .]

The uncoupling of system integration and social integration means at first only a differentiation between two types of action coordination, one coming about through the consensus of those involved, the other through functional interconnections of action. System-integrative mechanisms attach to the effects of action. As they work through action orientations in a subjectively inconspicuous fashion, they may leave the socially integrative contexts of action which they are parasitically utilizing structurally unaltered – it is this sort of intermeshing of system with social integration that we postulated for the development level of tribal societies. Things are different when system integration intervenes in the very forms of social integration. In this case, too, we have to do with latent functional interconnections, but the subjective inconspicuousness of systemic constraints that *instrumentalize* a communicatively structured lifeworld takes on the character of deception, of objectively false consciousness. The effects of the system on the lifeworld, which change the structure of contexts of action in socially integrated groups, have to remain hidden. The reproductive constraints that instrumentalize a lifeworld without weakening the illusion of its self-sufficiency have to hide, so to speak, in the pores of communicative action. This gives rise to a *structural violence* that, without becoming manifest as such, takes hold of the forms of intersubjectivity of possible understanding. Structural violence is exercised by way of systematic restrictions on communication; distortion is anchored in the formal conditions of communicative action in such a way that the interrelation of the objective, social, and subjective worlds gets prejudged for participants in a typical fashion.

The Theory of Communicative Action, vol. 2, pp. 153–5, 172–3, 185–7.

26

Marx and the Thesis of Internal Colonization

Marx was unable to conceive the transformation of concrete into abstract labor as a special case of the systemically induced reification of social relations in general because he started from the model of the purposive actor who, along with his products, is robbed of the possibility of developing his essential powers. The theory of value is carried through in action-theoretic concepts that make it necessary to approach the genesis of reification *below* the level of interaction, and to treat as derived phenomena the de-formation of interaction relations themselves – the deworlding of communciative action that is transferred over to media and the technicizing of the lifeworld that follows upon this. [. . .]

The three weaknesses of the theory of value that we have analyzed here explain why, despite its two-level concept of society combining system and lifeworld, the critique of political economy has been unable to produce a satisfactory account of late capitalism. The Marxian approach requires an economistically foreshortened interpretation of developed capitalist societies. Marx was right to assign an evolutionary primacy to the economy in such societies: the problems in this subsystem determine the path of development of the society as a whole. But this primacy should not mislead us into tailoring the complementary relationship between the economy and the state apparatus to a trivial notion of base and superstructure. As opposed to the monism of the theory of value, we have to allow for two steering media and four channels through which the two complementary subsystems subject the lifeworld to their imperatives. Reification effects can result in like manner from the bureaucratization and monetarization of public and private areas of life.

Marxian orthodoxy has a hard time explaining government interventionism, mass democracy, and the welfare state. The economistic approach breaks down in the face of the pacification of class conflict and the long-term success of reformism in European countries since World War II, under the banner of a social-democratic program in the broader sense. In what follows, I shall (1) indicate the theoretical deficits detrimental to Marx's attempts to explain late capitalism, in particular state interventionism, mass democracy, and the welfare state; and then (2) introduce a model that explains the compromise structures of late capitalism and the cracks within them; and finally (3) go back to the role of culture, to which the Marxian theory of ideology does not do justice.

(1) *Government interventionism.* If we take as a basis the model of two complementary subsystems, one of which presents the problems to the other, a crisis theory that proceeds only in economic terms proves to be unsatisfactory. Even if system problems arise in the first place from the crisis-ridden course of economic growth, economic disequilibria can be balanced through the state jumping into the functional gaps of the market. Of course, the substitution of governmental for market functions takes place under the proviso that the sovereign right of private enterprise in matters of investment be fundamentally safeguarded. Economic growth would lose its intrinsic capitalist dynamics and the economy would forfeit its primacy if the production process were *controlled* through the medium of power. The intervention of the state may not affect the division of labor between a market-dependent economy and an economically unproductive state. In all three central dimensions – guaranteeing by military and legal-institutional means the presuppositions for the continuance of the mode of production; influencing the business cycle; and attending to the infrastructure with a view to the conditions of capital realization – government intervention has the *indirect* form of manipulating the boundary conditions for the decisions of private enterprise, and the *reactive* form of strategies for avoiding its side effects or compensating for them. This refracted mode of employing administrative power is determined by the propelling mechanism of an economy steered via the money medium.

As a result of this structural dilemma, economically conditioned crisis tendencies are not only administratively processed, flattened out, and intercepted, but also are inadvertently displaced into the administrative system. They can appear in various forms there – for example, as conflicts between business-cycle policy and infrastructure policy, as an overuse of the resource "time" (national debt), as an overloading of bureaucratic planning capacities, and so forth. This can, in turn, call forth relief strategies aimed at shifting the burden of problems back onto the economic system. Claus Offe has been particularly concerned to explain this complicated pattern of crises and of maneuvers to deal with them – oscillating from one subsystem to the other, pushed from one dimension to the other.[1]

Mass democracy. If we start from a model with two steering media, namely money and power, then an economic theory of democracy developed in terms of Marxist functionalism is inadequate. In comparing these two media, we saw that the institutionalization of power is more demanding than that of money. Money is anchored in the lifeworld by the institutions of bourgeois private law; for this reason the theory of value can start from the contractual relation between the wage-laborer and the owner of capital. By contrast, the public-legal (in the sense of the law applying to public bodies) pendant of an organization of offices does not suffice for power; above and beyond this, a legitimation of the political order is needed. And only democratic procedures of political will-formation can in principle generate legitimacy under conditions of a rationalized lifeworld with highly individuated members, with norms that have become abstract, positive, and in need of justification, and with traditions that have, as regards their claim to authority, been reflectively refracted and set communicatively aflow.[2] In this respect, the organized labor movement aimed in the same direction as the bourgeois emancipation movements. In the end, the legitimation process is regulated – on the basis of freedom of organization and of belief, and by way of competition between parties – in the form of free, secret, and general elections. Of course, the political participation of citizens takes place under certain structural restrictions.

Between capitalism and democracy there is an *indissoluble* tension; in them two opposed principles of societal integration compete for primacy. If we look at the self-understanding expressed in the basic principles of democratic constitutions, modern societies assert the primacy of a lifeworld in relation to the subsystems separated out of its institutional orders. The normative meaning of democracy can be rendered in social-theoretical terms by the formula that the fulfillment of the functional necessities of *systemically* integrated domains of action shall find its limits in the integrity of the lifeworld, that is to say, in the requirements of domains of action dependent on *social* integration. On the other hand, the internal dynamics of the capitalist economic system can be preserved only insofar as the accumulation process is uncoupled from orientations to use value. The propelling mechanism of the economic system has to be kept as free as possible from lifeworld restrictions as well as from the demands for legitimation directed to the administrative system. The internal systemic logic of capitalism can be rendered in social-theoretical terms by the formula that the functional necessities of systemically integrated domains of action shall be met, if need be, even at the cost of *technicizing* the lifeworld. Systems theory of the Luhmannian sort transforms this practical postulate into a theoretical one and thus makes its normative content unrecognizable.

Offe has expressed the tension between capitalism and democracy, from the standpoint of the competition between two contrary principles of societal integration, in the following paradox:

> Capitalist societies are distinguished from all others not by the problem of their reproduction, that is, the reconciliation of social and system integration, but by the fact that they attempt to deal with what is in fact

the basic problem of all societies in a way that simultaneously entertains two solutions which logically preclude one another: the differentiation or privatization of production and its politicization or "socialization" (in the Marxian sense). The two strategies thwart and paralyze each other. As a result the system is constantly confronted with the dilemma of having to abstract from the normative rules of action and the meaning relations of subjects without being able to disregard them. The political neutralization of the spheres of labor, production, and distribution is simultaneously confirmed and repudiated.[3]

This paradox also manifests itself in the fact that if parties want to gain or retain the power of office, they have to secure the trust of private investors and of the masses simultaneously.

Above all, the two imperatives clash in the political-public sphere, where the autonomy of the lifeworld has to prove itself in the face of the administrative system. The "public opinion" that gets articulated there has a different meaning from the perspective of the lifeworld than it does from the systemic perspective of the state apparatus.[4] One or the other of these perspectives is adopted by political sociologists according to whether they take an action-theoretic or a systems-theoretic approach; the chosen perspective is then applied to support a pluralistic, or ideology-critical, or authoritarian approach. Thus, from one point of view, what opinion polls report as public opinion or the will of the voters, of parties and associations, counts as a pluralistic expression of a general interest; social consensus is regarded as the *first link* in the chain of political will-formation and as the *basis* of legitimation. From the other point of view, the same consensus counts as the *result* of engineering legitimation; it is regarded as the *last link* in the chain of production of mass loyalty, with which the political system outfits itself in order to make itself independent from lifeworld restrictions. These two lines of interpretation have been falsely opposed to one another as the normative versus the empirical approach to democracy. In fact, however, each of the two views contains only one aspect of mass democracy. The formation of will that takes place via competition between parties is a result of both – the pull of communication processes in which norms and values are shaped, on the one hand, and the push of organizational performances by the political system, on the other.

The political system produces mass loyalty in both a positive and a selective manner: positively through the prospect of making good on social-welfare programs, selectively through excluding themes and contributions from public discussion. This can be accomplished through a sociostructural filtering of access to the political public sphere, through a bureaucratic deformation of the structures of public communication, or through manipulative control of the flow of communication.

By a combination of such variables we can explain how the symbolic self-presentation of political elites in the public sphere can be largely uncoupled from real decision-making processes within the political system.[5] Corresponding to this, we find a segmenting of the role of the voter, to which political participation is generally restricted. In general, electoral decisions have influence only on the recruitment of leadership personnel; as far as the motives behind them are concerned, they are removed from the grasp of discursive will-formation. This arrangement amounts to a neutralization of the possibilities for political participation opened up by the role of citizen.[6]

Welfare state. If we begin with a model of the interchange of the formally organized domains of economics and politics, on the one side, and communicatively structured domains of the private and public spheres on the other, then we have to consider that problems arising in the sphere of social labor get shifted from private to public spheres of life and, under the conditions of competitive-democratic will-formation, are there transformed into mortgages on legitimation. The social burdens resulting from class conflict – and these are in the first instance private burdens – cannot be kept away from the political sphere. Thus does social welfare become the political content of mass democracy. This shows that the political system cannot emancipate itself without leaving a trace from its citizens' orientations to use values. It cannot produce mass loyalty in any desired amount, but must, in its social-welfare programs, also make offers that can be checked as to fulfillment.

The legal institutionalization of collective bargaining became the basis of a reform politics that has brought about a pacification of class conflict in the social-welfare state. The core of the matter is the legislation of rights and entitlements in the spheres of work and social welfare, making provision for the basic risks of the wage laborers' existence and compensating them for handicaps that arise from the structurally weaker market positions (of employees, tenants, consumers, etc.). Social-welfare policy heads off extreme disadvantages and insecurities without, naturally, affecting the structurally unequal property, income, and power relations. The regulations and performances of the social-welfare state are, however, not only oriented to goals of social adjustment through individual compensations, but also to overcoming collectively experienced, external effects – for example, in the ecologically sensitive areas of town planning and highway construction, energy and water policy, protection of the countryside, or in the areas of health, culture, and education.

Politics directed to expanding the social-welfare state are certainly faced with a dilemma, which is expressed at the fiscal level in the zero-sum game between public expenditures for social-welfare measures, on the one side, and expenditures aimed to promote business and to improve the infrastructure in ways that foster economic growth, on the other side. The dilemma consists in the fact that the social-welfare state is supposed to head off immediately negative effects on the lifeworld of a capitalistically organized occupational system, as well as the dysfunctional side effects thereupon of economic growth that is steered through capital accumulation, and it is supposed to do so without encroaching upon the organizational form, the structure, or the drive mechanism of economic production. Not the least among the reasons why it may not impair the conditions of stability and the requirements of mobility of capitalist growth is the following: adjustments to the pattern of distribution of social compensations trigger reactions on the part of privileged groups unless they can be covered by increases in the social product and thus do not affect the propertied classes; when this is not the case, such measures cannot fulfill the function of containing and mitigating class conflict.

Thus, not only is the *extent* of social-welfare expenditures subject to fiscal restrictions, the *kind* of social-welfare performance, the *organized way* in which life is provided for, has to fit into the structure of an interchange, via money and power, between formally organized domains of action and their environments.

(2) Insofar as the political system in developed capitalist societies manages to overcome the structural dilemmas accompanying government interventionism, mass democracy, and the welfare state, structures of late capitalism take shapes that have to appear as paradoxical from the perspective of a Marxian theory with a narrowly economic approach. The welfare-state pacification of class conflict comes about under the condition of a continuation of the accumulation process whose capitalist drive mechanism is protected and not altered by the interventions of the state. In the West, under both social-democratic and conservative governments, a reformism relying on the instruments of Keynesian economics has made this development into a program; since 1945, especially in the phase of reconstructing and expanding destroyed productive capacity, it has achieved unmistakable economic and sociopolitical successes. The societal structures that have crystallized out in the process should not, however, be interpreted in the manner of Austro-Marxist theoreticians such as Otto Bauer or Karl Renner, that is, as the result of a class compromise. For with the institutionalization of class conflict, the social antagonism bred by private disposition over the means of producing social wealth increasingly loses its structure-forming power for the lifeworlds of social groups, although it does remain constitutive for the structure of the economic system. Late capitalism makes use in its own way of the relative uncoupling of system and lifeworld. A class structure shifted out of the lifeworld into the system loses its historically palpable shape. The unequal distribution of social rewards reflects a structure of privilege that can no longer be traced back to class positions in any unqualified way. The old sources of inequality are, to be sure, not sealed off, but now there is interference with both welfare-state compensations

and inequalities of another sort. Disparities and conflicts among marginal groups are characteristic of this. The more the class conflict that is built into society through the private economic form of accumulation can be dammed up and kept latent, the more problems come to the fore that do not *directly* violate interest positions ascribable on a class-specific basis.

Here I shall not go into the difficult problem of how the composition rules for the pattern of social equality in late capitalism undergo change; I am interested rather in how a new type of reification effect arises in class-unspecific ways and why these effects – filtered, naturally, through the pattern of social inequality and spread around in a differential fashion – are today found above all in communicatively structured domains of action.

The welfare-state compromise alters the conditions of the four existing relations between system (economy and state) and lifeworld (private and public spheres), around which the roles of the employee and the consumer, the client of public bureaucracies and the citizen of the state, crystallize. In his theory of value Marx concentrated solely on the exchange of labor power for wages and found the symptoms of reification in the sphere of social labor. Before his eyes he had that historically limited type of alienation that Engels, for example, had described in *The Condition of the Working Class in England.*[7] From the model of alienated factory work in the early stages of industrialization, Marx developed a concept of alienation that he carried over to the proletarian lifeworld as a whole. This concept makes no distinction between the dislocation of traditional lifeworlds and the destruction of post-traditional lifeworlds. And it also does not discriminate between impoverishment, which concerns the material reproduction of the lifeworld, and disturbances in the symbolic reproduction of the lifeworld – in Weber's terms, between problems of outer and of inner need. But this type of alienation recedes further and further into the background as the welfare state becomes established.

In the social-welfare state, the roles provided by the occupational system become, so to speak, normalized. Within the framework of post-traditional lifeworlds, the structural differentiation of employment within organizations is no foreign element in any case; the burdens resulting from the character of heteronomously determined work are made at least subjectively bearable – if not through "humanizing" the work place, through providing monetary reward and legally guaranteed securities – and are largely headed off in this way, along with other disadvantages and risks stemming from the status of workers and employees. The role of employee loses its debilitating proletarian features with the continuous rise in the standard of living, however differentiated by stratification. As the private sphere is shielded against palpable consequences of the system imperatives at work, conflicts over distribution also lose their explosive power; it is only in dramatic, exceptional cases that they go beyond the institutional boundaries of collective bargaining and become a burning issue.

This new equilibrium between normalized occupational roles and upgraded consumer roles is, as we have seen, the result of a welfare arrangement that comes about under the legitimation conditions of mass democracy. The theory of value was wrong to ignore the interchange relations between the political system and the lifeworld. For the pacification of the sphere of social labor is only the counterpart to an equilibrium established on the other side, between an expanded, but at the same time neutralized, citizen's role and a blown-up client's role. The establishment of basic political rights in the framework of mass democracy means, on the one hand, a universalization of the role of citizen and, on the other hand, a segmenting of this role from the decision-making process, a cleansing of political participation from any participatory content. Legitimacy and mass loyalty form an alloy that is not analyzed by those involved and cannot be broken down into its critical components.

For this neutralization of the generalized role of citizen, the welfare state also pays in the coin of use values that come to citizens as clients of welfare-state bureaucracies. "Clients" are customers who enjoy the rewards of the welfare state; the client role is a companion piece that makes political participation that has been evaporated into an abstraction and robbed of its effectiveness acceptable. The negative side effects of institutionalizing an alienated mode of having a say in matters of public interest are passed off onto the client role in much the same way as the burdens of normalizing alienated labor are passed off onto the consumer role. It is primarily in these two channels that new conflict potentials of late capitalist society are gathering. With the exception of critical theorists such as Marcuse and Adorno, Marxists have found these new potentials vexing. Of course, the framework of the critique of instrumental reason within which those critical theorists operated has turned out to be too narrow. Only in the framework of a critique of functionalist reason can we give a plausible account of why, under the cover of a more or less successful welfare-state compromise, there should still be any conflicts breaking out at all – conflicts that do not appear primarily in class-specific forms and yet go back to a class structure that is displaced into systemically integrated domains of action. The explanation suggested by our model of late capitalist society – a model that is admittedly very stylized and that works with only a few, idealized assumptions – is the following.

Welfare-state mass democracy is an arrangement that renders the class antagonism still built into the economic system innocuous, under the condition, however, that the capitalist dynamics of growth, protected by measures of state intervention, do not grow weak. Only then is there a mass of compensation available that can be distributed according to implicitly agreed-upon criteria, in ritualized confrontations, and channeled into the roles of consumer and client in such a way that the structures of alienated labor and alienated political participation develop no explosive power. However, the politically supported, internal dynamics of the economic system result in a more or less continuous increase in system complexity – which means not only an *extension* of formally organized domains of action, but an increase in their internal *density* as well. This is true, in the first place, for relations within the subsystems of the economy and the public administration and for their relations with each other. It is this internal growth that explains the processes of concentration in commodity, capital, and labor markets, the centralization of private firms and public agencies, as well as part of the expansion in the functions and activities of the state (as manifested by the correlative rise in government budgets).

However, the growth of this whole complex has as much to do with the interchange of the subsystems with those spheres of the lifeworld that have gotten redefined as system environments – in the first instance, private households that have been converted over to mass consumption, and client relations that are coordinated with bureaucratic provisions for life.

On the basic assumptions of our model, these are the two channels through which the compensations flow, which the welfare state offers for the pacification of the sphere of social labor and the neutralization of participation in political decision-making processes. If we ignore for the moment crisis-laden disequilibria of the system that are passed on to the lifeworld in administratively processed forms, capitalist growth triggers conflicts within the lifeworld chiefly as a consequence of the expansion and the increasing density of the monetary-bureaucratic complex; this happens, first of all, where socially integrated contexts of life are redefined around the roles of consumer and client and assimilated to systemically integrated domains of action. Such processes have always been part of capitalist modernization; historically, they have been successful in overriding the defensive reaction of those affected so long as it was primarily a question of transferring the material reproduction of the lifeworld over to formally organized domains of action. Along the front between system and lifeworld, the lifeworld evidently offers stubborn and possibly successful resistance only when functions of symbolic reproduction are in question.

(3) Before getting into these empirical matters, we have to pick up a thread that we earlier laid aside. We interpreted Weber's thesis of the loss of freedom in terms of a systemically induced reification of communicatively structured domains of action; then, from our critical discussion of the theory of value, we arrived at hypotheses that might explain why there are reification tendencies at all in developed capitalist societies, even if in an altered form. But how does Weber's second cultural-critical thesis – which had to do with the disintegration of

religious-metaphysical world-views and with phenomena of a loss of meaning – fit together with this reception of Marx? In Marx and Lukács the theory of reification is supplemented and supported by a theory of class-consciousness. The latter is directed, in an ideology-critical fashion, against the dominant form of consciousness and reclaims for the other side certain privileged opportunities for critical insight. In the face of a class antagonism pacified by means of welfare-state measures, however, and in the face of the growing anonymity of class structures, the theory of class consciousness loses its empirical reference. It no longer has application to a society in which we are increasingly unable to identify strictly class-specific lifeworlds. Consistent with this, Horkheimer and his collaborators replaced it with a theory of mass culture.

Marx developed his dialectical concept of ideology with an eye to eighteenth-century bourgeois culture. These ideals of self-formation, which had found classic expression in science and philosophy, in natural right and economics, in art and literature, had entered into the self-understanding and the private lifestyles of the bourgeoisie and of an increasingly bourgeois nobility, as well as into the principles of public order. Marx recognized the ambivalent content of bourgeois culture. In its claims to autonomy and scientific method, to individual freedom and universalism, to radical, romantic self-disclosure, it is on the one hand, the result of cultural rationalization – having ceased to rely on the authority of tradition, it is sensitive to criticism and self-criticism. On the other hand, however, the normative contents of its abstract and unhistorical ideas, overshooting as they do existing social realities, not only support a critically transforming practice by providing some initial guidance, but also support an affirming and endorsing practice by providing a measure of idealistic transfiguration. The utopian-ideological double character of bourgeois culture has been worked out again and again from Marx to Marcuse.[8] This description applies to just those structures of consciousness that we would expect under the conditions of a modern form of understanding.

We designated as a "modern form of understanding" a structure of communication characterized in profane domains of activity by the facts that (1) communicative actions are increasingly detached from normative contexts and become increasingly dense, with an expanded scope for contingencies; and (2) forms of argumentation are institutionally differentiated, namely, theoretical discourse in the scientific enterprise, moral-practical discourse in the political public sphere and in the legal system, and aesthetic criticism in the artistic and literary enterprise. [...] In the early modern period, the realm of the sacred was not completely leveled down; in secularized form it lived on in the contemplation of an art that had not shed its aura, as well as in practically effective religious and philosophical traditions, in the transitional forms of a not yet fully secularized bourgeois culture. As this residue of the sacred gets flattened out, however, as the syndrome of validity-claims gets disentangled here as well, the "loss of meaning" that occupied Weber makes itself felt. The rationality differential that had always existed between the realms of the sacred and the profane now disappears. The rationality potential released in the profane realm had previously been narrowed down and neutralized by world-views. Considered in structural terms, these world-views were at a lower level of rationality than everyday consciousness; at the time, however, they were intellectually better worked through and articulated. What is more, mythical or religious world-views were so deeply rooted in ritual or cultic practices that the motives and value-orientations formed without coercion in collective convictions were sealed off from the influx of dissonant experiences, from the rationality of everyday life. This all changes with the secularization of bourgeois culture. The irrationally binding, sacrally preserved power of a level of rationality that had been superseded in everyday practice begins to wane. The substance of basic convictions that were culturally sanctioned and did not need to be argued for begins to evaporate.

From the logic of cultural rationalization we can project the vanishing point toward which cultural modernity is heading; as the rationality differential between the profane realm of action and a definitively disenchanted culture gets leveled out, the latter will lose the properties that made it capable of taking on ideological functions.

Of course, this state of affairs – which Daniel Bell has proclaimed as "The End of Ideology" – was a long time coming. The French Revolution, which was fought under the banner of bourgeois ideals, inaugurated the epoch of ideologically determined mass movements. The classical bourgeois emancipation movements gave rise to traditionalist reactions with the characteristics of a regression to the pre-bourgeois level of imitated substantiality. On the other hand, there was also a syndrome of heterogeneous modern reactions, ranging across a broad spectrum of scientific – mostly pseudo-scientific – popular views, from anarchism, communism, and socialism, through syndicalist, radical-democratic, and conservative-revolutionary orientations, to fascism and National Socialism. This was the second generation of ideologies that arose on the ground of bourgeois society. All differences in formal level and synthetic power notwithstanding, they have one thing in common. Unlike the classical bourgeois ideology, these world-views, rooted in the nineteenth century, work up specifically modern manifestations of withdrawal and deprivation – that is to say, deficits inflicted upon the lifeworld by societal modernization. This is the direction indicated, for instance, by the visionary desires for a moral or aesthetic renewal of the political public sphere or, more generally, for revitalizing a politics that has shrunk to administration. Thus, tendencies to moralization are expressed in the ideals of autonomy and participation that usually predominate in radical-democratic and socialist movements. Tendencies to aestheticization are expressed in needs for expressive

self-presentation and authenticity; they can predominate in both authoritarian movements (like fascism) and anti-authoritarian movements
(like anarchism). Such tendencies are in keeping with modernity
inasmuch as they do not turn to metaphysically or religiously satisfying
world-views to "salvage" the moral-practical and expressive moments
suppressed or neglected by the capitalist pattern of modernization; they
seek, instead, to establish them practically in the new life forms of a
society revolutionized in some way or other.

In spite of the differences in content, these world-views still share
with the ideologies of the first generation – the offspring of rational
natural law, of utilitarianism, of bourgeois social philosophy and philosophy of history in general – the *form* of totalizing conceptions of order
addressed to the political consciousness of comrades and partners in
struggle. It is just this form of a global interpretation of the whole,
drawn up from the perspective of the lifeworld and capable of integration, that had to break down in the communication structures of a
developed modernity. When the auratic traces of the sacred have been
lost and the products of a synthetic, world-picturing power of imagination have vanished, the form of understanding, now fully differentiated
in its validity basis, becomes so transparent that the communicative
practice of everyday life no longer affords any niches for the structural
violence of ideologies. The imperatives of autonomous subsystems then
have to exert their influence on socially integrated domains of action
from the outside, and *in a discernible fashion*. They can no longer hide
behind the rationality differential between sacred and profane realms
of action and reach inconspicuously through action orientations so as
to draw the lifeworld into intuitively inaccessible, functional interconnections.

If, however, the rationalized lifeworld more and more loses its structural possibilities for ideology formation, if the facts that speak for an
instrumentalizing of the lifeworld can hardly be interpreted away any
longer and ousted from the horizon of the lifeworld, one would expect
that the competition between forms of social and system integration
would openly come to the fore. But the late capitalist societies fitting
the description of "welfare-state pacification" do not confirm this
conjecture. They have evidently found some functional equivalent for
ideology formation. In place of the positive task of meeting a certain
need for interpretation by ideological means, we have the negative
requirement of preventing holistic interpretations from coming into
existence. The lifeworld is always constituted in the form of a global
knowledge intersubjectively shared by its members; thus, the desired
equivalent for no longer available ideologies might simply consist in the
fact that the everyday knowledge appearing in totalized form remains
diffuse, or at least never attains that level of articulation at which alone
knowledge can be accepted as valid according to the standards of

cultural modernity. *Everyday consciousness* is robbed of its power to synthesize; it becomes *fragmented.*

Something of this sort does in fact happen; the differentiation of science, morality, and art, which is characteristic of Occidental rationalism, results not only in a growing autonomy for sectors dealt with by specialists, but also in the splitting off of these sectors from a stream of tradition continuing on in everyday practice in a quasi-natural fashion. This split has been repeatedly experienced as a problem. The attempts at an *Aufhebung* of philosophy and art were rebellions against structures that subordinated everyday consciousness to the standards of exclusive expert cultures developing according to their own logics and that yet cut it off from any influx from them.[9] Everyday consciousness sees itself thrown back on traditions whose claims to validity have already been suspended; where it does escape the spell of traditionalism, it is hopelessly splintered. In place of "false consciousness" we today have a "fragmented consciousness" that blocks enlightenment by the mechanism of reification. It is only with this that the conditions for a *colonization of the lifeworld* are met. When stripped of their ideological veils, the imperatives of autonomous subsystems make their way into the lifeworld from the outside – like colonial masters coming into a tribal society – and force a process of assimilation upon it. The diffused perspectives of the local culture cannot be sufficiently coordinated to permit the play of the metropolis and the world market to be grasped from the periphery.

Thus, the theory of late capitalist reification, reformulated in terms of system and lifeworld, has to be supplemented by an analysis of cultural modernity, which replaces the now superseded theory of consciousness. Rather than serving a critique of ideology, this analysis would have to explain the cultural impoverishment and fragmentation of everyday consciousness. Rather than hunting after the scattered traces of revolutionary consciousness, it would have to examine the conditions for recoupling a rationalized culture with an everyday communication dependent on vital traditions.

Tendencies toward juridification

I have explained the symptoms of reification appearing in developed capitalist societies by the fact that the media-controlled subsystems of the economy and the state intervene with monetary and bureaucratic means in the symbolic reproduction of the lifeworld. According to our hypothesis, a "colonization of the lifeworld" can come about only

- when traditional forms of life are so far dismantled that the structural components of the lifeworld (culture, society, and personality) have been differentiated to a great extent;

- when exchange relations between the subsystems and the lifeworld are regulated through differentiated roles (for employment at organized workplaces, for the consumer demand of private households, for the relation of clients to government bureaucracies, and for formal participation in the legitimation process);
- when the real abstractions that make available the labor power of the employed and make possible the mobilization of the vote of the electorate are tolerated by those affected as a trade-off against social rewards (in terms of time and money);
- where these compensations are financed according to the welfare-state pattern from the gains of capitalist growth and are canalized into those roles in which, withdrawn from the world of work and the public sphere, privatized hopes for self-actualization and self-determination are primarily located, namely, in the roles of consumer and client.

Statements about an internal colonization of the lifeworld are at a relatively high level of generalization. This is not so unusual for social-theoretical reflection, as can be seen in the example of systems functionalism as well. But such a theory is always exposed to the danger of overgeneralization and so must be able to specify at least *the type* of empirical research that is appropriate to it. I shall therefore provide an example of the evidence by which the thesis of internal colonization can be tested: the juridification of communicatively structured areas of action. I choose this example because it offers no particularly serious problems in method or content. The development of law belongs to the undisputed and, since Durkheim and Weber, classical research areas of sociology.

If it is true that the symbolic reproduction of the lifeworld cannot be transposed onto the base of systemic integration without pathological consequences, and if precisely this trend is the unavoidable side effect of a successful welfare-state program, then in the areas of cultural reproduction, social integration, and socialization an assimilation to formally organized domains of action would have to take place under the conditions mentioned above. The social relations we call "formally organized" are those that are first constituted in forms of modern law. Thus it is to be expected that the changeover from social to system integration would take the form of juridification processes. The predicted reification effects would have to be demonstrated at the analytical level and, indeed, as being the symptomatic consequence of *a specific kind* of juridification. [. . .]

Norms that contain class conflict and enforce social-welfare measures have, from the perspective of their beneficiaries as well as from that of democratic law-givers, a freedom-guaranteeing character. However, this does not apply unambiguously to all welfare-state regulations. From the start, the *ambivalence of guaranteeing freedom and taking it away* has attached to the policies of the welfare state. The first wave of juridification constitutive of the relation between capital and wage-labor owed its ambivalence to a contradiction between, on the one hand, the socially emancipatory intent of the norms of bourgeois civil law and, on the other, its socially repressive effects on those who were forced to offer their labor power as a commodity. The net of welfare-state guarantees is meant to cushion the external effects of a production process based on wage labor. Yet the more closely this net is woven, the more clearly ambivalences of *another sort* appear. The negative effects of this – to date, final – wave of juridification do not appear as side effects; they result *from the form of juridification itself.* It is now the very means of guaranteeing freedom that endangers the freedom of the beneficiaries.

In the area of *public welfare policy* this situation has attracted wide attention under the title "juridification and bureaucratization as limits to welfare policy."[10] In connection with social-welfare law, it has been shown repeatedly that although legal entitlements to monetary income in case of illness, old age, and the like definitely signify historical progress when compared with the traditional care of the poor, this juridification of life-risks exacts a noteworthy price in the form of *restructuring interventions in the lifeworlds* of those who are so entitled. These costs ensue from the bureaucratic implementation and monetary redemption of welfare entitlements. The structure of bourgeois law dictates the formulation of welfare-state guarantees as *individual* legal entitlements under precisely *specified* general legal conditions.

In social-welfare law, *individualization* – that is, the attribution of entitlements to strategically acting legal subjects pursuing their private interests – may be more appropriate to the life situations requiring regulation than is the case, for instance, in family law. Nevertheless, the individualizing definition of, say, geriatric care has burdensome consequences for the self-image of the person concerned, and for his relations with spouse, friends, neighbors, and others; it also has consequences for the readiness of solidaristic communities to provide subsidiary assistance. A considerable compulsion toward the redefinition of everyday situations comes above all from the *specification of legal conditions* – in this case, the conditions under which social security will provide compensation:

> An insured case is normally understood as a "typical example of the particular contingency against which social security is supposed to provide protection." Compensation is made in the event of a valid claim to benefit. The juridification of social situation-definitions means introducing into matters of economic and social distribution an if-then structure of conditional law that is "foreign" to social relations, to social causes, dependencies and needs. This structure does not, however, allow for appropriate, and especially not for preventive, reactions to the causes of the situations requiring compensation.[11]

In the end, the *generality* of legal situation-definitions is tailored to *bureaucratic implementation*, that is, to the administration that deals with the social problem as presented by the legal entitlement. The situation to be regulated is embedded in the context of a life-history and of a concrete form of life; it has to be subjected to violent abstraction, not merely because it has to be subsumed under the law, but so that it can be dealt with administratively. The implementing bureaucracies have to proceed very selectively and *choose* from among the legally defined conditions of compensation those social exigencies that can at all be dealt with by means of bureaucratic power exercised according to law. Moreover, this suits the needs of a centralized and computerized handling of social exigencies by large, distant organizations. These organizations add a spatial and temporal element to the social and psychological distance of the client from the welfare bureaucracy.

Furthermore, the indemnification of the life-risks in question usually takes the *form of monetary compensation*. However, in such cases as reaching retirement or losing a job, the typical changes in life-situation and the attendant problems cannot as a rule be subjected to consumerist redefinition. To balance the inadequacy of these system-conforming compensations, *social services* have been set up to lend *therapeutic assistance*.

With this, however, the contradictions of welfare-state intervention are only reproduced at a higher level. The form of the administratively prescribed treatment by an expert is for the most part in contradiction with the aim of the therapy, namely, that of promoting the client's independence and self-reliance:

> The process of providing social services takes on a reality of its own, nurtured above all by the professional competence of public officials, the framework of administrative action, biographical and current "findings," the readiness and ability to cooperate of the person seeking the service or being subjected to it. In these areas too there remain problems connected with a class-specific utilization of such services, with the assignments made by the courts, the prison system and other offices, and with the appropriate location and arrangement of the services within the network of bureaucratic organizations of the welfare state; but beyond this, such forms of physical, psycho-social and emancipatory aid really require modes of operation, rationality criteria, and organizational forms that are foreign to bureaucratically structured administration.[12]

The ambivalence of the last juridification wave, that of the welfare state, can be seen with particular clarity in the paradoxical consequences of the social services offered by the therapeutocracy – from the prison system through medical treatment of the mentally ill, addicts, and the behaviorally disturbed, from the classical forms of social work through the newer psychotherapeutic and group-dynamic forms of support, pastoral care, and the building of religious groups, from youth work, public education, and the health system through general preventive measures of every type. The more the welfare state goes beyond pacifying the class conflict lodged in the sphere of production and spreads a net of client relationships over private spheres of life, the stronger are the anticipated pathological side effects of a juridification that entails both a bureaucratization and a monetarization of core areas of the lifeworld. The *dilemmatic structure of this type of juridification* consists in the fact that, while the welfare-state guarantees are intended to serve the goal of social integration, they nevertheless promote the disintegration of life-relations when these are separated, through legalized social intervention, from the consensual mechanisms that coordinate action and are transferred over to media such as power and money. In this sense, R. Pitschas speaks of the crisis of public-welfare policy as a crisis of social integration.[13]

For an empirical analysis of these phenomena, it is important to clarify the criteria on the basis of which the aspects of guaranteeing and taking away freedom can be separated. From the legal standpoint the first thing that presents itself is the classical division of fundamental rights into liberties and participatory rights; one might presume that the structure of bourgeois formal law becomes dilemmatic precisely when these means are no longer used to negatively demarcate areas of private discretion, but are supposed to provide positive guarantees of membership and participation in institutions and benefits. If this presumption proved true, then one would already expect a change from guaranteeing to taking away freedom at the third (democratizing) stage of juridification and not only at the fourth (welfare-state) stage. There are indeed indications that the *organization of the exercise of civil liberties* considerably restricts the possibilities for spontaneous opinion-formation and discursive will-formation through a segmentation of the voter's role, through the competition of leadership elites, through vertical opinion-formation in bureaucratically encrusted party apparatuses, through autonomized parliamentary bodies, through powerful communication networks, and the like. However, such arguments cannot be used to deduce aspects of taking away freedom from the very *form* of participatory rights, but only from the bureaucratic ways and means of their *implementation*. One can scarcely dispute the unambiguously freedom-guaranteeing character of the *principle* of universal suffrage, nor of the *principles* of freedom of assembly, of the press, and of opinion – which, under the conditions of modern mass communication, must also be interpreted as democratic participatory rights.

A different criterion, more sociological in nature and open to social-theoretic interpretation, takes us further: that is, the classification of legal norms according to whether they can be legitimized only through procedure in the positivist sense, or are amenable to substantive justification. If the legitimacy of a legal norm is brought into question, it is, in many cases, sufficient to refer to the formally correct genesis of the law, judicial decision, or administrative act. Legal positivism has conceptualized this as legitimation through procedure, though, of course, without seeing that this mode of legitimation is insufficient in itself and merely points to the need for justification of the legitimizing public authorities.[14] In the face of the changing and steadily increasing volume of positive law, modern legal subjects content themselves in actual practice with legitimation through procedure, for in many cases substantive justification is not only not possible, but is also, from the viewpoint of the lifeworld, meaningless. This is true of cases where the *law* serves as a means for organizing media-controlled subsystems that have, in any case, become autonomous in relation to the normative contexts of action oriented by mutual understanding. Most areas of economic, commercial, business, and administrative law fit here: the law is combined with the media of power and money in such a way that it takes on the role of a steering medium itself. Law as a medium, however, remains bound up with *law as an institution*. By legal *institutions* I mean legal norms that cannot be sufficiently legitimized through a positivistic reference to procedure. Typical of these are the bases of constitutional law, the principles of criminal law and penal procedure, and all regulation of punishable offenses close to morality (e.g., murder, abortion, rape, etc.). As soon as the validity of *these* norms is questioned in everyday practice, the reference to their legality no longer suffices. They need substantive justification, because they belong to the legitimate orders of the lifeworld itself and, together with informal norms of conduct, form the background of communicative action.

We have characterized modern law through a combination of principles of enactment and justification. This structure simultaneously makes possible a positivistic prolongation of the paths of justificatory reasoning and a moralizing intensification of the justification problematic, which is thereby shifted into the foundations of the legal system. We can now see how the uncoupling of system and lifeworld fits in with this legal structure. Law used as a steering medium is relieved of the problem of justification; it is connected with the body of law whose substance requires legitimation only through formally correct procedure. By contrast, legal institutions belong to the societal components of the lifeworld. Like other norms of conduct not covered by the sanctioning authority of the state, they can become moralized under appropriate circumstances. Admittedly, changes in the basis of legitimation do not directly affect the stock of legal norms, but they may provide the impetus for a legal (or, in the limiting case, a revolutionary) change in existing law.

As long as the law functions as a complex medium bound up with money and power, it extends to formally organized domains of action that, as such, are directly constituted in the forms of bourgeois formal law. By contrast, legal institutions have no *constitutive* power, but only a *regulative* function. They are embedded in a broader political, cultural, and social context; they stand in a continuum with moral norms and are superimposed on communicatively structured areas of action. They give to these informally constituted domains of action a binding form backed by state sanction. From this standpoint we can distinguish processes of juridification according to whether they are linked to antecedent institutions of the lifeworld and juridically superimposed on socially integrated areas of action, or whether they merely increase the density of legal relationships that are constitutive of systemically integrated areas of action. Here, the question of the appropriate mode of legitimation may serve as a first test. The technicized and de-moralized areas of law that grow along with the complexity of the economic and administrative systems have to be evaluated with respect to functional imperatives and in accordance with higher-order norms. Looked at historically, the continuous growth in positive law largely falls into this category and merely indicates an increased recourse to the medium of law. The epochal juridification waves are, on the other hand, characterized by *new legal institutions*, which are also reflected in the legal consciousness of everyday practice. Only with respect to this second category of juridification do questions of normative evaluation arise.

The first wave of juridification had a freedom-guaranteeing character to the extent that bourgeois civil law and a bureaucratic domination exercised by legal means at least meant emancipation from pre-modern relations of power and dependence. The three subsequent juridification waves guaranteed an increase in freedom insofar as they were able to restrain, in the interests of citizens and of private legal subjects, the political and economic dynamics that had been released by the legal institutionalization of the media of money and power. The step-by-step development toward the democratic welfare state is directed against those modern relations of power and dependence that arose with the capitalist enterprise, the bureaucratic apparatus of domination, and, more generally, the formally organized domains of action of the economy and the state. The inner dynamics of these action systems also unfold within the organizational forms of law, but in such a way that law here takes on the role of a steering medium rather than supplementing institutional components of the lifeworld.

In its role as a medium, existing law can be more or less functional, but outside of the horizon of the lifeworld it is meaningless to question the freedom-guaranteeing or freedom-reducing character of these norms. The ambivalence of guaranteeing/taking away freedom cannot be reduced to a dialectic between law as an institution and law as a medium, because the alternative between guaranteeing or taking away freedom is posed only from the viewpoint of the lifeworld, that is, only in relation to legal institutions.

So far we have proceeded on the assumption that law is used as a medium only within formally organized domains of action, and that as a steering medium it remains indifferent in relation to the lifeworld and to the questions of substantive justification that arise within its horizons. Welfare-state interventionism has since rendered this assumption invalid. Public welfare policy has to use the law precisely as a medium to regulate those exigencies that arise in communicatively structured areas of action. To be sure, the principle of social participation and social compensation is, like freedom of association, a constitutionally anchored institution that can connect up easily with the legitimate orders of the modern lifeworld. But social-welfare law, through which social compensation is implemented, differs from, for instance, the laws governing collective bargaining, through which freedom of association becomes effective, in one important respect: measures of social-welfare law (as a rule, compensatory payments) do not, like collective wage and salary agreements, intervene in an area that is *already* formally organized. Rather, they regulate exigencies that, as lifeworld situations, belong to a communicatively structured area of action. Thus, I should like to explain the type of reification effect exhibited in the case of public welfare policy by the fact that the *legal institutions* that guarantee social compensation become effective only through *social-welfare law used as a medium*. From the standpoint of action theory the paradox of this legal structure can be explained as follows. As a medium, social-welfare law is tailored to domains of action that are first constituted in legal forms of organization and that can be held together only by systemic mechanisms. At the same time, however, social-welfare law applies to situations embedded in informal lifeworld contexts.

In our context, government welfare policy serves only as an illustration. The thesis of internal colonization states that the subsystems of the economy and state become more and more complex as a consequence of capitalist growth, and penetrate ever deeper into the symbolic reproduction of the lifeworld. It should be possible to test this thesis sociologically wherever the traditionalist padding of capitalist modernization has worn through and central areas of cultural reproduction, social integration, and socialization have been openly drawn into the vortex of economic growth and therefore of juridification. This applies not only to such issues as protection of the environment, nuclear reactor security, data protection, and the like, which have been successfully dramatized in the public sphere. The trend toward juridification of informally regulated spheres of the lifeworld is gaining ground along a broad front – the more leisure, culture, recreation, and tourism recognizably come into the grip of the laws of the commodity economy and the definitions of mass consumption, the more the structures of the bourgeois family manifestly become adapted to the imperatives of the employment system, the more the school palpably takes over the functions of assigning job and life prospects, and so forth. [. . .]

If one studies the paradoxical structure of juridification in such areas as the family, the schools, social-welfare policy, and the like, the meaning of the demands that regularly result from these analyses is easy to decipher. The point is to protect areas of life that are functionally dependent on social integration through values, norms, and consensus formation, to preserve them from falling prey to the systemic imperatives of economic and administrative subsystems growing with dynamics of their own, and to defend them from becoming converted over, through the steering medium of the law, to a principle of sociation that is, for them, dysfunctional.

The Theory of Communicative Action, vol. 2, pp. 342–73.

Notes

1 Claus Offe, *Contradictions of the Welfare State* (Cambridge, Mass., 1984), and *Disorganized Capitalism* (Cambridge, Mass., 1985).

2 J. Habermas, "Legitimation Problems in the Modern State," in *Communication and the Evolution of Society* (Boston, 1979), pp. 178–205 [reading 23 above].

3 Claus Offe, "Ungovernability," in J. Habermas (ed.), *Observations on "The Spiritual Situation of the Age"* (Cambridge, Mass., 1984), pp. 67–88, here p. 85.

4 Niklas Luhmann, "Öffentliche Meinung," in *Politische Planung* (Opladen, 1971), pp. 9ff.

5 M. Edelman, *The Symbolic Uses of Politics* (Urbana, Ill., 1964); D.O. Sears, R.R. Lau, T.R. Tyler, and H.M. Allen, "Self-Interest vs. Symbolic Politics," *American Political Science Review*, 74, 1980: 670ff.

6 This neutralization is normally sufficient at least to prevent a basic empirical question that would affect the normative self-understanding of democracies from making its way into everyday political consciousness: "Whether a process moving along institutional lines yields up results of a consensus arrived at free from domination and for that reason vouchsafing legitimacy, or whether this process itself produces and enforces a passive mass loyalty more or less accepting of its institutional restrictions, and thus props itself up on a self-generated foundation of formally democratic [*scheindemokratischer*] acclamation." W.D. Narr and C. Offe, "Einleitung," in *Wohlfahrtsstaat und Massenloyalität* (Cologne, 1975), p. 28.

7 S. Marcus, *Engels, Manchester, and the Working Class* (London, 1974).

8 Herbert Marcuse, "The Affirmative Character of Culture," in *Negations* (Boston, 1968), pp. 88–133, *An Essay on Liberation* (Boston, 1969), and *Counterrevolution and Revolt* (Boston, 1972). See J. Habermas, "Herbert Marcuse: On Art and Revolution," in *Philosophical-Political Profiles* (Cambridge, Mass., 1983), pp. 165–70.

9 Corresponding to this direct intervention of experts into everyday life, and to the technocratic scientization of practice, are tendencies toward deprofessionalization, for which U. Oevermann is attempting to develop a theoretical explanation.

10 For the relevant literature, see E. Reidegeld, "Vollzugsdefizite sozialer Leistungen," in R. Voigt, *Verrechtlichung*, (Frankfurt, 1980), pp. 275ff.
11 For the relevant literature, see E. Reidegeld, "Vollzugsdefizite sozialer Leistungen," in R. Voigt, *Verrechtlichung*, (Frankfurt, 1980), pp. 277.
12 Ibid., p. 281.
13 "In the area where the constitutional state and the welfare state meet, social policy that uses 'active' social intervention in the state's organization of freedom threatens to overwhelm the individual's right to help himself. The state benefit system thereby not only undoes the distribution of responsibilities between state and society; by shaping social benefits, it moulds *whole patterns of life*. If the citizen's life is insured in legalized form against all vicissitudes, from before birth to after death – as the law governing survivors' benefits teaches – then the individual fits himself into these social shells of his existence. He lives his life free of material worries, but simultaneously suffers from an excess of government provisions and from a fear of losing them." R. Pitschas, "Soziale Sicherung durch fortschreitende Verrechtlichung," in Voigt, *Verrechtlichung*, p. 155.
14 See vol. 1 of this work, *Reason and the Rationalization of Society* (Boston, 1984), 1:264ff.

PART VIII

Critical Social Theory Today

Introduction

This part begins with the final section of The Theory of Communicative Action (reading 27), in which Habermas outlines his own program for critical theory in opposition to alternative programs in social theory and to the critical theory of the original Frankfurt School. In opposition both to Marxism itself and to early critical theory, Habermas aims "to free historical materialism from its philosophy-of-history ballast."[1] As in reading 26 in part VII, he brings his model to bear on some of the concrete problems of contemporary liberal democracies. Some of the theoretical themes return in Habermas's lecture series from the mid-1980s which was published as The Philosophical Discourse of Modernity. This book has attracted most attention for its critiques of Heidegger and of post-structuralism, but it also contains a more constructive theory of the ambivalent nature of modernity, which is illustrated here (readings 28–9) by the opening pages of the book and its final chapter.

One of the clearest ways of marking the difference between critical theory in Habermas's sense and what is often called critical theory in literary studies is in terms of their respective attitudes to modernity, the Enlightenment, and conceptions of the human subject. Whereas thinkers influenced by post-structuralism and postmodernism tend to be radically skeptical of all three, critical theorists in the Frankfurt tradition are more likely to argue that we should retain such notions, with all due caution in respect of their problematic aspects. For Habermas, modernity, with its ideals of enlightenment and individual freedom, is a "project" which requires completion. To do philosophical justice to this project, however, we must move away from what he variously calls the philosophy of consciousness, the philosophy of the subject, or subject-centred reason, to an alternative model based on the communicative relations between human subjects. Only in this way can we recover and reanimate what he calls the normative content of modernity.

The philosophical implications of this approach are developed more fully in Postmetaphysical Thinking (Cambridge: Polity, 1992). More recently, he has returned to some of these themes both in his political writings, notably in Die nachholende Revolution (Frankfurt: Suhrkamp,

1990), and in a substantial interview, conducted in 1991 and published in English in an extended form in 1994 with the title The Past as Future.

Note

1 *The Theory of Communicative Action*, vol. II, p. 383; see reading 27.

Further Reading

Maurizio Passerin d'Entrèves and Seyla Benhabib (eds), *Habermas and the Unfinished Project of Modernity: Critical Essays on the Philosophical Discourse of Modernity* (Cambridge: Polity, 1996).
William Outhwaite, "Nietzsche and Critical Theory" in Peter Sedgwick (ed.), *Nietzsche: A Critical Reader* (Oxford: Blackwell, 1995).
William Outhwaite, "Habermas: Modernity as Reflection," in Brian Cheyette and Laura Marcus (eds), *Modernity, Culture and "the Jew"* (California University Press, forthcoming).

27

The Tasks of a Critical Theory of Society

My purpose in discussing the thesis of internal colonization in connection with recent tendencies toward juridification in the Federal Republic of Germany was, among other things, to show by example how processes of real abstraction, to which Marx directed his attention, can be analyzed without our having any equivalent for his theory of value. This brings us back to the central question of whether, in the present state of the social sciences, it is necessary and possible to replace the theory of value, at least insofar as it enables us to connect theoretical statements about lifeworld and system to each other. As we have seen, Marx conceived the systemic context of capital self-realization as a fetishistic totality; from this there followed the methodological requirement that we decipher anything that might correctly be brought under a systems-theoretical description simultaneously as a process of reification of living labor. This far-reaching claim has to be dropped, however, if we see in the capitalist economic system not only a new formation of class relationships but an advanced level of system differentiation in its own right. Under these premises, the *semantic question* of how something can be translated from one language into the other can be converted into the *empirical question* of when the growth of the monetary-bureaucratic complex affects domains of action that cannot be transferred to system-integrative mechanisms without pathological side effects. The analysis of Parsonian media theory led me to the assumption that this boundary is overstepped when systemic imperatives force their way into domains of cultural reproduction, social integration, and socialization. This assumption needs to be tested empirically in connection with "real abstractions" detected in the core zones of the lifeworld. The semantic problem of connecting systems-theoretic and action-theoretic descriptions requires a solution that does not prejudge substantive questions.

I introduced the system concept of society by way of a *methodological objectification* of the lifeworld and justified the shift in perspective connected with this objectification – a shift from the perspective of a participant to that of an observer – in action-theoretic terms. Like the theory of value, this justification has the form of a conceptual explication. It is supposed to explain what it means for the symbolic reproduction of the lifeworld when communicative action is replaced by media-steered interaction, when language, in its function of coordinating action, is replaced by media such as money and power. Unlike the transformation of concrete into abstract labor, this does not *eo ipso* give rise to reifying effects. The conversion to another mechanism of action coordination, and thereby to another principle of sociation, results in reification – that is, in a pathological deformation of the communicative infrastructure of the lifeworld – only when the lifeworld cannot be withdrawn from the functions in question, when these functions cannot be painlessly transferred to media-steered systems of action, as those of material reproduction sometimes can. In this way phenomena of reification lose the dubious status of facts that can be inferred from economic statements about value relations by means of semantic transformations alone. "Real abstractions" now make up instead an object domain for empirical inquiry. They become the object of a research program that no longer has need of value theory or any similar translation tool.

In other respects a theory of capitalist modernization developed by means of a theory of communicative action does follow the Marxian model. It is *critical* both of contemporary social sciences and of the social reality they are supposed to grasp. It is critical of the reality of developed societies inasmuch as they do not make full use of the learning potential culturally available to them, but deliver themselves over to an uncontrolled growth of complexity. As we have seen, this increasing system complexity encroaches upon non-renewable supplies like a quasi-natural force; not only does it outflank traditional forms of life, it attacks the communicative infrastructure of largely rationalized lifeworlds. But the theory is also critical of social-scientific approaches that are incapable of deciphering the paradoxes of societal rationalization because they make complex social systems their object only from one or another abstract point of view, without accounting for the historical constitution of their object domain (in the sense of a reflexive sociology).[1] Critical social theory does not relate to established lines of research as a competitor; starting from its concept of the rise of modern societies, it attempts to explain the specific limitations and the relative rights of those approaches.

If we leave to one side the insufficiently complex approach of behaviorism, there are today three main lines of inquiry occupied with the phenomenon of modern societies. We cannot even say that they are in competition, for they scarcely have anything to say to one another. Efforts at theory comparison do not issue in reciprocal critique; fruitful critique that might foster a common undertaking can hardly be developed across these distances, but at most within one or another camp. There is a good reason for this mutual incomprehension: the object domains of the competing approaches do not come into contact, for they are the result of one-sided abstractions that unconsciously cut the ties between system and lifeworld constitutive for modern societies.

Taking as its point of departure the work of Max Weber, and also in part Marxist historiography, an approach – sometimes referred to as the history of society [*Gesellschaftsgeschichte*] – has been developed that is comparative in outlook, typological in procedure, and, above all, well informed about social history. The dynamics of class struggle are given greater or lesser weight according to the positions of such different authors as Reinhard Bendix, R. Lepsius, C. Wright Mills, Barrington Moore, and Hans-Ulrich Wehler; however, the theoretical core is always formed by assumptions about the structural differentiation of society in functionally specified systems of action. Close contact with historical research prevents the *theory of structural differentiation* from issuing in a more strongly theoretical program, for instance, in some form of systems functionalism. Rather, analysis proceeds in such a way that modernization processes are referred to the level of institutional differentiation. The functionalist mode of investigation is not so widely separated from the structuralist mode that the potential competition between the two conceptual strategies could develop. The modernization of society is, to be sure, analyzed in its various ramifications, but a one-dimensional idea of the whole process of structural differentiation predominates. It is not conceived as a second-order differentiation process, as an uncoupling of system and lifeworld that, when sufficiently advanced, makes it possible for media-steered subsystems to react back on structurally differentiated lifeworlds. As a result, the pathologies of modernity do not come into view as such from this research perspective; it lacks the conceptual tools to distinguish adequately between (1) the structural differentiation of the lifeworld, particularly of its societal components, (2) the growing autonomy of action systems that are differentiated out via steering media, as well as the internal differentiation of these subsystems, and finally (3) those differentiation processes that simultaneously dedifferentiate socially integrated domains of action in the sense of colonizing the lifeworld.

Taking as its point of departure neo-classical economic theory, on the one hand, and social-scientific functionalism, on the other, a *systems-theoretical approach* has established itself above all in economics and in the sciences of administration. These system sciences have, so to speak, grown up in the wake of the two media-steered subsystems. As long as they were occupied chiefly with the internal complexity of the economic and administrative systems, they could rest content with sharply idealized models. To the extent that they had to bring the restrictions of the relevant social environments into their analyses, however, there arose a need for an integrated theory that would also cover the interaction between the two functionally intermeshed subsystems of state and economy.

It is only with the next step in abstraction, which brought society as a whole under systems-theoretical concepts, that the system sciences overdrew their account. The systems theory of society first developed by Parsons and consistently carried further by Luhmann views the rise and development of modern society solely in the functionalist perspective of growing system complexity. Once systems functionalism is cleansed of the dross of the sociological tradition, it becomes insensitive to social pathologies that can be discerned chiefly in the structural features of socially integrated domains of action. It hoists the vicissitudes of communicatively structured lifeworlds up to the level of media dynamics; by assimilating them, from the observer perspective, to disequilibria in intersystemic exchange relations, it robs them of the significance of identity-threatening deformations, which is how they are experienced from the participant perspective.

Finally, from phenomenology, hermeneutics, and symbolic interactionism there has developed an *action-theoretical approach*. To the extent that the different lines of *interpretive sociology* proceed in a generalizing manner at all, they share an interest in illuminating structures of world-views and forms of life. The essential part is a theory of everyday life, which can also be linked up with historical research, as it is in the work of E.P. Thompson. To the extent that this is done, modernization processes can be presented from the viewpoint of the lifeworlds specific to different strata and groups; the everyday life of the subcultures dragged into these processes are disclosed with the tools of anthropological research. Occasionally these studies condense to fragments of history written from the point of view of its victims. Then modernization appears as the sufferings of those who had to pay for the establishment of the new mode of production and the new system of states in the coin of disintegrating traditions and forms of life. Research of this type sharpens our perception of historical asynchronicities; they provide a stimulus to critical recollection in Benjamin's sense. But it has as little place for the internal systemic dynamics of economic development, of nation- and state-building, as it does for the structural logics of rationalized lifeworlds. As a result, the subcultural mirrorings in which the sociopathologies of modernity are refracted and reflected retain the subjective and accidental character of *uncomprehended* events.

Whereas the theory of structural differentiation does not sufficiently separate systemic and lifeworld aspects, systems theory and action theory each isolates and overgeneralizes one of the two aspects. The methodological abstractions have the same result in all three cases. The theories of modernity made possible by these approaches remain insensitive to what Marx called "real abstractions;" the latter can be gotten at through an analysis that at once traces the rationalization of lifeworlds *and* the growth in complexity of media-steered subsystems, and that keeps the paradoxical nature of their interference in sight. As we have seen, it is possible to speak in a non-metaphorical sense of paradoxical conditions of life if the structural differentiation of life-worlds is described as rationalization. Social pathologies are not to be measured against "biological" goal states but in relation to the contra-dictions in which communicatively intermeshed interaction can get caught because deception and self-deception can gain objective power in an everyday practice reliant on the facticity of validity claims.

By "real abstractions" Marx was referring not only to paradoxes experienced by those involved as deformations of their lifeworld, but above all to paradoxes that could be gotten at only through an analysis of reification (or of rationalization). It is in this latter sense that we call "paradoxical" those situations in which systemic relief mechanisms made possible by the rationalization of the lifeworld turn around and overburden the communicative infrastructure of the lifeworld. After attempting to render a fourth approach to inquiry – the *genetic structuralism* of developmental psychology – fruitful for appropriating Weber's sociology of religion, Mead's theory of communication, and Durkheim's theory of social integration,[2] I proposed that we read the Weberian rationalization thesis in that way. The basic conceptual framework I developed by these means was, naturally, not meant to be an end in itself; rather, it has to prove itself against the task of explaining those pathologies of modernity that other approaches pass right by for methodological reasons.

It is just this that critical theory took as its task before it increasingly distanced itself from social research in the early 1940s. In what follows I will (1) recall the complex of themes that originally occupied critical theory, and (2) show how some of these intentions can be taken up without the philosophy of history to which they were tied. In the process, I shall (3) go into one topic at somewhat greater length: the altered significance of the critique of positivism in a postpositivist age.

(1) The work of the Institute for Social Research was essentially dominated by six themes until the early 1940s when the circle of collaborators that had gathered in New York began to break up. These research interests are reflected in the lead theoretical articles that appeared in the main part of the *Zeitschrift für Sozialforschung*. They have to do with (a) the forms of integration in postliberal societies, (b) family socialization and ego development, (c) mass media and mass culture, (d) the social psychology behind the cessation of protest, (e) the theory of art, and (f) the critique of positivism and science. This spectrum of themes reflects Horkheimer's conception of an interdisci-plinary social science. In this phase the central line of inquiry, which I characterized with the catchphrase "rationalization as reification", was to be worked out with the differentiated means of various disciplines.[3] Before the "critique of instrumental reason" contracted the process of reification into a topic for the philosophy of history again, Horkheimer and his circle had made "real abstractions" the object of empirical

inquiry. From this theoretical standpoint it is not difficult to see the unity in the multiplicity of themes enumerated above. [. . .] At that time critical theory was still based on the Marxist philosophy of history, that is, on the conviction that the forces of production were developing an objectively explosive power. Only on this presupposition could critique be restricted to "bringing to consciousness potentialities that have emerged within the maturing historical situation itself."[4] Without a *theory* of history there could be no immanent critique that applied to the manifestations of objective spirit and distinguished what things and human beings could be from what they actually were.[5] Critique would be delivered up to the reigning standards in any given historical epoch. The research program of the 1930s stood and fell with its historical-philosophical trust in the rational potential of bourgeois culture – a potential that would be released in social movements under the pressure of developed forces of production. Ironically, however, the critiques of ideology carried out by Horkheimer, Marcuse, and Adorno confirmed them in the belief that culture was losing its autonomy in postliberal societies and was being incorporated into the machinery of the eco-nomic-administrative system. The development of productive forces, and even critical thought itself, was moving more and more into a perspec-tive of bleak assimilation to their opposites. In the totally administered society only instrumental reason, expanded into a totality, found embodiment; everything that existed was transformed into a real abstraction. In that case, however, what was taken hold of and deformed by these abstractions escaped the grasp of empirical inquiry.

The fragility of the Marxist philosophy of history that implicitly serves as the foundation of this attempt to develop critical theory in interdis-ciplinary form makes it clear why it had to fail and why Horkheimer and Adorno scaled down this program to the speculative observations of the *Dialectic of Enlightenment*. Historical-materialist assumptions regarding the dialectical relation between productive forces and produc-tive relations had been transformed into pseudo-normative propositions concerning an objective teleology in history. This was the motor force behind the realization of a reason that had been given ambiguous expression in bourgeois ideals. Critical theory could secure its normative foundations only in a philosophy of history. But this foundation was not able to support an empirical research program.

This was also evident in the lack of a clearly demarcated object domain like the communicative practice of the everyday lifeworld in which rationality structures are embodied and processes of reification can be traced. The basic concepts of critical theory placed the conscious-ness of individuals directly vis-à-vis economic and administrative mech-anisms of integration, which were only extended inward, intraphysically. In contrast to this, the theory of communicative action can ascertain for itself the rational content of anthropologically deep-seated structures by means of an analysis that, *to begin with*, proceeds reconstructively, that is, unhistorically. It describes structures of action and structures of mutual understanding that are found in the intuitive knowledge of competent members of modern societies. There is no way back from them to a theory of history that does not distinguish between problems of developmental logic and problems of developmental dynamics.

In this way I have attempted to free historical materialism from its philosophy-of-history ballast.[6] Two abstractions are required for this: (i) abstracting the development of cognitive structures from the historical dynamic of events, and (ii) abstracting the evolution of society from the historical concretion of forms of life. Both help in getting beyond the confusion of basic categories to which the philosophy of history owes its existence.

A theory developed in this way can no longer start by examining concrete ideals immanent in traditional forms of life. It must orient itself to the range of learning processes that is opened up at a given time by a historically attained level of learning. It must refrain from critically evaluating and normatively ordering totalities, forms of life and cultures, and life-contexts and epochs *as a whole*. And yet it can take up some of the intentions for which the interdisciplinary research program of earlier critical theory remains instructive.

(2) Coming at the end of a complicated study of the main features of a theory of communicative action, this suggestion cannout count even as a "promissory note". It is less a promise than a conjecture. So as not to leave it entirely ungrounded, in what follows I will comment briefly on the theses mentioned above, and in the same order. With these illustrative remarks I also intend to emphasize the fully open character and the flexibility of an approach to social theory whose fruitfulness can be confirmed only in the ramifications of social and philosophical research. As to what social theory can accomplish in and of itself – it resembles the focussing power of a magnifying glass. Only when the social sciences no longer sparked a single thought would the time for social theory be past.

(a) *On the forms of integration in postliberal societies.* Occidental rationalism arose within the framework of bourgeois capitalist societies. For this reason, following Marx and Weber I have examined the initial conditions of modernization in connection with societies of this type and have traced the capitalist path of development. In postliberal societies there is a fork in this path: modernization pushes forward in one direction through endogenously produced problems of economic accumulation, in the other through problems arising from the state's efforts at rationalization. Along the developmental path of organized capitalism, a political order of welfare-state mass democracy took shape. In some places, however, under the pressure of economic crises, the mode of production, threatened by social disintegration, could be maintained for a time only in the political form of authoritarian or fascist orders. Along the developmental path of bureaucratic socialism a political order of dictatorship by state parties took shape. In recent years Stalinist domination by force has given way to more moderate, post-Stalinist regimes; the beginnings of a democratic workers' movement and of democratic decision-making processes within the Party are for the time visible only in Poland. Both the fascist and the democratic deviations from the two dominant patterns depend rather strongly, it seems, on national peculiarities, particularly on the political culture of the countries in question. At any rate, these branchings make historical specifications necessary even at the most general level of types of societal integration and of corresponding social pathologies. If we permit ourselves to simplify in an ideal-typical manner and limit ourselves to the two dominant variants of postliberal societies, and if we start from the assumption that alienation phenomena arise as systemically induced deformations of the lifeworld, then we can take a few steps toward a comparative analysis of principles of societal organizations, kinds of crisis tendency, and forms of social pathology.

On our assumption, a considerably rationalized lifeworld is one of the initial conditions for modernization processes. It must be possible to anchor money and power in the lifeworld as media, that is, to institutionalize them by means of positive law. If these conditions are met, economic and administrative systems can be differentiated out, systems that have a complementary relation to one another and enter into interchanges with their environments via steering media. At this level of system differentiation modern societies arise, first capitalist societies, and later – setting themselves off from those – bureaucratic-socialist societies. A capitalist path of modernization opens up as soon as the economic system develops its own intrinsic dynamic of growth and, with its endogenously produced problems, takes the lead, that is, the evolutionary primacy, for society as a whole. The path of modernization runs in another direction when, on the basis of state ownership of most of the means of production and an institutionalized one-party rule, the administrative action system gains a like autonomy in relation to the economic system.

To the extent that these organizational principles are established, there arise interchange relations between the two functionally interlocked subsystems and the societal components of the lifeworld in which the media are anchored [. . .]. The lifeworld, more or less relieved of tasks of material reproduction, can in turn become more differentiated in its symbolic structures and can set free the inner logic of development of cultural modernity. At the same time, the private and public spheres are now set off as the environments of the system. According to whether the economic system or the state apparatus attains evolutionary primacy, either private households or politically relevant memberships are the points of entry for crises that are shifted from the subsystems to the

lifeworld. In modernized societies disturbances in the material reproduction of the lifeworld take the form of stubborn systemic disequilibria;
the latter either take effect directly as *crisis* or call forth *pathologies* in
the lifeworld.

Steering crises were first studied in connection with the business cycle
of market economies. In bureaucratic socialism, crisis tendencies spring
from self-blocking mechanisms in planning administrations, as they do
on the other side from endogenous interruptions of accumulation
processes. Like the paradoxes of exchange rationality, the paradoxes of
planning rationality can be explained by the fact that rational action
orientations come into contradiction with themselves through unin-
tended systemic effects. These crisis tendencies are worked through not
only in the subsystem in which they arise, but also in the complementary
action system into which they can be shifted. Just as the capitalist
economy relies on organizational performances of the state, the socialist
planning bureaucracy has to rely on self-steering performances of the
economy. Developed capitalism swings between the contrary policies of
"the market's self-healing powers" and state interventionism.[7] The
structural dilemma is even clearer on the other side, where policy
oscillates hopelessly between increased central planning and decentral-
ization, between orienting economic programs toward investment and
toward consumption.

These *systemic disequilibria* become *crises* only when the performances of economy and state remain manifestly below an established
level of aspiration and harm the symbolic reproduction of the lifeworld
by calling forth conflicts and reactions of resistance there. It is the
societal components of the lifeworld that are directly affected by this.
Before such conflicts threaten core domains of social integration, they
are pushed to the periphery – before anomic conditions arise there are
appearances of withdrawal of legitimation or motivation [. . .]. But when
steering crises – that is, perceived disturbances of material reproduction
– are successfully intercepted by having recourse to lifeworld resources,
pathologies arise in the lifeworld. [. . .]

We can represent the replacement of steering crises with lifeworld
pathologies as follows: anomic conditions are avoided, and legitimations
and motivations important for maintaining institutional orders are
secured, at the expense of, and through the ruthless exploitation of,
other resources. Culture and personality come under attack for the sake
of warding off crises and stabilizing society [. . .]. Instead of manifestations of anomie (and instead of the withdrawal of legitimation and
motivation in place of anomie), phenomena of alienation and the
unsettling of collective identity emerge. I have traced such phenomena
back to a colonization of the lifeworld and characterized them as a
reification of the communicative practice of everyday life.

However, deformations of the lifeworld take the form of a reification
of communicative relations only in capitalist societies, that is, only

where the private household is the point of incursion for the displacement of crises into the lifeworld. This is not a question of the overextension of a single medium but of the monetarization and bureaucratization of the spheres of action of employees and of consumers, of citizens and of clients of state bureaucracies. Deformations of the lifeworld take a different form in societies in which the points of incursion for the penetration of crises into the lifeworld are politically relevant memberships. There too, in bureaucratic-socialist societies, domains of action that are dependent on social integration are switched over to mechanisms of system integration. But instead of the reification of communicative relations we find the shamming of communicative relations in bureaucratically desiccated, forcibly "humanized" domains of pseudo-political intercourse in an overextended and administered public sphere. This pseudo-politicization is symmetrical to reifying privatization in certain respects. The lifeworld is not directly assimilated to the system, that is, to legally regulated, formally organized domains of action; rather, systemically self-sufficient organizations are fictively put back into a simulated horizon of the lifeworld. While the system is draped out as the lifeworld, the lifeworld is absorbed by the system.[8]

(b) *Family socialization and ego development.* The diagnosis of an uncoupling of system and lifeworld also offers a different perspective for judging the structural change in family, education, and personality development. For a psychoanalysis viewed from a Marxist standpoint, the theory of the Oedipus complex, interpreted sociologically, was pivotal for explaining how the functional imperatives of the economic system could establish themselves in the superego structures of the dominant social character. Thus, for example, Löwenthal's studies of drama and fiction in the nineteenth century served to show in detail that the constraints of the economic system – concentrated in status hierarchies, occupational roles, and gender stereotypes – penetrated into the innermost aspects of life history via intrafamilial dependencies and patterns of socialization. The intimacy of highly personalized relations merely concealed the blind force of economic interdependencies that had become autonomous in relation to the private sphere – a force that was experienced as "fate".

Thus the family was viewed as the agency through which systemic imperatives influenced our instinctual vicissitudes; its communicative internal structure was not taken seriously. Because the family was always viewed only from functionalist standpoints and was never given its own weight from structuralist points of view, the epochal changes in the bourgeois family could be misunderstood; in particular, the results of the leveling out of paternal authority could be interpreted wrongly. It seemed as if systemic imperatives now had the chance – by way of a mediatized family – to take hold directly of intrapsychic events, a process that the soft medium of mass culture could at most slow down. If, by contrast, we *also* recognize in the structural transformation of the bourgeois family the inherent rationalization of the lifeworld; if we see that, in egalitarian patterns of relationship, in individuated forms of intercourse, and in liberalized child-rearing practices, some of the potential for rationality ingrained in communicative action is *also* released; then the changed conditions of socialization in the middle-class nuclear family appear in a different light.

Empirical indicators suggest the growing autonomy of a nuclear family in which socialization processes take place through the medium of largely deinstitutionalized communicative action. Communicative infrastructures are developing that have freed themselves from latent entanglements in systemic dependencies. The contrast between the *homme* who is educated to freedom and humanity in the intimate sphere and the *citoyen* who obeys functional necessities in the sphere of social labor was always an ideology. But it has now taken on a different meaning. Familial lifeworlds see the imperatives of the economic and administrative systems coming at them from outside, instead of being mediatized by them from behind. In the families and their environments we can observe a polarization between communicatively structured and formally organized domains of action; this places socialization processes under different conditions and exposes them to a different type of danger. This view is supported by two rough sociopsychological clues: the diminishing significance of the Oedipal problematic and the growing significance of adolescent crises.

For some time now, psychoanalytically trained physicians have observed a symptomatic change in the typical manifestations of illness. Classical hysterias have almost died out; the number of compulsion neuroses is drastically reduced; on the other hand, narcissistic disturbances are on the increase.[9] Christopher Lasch has taken this symptomatic change as the occasion for a diagnosis of the times that goes beyond the clinical domain.[10] It confirms the fact that the significant changes in the present escape sociopsychological explanations that start from the Oedipal problematic, from an internalization of societal repression which is simply masked by parental authority. The better explanations start from the premise that the communication structures that have been set free in the family provide conditions for socialization that are as demanding as they are vulnerable. The potential for irritability grows, and with it the probability that instabilities in parental behavior will have a comparatively strong effect – a subtle neglect.

The other phenomenon, a sharpening of the adolescence problematic, also speaks for the socializatory significance of the uncoupling of system and lifeworld.[11] Systemic imperatives do not so much insinuate themselves into the family, establish themselves in systematically distorted communication, and inconspicuously intervene in the formation of the self as, rather, openly come at the family from outside. As a result, there is a tendency toward disparities between competences, attitudes, and motives, on the one hand, and the functional requirements of adult roles on the other. The problems of detaching oneself from the family and forming one's own identity have in any case turned adolescent development (which is scarcely safeguarded by institutions anymore) into a critical test for the ability of the coming generation to connect up with the preceding one. When the conditions of socialization in the family are no longer functionally in tune with the organizational membership conditions that the growing child will one day have to meet, the problems that young people have to solve in their adolescence become insoluble for more and more of them. One indication of this is the social and even political significance that youth protest and with-drawal cultures have gained since the end of the 1960s.[12]

This new problem situation cannot be handled with the old theoretical means. If we connect the epochal changes in family socialization with the rationalization of the lifeworld, socializatory interaction becomes the point of reference for the analysis of ego development, and systematically distorted communication – the reification of interpersonal relations – the point of reference for investigating pathogenesis. The theory of communicative action provides a framework within which the structural model of ego, id, and superego can be recast.[13] Instead of an instinct theory that represents the relation of ego to inner nature in terms of a philosophy of consciousness – on the model of relations between subject and object – we have a theory of socialization that connects Freud with Mead, gives structures of intersubjectivity their due, and replaces hypotheses about instinctual vicissitudes with assump-tions about identity formation.[14] This approach can (i) appropriate more recent developments in psychoanalytic research, particularly the theory of object relations[15] and ego psychology,[16] (ii) take up the theory of defense mechanisms[17] in such a way that the interconnections between intrapsychic communication barriers and communication disturbances at the interpersonal level become comprehensible,[18] and (iii) use the assumptions about mechanisms of conscious and unconscious mastery to establish a connection between orthogenesis and pathogenesis. The cognitive and sociomoral development studied in the Piagetian tradition[19] takes place in accord with structural patterns that provide a reliable foil for intuitively recorded clinical deviations.

(c) *Mass media and mass culture.* With its distinction between system and lifeworld, the theory of communicative action brings out the independent logic of socializatory interaction; the corresponding distinc-tion between two contrary types of communication medium makes us sensitive to the ambivalent potential of mass communications. The theory makes us skeptical of the thesis that the essence of the public sphere has been liquidated in postliberal societies. According to Hork-heimer and Adorno, the communication flows steered via mass media *take the place of* those communication structures that had once made possible public discussion and self-understanding by citizens and private individuals. With the shift from writing to images and sounds, the electronic media – first film and radio, later television – present themselves as an apparatus that completely permeates and dominates the language of everyday communication. On the one hand, it transforms the authentic content of modern culture into the sterilized and ideologically effective stereotypes of a mass culture that merely replicates what exists; on the other hand, it uses up a culture cleansed of all subversive and transcending elements for an encompassing system of social controls, which is spread over individuals, in part reinforcing their weakened internal behavioral controls, in part replacing them. The mode of functioning of the culture industry is said to be a mirror image of the psychic apparatus, which, as long as the internalization of paternal authority was still functioning, had subjected instinctual nature to the control of the superego in the way that technology had subjected outer nature to its domination.

Against this theory we can raise the empirical objections that can always be brought against stylizing oversimplifications – that it proceeds ahistorically and does not take into consideration the structural change in the bourgeois public sphere; that it is not complex enough to take account of the marked national differences – from differences between private, public-legal, and state-controlled organizational structures of broadcasting agencies, to differences in programing, viewing practices, political culture, and so forth. But there is an even more serious objection, an objection in principle, that can be derived from the dualism of media discussed above.

I distinguished two sorts of medium that can ease the burden of the (risky and demanding) coordinating mechanism of reaching understanding: on the one hand, steering media, via which subsystems are differentiated out of the lifeworld; on the other hand, generalized forms of communication, which do not replace reaching agreement in language but merely condense it, and thus remain tied to lifeworld contexts. Steering media uncouple the coordination of action from building consensus in language altogether and neutralize it in regard to the alternative of coming to an agreement or failing to do so. In the other case we are dealing with a specialization of linguistic processes of consensus formation that remains dependent on recourse to the resources of the lifeworld background. The mass media belong to these generalized forms of communication. They free communication processes from the provinciality of spatiotemporally restricted contexts and permit public spheres to emerge, through establishing the abstract simultaneity of a virtually present network of communication contents far removed in space and time and through keeping messages available for manifold contexts.

These media publics hierarchize and at the same time remove restrictions on the horizon of possible communication. The one aspect cannot be separated from the other – and therein lies their ambivalent potential. Insofar as mass media one-sidedly channel communication flows in a centralized network – from the center to the periphery or from above to below – they considerably strengthen the efficacy of social controls. But tapping this authoritarian potential is always precarious because there is a counterweight of emancipatory potential built into communication structures themselves. Mass media can simultaneously contextualize and concentrate processes of reaching understanding, but it is only in the first instance that they relieve interaction from yes/no responses to criticizable validity-claims. Abstracted and clustered though they are, these communications cannot be reliably shielded from the possibility of opposition by responsible actors.

When communications research is not abridged in an empiricist manner and allows for dimensions of reification in communicative everyday practice,[20] it confirms this ambivalence. Again and again reception research and program analysis have provided illustrations of the theses in culture criticism that Adorno, above all, developed with a certain overstatement. In the meantime, the same energy has been put into working out the contradictions resulting from the facts that:

- the broadcasting networks are exposed to competing interests; they are not able to smoothly integrate economic, political and ideological, professional and aesthetic viewpoints,[21]
- normally the mass media cannot, without generating conflict, avoid the obligations that accrue to them from their journalistic mission and the professional code of journalism;[22]
- the programs do not only, or even for the most part, reflect the standards of mass culture;[23] even when they take the trivial forms of popular entertainment, they may contain critical messages – "popular culture as popular revenge;"[24]
- ideological messages miss their audience because the intended meaning is turned into its opposite under conditions of being received against a certain subcultural background;[25]
- the inner logic of everyday communicative practice sets up defenses against the direct manipulative intervention of the mass media;[26]
- the technical development of electronic media does not necessarily move in the direction of centralizing networks, even though "video pluralism" and "television democracy" are at the moment not much more than anarchist visions.[27]

(d) *Potentials for protest.* My thesis concerning the colonization of the lifeworld, for which Weber's theory of societal rationalization served as a point of departure, is based on a critique of functionalist reason, which agrees with the critique of instrumental reason only in its intention and in its ironic use of the word "reason." One major difference is that the theory of communicative action conceives of the lifeworld as a sphere in which processes of reification do not appear as mere reflexes – as manifestations of a repressive integration emanating from an oligopolistic economy and an authoritarian state. In this respect, the earlier critical theory merely repeated the errors of Marxist functionalism.[28] My references to the socializatory relevance of the uncoupling of system and lifeworld and my remarks on the ambivalent potentials of mass media and mass culture show the private and public spheres in the light of a rationalized lifeworld in which system imperatives *clash with* independent communication structures. The transposition of communicative action to media-steered interactions and the deformation of the structures of a damaged intersubjectivity are by no means predecided processes that might be distilled from a few global concepts. The analysis of lifeworld pathologies calls for an (unbiased) investigation of tendencies *and* contradictions. The fact that in welfare-state mass democracies class conflict has been institutionalized and thereby pacified does not mean that protest potential has been altogether laid to rest. But the potentials for protest emerge now along different lines of conflict – just where we would expect them to emerge if the thesis of the colonization of the lifeworld were correct.

In the past decade or two, conflicts have developed in advanced Western societies that deviate in various ways from the welfare-state pattern of institutionalized conflict over distribution. They no longer flare up in domains of material reproduction; they are no longer channeled through parties and associations; and they can no longer be allayed by compensations. Rather, these new conflicts arise in domains of cultural reproduction, social integration, and socialization; they are carried out in subinstitutional – or at least extraparliamentary – forms of protest; and the underlying deficits reflect a reification of communicatively structured domains of action that will not respond to the media of money and power. The issue is not primarily one of compensations that the welfare state can provide, but of defending and restoring endangered ways of life. In short, the new conflicts are ignited not by distribution problems but by questions having to do with the grammar of forms of life.

This new type of conflict is an expression of the "silent revolution" in values and attitudes that R. Inglehart has observed in entire populations.[29] Studies by Hildebrandt and Dalton, and by Barnes and Kaase, confirm the change in themes from the "old politics" (which turns on questions of economic and social security, internal and military security) to a "new politics."[30] The new problems have to do with quality of life, equal rights, individual self-realization, participation, and human rights. In terms of social statistics, the "old politics" is more strongly supported by employers, workers, and middle-class tradesmen, whereas the new politics finds stronger support in the new middle classes, among the younger generation, and in groups with more formal education. These phenomena tally with my thesis regarding internal colonization.

If we take the view that the growth of the economic-administrative complex sets off processes of erosion in the lifeworld, then we would expect old conflicts to be overlaid with new ones. A line of conflict forms between, on the one hand, a center composed of strata *directly* involved in the production process and interested in maintaining capitalist growth as the basis of the welfare-state compromise, and, on the other hand, a periphery composed of a variegated array of groups that are lumped together. Among the latter are those groups that are further removed from the "productivist core of performance" in late capitalist societies,[31] that have been more strongly sensitized to the self-destructive consequences of the growth in complexity or have been more strongly affected by them. The bond that unites these heterogeneous groups is the critique of growth. Neither the bourgeois emancipation movements nor the struggles of the organized labor movement can serve as a model for this protest. Historical parallels are more likely to be found in the social-romantic movements of the early industrial period, which were supported by craftsmen, plebians, and workers, in the defensive movements of the populist middle class, in the escapist movements (nourished by bourgeois critiques of civilization) undertaken by reformers, the *Wandervögel*, and the like.

The current potentials for protest are very difficult to classify, because scenes, groupings, and topics change very rapidly. To the extent that organizational nuclei are formed at the level of parties or associations, members are recruited from the same diffuse reservoir.[32] The following catchphrases serve at the moment to identify the various currents in the Federal Republic of Germany: the antinuclear and environmental movements; the peace movement (including the theme of north–south conflict); single-issue and local movements; the alternative movement (which encompasses the urban "scene", with its squatters and alternative projects, as well as the rural communes); the minorities (the elderly, gays, handicapped, and so forth); the psychoscene, with support groups and youth sects; religious fundamentalism; the tax-protest movement, school protest by parents' associations, resistance to "modernist" reforms; and, finally, the women's movement. Of international significance are the autonomy movements struggling for regional, linguistic, cultural, and also religious independence.

In this spectrum I will differentiate emancipatory potentials from potentials for resistance and withdrawal. After the American civil rights movement – which has since issued in a particularistic self-affirmation of black subcultures – only the feminist movement stands in the tradition of bourgeois-socialist liberation movements. The struggle against patriarchal oppression and for the redemption of a promise that has long been anchored in the acknowledged universalistic foundations of morality and law gives feminism the impetus of an offensive movement, whereas the other movements have a more defensive character. The resistance and withdrawal movements aim at stemming formally organized domains of action for the sake of communicatively structured domains, and not at conquering new territory. There is an element of particularism that connects feminism with these movements; the emancipation of women means not only establishing formal equality and eliminating male privilege, but overturning concrete forms of life marked by male monopolies. Furthermore, the historical legacy of the sexual division of labor to which women were subjected in the bourgeois nuclear family has given them access to contrasting virtues, to a register of values complementary to those of the male world and opposed to a one-sidedly rationalized everyday practice.

Within resistance movements we can distinguish further between the defense of traditional and social rank (based on property) and a defense that already operates on the basis of a rationalized lifeworld and tries out new ways of cooperating and living together. This criterion makes it possible to demarcate the protest of the traditional middle classes against threats to neighborhoods by large technical projects, the protest of parents against comprehensive schools, the protest against taxes (patterned after the movement in support of Proposition 13 in California), and most of the movements for autonomy, on the one side, from the core of a new conflict potential, on the other: youth and alternative movements for which a critique of growth sparked by themes of ecology and peace is the common focus. It is possible to conceive of these conflicts in terms of resistance to tendencies toward a colonization of the lifeworld, as I hope now to indicate, at least in a cursory way. The objectives, attitudes, and ways of acting prevalent in youth protest groups can be understood, to begin with, as reactions to certain problem situations that are perceived with great sensitivity.

"Green" problems. The intervention of large-scale industry into ecological balances, the growing scarcity of non-renewable natural resources, as well as demographic developments present industrially developed societies with major problems; but these challenges are abstract at first and call for technical and economic solutions, which must in turn be globally planned and implemented by administrative means. What sets off the protest is rather the tangible destruction of the urban environment; the despoliation of the countryside through housing developments, industrialization, and pollution; the impairment of health through the ravages of civilization, pharmaceutical side effects, and the like – that is, developments that noticeably affect the organic foundations of the lifeworld and make us drastically aware of standards of livability, of inflexible limits to the deprivation of sensual-aesthetic background needs.

Problems of excessive complexity. There are certainly good reasons to fear military potentials for destruction, nuclear power plants, atomic waste, genetic engineering, the storage and central utilization of private data, and the like. These real anxieties are combined, however, with the terror of a new category of risks that are literally invisible and are comprehensible only from the perspective of the system. These risks invade the lifeworld and at the same time burst its dimensions. The anxieties function as catalysts for a feeling of being overwhelmed in view of the possible consequences of processes for which we are morally accountable – since we do set them in motion technically and politically – and yet for which we can no longer take moral responsibility – since their scale has put them beyond our control. Here resistance is directed against abstractions that are forced upon the lifeworld, although they go beyond the spatial, temporal, and social limits of complexity of even highly differentiated lifeworlds, centered as these are around the senses.

Overburdening the communicative infrastructure. Something that is expressed rather blatantly in the manifestations of the psychomovement and renewed religious fundamentalism is also a motivating force behind most alternative projects and many citizens' action groups – the painful manifestations of deprivation in a culturally impoverished and one-sidedly rationalized practice of everyday life. For this reason, ascriptive characteristics such as gender, age, skin color, neighborhood or locality, and religious affiliation serve to build up and separate off communities, to establish subculturally protected communities supportive of the search for personal and collective identity. The revaluation of the particular, the natural, the provincial, of social spaces that are small enough to be familiar, of decentralized forms of commerce and despe-cialized activities, of segmented pubs, simple interactions, and dediffer-entiated public spheres – all this is meant to foster the revitalization of possibilities for expression and communication that have been buried alive. Resistance to reformist interventions that turn into their opposite, because the means by which they are implemented run counter to the declared aims of social integration, also belongs in this context.

The new conflicts arise along the seams between system and lifeworld. Earlier I described how the interchange between the private and public spheres, on the one hand, and the economic and administrative action systems, on the other, takes place via the media of money and power, and how it is institutionalized in the roles of employees and consumers, citizens and clients of the state. It is just these roles that are the targets of protest. Alternative practice is directed against the profit-dependent instrumentalization of work in one's vocation, the market-dependent mobilization of labor power, against the extension of pressures of competition and performance all the way down into elementary school. It also takes aim at the monetarization of services, relationships, and time, at the consumerist redefinition of private spheres of life and personal lifestyles. Furthermore, the relation of clients to public service agencies is to be opened up and reorganized in a participatory mode, along the lines of self-help organizations. It is above all in the domains of social policy and health policy (e.g., in connection with psychiatric care) that models of reform point in this direction. Finally, certain forms of protest negate the definitions of the role of citizen and the routines for pursuing interests in a purposive-rational manner – forms ranging from the undirected explosion of disturbances by youth ("Zürich is burning!"), through calculated or surrealistic violations of rules (after the pattern of the American civil rights movement and student protests), to violent provocation and intimidation.

According to the programmatic conceptions of some theoreticians, a partial disintegration of the social roles of employees and consumers, of clients and citizens of the state, is supposed to clear the way for counterinstitutions that develop from within the lifeworld in order to set limits to the inner dynamics of the economic and political-administrative action systems. These institutions are supposed, on the one hand, to divert out of the economic system a second, informal sector that is no longer oriented to profit and, on the other hand, to oppose to the party system new forms of a "politics in the first person," a politics that is expressive and at the same time has a democratic base. Such institutions would reverse just those abstractions and neutralizations by which in modern societies labor and political will-formation have been tied to media-steered interaction. The capitalist enterprise and the mass party (as an "ideology-neutral organization for acquiring power") generalize their points of social entry via labor markets and manufactured public spheres; they treat their employees and voters as abstract labor power and voting subjects; and they keep at a distance – as environments of the system – those spheres in which personal and collective identities can alone take shape. By contrast, the counterinstitutions are intended to dedifferentiate some parts of the formally organized domains of action, remove them from the clutches of the steering media, and return these "liberated areas" to the action-coordinating mechanism of reaching understanding.

However unrealistic these ideas may be, they are important for the polemical significance of the new resistance and withdrawal movements reacting to the colonization of the lifeworld. This significance is obscured, both in the self-understanding of those involved and in the ideological imputations of their opponents, if the communicative rationality of cultural modernity is rashly equated with the functionalist rationality of self-maintaining economic and administrative action systems – that is, whenever the rationalization of the lifeworld is not carefully distinguished from the increasing complexity of the social system. This confusion explains the fronts – which are out of place and obscure the real political oppositions – between the antimodernism of the Young Conservatives and the neo-conservative defense of postmodernity that robs a modernity at variance with itself of its rational content and its perspectives on the future.[33]

(3) In this work I have tried to introduce a theory of communicative action that clarifies the normative foundations of a critical theory of society. The theory of communicative action is meant to provide an alternative to the philosophy of history on which earlier critical theory still relied, but which is no longer tenable. It is intended as a framework

within which interdisciplinary research on the selective pattern of capitalist modernization can be taken up once again. The illustrative observations (a) through (d) were meant to make this claim plausible. The two additional themes (e) and (f) are a reminder that the investigation of what Marx called "real abstraction" has to do with the social-scientific tasks of a theory of modernity, not the philosophical. Social theory need no longer ascertain the normative contents of bourgeois culture, of art and of philosophical thought, in an indirect way, that is, by way of a critique of ideology. With the concept of a communicative reason ingrained in the use of language oriented to reaching understanding, it again expects from philosophy that it take on systematic tasks. The social sciences can enter into a cooperative relation with a philosophy that has taken up the task of working on a theory of rationality.

It is no different with modern culture as a whole than it was with the physics of Newton and his heirs: modern culture is as little in need of a philosophical grounding as science. As we have seen, in the modern period culture gave rise of itself to those structures of rationality that Weber then discovered and described as value spheres. With modern science, with positive law and principled secular ethics, with autonomous art and institutionalized art criticism, three moments of reason crystallized without help from philosophy. Even without the guidance of the critiques of pure and practical reason, the sons and daughters of modernity learned how to divide up and develop further the cultural tradition under these different aspects of rationality – as questions of truth, justice, or taste. More and more the sciences dropped the elements of world-views and do without an interpretation of nature and history as a whole. Cognitive ethics separates off problems of the good life and concentrates on strictly deontological, universalizable aspects, so that what remains from the good is only the just. And an art that has become autonomous pushes toward an ever purer expression of the basic aesthetic experiences of a subjectivity that is decentered and removed from the spatiotemporal structures of everyday life. Subjectivity frees itself here from the conventions of daily perception and of purposive activity, from the imperatives of work and of what is merely useful.

These magnificent "one-sidednesses," which are the signature of modernity, need no foundation and no justification in the sense of a transcendental grounding, but they do call for a self-understanding regarding the character of this knowledge. Two questions must be answered: (a) whether a reason that has objectively split up into its moments can still preserve its unity, and (b) how expert cultures can be mediated with everyday practice. The reflections offered in the first and third chapters [see readings 11–13] are intended as a provisional account of how formal pragmatics can deal with these questions. With that as a basis, the theory of science, the theory of law and morality, and aesthetics, in cooperation with the corresponding historical disciplines, can then reconstruct both the emergence and the internal history of those modern complexes of knowledge that have been differentiated out, each under a different single aspect of validity – truth, normative rightness, or authenticity.

The mediation of the moments of reason is no less a problem than the separation of the aspects of rationality under which questions of truth, justice, and taste were differentiated from one another. The only protection against an empiricist abridgement of the rationality problematic is a steadfast pursuit of the tortuous routes along which science, morality, and art communicate with one another. In each of these spheres, differentiation processes are accompanied by countermovements that, under the primacy of one dominant aspect of validity, bring back in again the two aspects that were at first excluded. Thus nonobjectivist approaches to research within the human sciences bring viewpoints of moral and aesthetic critique to bear[34] – without threatening the primacy of questions of truth; only in this way is critical social theory made possible. Within universalistic ethics the discussion of the ethics of responsibility and the stronger consideration given to hedonistic motives bring the calculation of consequences and the interpretation of needs into play[35] – and they lie in the domains of the cognitive and the expressive; in this way materialist ideas can come in without threatening the autonomy of the moral.[36] Finally, post-avant-garde art is characterized by the coexistence of tendencies toward realism and engagement with those authentic continuations of classical modern art that distilled out the independent logic of the aesthetic[37]; in realist art and *l'art engagé*, moments of the cognitive and of the moral-practical come into play again in art itself, and at the level of the wealth of forms that the avant-garde set free. It seems as if the radically differentiated moments of reason want in such countermovements to point toward a unity – not a unity that could be had at the level of world-views, but one that might be established *this side* of expert cultures, in a non-reified communicative everyday practice.

How does this sort of affirmative role for philosophy square with the reserve that critical theory always maintained in regard to both the established scientific enterprise and the systematic pretensions of philosophy? Is not such a theory of rationality open to the same objections that pragmatism and hermeneutics have brought against every kind of foundationalism?[38] Do not investigations that employ the concept of communicative reason without blushing bespeak universalistic justificatory claims that will have to fall to those – only too well-grounded – metaphilosophical doubts about theories of absolute origins and ultimate grounds? Have not both the historicist enlightenment and materialism forced philosophy into a self-modesty for which the tasks of a theory of rationality must already appear extravagant? The theory of communicative action aims at the moment of unconditionality that, with criticizable validity-claims, is built into the conditions of processes of consensus formation. *As claims* they transcend all limitations of space and time, all the provincial limitations of the given context. Rather than answer these questions here with arguments already set out in the introductory chapter [...], I shall close by adding two methodological arguments that speak against the suspicion that the theory of communicative action is guilty of foundationalist claims.

First we must see how philosophy changes its role when it enters into cooperation with the sciences. As the "feeder" (*Zubringer*) for a theory of rationality, it finds itself in a division of labor with reconstructive sciences; these sciences take up the pre-theoretical knowledge of competently judging, acting, and speaking subjects, as well as the collective knowledge of traditions, in order to get at the most general features of the rationality of experience and judgment, action and mutual understanding in language. In this context, reconstructions undertaken with philosophical means also retain a hypothetical character; precisely because of their strong universalistic claims, they are open to further, indirect testing. This can take place in such a way that the reconstructions of universal and necessary presuppositions of communicative action, of argumentative speech, of experience and of objectivating thought, of moral judgments and of aesthetic critique, enter into empirical theories that are supposed to explain *other* phenomena – for example, the ontogenesis of language and of communicative abilities, of moral judgment and social competence; the structural transformation of religious-metaphysical world-views; the development of legal systems or of forms of social integration generally.

From the perspective of the history of theory, I have taken up the work of Mead, Weber, and Durkheim and tried to show how in their approaches, which are simultaneously empirical and reconstructive, the operations of empirical science and of philosophical conceptual analysis intermesh. The best example of this cooperative division of labor is Piaget's genetic theory of knowledge.[39]

A philosophy that opens its results to indirect testing in this way is guided by the fallibilistic consciousness that the theory of rationality it once wanted to develop on its own can now be sought only in the felicitous coherence of different theoretical fragments. Coherence is the sole criterion of considered choice at the level on which mutually fitting theories stand to one another in relations of supplementing and reciprocally presupposing, for it is only the individual propositions derivable from theories that are true or false. Once we have dropped foundationalist claims, we can no longer expect a hierarchy of sciences; theories – whether social-scientific or philosophical in origin – have to fit with one another, unless one puts the other in a problematic light and we have to see whether it suffices to revise the one or the other.

The test case for a theory of rationality with which the modern understanding of the world is to ascertain its own universality would certainly include throwing light on the opaque figures of mythical thought, clarifying the bizarre expressions of alien cultures, and indeed in such a way that we not only comprehend the learning processes that separate "us" from "them," but also become aware of what we have *unlearned* in the course of this learning. A theory of society that does not close itself off a priori to this possibility of unlearning has to be critical also in relation to the pre-understanding that accrues to it from its own social setting, that is, it has to be open to self-criticism. Processes of unlearning can be gotten at through a critique of deformations that are rooted in the selective exploitation of a potential for rationality and mutual understanding that was once available but is now buried over.

There is also another reason why the theory of society based on the theory of communicative action cannot stray into foundationalist byways. Insofar as it refers to structures of the lifeworld, it has to explicate a background knowledge over which no one can dispose at will. The lifeworld is at first "given" to the theoretician (as it is to the layperson) as his or her own, and in a paradoxical manner. The mode of pre-understanding or of intuitive knowledge of the lifeworld from within which we live together, act and speak with one another, stands in peculiar contrast, as we have seen, to the explicit knowledge of something. The horizontal knowledge that communicative everyday practice *tacitly* carries with it is paradigmatic for the *certainty* with which the lifeworld background is present; yet it does not satisfy the criterion of knowledge that stands in internal relation to validity-claims and can therefore be criticized. That which stands beyond all doubt seems as if it could never become problematic; as what is simply unproblematic, a lifeworld can at most fall apart. It is only under the pressure of approaching problems that relevant components of such background knowledge are torn out of their unquestioned familiarity and brought to consciousness as something in need of being ascertained. It takes an earthquake to make us aware that we had regarded the ground on which we stand every day as unshakable. Even in situations of this sort, only a small segment of our background knowledge becomes uncertain and is set loose after having been enclosed in complex traditions, in solidaric relations, in competences. If the objective occasion arises for us to arrive at some understanding about a situation that has become problematic, background knowledge is transformed into explicit knowledge only in a piecemeal manner.

This has an important methodological implication for sciences that have to do with cultural tradition, social integration, and the socialization of individuals – an implication that became clear to pragmatism and to hermeneutic philosophy, each in its own way, as they came to doubt the possibility of Cartesian doubt. Alfred Schutz, who so convincingly depicted the lifeworld's mode of unquestioned familiarity, nevertheless missed just this problem: whether a lifeworld, in its opaque taken-for-grantedness, eludes the phenomenologist's inquiring gaze or is opened up to it does not depend on just *choosing* to adopt a theoretical attitude. The totality of the background knowledge constitutive for the construction of the lifeworld is no more at his disposition than at that of any social scientist – unless an objective challenge arises, in the face of which the lifeworld as a whole becomes problematic. Thus a theory that wants to ascertain the general structures of the lifeworld cannot adopt a transcendental approach; it can only hope to be equal to the *ratio essendi* of its object when there are grounds for assuming that the objective context of life in which the theoretician finds himself is opening up to him its *ratio cognoscendi*.

This implication accords with the point behind Horkheimer's critique of science in his programmatic essay "Traditional and Critical Theory:"

> The traditional idea of theory is abstracted from scientific activity as it is carried on within the division of labor at a particular stage in the latter's development. It corresponds to the activity of the scholar which takes place alongside all the other activities of society, but in no immediately clear connection with them. In this view of theory, therefore, the real social function of science is not made manifest; it conveys not what theory means in human life, but only what it means in the isolated sphere in which, for historical reasons, it comes into existence.[40]

As opposed to this, critical social theory is to become conscious of the self-referentiality of its calling; it knows that in and through the very act of knowing it belongs to the objective context of life that it strives to grasp. The context of its emergence does not remain external to the theory; rather, the theory takes this reflectively up into itself: "In this intellectual activity the needs and goals, the experiences and skills, the customs and tendencies of the contemporary form of human existence have all played their part."[41] The same holds true for the context of application: "As the influence of the subject matter on the theory, so also the application of the theory to the subject matter is not only an intrascientific process but a social one as well."[42]

In his famous methodological introduction to his critique of political economy of 1857, Marx applied the type of reflection called for by Horkheimer to one of his central concepts. He explained there why the basic assumptions of political economy rest on a seemingly simple abstraction, which is in fact quite difficult:

> It was an immense step forward for Adam Smith to throw out every limiting specification of wealth-creating activity – not only manufacturing, or commercial, or agricultural labor, but one as well as the others, labor in general. With the abstract universality of wealth-creating activity we now have the universality of the object defined as wealth, the product as such or again labor as such, but labor as past objectified labor. How difficult and great this transition was may be seen from how Adam Smith himself from time to time still falls back into the Physi-

ocratic system. Now it might seem that all that had been achieved thereby was to discover the abstract expression for the simplest and most ancient relation in which human beings – in whatever form of society – play the role of producers. This is correct in one respect. Not in another ... Indifference toward specific labors corresponds to a form of society in which individuals can with ease transfer from one labor to another, and where the specific kind is a matter of chance for them, hence of indifference. Not only the category "labour", but labor in reality has here become the means of creating wealth in general, and has ceased to be organically linked with particular individuals in any specific form. Such a state of affairs is at its most developed in the modern form of existence of bourgeois society – in the United States. Here, then, for the first time, the point of departure of modern economics, namely the abstraction of the category "labour", "labour as such", labor pure and simple, becomes true in practice.[43]

Smith was able to lay the foundations of modern economics only after a mode of production arose that, like the capitalist mode with its differentiation of an economic system steered via exchange value, forced a transformation of concrete activities into abstract performances, intruded into the world of work with this real abstraction, and thereby created a problem for the workers themselves: "Thus the simplest abstraction which modern economics places at the head of its discussions and which expresses an immeasurably ancient relation valid in all forms of society, nevertheless achieves practical truth as an abstraction only as a category of the most modern society."[44] A theory of society that claims universality for its basic concepts, without being allowed simply to bring them to bear upon their object in a conventional manner, remains caught up in the self-referentiality that Marx demonstrated in connection with the concept of abstract labor. As I have argued above, when labor is rendered abstract and indifferent, we have a special case of the transference of communicatively structured domains of action over to media-steered interaction. This interpretation decodes the deformations of the lifeworld with the help of another category, namely, "communicative action." What Marx showed to be the case in regard to the category of labor holds true for this as well: "how even the most abstract categories, despite their validity – precisely because of their abstractness – for all epochs, are nevertheless, in the specific character of this abstraction, themselves likewise a product of historical relations, and possess their full validity only for and within these relations."[45] The theory of communicative action can explain why this is so: the development of society must *itself* give rise to the problem situations that *objectively* afford contemporaries a privileged access to the general structures of the lifeworld.

The theory of modernity that I have here sketched in broad strokes permits us to recognize the following: In modern societies there is such an expansion of the scope of contingency for interaction loosed from normative contexts that the inner logic of communicative action "becomes practically true" in the deinstitutionalized forms of intercourse of the familial private sphere as well as in a public sphere stamped by the mass media. At the same time, the systemic imperatives of autonomous subsystems penetrate into the lifeworld and, through monetarization and bureaucratization, force an assimilation of communicative action to formally organized domains of action – even in areas where the action-coordinating mechanism of reaching understanding is functionally necessary. It may be that this provocative threat, this challenge that places the symbolic structures of the lifeworld as a whole in question, can account for why they have become accessible to us.

The Theory of Communicative Action, vol. 2, pp. 374–403.

Notes

1 A. Gouldner, *The Coming Crisis of Western Sociology* (New York, 1970), pp. 25ff; B. Gruenberg, "The Problem of Reflexivity in the Sociology of Science," *Philosophy of Social Science*, 8, 1978: 321ff.

2 W. Mayrl, "Genetic Structuralism and the Analysis of Social Consciousness," *Theory and Society*, 5, 1978: 20ff.

3 H. Dubiel, *Theory and Politics: Studies in the Development of Critical Theory* (Cambridge, Mass.: MIT Press, 1985), pt 2.

4 H. Marcuse, "Philosophy and Critical Theory," in *Negations* (Boston, 1968), pp. 134–58, here p. 158.

5 Ibid.

6 See *Communication and the Evolution of Society*, esp. chs 3 and 4.

7 On the discussion of the breakdown of Keynesian economic policy in the West, see P.C. Roberts, "The Breakdown of the Keynesian Model," *Public Interest*, 1978: 20ff; J.A. Kregel, "From Post-Keynes to Pre-Keynes," *Social Research*, 46, 1979: 212ff; J.D. Wisman, "Legitimation, Ideology-Critique and Economics," *Social Research*, 46, 1979: 291ff; P. Davidson, "Post Keynesian Economics," *Public Interest*, 1980: 151ff.

8 A. Arato, "Critical Sociology and Authoritarian State Socialism," in D. Held and J. Thompson (eds), *Habermas: Critical Debates* (Cambridge, Mass., 1982), pp. 196–218.

9 H. Kohut, *Narzissmus, eine Theorie der Behandlung narzistischer Persönlichkeitsstörungen* (Frankfurt, 1973) and *Die Heilung des Selbst* (Frankfurt, 1979).

10 Christopher Lasch, *The Culture of Narcissism* (New York, 1978).

11 P. Blos, *On Adolescence* (New York, 1962); Erik Erikson, *Identity and the Life Cycle* (New York, 1959).

12 See R. Döbert and G. Nunner-Winkler, *Adoleszenzkrise and Identitätsbildung* (Frankfurt, 1975); T. Ziehe, *Pubertät und Narzissmus* (Frankfurt, 1975); R.M. Merelman, "Moral Development and Potential Radicalism in Adolescence," *Youth and Society*, 9, 1977: 29ff; C.A. Rootes, "Politics of Moral Protest and Legitimation Problems of the Modern Capitalist State," *Theory and Society*, 9, 1980: 473ff.

13 See *Knowledge and Human Interests*, esp. chs 10–12.
14 J. Habermas, "Moral Development and Ego Identity," in *Communication and the Evolution of Society*, pp. 69–94; R. Keagan, *The Evolving Self* (Cambridge, Mass., 1981).
15 W.R.D. Fairbane, *An Object Relations Theory of Personality* (London, 1952); D.W. Winnicott, *The Maturational Process and the Facilitating Environment* (New York, 1965).
16 See E. Jacobson, *The Self and the Object World* (New York, 1964); M. Mahler, *Symbiose und Individuation*, 2 vols (Stuttgart, 1972); H. Kohut, *Narzissmus*; H. Kohut, *Introspektion, Empathie und Psychoanalyse* (Frankfurt, 1976); O. Kernberg, *Borderline-Störungen und pathologischer Narzissmus* (Frankfurt, 1978).
17 A. Freud, *The Ego and the Mechanisms of Defense* (New York, 1946); D.R. Miller and G.E. Swanson, *Inner Conflict and Defense* (New York, 1966); L.B. Murphy, "The Problem of Defense and the Concept of Coping," in E. Antyony and C. Koipernik (eds), *The Child in His Family* (New York, 1970); N. Haan, "A Tripartite Model of Ego-Functioning," *Journal of Neurological Mental Disease*, 148, 1969: 14ff.
18 R. Dobert, G. Nunner-Winkler, and J. Habermas (eds), *Entwicklung des Ichs* (Cologne, 1977); R.L. Selman, *The Growth of Interpersonal Understanding* (New York, 1980).
19 W. Damon (ed), *New Directions for Child Development*, 2 vols (San Francisco, 1978); H. Furth, *Piaget and Knowledge* (Chicago, 1981).
20 C.W. Mills, *Politics, Power and People* (New York, 1963); B. Rosenberg and D. White (eds), *Mass Culture* (Glencoe, Ill., 1957); A. Gouldner, *The Dialectics of Ideology and Technology* (New York, 1976); E. Barnouw, *The Sponser* (New York, 1977); D. Smythe, "Communications: Blind Spot of Western Marxism," *Canadian Journal of Political and Social Theory*, 1, 1977; T. Gitlin, "Media Sociology: The Dominant Paradigm," *Theory and Society*, 6, 1978: 205ff.
21 D. Kellner, "Network Television and American Society: Introduction to a Critical Theory of Television," *Theory and Society*, 10, 1981: 31ff.
22 Ibid., pp. 38ff.
23 A Swingewood, *The Myth of Mass Culture* (London, 1977).
24 D. Kellner, "TV, Ideology and Emancipatory Popular Culture," *Socialist Review*, 45, 1979: 13ff.
25 D. Kellner, "Kulturindustrie und Massenkommunikation: Die kritische Theorie und ihre Folgen," in W. Bonss and A. Honneth (eds), *Sozialforschung als Kritik* (Frankfurt, 1982), pp. 482–515.
26 From Lazarfeld's early radio studies on the dual character of communication flows and the role of opinion leaders, the independent weight of everyday communication in relation to mass communication has been confirmed again and again: "In the last analysis it is people talking with people more than people listening to, or reading, or looking at the mass media that really causes opinions to change." Mills, *Power, Politics and People*, p. 590. See P. Lazarsfeld, B. Berelson, and H. Gaudet, *The People's Choice* (New York, 1948); P. Lazarsfeld and E. Katz, *Personal Influence* (New York, 1955). Compare O. Negt and A. Kluge, *Öffentlichkeit und Erfahrung* (Frankfurt, 1970), and *Geschichte und Eigensinn* (Munich, 1981).
27 H.M. Enzenberger, "Baukasten zu einer Theorie der Mieden," in *Palaver* (Frankfurt, 1974), pp. 91ff.

28 S. Benhabib, "Modernity and the Aporias of Critical Theory," *Telos*, 49, 1981: 38–60.

29 R. Inglehart, "Wertwandel und politisches Verhalten," in J. Matthes (ed), *Sozialer Wandel in Westeuropa* (Frankfurt, 1979).

30 K. Hildebrandt and R.J. Dalton, "Die neue Politik," *Politische Vierteljahres-schrift*, 18, 1977: 230ff; S.H. Barnes, M. Kaase et al., *Political Action* (Beverly Hills/London, 1979).

31 J. Hirsch, "Alternativbewegung: Eine politische Alternative," in R. Roth (ed.), *Parlamentarisches Ritual und politische Alternativen* (Frankfurt, 1980).

32 On the dual economy, see A. Gorz, *Abschied vom Proletariat* (Frankfurt, 1980).

33 J. Habermas, "Modernity versus Postmodernity," *New German Critique*, 22, 1981: 3–14.

34 R. Bernstein, *The Restructuring of Social and Political Theory* (Philadelphia, 1976).

35 In "The Methodological Illusions of Modern Political Theory," *Neue Hefte für Philosophie*, 21, 1982: 47–74, Seyla Benhabib stresses the fact that the discourse theory of ethics proposed by K.-O. Apel and myself treats calculations of consequences and, above all, interpretations of needs as essential elements of moral argumentation. See K.-O. Apel, "Sprechakt-theorie und transzendentale Sprachpragmatik, zur Frage ethischer Normen," in K.-O. Apel (ed.), *Sprachpragmatik und Philosophie* (Frankfurt, 1976), pp. 10–173; J. Habermas, *Moral Consciousness and Communicative Action*.

36 On this point, Max Horkheimer's essay "Materialismus und Moral," *Zeitschrift für Sozialforschung*, 2, 1933: 263ff is still worth reading.

37 P. Bürger, *Theory of the Avant-Garde* (Minneapolis, 1984).

38 R. Rorty, *Philosophy and the Mirror of Nature* (Princeton, 1979).

39 R.F. Kitchener, "Genetic Epistemology, Normative Epistemology, and Psychologism," *Synthese*, 45, 1980: 257ff.

40 In M. Horkheimer, *Critical Theory* (New York, 1972), pp. 188–243, here p. 197.

41 Ibid., p. 205.

42 Ibid., p. 196. I once characterized the relation between social theory and social practice in the same way: "Historical materialism aims at achieving an explanation of social evolution which is so comprehensive that it encompasses the theory's own contexts of origin and application. The theory specifies the conditions under which a self-reflection of the history of the species has become objectively possible. At the same time it names those to whom the theory is addressed, who can with its help gain enlightenment about themselves and their emancipatory role in the process of history. With this reflection on the context of its origin and this anticipation of the context of its application, the theory understands itself as a necessary catalytic moment in the very complex of social life that it analyzes; and it analyzes this complex as an integral network of coercion, from the viewpoint of its possible transformation." *Theory and Practice* (Boston, 1973), pp. 2–3.

43 K. Marx, *Grundrisse* (Harmondsworth, 1973), pp. 104–5.

44 Ibid., p. 105.

45 Ibid.

28

Modernity's Consciousness of Time and Its Need for Self-Reassurance

I

In his famous introduction to the collection of his studies on the sociology of religion, Max Weber takes up the "problem of universal history" to which his scholarly life was dedicated, namely, the question why, outside Europe, "the scientific, the artistic, the political, or the economic development . . . did not enter upon that path of rationalization which is peculiar to the Occident?"[1] For Weber, the intrinsic (that is, not merely contingent) relationship between modernity and what he called "Occidental rationalism" was still self-evident.[2] He described as "rational" the process of disenchantment which led in Europe to a disintegration of religious world-views that issued in a secular culture. With the modern empirical sciences, autonomous arts, and theories of morality and law grounded on principles, cultural spheres of value took shape which made possible learning processes in accord with the respective inner logics of theoretical, aesthetic, and moral-practical problems.

What Weber depicted was not only the secularization of Western *culture*, but also and especially the development of modern *societies* from the viewpoint of rationalization. The new structures of society were marked by the differentiation of the two functionally intermeshing systems that had taken shape around the organizational cores of the capitalist enterprise and the bureaucratic state apparatus. Weber understood this process as the institutionalization of purposive-rational economic and administrative action. To the degree that everyday life was affected by this cultural and societal rationalization, traditional forms of life – which in the early modern period were differentiated primarily according to one's trade – were dissolved. The modernization of the lifeworld is not determined only by structures of purposive rationality. Emile Durkheim and George Herbert Mead saw rationalized lifeworlds as characterized by the reflective treatment of traditions that have lost their quasi-natural status; by the universalization of norms of action and the generalization of values, which set communicative action free from narrowly restricted contexts and enlarge the field of options; and finally, by patterns of socialization that are oriented to the formation of abstract ego-identities and force the individuation of the growing child. This is, in broad strokes, how the classical social theorists drew the picture of modernity.

Today Max Weber's theme appears in another light; this is as much the result of the labors of those who invoke him as of the work of his critics. "Modernization" was introduced as a technical term only in the 1950s. It is the mark of a theoretical approach that takes up Weber's problem but elaborates it with the tools of social-scientific functionalism. The concept of modernization refers to a bundle of processes that are cumulative and mutually reinforcing: to the formation of capital and the mobilization of resources; to the development of the forces of production and the increase in the productivity of labor; to the establishment of centralized political power and the formation of national identities; to the proliferation of rights of political participation, of urban forms of life, and of formal schooling; to the secularization of values and norms; and so on. The theory of modernization performs two abstractions on Weber's concept of "modernity." It dissociates "modernity" from its modern European origins and stylizes it into a spatiotemporally neutral model for processes of social development in general. Furthermore, it breaks the internal connections between modernity and the historical context of Western rationalism, so that processes of modernization can no longer be conceived of as rationalization, as the historical objectification of rational structures. James Coleman sees in this the advantage that a concept of modernization generalized in terms of a theory of evolution is no longer burdened with the idea of a completion of modernity, that is to say, of a goal state after which "postmodern" developments would have to set in.[3]

Indeed it is precisely modernization research that has contributed to the currency of the expression "postmodern" even among social scientists. For in view of an evolutionarily autonomous, self-promoting modernization, social-scientific observers can all the more easily take leave of the conceptual horizon of Western rationalism in which modernity arose. But as soon as the internal links between the concept of modernity and the self-understanding of modernity gained within the horizon of Western reason have been dissolved, we can relativize the, as it were, automatically continuing process of modernization from the distantiated standpoint of a postmodern observer. Arnold Gehlen brought this down to the formula: The premises of the Enlightenment are dead; only their consequences continue on. From this perspective, a self-sufficiently advancing modernization of society has separated itself from the impulses of a cultural modernity that has seemingly become obsolete in the meantime; it only carries out the functional laws of economy and state, technology and science, which are supposed to have amalgamated into a system that cannot be influenced. The relentless acceleration of social processes appears as the reverse side of a culture that is exhausted and has passed into a crystalline state. Gehlen calls modern culture "crystallized" because "the possibilities implanted in it have all been developed in their basic elements. Even the counterpossibilities and antitheses have been uncovered and assimilated, so that henceforth changes in the premises have become increasingly unlikely . . . If you have this impression, you will perceive crystallization . . . even in a realm as astonishingly dynamic and full of variety as that of modern painting."[4] Because "the history of ideas has concluded," Gehlen can observe with a sigh of relief that "we have arrived at *posthistoire.*" With Gottfried Benn* he imparts the advice: "Count up your supplies." This *neo-conservative* leave-taking from modernity is directed, then, not to the unchecked dynamism of societal modernization but to the husk of a cultural self-understanding of modernity that appears to have been overtaken.

In a completely different political form, namely an anarchist one, the idea of postmodernity appears among theoreticians who do not see that any uncoupling of modernity and rationality has set in. They, too, advertise the end of the Enlightenment; they, too, move beyond the horizon of the tradition of reason in which European modernity once understood itself; and they plant their feet in *posthistoire.* But unlike the neo-conservative, the anarchist farewell to modernity is meant for society and culture in the same degree. As that continent of basic concepts bearing Weber's Occidental rationalism sinks down, reason makes known its true identity – it becomes unmasked as the subordinating and at the same time itself subjugated subjectivity, as the will to instrumental mastery. The subversive force of this critique, which pulls away the veil of reason from before the sheer will to power, is at the same time supposed to shake the iron cage in which the spirit of modernity has been objectified in societal form. From this point of view, the modernization of society cannot survive the end of the cultural modernity from which it arose. It cannot hold its own against the "primordial" anarchism under whose sign postmodernity marches.

However distinct these two readings of the theory of postmodernity are, both reject the basic conceptual horizon within which the self-understanding of European modernity has been formed. Both theories of postmodernity pretend to have gone beyond this horizon, to have left it behind as the horizon of a past epoch. Hegel was the first philosopher to develop a clear concept of modernity. We have to go back to him if we want to understand the internal relationship between modernity and rationality, which, until Max Weber, remained self-evident and which today is being called into question. We have to get clear on the Hegelian concept of modernity to be able to judge whether the claim of those who base their analyses on other premises is legitimate. At any rate, we cannot dismiss a priori the suspicion that postmodern thought merely claims a transcendent status, while it remains in fact dependent on presuppositions of the modern self-understanding that were brought to light by Hegel. We cannot exclude from the outset the possibility that neo-conservatism and aesthetically inspired anarchism, in the name of a farewell to modernity, are merely trying to revolt against it once again. It could be that they are merely cloaking their complicity with the venerable tradition of counter-Enlightenment in the garb of post-Enlightenment.

The Philosophical Discourse of Modernity, I, pp. 1–4.

Notes

1 Max Weber, *The Protestant Ethic and the Spirit of Capitalism* (New York, 1958), p. 25.
2 On this see *The Theory of Communicative Action*, vol. 1, ch. 2.
3 See the article on "Modernization" by James Coleman in *The Encyclopedia of the Social Sciences* (New York: Macmillan and Free Press, 1968), vol. 10, at p. 397.
4 Arnold Gehlen, "Über kulturelle Kristallisation," in *Studien zur Anthropologie* (Neuwied, 1963), p. 321. [On Gehlen's conservative philosophical anthropology, see Habermas's article in *Philosophical-Political Profiles*, pp. 111–28; also Axel Honneth and Hans Joas, *Social Action and Human Nature* (Cambridge: Cambridge University Press, 1988).]

29

The Normative Content of Modernity

I

The radical critique of reason exacts a high price for taking leave of modernity. In the first place, these discourses can and want to give no account of their own position. Negative dialectics, genealogy, and deconstruction alike avoid those categories in accord with which modern knowledge has been differentiated – by no means accidentally – and on the basis of which we today understand texts. They cannot be unequivocally classified with either philosophy or science, with moral and legal theory, or with literature and art. At the same time, they resist any return to forms of religious thought, whether dogmatic or heretical. So an incongruity arises between these "theories," which raise validity-claims only to renounce them, and the kind of institutionalization they undergo within the business of science. There is an asymmetry between the rhetorical gesture with which these discourses demand understanding and the critical treatment to which they are subjected institutionally, for example in the framework of an academic lecture. No matter whether Adorno paradoxically reclaims truth-validity, or Foucault refuses to draw consequences from manifest contradictions; no matter whether Heidegger and Derrida evade the obligation to provide grounds by fleeing into the esoteric or by fusing the logical with the rhetorical: There always emerges a symbiosis of incompatibles, an amalgam that resists "normal" scientific analysis at its core. Things are only shifted to a different place if we change the frame of reference and no longer treat the same discourse as philosophy or science, but as a piece of literature. That the self-referential critique of reason is located everywhere and nowhere, so to speak, in discourses without a place, renders it almost immune to competing interpretations. Such discourses unsettle the institutionalized standards of fallibilism; they always allow for a final word, even when the argument is already lost: that the opponent has misunderstood the meaning of the language game and has committed a category mistake in the *sorts* of response he has been making.

The variations of a critique of reason with reckless disregard for its own foundations are related to one another in another respect as well. They are guided by normative intuitions that go beyond what they can accommodate in terms of the indirectly affirmed "other of reason." Whether modernity is described as a constellation of life that is reified and used, or as one that is technologically manipulated, or as one that is totalitarian, rife with power, homogenized, imprisoned – the denunciations are constantly inspired by a special sensitivity for complex injuries and subtle violations. Inscribed in this sensitivity is the picture of an undamaged intersubjectivity that the young Hegel first projected as an ethical totality. With the counterconcepts (injected as empty formulas) of being, sovereignty, power, difference, and non-identity, this critique points to the contents of aesthetic experience; but the values derived therefrom and explicitly laid claim to – the values of grace and illumination, ecstatic rapture, bodily integrity, wish-fulfillment, and caring intimacy – do not cover the moral change that these authors tacitly envision in connection with a life practice that is intact – and not only in the sense of reconciling inner nature. Between the declared normative foundations and the concealed ones there is a disparity that can be explained by the *undialectical* rejection of subjectivity. Not only the devastating consequences of an objectifying relation-to-self are condemned along with this principle of modernity, but also the *other* connotations once associated with subjectivity as an unredeemed promise: the prospect of a self-conscious practice, in which the solidary self-determination of all was to be joined with the self-realization of each. What is thrown out is precisely what a modernity reassuring itself once meant by the concepts of self-consciousness, self-determination, and self-realization.

A further defect of these discourses is explained by their totalizing repudiation of modern forms of life: Although they are interesting in regard to fundamentals, they remain undifferentiated in their results. The criteria according to which Hegel and Marx, and even Max Weber and Lukács, distinguished between emancipatory-reconciling aspects of social rationalization and repressive-alienating aspects have been blunted. In the meantime, critique has taken hold of and demolished the sorts of concept by which those aspects could be distinguished from one another so that their paradoxical entanglement became visible. Enlightenment and manipulation, the conscious and the unconscious, forces of production and forces of destruction, expressive self-realization and repressive desublimation, effects that ensure freedom and those that remove it, truth and ideology – now all these moments flow into one another. They are not linked to one another as, say, conflicting elements in a disastrous functional context – unwilling accomplices in a contradictory process permeated by oppositional conflict. Now the differences and oppositions are so undermined and even collapsed that critique can no longer discern contrasts, shadings, and ambivalent tones within the flat and faded landscape of a totally administered, calculated, and power-laden world. To be sure, Adorno's theory of the administered world and Foucault's theory of power are more fertile, and simply more informative, than Heidegger's or Derrida's lucubrations on technology as an instrumental frame [*Gestell*] or on the totalitarian nature of the political order. But they are all insensitive to the highly *ambivalent* content of cultural and social modernity. This leveling can also be seen in the diachronic comparison of modern forms of life with pre-modern ones. The high price earlier exacted from the mass of the population (in the dimensions of bodily labor, material conditions, possibilities of individual choice, security of law and punishment, political participation, and schooling) is barely even noticed.

It is worthy of note that in the various approaches to the critique of reason, no systematic place is envisaged for everyday practice. Pragmatism, phenomenology, and hermeneutic philosophy have bestowed an epistemological status upon the categories of everyday action, speech, and common life. Marx even singled out everyday practice as the locus where the rational content of philosophy was supposed to flow into the life forms of an emancipated society. But Nietzsche so directed the gaze of his successors to the phenemona of the extraordinary that they contemptuously glide over the practice of everyday life as something derivative or inauthentic. [...] In communicative action the creative moment of the linguistic constitution of the world forms *one syndrome* with the cognitive-instrumental, moral-practical, and expressive moments of the intramundane linguistic functions of representation, interpersonal relation, and subjective expression. In the modern world, "value-spheres" have been differentiated out from each of these moments – namely, on the one hand, art, literature, and a criticism specialized in questions of taste, around the axis of *world-disclosure*; and, on the other hand, problem-solving discourses specialized in questions of truth and justice, around the axis of *intramundane learning processes*. These knowledge systems of art and criticism, science and philosophy, law and morality, have become the more split off from ordinary communication the more strictly and one-sidedly they each have to do with one linguistic function and one aspect of validity. But they should not be considered on account of this abstraction per se as phenomena of decline symptomatic of subject-centered reason.

To Nietzscheanism, the differentiation of science and morality appears as the formative process of a reason that at once usurps and stifles the poetic, world-disclosing power of art. Cultural modernity seems a realm of horrors, marked by the totalitarian traits of a subject-centered reason that structurally overburdens itself. Three simple facts are filtered out of this picture: First, the fact that those aesthetic experiences in the light of which true nature is supposed to reveal itself to an exclusive reason are due to the same process of differentiation as science and morality. Then the fact that cultural modernity also owes its division into special discourses for questions of taste, truth, and justice to an increase in knowledge that is hard to dispute. And especially the fact that it is only the modalities of interchange between these knowledge systems and everyday practice that determine whether the gains from such abstraction affect the lifeworld destructively.

From the viewpoint of individual cultural spheres of value, the syndrome of the everyday world appears as "life" or as "practice" or as "ethos," over against which stands "art" or "theory" or "morality". We have already spoken about the mediating roles of criticism and philosophy in another context. For criticism, the relationship between "art" and "life" is just as problematic as the relationship between "theory" and "practice" or between "morality" and "ethos" is for philosophy. The *unmediated* transposition of specialized knowledge into the private and public spheres of the everyday world can endanger the autonomy and independent logics of the knowledge systems, on the one hand, and it can violate the integrity of lifeworld contexts, on the other. A knowledge specialized in only one validity-claim, which, without sticking to its specific context, bounces across the whole spectrum of validity, unsettles the equilibrium of the lifeworld's communicative infrastructure. Insufficiently complex incursions of this sort lead to the aestheticizing, or the scienticizing, or the moralizing of particular domains of life and give rise to effects for which expressivist countercultures, technocratically carried out reforms, or fundamentalist movements can serve as drastic examples.

The profounder paradoxes of *societal* rationalization, however, are still not even touched by the complicated relationships between ordinary and expert *cultures*. They have to do with the systematically induced reification of everyday practice, to which I will return presently. However, the very first steps along the path to differentiation in the picture of the ambiguously rationalized lifeworld of modern societies already bring to our awareness the problem that will concern us in this last lecture.

Dedifferentiations are built into the leveling critique of reason only on the basis of descriptions that are guided in turn by normative intuitions. This normative content has to be acquired and justified from the rational potential inherent in everyday practice, if it is not to remain arbitrary. The concept of a communicative reason that transcends subject-centered reason, which I have provisionally introduced, is intended to lead away from the paradoxes and levelings of a self-referential critique of reason. On another front, it has to be upheld against the competing approach of a systems theory that utterly shoves the problematic of rationality aside, strips away *any* notion of reason as an old European drag, and then light-footedly takes over from the philosophy of the subject (as well as from the theory of power advanced by its sharpest opponents). This double battlefront makes the rehabilitation of the concept of reason a doubly risky business. It has to protect itself on both flanks from getting caught in the traps of the kind of subject-centered thinking that failed to keep the unforced force of reason free both from the *totalitarian* characteristics of an *instrumental* reason that objectifies everything around it, itself included, and from the *totalizing* characteristics of an *inclusive* reason that incorporates everything and, as a unity, ultimately triumphs over every distinction. Praxis philosophy hoped to derive the normative content of modernity from the reason embodied in the mediations of social practice. If the basic concept of communicative action replaces that of social labor, is the totality-perspective built into that concept radically altered?

II

According to Marx, social praxis extends in the dimensions of historical time and space; within the horizon of a surrounding *nature-in-itself*, which also cosmically encompasses the history of the species, it mediates the *subjective nature* of cooperating individuals with the *nature objectivated* by our bodily interventions. The mediating process of labor is therefore related to nature under three different aspects: to the *experienced* needs and desires of subjective nature; to the objective nature *apprehended* and *elaborated through objectification;* to the nature *presupposed* by labor as its horizon and foundation. [. . .] labor is thereby interpreted along the lines of an aesthetics of production and portrayed as a circular process of externalizing, objectifying, and appropriating essential forces. Accordingly, the process of the self-mediation of nature assumes into itself the *self-realization* of the acting *subjects* functioning within it. Both are processes of self-generation; they are produced out of their own products. Similarly, the society issuing from this praxis is conceived as a product of the forces and relationships of production created within it and by it. This figure of thought from praxis philosophy forces us to permit the moments of labor and nature – initially related distinctly to one another – to be absorbed into the totality of a self-referential process of reproduction. Ultimately, it is nature itself that reproduces itself through the reproduction of the subject-writ-large, society, and of the subjects active within it. Marx did not escape the totality thinking of Hegel. This changes if social praxis is no longer thought of primarily as a labor process.

The complementary concepts of communicative action and lifeworld introduce a difference that – unlike the difference between labor and nature – is not reabsorbed into a higher unity as its moments. To be sure, the reproduction of the lifeworld is nourished by the contributions of communicative action, even as the latter is dependent in turn upon the resources of the lifeworld. But we should not think of this circular process on the model of self-generation, as a production out of its own products, and then associate it with self-realization. Otherwise, we would hypostatize the process of mutual understanding into an event of mediation (as happens to the labor process in praxis philosophy) and inflate the lifeworld into the totality of a higher-level subject (as happens to spirit in the philosophy of reflection). The difference between lifeworld and communicative action is not taken back in any unity; it is even *deepened* to the extent that the reproduction of the lifeworld is no longer merely routed *through* the medium of action oriented toward reaching an understanding, but is saddled *on* the interpretative performances of its agents. To the degree that the yes/no decisions that sustain the communicative practice of everyday life do not derive from an ascribed normative consensus, but emerge from the cooperative interpretative processes of the participants themselves, *concrete* forms of life and *universal* structures of the lifeworld become separated. Naturally, there are family resemblances among the plurality of totalities of life forms; they overlap and interlock, but they are not embraced in turn by some super-totality. Multiplicity and diffusion arise in the course of an abstraction process through which the *contents* of particular lifeworlds are set off ever more starkly from the universal *structures* of the lifeworld.

Considered as a *resource*, the lifeworld is divided in accord with the "given" components of speech acts (that is, their propositional, illocutionary, and intentional components) into culture, society, and person. I call *culture*[1] the store of knowledge from which those engaged in communicative action draw interpretations susceptible of consensus as they come to an understanding about something in the world. I call *society* (in the narrower sense of a component of the lifeworld) the legitimate orders from which those engaged in communicative action gather a solidarity, based on belonging to groups, as they enter into interpersonal relationships with one another. *Personality* serves as a term of art for acquired competences that render a subject capable of speech and action and hence able to participate in processes of mutual understanding in a given context and to maintain his own identity in the shifting contexts of interaction. This conceptual strategy breaks with the traditional conception – also held by the philosophy of the subject and praxis philosophy – that societies are composed of collectivities and these in turn of individuals. Individuals and groups are "members" of a lifeworld only in a metaphorical sense.

The symbolic reproduction of the lifeworld does take place as a circular process. The structural nuclei of the lifeworld are "made possible" by their correlative processes of reproduction, and these in turn are "made possible" by contributions of communicative action. *Cultural reproduction* ensures that (in the semantic dimension) newly arising situations can be connected up with existing conditions in the world; it secures the continuity of tradition and a coherency of knowledge sufficient for the consensus needs of everyday practice. *Social integration* ensures that newly arising situations (in the dimension of social space) can be connected up with existing conditions in the world; it takes care of the coordination of action by means of legitimately regulated interpersonal relationships and lends constancy to the identity of groups. Finally, the *socialization* of members ensures that newly arising situations (in the dimension of historical time) can be connected up with existing world conditions; it secures the acquisition of generalized capacities for action for future generations and takes care of harmonizing individual life-histories and collective life forms. Thus, interpretative schemata susceptible of consensus (or "valid knowledge"), legitimately ordered interpersonal relationships (or "solidarities"), and capacities for interaction (or "personal identities") are renewed in these three processes of reproduction.

If this is accepted as a theoretical description of a balanced and undistorted reproduction of the lifeworld, we can pursue the following question, first of all by means of a thought experiment: In which direction would the structures of the lifeworld have to vary if the undistorted reproduction of a concrete life form were to be less and less guaranteed by traditional, customary, time-tested, and consensual stocks of knowledge and had to be secured instead by a risky search for consensus, that is, by the cooperative achievements of those engaged in communicative action themselves?

This is certainly an idealized projection, but not an utterly arbitrary one, since actual lines of development in modern lifeworlds stand out against the background of this thought experiment: the abstraction of *universal* lifeworld structures from the particular configurations of totalities of forms of life that arise only as plural. On the cultural level, the traditional nuclei that guarantee identity separate off from the concrete contents with which they were once closely woven in mythical world-views. They shrink to abstract elements such as concepts of the objective, social, and subjective worlds, presuppositions of communication, procedures of argumentation, abstract basic values, etc. On the level of society, general principles are crystallized out of the particular contexts to which they were once bound in primitive societies. In modern societies, principles of legality and morality prevail which are less and less tailored to particular life forms. On the level of personality, the cognitive structures acquired in the process of socialization are dissociated ever more emphatically from the contents of cultural knowledge with which they were initially integrated in "concrete thinking." The objects with respect to which formal competences can be exercised become ever more variable. If we single out of these trends only the degree of freedom gained by the structural components of the lifeworld, the following vanishing points result: for culture, a condition of the constant revision of traditions that have been unthawed, that is, that have become reflective; for society, a condition of the dependence of legitimate orders upon formal and ultimately discursive procedures for establishing and grounding norms; for personality, a condition of the risk-filled self-direction of a highly abstract ego-identity. There arise structural pressures toward the critical dissolution of guaranteed knowledge, the establishment of generalized values and norms, and self-directed individuation (since abstract ego-identities point toward self-realization in autonomous life projects).

This separation of form and content is a distant reminder of the traditional determination of a "rational practice:" Self-consciousness returns in the form of a culture become reflexive; self-determination in the form of generalized values and norms; self-realization in that of the advanced individuation of socialized subjects. But the growth in reflexivity, in universalism, and in individuation undergone by the structural core of the lifeworld in the course of its differentiation now no longer fits the description of an intensification within the dimensions of the subject's relation-to-self. And only under this description – that is, from the perspective of the philosophy of the subject – could societal rationalization, the unfolding of the rational potential of social practice, be represented as the self-reflection of a societal macrosubject. The theory of communication can do without this figure of thought. Now the increasing reflexivity of culture, the generalization of values and norms, and the heightened individuation of socialized subjects, the enhancement of critical consciousness, autonomous will-formation, and individuation – that is, the strengthening of the moments of rationality once attributed to the practice of subjects – takes place under conditions of an ever more extensive and ever more finely woven net of linguistically generated intersubjectivity. Rationalization of the lifeworld means differentiation and condensation at once – a thickening of the floating web of intersubjective threads that simultaneously holds together the ever more sharply differentiated components of culture, society, and person. The reproductive mode of the lifeworld does not change linearly in the direction indicated by the catchwords "reflexivity," "abstract universalism," and "individuation." Rather, the rationalized lifeworld secures the continuity of its contexts of meaning with the discontinuous tools of critique; it preserves the context of social integration by the risky means of an individualistically isolating universalism; and it sublimates the overwhelming power of the genealogical nexus into a fragile and vulnerable universality by means of an extremely individualized socialization. The more abstractly the differentiated structures of the lifeworld operate in the ever more particularized forms of life, the more the rational potential of action oriented toward reaching understanding evolves solely by these *means*. This can be clarified by the following thought experiment.

Continuities in the semantic field would not have to be severed even if cultural reproduction could now occur *only* by way of critique. In a structurally differentiated lifeworld, the development of the potential for negation inherent in the process of reaching agreement in language becomes a *necessary* condition for texts to connect up with one another and for traditions – which live, of course, from the power of conviction – to continue. Nor would the intersubjective net knit together in social space out of relations of reciprocal recognition have to be torn apart if social integration could now occur *only* by way of a universalism that was abstract and at the same time individualistically tailored. The procedures of discursive will-formation established in the structurally differentiated lifeworld are set up to secure the social bond of all with all precisely through equal consideration of the interests of each individual. This means that as a participant in discourses, the individual, with his irreplaceable "yes" or "no," is only fully on his own under the presupposition that he remains bound to a universal community by way of a cooperative quest for truth. Not even the substance of the universal within the historical succession of generations would have to dissolve away into nothing if processes of socialization could now advance *only* across the threshold of extreme individuation. In the structurally differentiated lifeworld, we merely acknowledge a principle that was in operation from the beginning: to wit, that socialization takes place in the same proportion as individuation, just as, inversely, individuals are constituted socially. With the system of personal pronouns, a relentless pressure toward individuation is built into the use of language oriented toward mutual understanding that is proper to socializing interaction. At the same time, the force of an intersubjectivity pressing toward socialization comes to the fore through the same linguistic medium.

Figures of thought from the theory of intersubjectivity thus render intelligible why critical testing and a fallibilist consciousness even enhance the continuity of a tradition that has stripped away its quasi-natural state of being. They make comprehensible why abstract, universalistic procedures for discursive will-formation even strengthen solidarity in life-contexts that are no longer legitimated by tradition. They help us to understand why an expanded scope for individuation and self-realization even condenses and stabilizes a process of socialization detached from fixed models of socialization.

If one retrieves the normative content of modernity in this manner – a content that gets away from the concepts of praxis philosophy, if not from its intentions – the three moments once assembled into the "dialectic of enlightenment" now fall apart: As the principle of modernity, subjectivity was supposed to determine its normative content as well; at the same time, subject-centered reason led to abstractions that fragmented the ethical totality; and yet only self-reflection, which emanated from subjectivity and strove to get beyond its narrow-mindedness, supposedly proved itself equal to the task of reconciliation. In its own way, praxis philosophy made this program its own. For Marx, the analysis of class antagonisms, their revolutionary overthrow, and the unleashing of the emancipatory content of stored-up forces of production were three conceptually interconnected moments. In this respect, the notion of reason derived from the structures of linguistically generated intersubjectivity and concretized in terms of rationalization processes in the lifeworld provides no equivalent for the concept of an intrinsically rational praxis that was deployed in the philosophy of history. As soon as we give up praxis philosophy's understanding of society as a self-referential subject-writ-large, encompassing all individual subjects, the corresponding models for the diagnosis and mastery of crisis – division and revolution – are no longer applicable. Because the successive releasing of the rational potential inherent in communicative action is no longer thought of as self-reflection writ large, this specification of the normative content of modernity can prejudice neither the conceptual tools for diagnosing crises nor the way of overcoming them.

The probability of conflict-free reproduction by no means increases with the degree of rationalization of the lifeworld – it is only that the level at which conflicts can arise is shifted. With the differentiation of the structures of the lifeworld, the forms in which social pathologies appear are multiplied according to which aspects of which structural factors are insufficiently taken care of: Loss of meaning, conditions of anomie, and psychopathologies are the most obvious kinds of symptom, but not the only ones. As a result, the causes of social pathologies, which in the model of a division within a macrosubject are still *clustered* around class antagonism, now break up into widely scattered historical contingencies. The pathological characteristics of modern societies now fit into patterns only to the extent that a predominance of economic and bureaucratic rationality – of cognitive-instrumental forms of rationality generally – makes itself felt. The jagged profile of rationality potentials that *have been unevenly exploited* excludes from our explanatory approach the idea of a stagnated circular process of self-mediation in a *divided* macrosubject.[2]

It is obvious that with these considerations we have not yet touched at all on the question from which praxis philosophy started. As long as we leave the material reproduction of the lifeworld out of consideration, as we have until now, we will not even reach the level of the older problematic. Indeed, Marx selected "labor" as his basic category because he could see how the structures of bourgeois society were *ever more strongly* stamped by abstract labor, that is, by the type of gainful labor steered by the market, valorized in a capitalist fashion, and organized into businesses. In the meantime, this tendency has clearly slackened.[3] But the *type* of social pathology analyzed by Marx in terms of the real abstractions characteristic of alienated labor has not thereby disappeared.

III

The approach of communication theory seems to be able to salvage the normative content of modernity only at the cost of idealist abstractions. Once again suspicion is cast on the purism of a purely communicative reason – this time on an abstract description of rationalized lifeworlds that does not take into account the constraints of material reproduction. In order to defuse this suspicion, we have to show that the theory of communication can contribute to explaining how it is that in the modern period an economy organized in the form of markets is functionally intermeshed with a state that has a monopoly on power, how it gains autonomy as a piece of norm-free sociality over against the lifeworld, and how it opposes its own imperatives based on system maintenance to the rational imperatives of the lifeworld. Marx was the first to analyze this conflict between system imperatives and lifeworld imperatives, in the form of a dialectic of dead labor and living labor, of abstract labor and concrete labor; and he vividly illustrated it with materials from social history concerning the irruption of new modes of production into traditional lifeworlds. Meanwhile, the kind of system rationality that first became evident in the independent logic of capital self-realization has taken over other domains of action as well.

No matter how structurally differentiated lifeworlds may be, no matter whether they have developed highly specialized subsystems (and subparts of subparts of subsystems) for the functional domains of cultural reproduction, social integration, and socialization – the complexity of any lifeworld is narrowly restricted by the limits of the strain that can be placed upon the mechanism of mutual understanding. In the degree that a lifeworld is rationalized, the expenditure of understanding borne by the communicative agents themselves increases. This also increases the risk of dissent in a communication that generates a bonding effect only via the double negation of validity claims. Ordinary language is a risky mechanism for coordinating action; it is also expensive, immobile, and restricted in what it can accomplish. The meaning of the individual speech act cannot be detached from the lifeworld's complex horizon of meaning; it remains entwined with the intuitively present background knowledge of interaction participants. The plenitude of connotations, the functional richness, and the capacity for variation proper to the use of language oriented toward mutual understanding are only the reverse side of a relationship to totality that does not allow for any arbitrary expansion of the capacity to achieve understanding in everyday practice.

Because lifeworlds can afford only a restricted outlay for coordination and understanding, at a certain level of complexity ordinary language has to be disencumbered by the sorts of special language that Talcott Parsons studied in connection with the example of money. When the medium for coordinating action no longer has to be called upon for *all* linguistic functions at once, then there is a disburdening effect. The binding of communicatively guided action to contexts of the lifeworld is also reduced by the partial replacement of ordinary language. Social processes set free in this way become "deworlded," that is, released from those relationships to the totality and those structures of intersubjectivity by which culture, society, and personality are interlaced with one another. Functions of material reproduction are especially open to this kind of disburdening because they do not per se need to be fulfilled by communicative actions. Changes in conditions in the material substrate can be traced back directly to the aggregate results and consequences of goal-directed interventions in the objective world. To be sure, these teleological actions need coordination too; they have to be socially integrated. But the integration can occur by way of an *impoverished* and *standardized* language that coordinates functionally specialized activities – for instance, the production and distribution of goods and services – without burdening social integration with the expense of risky and uneconomical processes of mutual understanding, and without connecting up with processes of cultural transmission and socialization through the medium of ordinary language. Evidently the medium of money satisfies these conditions for a specially encoded steering language. It has branched off from normal language as a special code that is tailored to special situations (of exchange); it conditions decisions for action on the basis of a built-in preference structure (of supply and demand), in a way that is effective for coordination but without having to lay claim to the resources of the lifeworld.

However, money makes possible not only specifically deworlded forms of interaction, but the formation of a functionally specialized system that articulates its relationships to the environment via money. Considered historically, capitalism saw the rise of an economic system that regulates internal exchanges as well as interchanges with its non-economic environments (private households and the state) through monetary channels. The institutionalization of wage labor on the one hand, and that of a state based on taxation on the other, was as constitutive of the new mode of production as was the organizational form of the capitalist enterprise inside the economic system. Complementary environments were formed in the measure that the productive process was shifted over to wage-labor and the apparatus of government was linked to production via taxes on those employed. On the one side, the state apparatus became dependent upon a media-steered economic system; this led, among other things, to the assimilation of official and personal power to the structure of a steering medium; that is, power became assimilated to money. On the other side, traditional forms of labor and of life broke down under the grip of gainful labor organized in business enterprises. The plebeianizing of the rural population and the proletarianizing of the labor force highly concentrated in cities became the first exemplary case of a systemically induced reification of everyday practice.

With exchange processes operating through media there emerges in modern societies a third level of autonomous functional contexts – above the level of simple interactions as well as beyond the level of forms of organization still bound to the lifeworld. Contexts of interaction that have gained autonomy as subsystems and that go beyond the horizon of the lifeworld congeal into the second nature of a norm-free sociality. This decoupling of system from lifeworld is experienced within modern lifeworlds as a *reification of life forms*. Hegel reacted to this basic experience with the concept of the "positive" and the idea of a dirempted ethical totality; Marx started more specifically from alienated industrial labor and class antagonisms. Operating under premises of the philosophy of the subject, they both nevertheless underestimated the independent logic of systemically integrated domains of action that are dissociated from structures of intersubjectivity to such an extent that they no longer exhibit any structural analogies with socially integrated domains of action differentiated *within* the lifeworld. For Hegel and Marx, the system of needs or capitalist society arose from processes of abstraction that still pointed to ethical totality or rational praxis and remained subject to their structures. These abstractions constituted non-independent moments within the self-relation and self-movement of a higher-level subject, into which they would flow once again. In Marx, this overcoming [*Aufhebung*] takes the shape of a revolutionary praxis, which breaks the systemic logic of capital's self-realization, brings the independent economic process back into the horizon of the lifeworld again, and frees the realm of freedom from the dictates of the realm of necessity. In attacking the private ownership of the means of production, the revolution simultaneously strikes at the institutional foundations of the medium through which the capitalist economy was differentiated out. The lifeworld rigidified under the law of value is to be given back its spontaneity; at that very moment, the objective illusion of capital will dissolve away into nothing.

As we have seen, this melting down of systemically reified domains of action into a spontaneous relation-to-self of spirit or of society already met with strong opposition from the right Hegelians of the first generation. Against the dedifferentiation of state and society, they insisted on the objective distinction between the societal system and the governmental subject. Their neo-conservative successors gave this thesis an affirmative twist. Hans Freyer and Joachim Ritter saw in the dynamic of the reification of culture and society only the reverse side of the constitution of a realm of subjective freedom worth striving for. Arnold Gehlen criticized even the latter as an empty subjectivity released from all objective imperatives. Even those who, following Lukács, fastened upon the concept of reification came to agree more and more with their opponents in their description; they were increasingly impressed with the impotence of subjects in relation to the feedback processes of self-regulating systems, over which they could have no influence. It makes almost no difference whether the one indicts as a negative totality what the other celebrates as a crystallization; or whether the one denounces as reification what the other technocratically lays down as the law of reality. For decades, this trend in the social-theoretical diagnosis of the age has been heading toward the point that systems functionalism makes into its own point: It allows the subjects themselves to degenerate into systems. It tacitly sets a seal on "the end of the individual," which Adorno encircled with his negative dialectic and protested against as a self-inflicted fate. Niklas Luhmann simply presupposes that the structures of intersubjectivity have collapsed and that individuals have become disengaged from their lifeworlds – that personal and social systems form environments for each other.[4] The barbaric condition predicted by Marx in case revolutionary praxis failed is characterized by a complete subsumption of the lifeworld under the imperatives of a valorization process decoupled from use values and concrete labor. Undisturbed by this, systems functionalism proceeds from the assumption that this condition has already set in – not merely at the entrance to the capitalist economy, but in the forecourts of *every* functional system. The marginalized lifeworld could survive only if it were to be transformed in turn into a media-steered subsystem and if it were to shed everyday communicative practice like a snakeskin.

On the one hand, Luhmann's version of systems functionalism takes up the heritage of the philosophy of the subject; it replaces the self-relating subject with a self-relating system. On the other hand, it radicalizes Nietzsche's critique of reason by withdrawing any kind of claim to reason along with the relationship to the totality of the lifeworld.

The fact that Luhmann draws upon the reflective content of these two opposed traditions and brings motifs from Kant and Nietzsche together in a cybernetic language game indicates the level at which he establishes social systems theory. Luhmann takes the same characteristics that Foucault attributed to discourse formations with the help of a transcendental-historical concept of power and transfers them to meaning-elaborating systems that operate in a self-relating fashion.[5] Since he also relinquishes the intention of a critique of reason together with the concept of reason, he can turn all the statements that Foucault made by way of denunciation into descriptive ones. In this respect, Luhmann pushes the neo-conservative affirmation of social modernity to a peak, and also to heights of reflection where everything the advocates of postmodernity could come up with has already been thought of – without any complaints and in a more differentiated manner. Moreover, systems functionalism is not open to the objection of being unable to give an account of its own status; it places itself without any hesitation within the system of science and comes forward with a claim to "disciplinary universality." Nor can it be charged with a tendency toward leveling. At most, Luhmann's theory, which is today incomparable when it comes to its power of conceptualization, its theoretical imaginativeness, and its capacity for processing information, raises doubts as to whether the price for its "gains in abstraction" is not too high. The tireless shredding machine of reconceptualization separates out the "undercomplex" lifeworld as an indigestible residue – precisely the realm of phenomena of interest to a social theory that has not burned all bridges to the pre-scientific experience of crisis.

In regard to the capitalist economy, Marx did not distinguish between the new level of system differentiation brought about by a media-steered economic system and the class-specific forms of its institutionalization. For him, abolishing class structures and melting down the independent systemic logic of functionally differentiated and reified domains of interaction formed a single syndrome. Luhmann commits a complementary error. Faced with the new level of the differentiation of systems, he overlooks the fact that media such as money and power, via which functional systems set themselves off from the lifeworld, have in turn to be institutionalized in the lifeworld. This is why the class-specific distributive effects of the media's being anchored in property laws and constitutional norms do not come into view at all. "Inclusion," in the sense of the equal rights of all individuals to access to all functional systems, thus appears as a systemically necessary outcome of the process of differentiation.[6] Whereas for Marx systemically autonomous functional contexts go up in smoke after a successful revolution, for Luhmann the lifeworld now has already lost all significance in the functionally differentiated societies of the modern world. What disappears from both perspectives is the mutual interpenetration and opposition of system and lifeworld imperatives, which explains the double-front character of societal modernization.

The paradoxes of societal rationalization, which I have developed elsewhere, may be summarized in an oversimplified way as follows. The rationalization of the lifeworld had to reach a certain maturity before the media of money and power could be legally institutionalized in it. The two functional systems of the market economy and the administrative state, which grew beyond the horizon of the political orders of stratified class societies, destroyed the traditional life forms of old European society to begin with. The internal dynamic of these two functionally intermeshed subsystems, however, also reacts back upon the rationalized life forms of modern society that made them possible, to the extent that processes of monetarization and bureaucratization penetrate the core domains of cultural reproduction, social integration, and socialization. Forms of interaction shaped by these media cannot encroach upon realms of life that by their function are dependent on action oriented to mutual understanding without the appearance of pathological side effects. In the political systems of advanced capitalist societies, we find compromise structures that, historically considered, can be conceived of as reactions on the part of the lifeworld to the independent systemic logic and growth in complexity proper to the capitalist economic process and a state apparatus with a monopoly on force. These origins have left their traces on the options that remain open to us in a social-welfare state in crisis.[7]

The options are determined by the logic of a politics adjusted to the system imperatives of economy and state. The two media-steered subsystems, which constitute environments for one another, are supposed to be intelligently attuned to one another – and not simply to reciprocally externalize their costs so as to burden a total system incapable of self-reflection. Within the scope of such a politics, only the correctly dosed distribution of problems as between the subsystems of state and economy is in dispute. One side sees the causes of crisis in the unleashing of the dynamics proper to the economy; the other side, in the bureaucratic fetters imposed on the former. The corresponding therapies are a social subduing of capitalism or a displacement of problems from administrative planning back to the market. The one side sees the source of the systemically induced disturbances of everyday life in monetarized labor power; the other, in the bureaucratic crippling of personal initiative. But both sides agree in assigning a merely passive role to the vulnerable domains of lifeworld interaction as against the motors of societal modernization: state and economy.

Meanwhile, the legitimists of the social-welfare state are everywhere in retreat, while the neo-conservatives complacently undertake to terminate the social-welfare-state compromise – or at least to redefine its conditions. In return for an energetic improvement of the valorization conditions of capital, neo-conservatives accept in the bargain costs that can be shifted in the short term to the lifeworld of the underprivileged and marginalized, but also risks that rebound upon society as a whole. There arise the new class structures of a society segmented on its ever widening margins. Economic growth is kept going by innovations that for the first time are *intentionally* tied to an armaments spiral that has gone out of control. At the same time, the intrinsic normative logic of rationalized lifeworlds now finds expression, however selectively, not only in the classical demands for more distributive justice, but in the wide spectrum of so-called postmaterial values, in the interest in conserving the natural bases of human life and in preserving the internal communicative structures of highly differentiated life forms. So it is that system imperatives and lifeworld imperatives form new frictional surfaces that spark new conflicts which cannot be dealt with in the existing compromise structures. The question posed today is whether a new compromise can be arranged in accord with the old rules of system-oriented politics – or whether the crisis management attuned to crises that are systemically caused and perceived as systemic will be undermined by social movements no longer oriented to the system's steering needs, but to the *processes at the boundaries* between system and lifeworld.

IV

With this question we touch upon the other moment – the possibility of mastering crises in grand format, for which praxis philosophy once offered the means of revolutionary praxis. If society as a whole is no longer thought of as a higher-level subject that knows itself, determines itself, and realizes itself, there are no paths of relation-to-self upon which the revolutionaries could enter in order to work with, for, and on the crippled macrosubject. Without a self-relating macrosubject, anything like a self-reflective knowledge on the part of the social totality is just as *inconceivable* as society's having an influence upon itself. As soon as the higher-level intersubjectivity of public processes of opinion and consensus formation takes the place of the higher-level subject of society as a whole, relationships-to-self of this kind lose their meaning. It is questionable whether under these changed premises it still makes any sense to speak of a "society exercising influence upon itself."

For a society to influence itself in this sense it must have, on the one hand, a reflexive center, where it builds up a knowledge of itself in a process of self-understanding, and, on the other hand, an executive system that, as a part, can act for the whole and influence the whole. Can modern societies meet these conditions? Systems theory projects a picture of them as acentric societies "without central organs."[8] On this account, the lifeworld has disintegrated without remainder into the functionally specialized subsystems such as economy, state, education, science, etc. These systemic monads, which have replaced withered intersubjective relationships with functional connections, are symmetrically related to one another, but their precarious equilibrium is not susceptible of being regulated for society as a whole. They must reciprocally balance one another, since none of the total societal functions that come to the fore with them attains a *primacy* for society as a whole. None of the subsystems could occupy the top of a hierarchy and represent the whole the way the emperor could once do for the empire in stratified societies. Modern societies no longer have at their disposal an authoritative center for self-reflection and steering.

From the viewpoint of systems theory, only the subsystems develop anything like a *self-consciousness*, and they do so only in view of their *own* function. The whole is reflected in the partial system's self-consciousness only from the perspective of that system, as its respective social *environment*:

> Hence, a consensus functional for society as a whole about what is and what is valid is difficult, in fact impossible; what is used as a consensus

functions in the form of a recognized provisional arrangement. In addition to this, there are the really productive syntheses of reality that are functionally specific at the levels of complexity that individual functional systems can achieve for themselves but can no longer add up to a comprehensive world-view in the sense of a *congregatio corporum*, or a *universitas rerum*.[9]

Luhmann elaborates on this "provisional arrangement" in a footnote as follows: "It was a peculiar decision of Husserlian philosophy, with considerable ramifications for sociological discussions, to endow this provisional arrangement with the status of an ultimately valid basis of a concrete a priori by giving it the title of 'lifeworld.'" It is sociologically untenable to postulate for the lifeworld any kind of "primacy in being."

The legacy of Husserlian apriorism may mean a burden for various versions of social phenomenology; but the communications-theoretic concept of the lifeworld has been freed from the mortgages of transcendental philosophy. If one is to take the basic fact of *linguistic* socialization into account, one will be hard put to do without this notion. Participants in interaction cannot carry out speech acts that are effective for coordination unless they impute to everyone involved an intersubjectively shared lifeworld that is angled toward the situation of discourse and anchored in bodily centers. For those acting in the first-person singular or plural with an orientation to mutual understanding, each lifeworld constitutes a totality of meaning relations and referential connections with a zero point in the coordinate system shaped by historical time, social space, and semantic field. Moreover, the different lifeworlds that collide with one another do not stand *next to each other* without any mutual understanding. As totalities, they follow the pull of their claims to universality and work out their differences until their horizons of understanding "fuse" with one another, as Gadamer puts it. Consequently, even modern, largely decentered societies maintain in their everyday communicative action a virtual center of self-understanding, from which even functionally specified systems of action remain within intuitive reach, as long as they do not outgrow the horizon of the lifeworld. This center is, of course, a projection, but it is an effective one. The polycentric projections of the totality – which anticipate, outdo, and incorporate one another – generate competing centers. Even collective identities dance back and forth in the flux of interpretations, and are actually more suited to the image of a fragile network than to that of a stable center of self-reflection.

Nevertheless, everyday practice affords a locus for spontaneous processes of self-understanding and identity formation, even in non-stratified societies that no longer have a knowledge of themselves available in the traditional forms of representative self-presentation. Even in modern societies, a diffuse common consciousness takes shape from the polyphonous and obscure projections of the totality. This common consciousness can be concentrated and more clearly articulated around specific themes and ordered contributions; it achieves greater clarity in the higher-level, concentrated communicative processes of a public sphere. Technologies of communication – such as book publishing and the press, first of all, and then radio and television – make utterances available for practically any context, and make possible a highly differentiated network of public spheres – local and transregional, literary, scientific, and political, within parties or associations, media-dependent or subcultural. Within these public spheres, processes of opinion and consensus formation, which depend upon diffusion and mutual interpenetration no matter how specialized they are, get institutionalized. The boundaries are porous; each public sphere is open to other public spheres. To their discursive structures they owe a universalist tendency that is hardly concealed. All partial public spheres point to a comprehensive public sphere in which society as a whole fashions a knowledge of itself. The European Enlightenment elaborated this experience and took it up into its programmatic formulas.

What Luhmann calls "the consensus functioning for the whole of society" is context-dependent and fallible – provisional in fact. But this reflexive knowledge on the part of society as a whole *exists*. Only now it is due to the higher-level intersubjectivity of public spheres and hence can no longer satisfy the sharp criteria of self-reflection by a higher-level subject. Of course, such a center of self-understanding is insufficient for a society to exercise influence over itself; for this, it would also require a central steering authority that could receive and translate into action the knowledge and the impulses from the public sphere.

According to the normative ideas of our political tradition, the democratically legitimated apparatus of state – having been shifted from the sovereignty of princes to the sovereignty of the people – is supposed to be able to put into effect the opinion and will of the citizenry as a public. The citizens themselves participate in the formation of collective consciousness, but they cannot act collectively. Can the government do so? "Collective action" would mean that the government would transpose the intersubjectively constituted self-knowledge of society organizationally into the self-determination of society. And yet, even on systems-theoretic grounds, one has to doubt this possibility. As a matter of fact, today politics has become an affair of a functionally specialized subsystem; and the latter does not dispose over the measure of autonomy relative to the other subsystems that would be required for central steering, that is, for an influence of society as a totality upon itself, an influence that comes from it and goes back to it.

In modern societies, there obviously exists an asymmetry between the (weak) capacities for intersubjective self-understanding and the (missing) capacities for the self-organization of society as a whole. Under these changed premises, there is no equivalent for the philosophy of the subject's model of self-influence in general and for the Hegelian-Marxist understanding of revolutionary action in particular.

This insight has come into broad effect, carried along by a specific experience that labor parties and unions have had, above all, in their attempts to realize the social-welfare-state project since the end of World War II. I am talking neither about the economic problems that cropped up as a result of successful social-welfare legislation during the period of reconstruction, nor about the limits upon the power and the ability of planning administrations to intervene, nor about problems of *steering* at all. I mean, rather, a characteristic transformation in the perception of the democratically legitimated state power that had to be brought to bear in pursuing the goal of "socially taming" the nature-like capitalist economic system, and especially the goal of neutralizing the destructive side effects of its crisis-filled expansion on the existence and lifeworld of dependent workers.[10] Advocates of the social-welfare state regarded it as unproblematic that an active government should intervene not only in the economic cycle but also in the life-cycle of its citizens – the goal indeed was to reform the living conditions of the citizens by way of reforming the conditions of labor and employment. Underlying this was the democratic tradition's idea that society could exercise an influence over itself by the neutral means of political-administrative power. Just this expectation has been disappointed.

In the meantime, an increasingly dense network of legal norms, of governmental and paragovernmental bureaucracies, has been drawn over the everyday life of its actual and potential clients. Extensive discussions about legal regulation and bureaucratization in general, about the counterproductive effects of government welfare policies in particular, about the professionalization and scientization of social services have drawn attention to circumstances that make one thing clear: The legal-administrative means of translating social-welfare programs into action are not some passive, as it were, propertyless medium. They are connected, rather, with a praxis that involves isolation of facts, normalization, and surveillance, the reifying and subjectivating violence of which Foucault has traced right down into the most delicate capillary tributaries of everyday communication. The deformations of a lifeworld that is regulated, fragmented, monitored, and looked after are surely more subtle than the palpable forms of material exploitation and impoverishment; but internalized social conflicts that have shifted from the corporeal to the psychic are not therefore less destructive.

Today one sees the contradiction inherent in the social-welfare-state project as such. Its substantive goal was to set free life forms structured in an egalitarian way, which were supposed at the same time to open up space for individual self-realization and spontaneity; but too great a demand was placed upon the medium of power in expecting it to call forth new forms of life. Once the state has been differentiated out as one among many media-steered functional systems, it should no longer be regarded as the central steering authority in which society brings together its capabilities for organizing itself. A functional system that has grown beyond the horizon of the lifeworld and become independent, that shuts itself off from perspectives of society as a whole, and that can perceive society as a whole only from the perspective of a subsystem, stands over against processes of opinion- and will-formation in a general public sphere, which, however diffuse, are still directed to society as a whole.

A new, as it were stereoscopically sharpened, view of "the political" emerges from the historical disillusionment with a bureaucratically coagulated social-welfare-state project. In addition to the independent systemic logic of a power medium that only seems to be usable in a purposive-rational manner, another dimension becomes visible. The public sphere as political, in which complex societies can acquire normative distance from themselves and work out experiences of crisis collectively, takes on a remoteness from the political system similar to the remoteness it previously had from the economic system. The political system has acquired a similarly problematic character, or at least one with two battlefronts. Now it is itself perceived as a source of steering problems, and not simply as a means for the solution of problems. Thus, we have become conscious of *the difference between steering problems and problems of mutual understanding*. We can see the difference between systemic disequilibria and lifeworld pathologies, between disturbances of material reproduction and deficiencies in the symbolic reproduction of the lifeworld. We come to recognize the distinction between the deficits that inflexible structures of the lifeworld can cause in the maintenance of the systems of employment and domination (via the withdrawal of motivation or legitimation), on the one hand, and manifestations of a colonization of the lifeworld by the imperatives of functional systems that externalize their costs, on the other. Such phenomena demonstrate once more that the achievements of steering and those of mutual understanding are resources that cannot be freely substituted for one another. Money and power can neither buy nor compel solidarity and meaning. In brief, the result of the process of disillusionment is a new state of consciousness in which the social-welfare-state project becomes reflexive to a certain extent and aims at taming not just the capitalist economy, but the state itself.

However, if not only capitalism but also the interventionist state itself is to be "socially tamed," the task has to be defined anew. The welfare-state project entrusted the planning capacity of public administrations with having a stimulating influence upon the self-steering mechanism of a *different* subsystem. If this "regulation," applied so very indirectly, is now supposed to extend to the organizational performances of the state, the mode of influence may not be specified again as indirect steering, for a new *steering* potential could only be furnished by *another* subsystem. Even if we could come up with a supplementary system of this sort, after a further round of disappointment and distantiation we would again face the problem that *perceptions of crises in the lifeworld* cannot be translated without remainder into *systems-related problems of steering.*

Instead, it is a question of building up restraining barriers for the exchanges between system and lifeworld and of building in sensors for the exchanges between lifeworld and system. At any rate, limit problems of this sort are posed as soon as a highly rationalized lifeworld is to be shielded against the intolerable imperatives of the occupational system or against the penetrating side effects of the administrative provision for life. The systemic spell cast by the capitalist labor market over the life-histories of those able to work, by the network of responsible, regulating, and supervising public authorities over the life forms of their clients, and by the now autonomous nuclear arms race over the life-expectancy of peoples, cannot be broken by systems learning to function better. Rather, impulses from the lifeworld must be able to enter into the self-steering of functional systems. Of course, this would require altering the relationship between autonomous, self-organized public spheres, on the one hand, and realms of action steered by money and power, on the other, or in other words: a new division of powers within the dimension of social integration. The socially integrating power of solidarity would have to be in a position to assert itself against the systemically integrating steering media of money and power.

I call those public spheres autonomous which are neither bred nor kept by a political system for purposes of creating legitimation. Centers of concentrated communication that arise spontaneously out of micro-domains of everyday practice can develop into autonomous public spheres and consolidate as self-supporting higher-level intersubjectives only to the degree that the lifeworld potential for self-organization and for the self-organized use of the means of communication are utilized. Forms of self-organization strengthen the collective capacity for action. Grassroots organizations, however, may not cross the threshold to the formal organization of independent systems. Otherwise they will pay for the indisputable gain in complexity by having organizational goals detached from the orientations and attitudes of their members and dependent instead upon imperatives of maintaining and expanding organizational power. The lack of symmetry between capacities for self-reflection and for self-organization that we have ascribed to modern societies as a whole is repeated on the level of the self-organization of processes of opinion and will-formation.

This need not be an obstacle, if one considers that the indirect influence of functionally differentiated subsystems on the individual mechanisms of self-steering means something altogether different from the goal-oriented influence of society upon itself. Their self-referential closedness renders the functional systems of politics and economics immune against attempts at intervention in the sense of *direct* interventions. Yet this same characteristic also renders systems sensitive to stimuli aimed at increasing their capacity for self-reflection, that is, their sensitivity to the reactions of the environment to their own activities. Self-organized public spheres must develop the prudent combination of power and intelligent self-restraint that is needed to sensitize the self-steering mechanisms of the state and the economy to the goal-oriented outcomes of radical democratic will-formation. In place of the model of society influencing itself, we have the model of boundary conflicts – which are held in check by the lifeworld – between the lifeworld and two subsystems that are superior to it in complexity and can be influenced by it only indirectly, but on whose performances it at the same time depends.

Autonomous public spheres can draw their strength only from the resources of largely rationalized lifeworlds. This holds true especially for culture, that is to say, for science's and philosophy's potential for interpretations of self and world, for the enlightenment potential of strictly universalistic legal and moral representations, and, not least, for the radical experiential contents of aesthetic modernity. It is no accident that social movements today take on cultural-revolutionary traits. Nonetheless, a structural weakness can be noticed here that is indigenous to all modern lifeworlds. Social movements get their thrust-power from threats to well-defined collective identities. Although such identities always remain tied to the particularism of a special form of life, they have to assimilate the normative content of modernity – the fallibilism, universalism, and subjectivism that undermine the force and concrete shape of any given particularity. Until now, the democratic, constitutional nation-state that emerged from the French Revolution was the only identity formation successful on a world-historical scale that could unite these two moments of the universal and the particular without coercion. The Communist Party has been unable to replace the identity of the nation-state. If not in the nation, in what other soil can universalistic value-orientations today take root?[11] The Atlantic community of values crystallized around NATO is hardly more than a propaganda formula for ministers of defense. The Europe of de Gaulle and Adenauer merely furnishes the superstructure for the basis of trade relations. Quite recently, left intellectuals have been projecting a completely different design as a counterimage to the Europe of the Common Market.

The dream of such a completely different European identity, which assimilates in a decisive way the legacy of Occidental rationalism, is taking shape at a time when the United States is getting ready to fall back into the illusions of the early modern period under the banner of a "second American Revolution." In the utopias painted in the old romances about the state, rational forms of life entered into a deceptive symbiosis with the technological mastery of nature and the ruthless mobilization of social labor power. This equation of happiness and emancipation with power and production has been a source of irritation for the self-understanding of modernity from the start – and it has called forth two centuries of criticism of modernity.

But the same utopian (in the bad sense) gestures of mastery are living on now in a caricature that moves the masses. The science fiction of Star Wars is just good enough for the ideology planners to spark – with the macabre vision of a militarized space – an innovative thrust that would give the colossus of worldwide capitalism sufficient footing for its next round of technological development. Old Europe could only find its way clear to a new identity if it opposed to this short circuit of economic growth, arms race, and "traditional values" the vision of breaking out of these self-inflicted systemic constraints, if it put an end to the confused idea that the normative content of modernity that is stored in rationalized lifeworlds could be set free only by means of ever more complex systems. The idea that the capacity to compete on an international scale – whether in markets or in outer space – is indispensable for our very survival is one of those everyday certitudes in which systemic constraints are condensed. Each one justifies the expansion and intensification of its own forces by the expansion and intensification of the forces of the others, as if it were not the ground rules of social Darwinism that are at the bottom of the play of forces. Modern Europe has created the spiritual presuppositions and the material foundations for a world in which this mentality has taken the place of reason. That is the real heart of the critique of reason since Nietzsche. Who else but Europe could draw from *its own* traditions the insight, the energy, the courage of vision – everything that would be necessary to strip from the (no longer metaphysical, but metabiological) premises of a blind compulsion to system maintenance and system expansion their power to shape our mentality.

The Philosophical Discourse of Modernity, XII, pp. 336–67.

Notes

1 I base what follows on the more complete account in *The Theory of Communicative Action*, vol. II, p. 138.

2 The ideologies that cover up repressed antagonisms can no longer be ascribed to the false consciousness of collectives; they are traced back to patterns of systematically distorted, everyday communication. It is here that the external organization of discourse exerts a pressure upon the internal organization of discourse that cannot be concealed in any other way, and twists it so as to break the internal connections between meaning and validity, meaning and intention, and meaning and action. (Compare Jürgen Habermas, "Überlegungen zur Kommunikationspathologie," in *Vorstudien und Ergänzungen zur Theorie des kommunikativen Handelns* (Frankfurt,

1984, pp. 226ff.) And it is here, in distorted communication, that we can recognize Hegel's bifurcated ethical totality and Marx's alienated praxis as forms of damaged intersubjectivity. Foucault's analyses of discourses would also have to be retrieved on this level, by means of formal pragmatics.

3 Claus Offe, "Work: The Key Sociological Category?", in *Disorganized Capitalism* (Cambridge, Mass. and Oxford, 1985), pp. 129–50.
4 See the excursus on Luhmann in *The Philosophical Discourse of Modernity*, pp. 368–85.
5 Axel Honneth, *Critique of Power*, has drawn my attention to this.
6 Niklas Luhmann, *Politische Theorie im Wohlfahrtsstaat* (Munich, 1981), pp. 25ff.
7 See the analyses by Claus Offe in "Some Contradictions of the Modern Welfare State," in *Contradictions of the Welfare State* (Cambridge, Mass. and London, 1984), pp. 147–61.
8 Luhmann, *Politische Theorie im Wohlfahrtsstaat*, p. 22.
9 Niklas Luhmann, *Gesellschaftsstruktur and Semantik*, vol. 1 (Frankfurt, 1980), p. 33.
10 I am basing what follows on the title essay in my book *The New Conservatism*.
11 Compare Jürgen Habermas, "Können komplexe Gesellschaften eine vernünftige Identität ausbilden?," in *Zur Rekonstruktion des historischen Materialismus* (Frankfurt, 1976), pp. 92ff; partially translated as "On Social Identity," *Telos*, 19, 1974: 91–103.

Select Bibliography of Habermas's Writings

A full list of works by and on Habermas can be found in René Görtzen, *Jürgen Habermas: Eine bibliographie seiner Schriften und der Sekundärliteratur 1952–1981* (Frankfurt: Suhrkamp,) 1982. A shorter version is appended to Arie Brand, *The Force of Reason: An Introduction to Habermas' Theory of Communicative Action* (Sydney: Allen and Unwin, 1990). See also the entry on Habermas in Stuart Brown, Diané Collinson, and Robert Wilkinson (eds), *Dictionary of Twentieth-Century Philosophers* (London: Routledge, 1996).

1962 *Strukturwandel der Öffentlichkeit.* Neuwied/Berlin: Luchterhand; 2nd edn Frankfurt: Suhrkamp, 1989. Tr. by Thomas Burger as *The Structural Transformation of the Public Sphere.* Cambridge: Polity, 1989.

1963 *Theorie und Praxis.* Neuwied/Berlin: Luchterhand. Tr. by John Viertel as *Theory and Practice.* London: Heinemann, 1974.

1968 *Technik und Wissenschaft als Ideologie.* Frankfurt: Suhrkamp. Part tr. by Jeremy J. Shapiro in Jürgen Habermas, *Toward a Rational Society.* London: Heinemann, 1971.

1968 *Erkenntnis und Interesse.* Frankfurt: Suhrkamp. Tr. by Jeremy J. Shapiro as *Knowledge and Human Interests.* London: Heinemann, 1971.

1971 (with Niklas Luhmann) *Theorie der Gesellschaft oder Sozialtechnologie: Was Leistet die Systemforschung?* Frankfurt: Suhrkamp.

1971 *Zur Logik der Sozialwissenschaften,* 2nd edn. Frankfurt: Suhrkamp. Tr. by Shierry Weber Nicholsen and Jerry A. Stark as *On the Logic of the Social Sciences.* Cambridge: Polity, 1988.

1971 *Philosophisch-Politische Profile.* Frankfurt: Suhrkamp. Part tr. by Thomas McCarthy as *Philosophical-Political Profiles.* London: Heinemann, 1983.

1973 "A Postscript to *Knowledge and Human Interests,*" *Philosophy of the Social Sciences,* 3, 2: 157–85.

1973 *Legitimationsprobleme im Spätkapitalismus.* Frankfurt: Suhrkamp. Tr. by Thomas McCarthy as *Legitimation Crisis.* London: Heinemann, 1976.

1973 "What does a crisis mean today?," *Social Research,* Winter. Reprinted in P. Connerton (ed.), *Critical Sociology.* Harmondsworth: Penguin, 1976.

1973 *Kultur und Kritik.* Frankfurt: Suhrkamp.

1974   "The Public Sphere", *New German Critique*, 1, 3: 49–55.
1974   "Können Komplexe Gesellschaften eine vernünftige Identität ausbilden?," in Habermas and D. Henrich, *Zwei Reden*. Frankfurt: Suhrkamp.
1976   *Zur Rekonstruktion des historischen Materialismus*. Frankfurt: Suhrkamp. Part tr. by Frederick G. Lawrence as *Communication and the Evolution of Society*. Boston: Beacon Press, 1979.
1981   *Theorie des kommunikativen Handelns*, 2 vols. Frankfurt: Suhrkamp, Tr. by Thomas McCarthy as *The Theory of Communicative Action*, 2 vols. (London: Heinemann, 1984 and Cambridge: Polity, 1987).
1982   "Objektivismus in den Sozialwissenschaften," in *Zur Logik der Sozialwissenschaften*, 5th edn. Frankfurt: Suhrkamp.
1982   "The Entwinement of Myth and Enlightenment," *New German Critique* 26: 13–20.
1983   *Moralbewußtsein und kommunikatives Handeln*. Frankfurt: Suhrkamp. Tr. by Christian Lenhardt and Shierry Weber Nicholsen as *Moral Consciousness and Communicative Action*. Cambridge: Polity, 1989.
1984   *Vorstudien and Ergänzungen zur Theorie des Kommunikativen Handelns*. Frankfurt: Suhrkamp, 82.
1985   "Moral und Sittlichkeit. Hegels Kantkritik im Lichte der Diskursethik,", *Merkur*, 39, 12, Dec. (Included in *Moral Consciousness and Communicative Action*. Cambridge: Polity, 1989).
1985   "Modernity – An Incomplete Project." Reprinted in Hal Foster (ed.), *Postmodern Culture*. London: Pluto.
1985   *Die neue Unübersichtlichkeit*. Frankfurt: Suhrkamp, Tr. by Shierry Weber Nicholsen as *The New Conservatism*. Cambridge: Polity, 1989.
1985   *Der Philosophische Diskurs der Moderne*. Frankfurt: Suhrkamp. Tr. by Frederick G. Lawrence as *The Philosophical Discourse of Modernity*. Cambridge: Polity, 1987.
1988   *Nachmetaphysisches Denken*. Frankfurt: Suhrkamp. Tr. by William Mark Hohengarten as *Postmetaphysical Thinking*. Cambridge: Polity, 1992.
1988   "Law and Morality", *Tanner Lectures on Human Values*, VIII: 217–79.
1989   "Towards a Communication Concept of Rational Will Formation," *Ratio Juris*, 2, July: 144–54.
1989   "Volkssouveränität als Verfahren," *Merkur*, 43, 6: 465–77.
1990   *Die nachholende Revolution*. Frankfurt: Suhrkamp.
1990   "Remarks on the Discussion", *Theory, Culture and Society*, 7, 4: 127–32.
1991   *Erläuterungen zur Diskursethik*. Frankfurt: Suhrkamp. Tr. by Ciaran Cronin as *Justification and Application*. Cambridge: Polity, 1993.
1991   *Vergangenheit als Zukunft*, ed. Michael Heller. Zürich: Pendo; 2nd edn Munich: Piper, 1993. Tr. by Max Pensky as *The Past as Future*. Cambridge: Polity, 1994.
1992   *Faktizität und Geltung*. Frankfurt: Suhrkamp. Tr. by William Rehg as *Between Facts and Norms*. Cambridge: Polity, 1996.

Glossary

Civil Society Originally used in English to refer to the entire non-state sphere. The equivalent German term *bürgerliche Gesellschaft* comes to refer, with Hegel, to the domain of contractual (especially economic) relations and, with Marx, to bourgeois or capitalist society. With the revival of the term in the 1980s to refer to the sphere of independent associations, in and against the state socialist dictatorships, German writers, including Habermas, have tended to use the English term or the German neologism *Zivilgesellschaft*. See Jean Cohen and Andrew Arato, *Civil Society and Political Theory* (Cambridge, Mass.: MIT Press, 1992).

Decisionism See *Value-freedom*

Discourse Used by Habermas in a semi-technical sense to refer to the systematic examination of problematized validity-claims; see reading 10, n. 2. Also more generally as in "discourse ethics." See also *validity*.

Domination (Herrschaft) Distinguished from power by Max Weber and later writers to indicate a relatively systematic exercise of power or authority. This term, central to critical theory, also appears in translations as "rule" or "authority." The latter usage is misleading, however, if authority is understood to be legitimate; domination can be either legitimate or illegitimate. See also *Legitimacy*.

Hermeneutics The science or art of interpretation, of texts or of human actions and cultural products. Habermas accepts Gadamer's critique of objectivist hermeneutics, while taking issue with his thesis of the "universality" of hermeneutics. See Josef Bleicher, *Contemporary Hermeneutics* (London: Routledge, 1980).

Historicism (Historismus) The relativistic nineteenth-century doctrine that historical epochs are radically distinct from one another and must be understood in their own terms. See Friedrich Meinecke, *Historism: The Rise of a New Historical Outlook* (London: Routledge, 1972).

Juridification (Verrechtlichung) The subordination of social relations to legal regulation, as in family law. Cf. reading 26.

Law (Recht) The German term is close to "justice" (*Gerechtigkeit*); thus Hegel's principal work of legal and political philosophy is usually translated as *The Philosophy of Right*, and German writers often use a qualifying adjective such as "codified" to distinguish actual laws from, for example, natural law. "Rights" in English has a more individualistic connotation than "*Rechte;*" hence the use of the term "*subjektive Rechte*" as an equivalent to "rights." The "*Rechtsstaat,*" sometimes translated as the "constitutional state," is one governed by the rule of law.

Legitimacy As Habermas notes, the use of this term has bifurcated, under Max Weber's influence, into a normative concept of the "rightness" of an order or a regime, and a more empirical sense in which it means nothing more than factual support, or what in the German context tends to be described as "mass loyalty" (*Massenloyalität*). Economic success and state propaganda may make a regime legitimate in the second sense, but not the first. Where Habermas and others refer to the procurement (*Beschaffung*) of legitimacy, it is more often the empirical sense which is intended. See also, however, Habermas's remark in reading 15, p. 182.

Lifeworld (Lebenswelt) Used by Husserl to refer to the world as given in experience, prior to the operations of science or phenomenological philosophy. Habermas draws in particular on Husserl's usage in *The Crisis of the European Sciences and Transcendental Phenomenology* (1938; tr. by David Carr (Evanston, Ill.: Northwestern University Press, 1970)), and extends it further to refer to relatively informal ways of life, contrasted with market and administrative systems, as well as to a cognitive "horizon of meaning." The different status of these two senses has given rise to some misunderstandings in the reception of Habermas's work.

Media Used by Habermas to refer both to the "mass media" and to "steering media" – what Talcott Parsons called "symbolically generalized media of communication" such as power and money. See *The Theory of Communicative Action*, vol. II, pp. 165 and 154; above, p. 279.

Neo-Kantianism Philosophical movement(s) aiming to "return" to Kantian questions in the late nineteenth and early twentieth centuries. German neo-Kantianism was divided into two branches: the "Marburg School" of Hermann Cohen (1842–1918) and Paul Natorp (1854–1924), which was mainly concerned with the theory of knowledge and the philosophy of science, and the "Heidelberg" or "Baden" School of Wilhelm Windelband (1848–1915) and Heinrich Rickert (1863–1936). Rickert's theory of values which govern the selection of phenomena for scientific inquiry was the major influence on Max Weber's philosophy of science and on the methodological dualism of the natural and social sciences examined by Habermas in *On the Logic of the Social Sciences*. For a characteristically brilliant critique of neo-Kantian influences on sociology, Habermas included, see Gillian Rose, *Hegel Contra Sociology* (London: Athlone Press, 1981), ch. 1. See also Andrew Arato, "The Neo-Idealist Defence of Intersubjectivity," *Telos*, 21, 1974: 108–61. See also *phenomena, value-freedom*.

Phenomena Often used by Habermas to indicate Kant's distinction between objects of perception and "things in themselves" or noumena.

Practical Habermas mostly uses this term in the sense of Kant's concept of practical reason, which refers to the moral-political domain. He often uses the word "technical" to refer to what in English would often be called practical or pragmatic matters. See, in particular, *Knowledge and Human Interests*.

Public sphere (Öffentlichkeit) Translated as "the public sphere" in the title of Habermas's book, *Öffentlichkeit* also means publicness or publicity. The term has been more contentious in German than in English usage, with some writers, including Habermas, differentiating between what is genuinely public, in the sense of citizenship or civil society, and what is merely generalized, as in "public opinion," or out in the open (see *Structural Transformation of the Public Sphere*, pp. 236–7). This parallels the distinction between genuine legitimacy and "mass loyalty." See also *civil society, legitimacy*.

Reflection (Reflexion) Used both in the general sense of a reflective or thoughtful attitude and, following Kant and Hegel, to refer to the critical examination of thought and other activities. Reflecting on his own earlier use of the terms "reflection" and "critique" in *Knowledge and Human Interests*, Habermas came to distinguish between emancipatory reflection and the reconstruction of a capacity such as language use. (See "reading 8; for an overview of Habermas's use of the term, see my chapter "Habermas: Modernity as Reflection," in Brian Cheyette and Laura Marcus (eds), *Modernity, Culture and "the Jew"* (California University Press, forthcoming).) Reflection in the optical sense, or that of the standard Marxist-Leninist theory of knowledge, is normally *Widerspiegelung* in German, though Adorno, for example, played on the double sense of reflection; on this, see Gilliam Rose, *The Melancholy Science: An Introduction to the Thought of Theodor W. Adorno* (London: Macmillan, 1978), p. 54.

Subject Although Habermas, unlike many French thinkers, does not question the very notion of subjectivity, he is critical of traditional conceptions of the human subject and its consciousness. His concept of communicative rationality is developed in opposition to what he calls "subject-centered" reason or the "philosophy of the subject."

Validity (Geltung) This neo-Kantian concept plays a key role in Habermas's thinking. In *Knowledge and Human Interests*, the knowledge-guiding interest in prediction and control determines the "meaning of the validity" (*Geltungssinn*) of the statements of empirical science. Habermas's later thought is based on the concept of validity-claims which are raised or presupposed in speech; these can then be redeemed or "cashed in" (*eingelöst*). For a critique, see Gillian Rose, *Hegel Contra Sociology* (London: Athlone Press, 1981), ch. 1. See also neo-Kantianism.

Value-freedom (Wertfreiheit) Sometimes also known in English as "ethical neutrality," this is the doctrine, now mainly associated with Max Weber and with positivist social science, that value-judgments should be kept out of science. For Weber, this also meant that science should be kept out of our value-judgments: we should not attempt to give them a spurious support from the factual conclusions of natural or social science but should recognize the element of existential choice between competing values. Habermas calls this position "decisionistic" – see reading 7. Habermas regards the separation of fact from value as "less a result than a problem," and his theory of cognitive interests is an attempt to address some of these complexities. Although he does not accept the ideal of value-free science in a simple sense, he applies a more pragmatic distinction between his own theoretical work and his more political writings.

Understanding (Verstehen) The German word is often used in English to refer to the interpretation of the actions of others and of social and cultural phenomena more generally, where this is distinguished from a "natural-scientific" method of explanation based on the discovery of law-like regularities. Habermas believes that understanding in this sense is a constitutive element of all social science. See William Outhwaite, *Understanding Social Life: The Method Called Verstehen* (London: Allen & Unwin, 1975; 2nd edn Lewes: Jean Stroud, 1986); Fred Dallmayr and Thomas McCarthy (eds), *Understanding and Social Inquiry* (Notre Dame, Ind.: Notre Dame University Press, 1977).

Vienna circle Group of philosophers and scientists in the 1920s and 1930s committed to logical empiricism and "unified science."

Biographical Notes

Apel, Karl-Otto (1922–) German philosopher; critical theorist.

Arendt, Hannah (1906–75) German-American political philosopher.

Austin, J. L. (1911–60) British philosopher of language; founder, following Wittgenstein, of "ordinary-language philosophy."

Benn, Gottfried (1886–1956) German poet and essayist.

Brocker, Walter (1902–) German philosopher and historian of philosophy.

Carnap, Rudolf (1891–1970) German-American philosopher; member of Vienna circle.

Cassirer, Ernst (1875-1945) German neo-Kantian philosopher and historian of philosophy.

Chomsky, Noam (1859–1952) American pragmatist philosopher.

Easton, David (1917–) American political scientist; system theorist.

Edelman, Murray (1919–) American political scientist; theorist of political ritual.

Ellul, Jacques (1912–) French political theorist.

Gadamer, Hans-Georg (1900–) German hemeneutic theorist.

Garfinkel, Howard (1917–) American sociologist of everyday life; founder of "ethnomethodology."

Gehlen, Arnold (1904–) German sociologist and philosophical anthropologist.

Goffman, Erving (1922–82) American sociologist of everyday life.

Hare, R. M. (1919–) British moral philosopher.

Hartmann, Nikolai (1882–1969) German existentialist philosopher and psychologist.

Kautsky, Karl (1854–1938) German socialist thinker and politician.

Kohlberg, Lawrence (1927–) American psychologist.

Lorenzen, Paul (1915–) German philosopher of science and ethics.

Luhmann, Niklas (1927–) German sociologist; system theorist.

Marcuse, Herbert (1898–1979) German philosopher; member of Frankfurt School.

McPherson, C. B. (1911–87) Canadian political theorist.

Mead, George Herbert (1863–1931) American pragmatist philosopher and sociologist.

Mills, C. Wright (1916–62) American sociologist.

Morris, Charles (1901–) American pragmatist philosopher.

Offe, Claus (1940–) German sociologist; critical theorist.

Parsons, Talcott (1902–79) American sociologist, structural-functionalist system theorist.

Peirce, C. S. (1839–1914) American pragmatist philosopher.

Piaget, Jean (1896–1980) Swiss psychologist and structuralist philosopher.

Popper, Karl (1902–94) Austrian-British philosopher.

Rawls, John (1921–) American moral philosopher.

Rickert, Heinrich (1863–1936) German neo-Kantian philosopher.

Ritter, Joachim (1903–) German historian of philosophy.

Ryle, Gilbert (1900–76) British analytic philosopher.

Scheler, Max (1874–1928) German philosopher and sociologist.

Schelsky, Helmut (1919–93) German sociologist.

Schmitt, Carl (1888–1985) German philosopher and legal theorist.

Schumpeter, Joseph (1883–1950) Austrian economist and social theorist.

Schutz, Alfred (1899–1959) Austrian-American philosopher and sociologist; founder of phenomenological sociology.

Strauss, Leo (1899–1973) American political philosopher.

Tarde, Gabriel (1843–1904) French sociologist; theorist of crowd psychology.

Taylor, Charles (1931–) Canadian philosopher and politician.

Toulmin, Stephen (1922–) British philosopher.

Wallerstein, Immanuel (1930–) American historian.

Wellmer, Albrecht (1933–) German philosopher; critical theorist.

Wittgenstein, Ludwig (1889–1951) Austrian-British philosopher; associated with the Vienna circle; later provided the basis for "ordinary-language philosophy."

Index

Note: Page numbers in *italics* refer to the editor's comments.